WORK & Society

Viktor Wang

innovativeink PUBLISHING
A Division of Kendall Hunt

innovativeink PUBLISHING
A Division of Kendall Hunt

www.innovativeinkpublishing.com
Send all inquiries to:
4050 Westmark Drive
Dubuque, IA 52004-1840

Print ISBN: 979-8-7657-9996-3
Ebook ISBN: 979-8-7657-9997-0

Published in the United States of America

Contents

Chapter 1: Work and Its Implications in a Global Society 1

Dayna Lynn Mitchell, California State Polytechnic University, Pomona, USA

ABSTRACT

Work transcends geographical boundaries in today's interconnected world, emerging as a multifaceted phenomenon with significant global implications. Technological advancements, globalization, and evolving economic landscapes have fundamentally reshaped the nature of work, influencing its perception, organization, and execution across diverse cultures and societies. This chapter delves into the dimensions of work in a global society, examining its economic, social, and ethical implications. We explore the impact of globalization on labor markets, the role of technological advancements in shaping the future of work, and the importance of diversity and inclusion in multicultural workplaces. Additionally, we address the ethical responsibilities of organizations, the significance of ethical leadership, and the role of education in preparing individuals for the global workforce. By understanding these complex interactions, we can navigate the challenges and opportunities presented by work in a global society, fostering more inclusive, productive, and ethical work environments.

Michelle I. Caron and Zuzana P. Buzzell, Southern New Hampshire University, USA

ABSTRACT

Multicultural diversity is a vital aspect of the global workforce. Growing interdependence among nations, economies, and cultures drives globalization, which promotes multicultural diversity. This chapter delves into the importance of multicultural diversity, benefits and challenges to the global workforce, and strategies for fostering multicultural diversity to identify unique solutions, increase market competitiveness, attract and retain talent, and build cultural competence. Organizations must acquire these competencies to enable them to effectively lead, collaborate, and communicate with internal and external stakeholders from varied cultural, ethnic, and racial backgrounds. Finding unity in the diversity of the competitive global landscape has the power to build and sustain dynamic capabilities, enhance brand reputation, and attract top talent from every sector of the global workforce.

Steve Lambert, University of Chester, United Kingdom

ABSTRACT

This chapter, "The Cultural and Social Status of Jobs," explores the intricate relationship between employment, cultural perceptions, and social status. Employment plays a crucial role in determining an individual's social position, heavily influenced by education, income, occupational prestige,

ernization has affected labor across cultures, focusing on the tension between traditional values and modern economic imperatives.

Gabriele Strohschen, DePaul University, USA
with contributions by Brigitte Bartsch, PiChi Han, Kenneth Elazier, Zaya Khananu, and Vincent Wiggins[1]

ABSTRACT

This chapter explores the multifaceted concept of work across various political and economic systems, focusing on democratic capitalism, dictatorship, Islamic fundamentalism, and socialism. Through personal narratives and theoretical insights, the chapter provides an examination of how work is defined, valued, and practiced within these contrasting systems. By presenting firsthand accounts from individuals living under different regimes, the chapter uncovers the relationship between political ideologies, economic structures, and workplace dynamics.

The narratives reflect a range of experiences shaped by each system's approach to freedom, education, labor rights, and the distribution of resources. These experiences offer insight into the inherent challenges and opportunities workers face globally, revealing how socio-cultural, religious, and political factors influence one's understanding of work. The chapter emphasizes the importance of understanding these perspectives as essential to fostering international dialogue, lifelong learning, and preparing for a 21st-century global workforce.

Ultimately, this chapter aims to stimulate critical thinking about how diverse political-economic systems impact not only individual lives but also the possibility of achieving a peaceful, interconnected global society. By examining these varied contexts, it urges readers to engage in further research and reflection on the evolving nature of work in a globalizing world.

1

social psychology factors emphasize the role of social norms and cultural contexts. Additionally, the chapter delves into the direct effects of climate on job satisfaction, organizational commitment, and work motivation, illustrating how temperature and seasonal changes affect employee performance and well-being. The indirect impacts through economic and environmental stressors are also discussed, linking job security, mental health, and organizational support with climatic conditions. Organizational strategies for fostering supportive cultures and implementing flexible work arrangements are proposed to mitigate climate-related impacts on work attitudes. Through comprehensive theoretical frameworks and empirical research, this chapter provides a deeper understanding of the complex interplay between climate and work, proposing strategies to enhance productivity and employee well-being in varying climatic scenarios.

Ted Fleming, Maynooth University, Ireland

ABSTRACT

The well-known photograph, 'Lunch atop a skyscraper' shows construction workers sitting on a beam 800 feet high on top of Rockefeller Centre, New York. The picture is part of a publicity shot promoting the building as it was being built in 1932 (Cross, 2003). Today visitors can replicate the experience in a tourist attraction called "The Beam" (Rahmanan, 2023). It seems that at least one of the men was Irish (Ó Cualáin, 2012). This photograph of a confident America expanding upward required workers. Emigration from Ireland began in the 1720s and by 1790 almost half a million of the 3 million Americans were Irish. Millions emigrated from the early 19th century, driven by poverty; in the 1850s by famine; attracted by promises of work and a better life. The impact on the industrial, social and political life of both the United States and Ireland was significant. In this chapter, I will map the story of work and society in Ireland and create an awareness that this story is best understood as a long historical journey through colonial (including famine) exploitation, independence, the famous Celtic Tiger, and its demise until today. Work and society in Ireland have reached a place where emigration is historically low, as is unemployment. Never before have so many immigrants re-defined work and society leading to historically high population levels. Despite the obvious success of the model of work in Ireland, there still remain serious problems of housing, homelessness, and relative poverty and inequality. This entire experience, over almost 200 years, is outlined in this chapter and leads toward a critical work theory.

ABSTRACT

This chapter examines the evolution and current state of work in Australia, exploring its historical context, key characteristics, and future trends. It traces the country's economic development from early reliance on agriculture and mining to its current service-based economy, highlighting the impact of significant events such as world wars, immigration policies, and economic reforms. The chapter discusses distinctive features of Australian work culture, including its strong labor laws, union presence, and emphasis on work-life balance. Two major trends shaping the future of work in Australia are analyzed in depth: digitalization and the gig economy. The chapter explores the implications of artificial intelligence and automation on job roles, emphasizing the need for reskilling and adaptation in the workforce. It also examines the rise of the gig economy, discussing its opportunities for flexible work and its challenges for worker protection and regulation. The chapter concludes by considering the future of work in Australia, highlighting the importance of agility in government policy, education, and individual skills development. It underscores the need for conscious technology design that enhances rather than replaces human work and emphasizes the importance of inclusion and diversity in shaping equitable work opportunities. Overall, the chapter provides a comprehensive overview of the dynamic nature of work in Australia and its broader implications for society and the economy.

ABSTRACT

This chapter emphasizes employers' pivotal role in cultivating a healthy work ethic among employees. Drawing on Pech's (2009) case study, it demonstrates how engaged workers can transition from unproductive to highly productive. Leaders must assess their practices, decisions, and inclusivity to combat disengagement and foster a positive workplace. Tailoring strategies based on the distinction between healthy and misguided work ethics—where X theory individuals may require more guidance and Y theory individuals benefit from autonomy—supports employee retention and drives innovation. In a diverse global workforce, understanding cultural values and motivators is crucial for fostering strong work ethics (Association for Talent Development, n.d.; Rannala, Gorman, Tierney, Guðmundsson, Hickey., & Corney, 2024) through training and development. Ethical leaders who respect these differences create environments conducive to innovation and best practices. As technology advances, traditional work ethics evolve, with higher education pivotal in nurturing ethical leaders who facilitate employee learning and work ethic growth. Prioritizing work ethic in education and training programs is essential, equipping individuals with skills like dependability, initiative, and interpersonal competence crucial for success in the 21st century. The evolving role of graduates underscores the importance of cultivating a work ethic tied to professionalism. Effective leadership in these programs fosters trust, credibility, and motivation, essential for organizational growth and innovation. Recognizing work ethic as a cornerstone, nearly nine out of ten hiring managers prioritize it in hiring decisions, underscoring its significance in preparing future professionals.

Foreword by Dr. Paul A. Bott

As the former Department Chair of Professional Studies at California State University, Long Beach, I had the privilege of overseeing the largest Workforce Education department on the West Coast. My tenure involved a critical task: expanding our department's reach, even as we successfully recruited nearly 2,000 adult learners. One of the strategies we employed to increase our Full-Time Equivalent Students (FTES) was to develop innovative General Education courses. Among these, "Working Around the World" was one of three new courses I designed to address the evolving needs of our diverse student body.

Despite our efforts, finding a suitable textbook for this course proved challenging. We needed a resource that could comprehensively address the complexities of work in a global context, encompassing diverse cultural, economic, and social perspectives. It is with great enthusiasm that I introduce Dr. Viktor Wang's edited volume, which I believe serves as the definitive textbook for this course. This volume represents a significant contribution to our understanding of global work dynamics.

The chapters within this book offer invaluable insights into various dimensions of work, from its implications in a global society to the impacts of multicultural diversity, technological advancements, and the effects of climate on work attitudes. Each chapter, meticulously crafted by leading experts, explores critical themes such as the evolution of gender-specific occupations, the interplay between work and societal values, and the challenges posed by immigration and migration. By examining work through these diverse lenses, the book not only addresses historical and contemporary issues but also provides a forward-looking perspective on the future of work in a rapidly changing world.

Dr. Wang's volume stands out not only for its comprehensive coverage but also for its ability to synthesize complex information into accessible and engaging content. This book will undoubtedly become an essential resource for students, educators, and professionals alike, offering a deep understanding of the global workforce's multifaceted nature. I hope that this textbook will inspire further exploration and discussion, fostering a more inclusive and informed approach to understanding work in our interconnected world.

I am delighted to see this volume come to fruition and am confident that it will greatly enhance the learning experience for those studying the global dimensions of work. Dr. Wang and his contributors have provided us with a remarkable tool for navigating the complexities of work in a global society, and I am honored to commend it as a significant academic resource.

Dr. Paul A. Bott,

Department Chair/Professor Emeritus of Professional Studies
California State University, Long Beach, USA

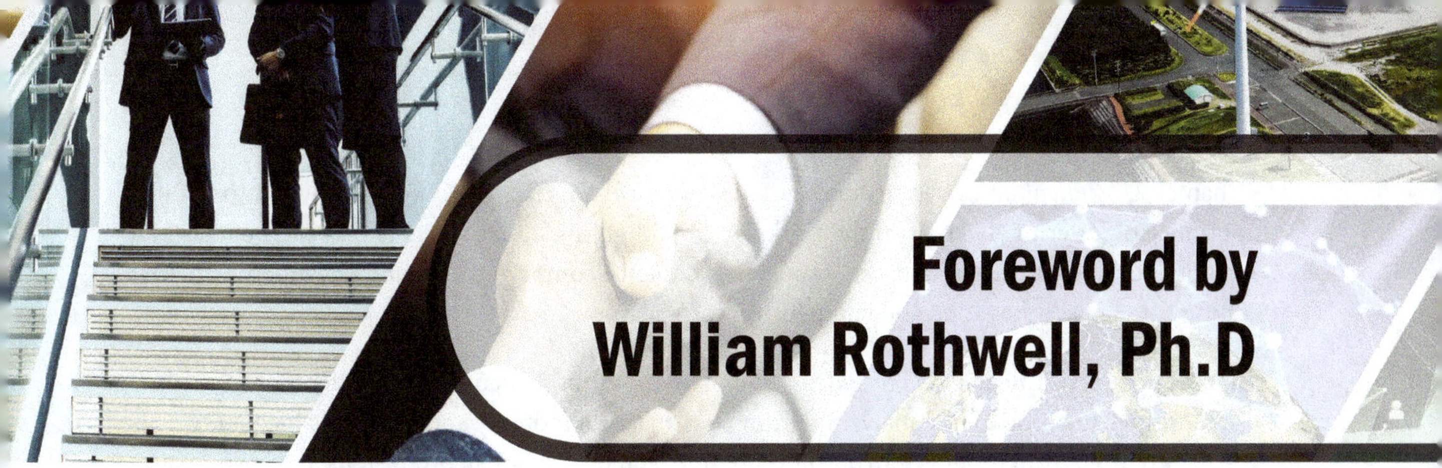

Foreword by William Rothwell, Ph.D

In an era of unprecedented global connectivity, the concept of a "global village" has become more relevant than ever. As a distinguished professor of education at Penn State University, USA, I have had the privilege of delivering training on every continent. This international exposure has underscored a critical realization: preparing our students for the global workforce requires cultivating their perceptions of work long before they enter the professional world. With nearly 9 million Americans living abroad and over 45 million foreign-born residents in the United States as of 2021, the diversity of our societies is reshaping the workforce landscape.

The metaphor of the United States as a "tossed salad"—where each ingredient retains its uniqueness—aptly captures the multicultural fabric of our society, contrasting the older "melting pot" concept. This analogy underscores the importance of preserving distinct cultural identities while promoting integration. In our globalized society, students must understand how religion, language, culture, politics, economics, and the environment shape work and workplace perceptions worldwide.

I am thrilled to introduce *Work and Society*, edited by Dr. Viktor Wang. This comprehensive volume is designed as a definitive textbook for the course *Working Around the World*. It addresses the intricate and multifaceted nature of work in a global context, filling a significant gap in the literature.

Each chapter of this book provides a valuable perspective on work in modern society. Chapter 1, *Work and Its Implications in a Global Society*, explores the transformative effects of technology, globalization, and evolving economic landscapes on work across various cultures, shedding light on the complex ethical and social dimensions of work today.

Chapter 2, *Multicultural Diversity and Its Implications in the Global Workforce*, delves into the importance of fostering diversity in the workplace, highlighting both the challenges and benefits of a multicultural workforce. It outlines strategies to enhance communication and collaboration across cultures to boost innovation and competitiveness.

In Chapter 3, *The Cultural and Social Status of Jobs*, the author discusses how different societies assign prestige to occupations, analyzing the impact on social mobility and economic inequality. This chapter offers critical insights into promoting equity and respect for all professions in the workplace.

Chapter 4, *Working in Modernity: Similarities and Differences between Work and Society in the United States and Other Countries*, provides a comparative analysis of work practices in various countries, emphasizing the influence of modernity on global labor markets.

Chapter 5, *Work under Democratic Capitalism, Dictatorship, Islamic Fundamentalism, and Socialism*, takes a deep dive into how different political and economic systems shape work, labor rights, and social dynamics, highlighting the diverse global perspectives on work.

The Effects of Immigration and Migration on Work, covered in Chapter 6, investigates the complex effects of migration on labor markets and socio-political dynamics in the U.S., Mexico, China, and other countries, offering a comparative lens on how immigration policies shape the workforce.

Chapter 7, *The Effects of Climate on People's Attitudes Toward Work*, examines how environmental factors and climate variations impact job satisfaction and performance, proposing strategies for organizations to mitigate these effects.

Chapter 8, *Work and the Socio-Economic Structure of Ireland*, presents a critical analysis of Ireland's historical and contemporary labor market, highlighting the impact of emigration, economic shifts, and cultural transformations on the workforce.

Chapters 9 and 10 offer fascinating insights into the evolution of gender-specific occupations and the influence of art, music, and religion on workplace practices. These chapters showcase how cultural norms, economic shifts, and creative practices shape workplace dynamics and influence gender roles across various societies.

In Chapter 11, *The Nature of Work in Australia and Its Implications*, the book examines the unique characteristics of the Australian labor market, focusing on the future of work in the face of digitalization, artificial intelligence, and the gig economy.

Finally, Chapter 12, *Ethical Work Practices*, underscores the role of employers in fostering ethical leadership and creating work environments that promote a healthy work ethic, a critical aspect of preparing individuals for the challenges of the 21st-century workforce.

Work and Society is an essential resource for educators, students, and practitioners seeking to understand the complexities of work in our interconnected world. It offers a comprehensive framework for examining the cultural, economic, and social factors that shape the modern workplace and provides the tools necessary for navigating the challenges and opportunities that lie ahead.

Sincerely,

William Rothwell, Ph.D., Distinguished Professor of Education
Penn State University, USA

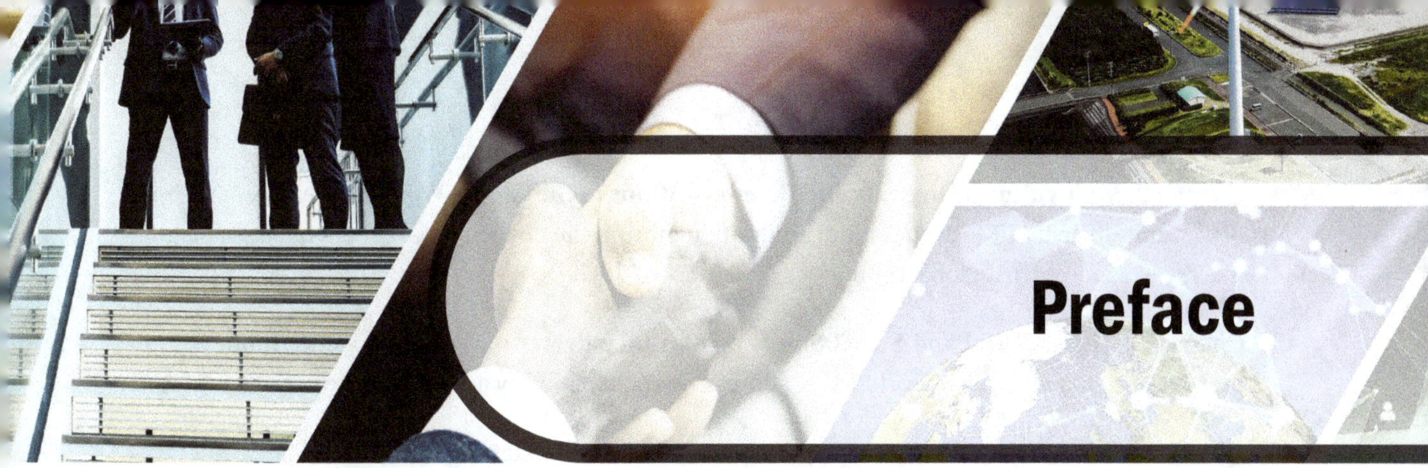

Preface

In 2021, I embarked on a transformative journey by joining California State University, San Bernardino as a faculty member and Career and Technical Education (CTE) coordinator. Returning to California after a decade of experience elsewhere, my focus was on expanding and enhancing the CTE program to meet the dynamic demands of modern education. This process involved strategic enrollment growth, and despite recruiting 180 students, a significant portion of these were non-traditional learners whose enrollment did not contribute to Full-Time Equivalent Students (FTES), presenting challenges in sustaining program growth.

Recognizing the need to adapt and innovate, I initiated the development of three new General Education (GE) courses, including *Working Around the World*, designed to broaden perspectives on work within a global context. This book, *Work and Society*, was conceived as the definitive textbook for that course, addressing critical gaps in understanding the interplay between work, society, and global dynamics.

The chapters of *Work and Society* offer readers comprehensive insights into how work intersects with societal, cultural, and economic factors in a rapidly globalizing world. Each chapter critically examines these interactions, providing a robust framework for understanding work within different national and cultural contexts.

Chapter 1: **Work and Its Implications in a Global Society** introduces the global forces shaping work today, such as technological advancements and globalization, while emphasizing diversity, inclusion, and ethical leadership in future work environments.

Chapter 2: **Multicultural Diversity and Its Implications in the Global Workforce** explores the role of cultural diversity in fostering innovation, highlighting the challenges and benefits of managing diverse workforces in a global economy.

Chapter 3: **The Cultural and Social Status of Jobs** investigates how societal values influence job prestige, emphasizing the importance of addressing social mobility and inequality in the workforce.

Chapter 4: **Similarities and Differences between Work and Society in the United States and Other Countries** offers a comparative analysis of work practices, revealing how different cultural perspectives shape workforce integration and preparedness.

Chapter 5: **Work under Democratic Capitalism, Dictatorship, Islamic Fundamentalism, and Socialism** provides a cross-cultural examination of how gender roles and work expectations evolve under different political and economic systems.

Chapter 6: **The Effects of Immigration and Migration on Work** delves into the global labor market, illustrating how migration reshapes economies and labor forces across the United States, Mexico, China, India, and beyond.

Chapter 7: **The Effects of Climate on People's Attitudes Toward Work** examines the impact of environmental factors on workplace attitudes, offering organizational strategies to mitigate the effects of climate change on job performance and satisfaction.

Chapter 8: **Work and the Economic Structure of a Business and Ireland** analyzes how Ireland's economic policies and globalization have influenced its labor market, contributing to a deeper understanding of regional work practices.

Chapter 9: **The Evolution of Gender-Specific Occupations in Various Cultures** explores the shifts in gender roles within the workforce, highlighting progress and ongoing challenges in achieving gender equity in the U.S., India, and Japan.

Chapter 10: **The Effects of the Practice of Art, Music, and Religion on the Practices of Work** examines how cultural elements, such as art, music, and religion, influence workplace behaviors and organizational culture, fostering creativity and ethical practices.

Chapter 11: **Work and Its Implications in Australia** offers an in-depth analysis of the evolution of work in Australia, focusing on the impact of technological and cultural shifts on workforce development.

Chapter 12: **Ethical Work Practices** emphasizes the importance of ethical leadership in cultivating a positive and productive work environment, stressing cultural values and motivators in shaping work ethics.

Work and Society serves as a vital resource for educators, practitioners, and policymakers seeking to understand the complexities of work in a globalized world. It provides essential insights into fostering inclusive, equitable, and ethical work environments across diverse cultural contexts.

Dr. Viktor Wang, Professor,
California State University, San Bernardino, USA

Editor and Contributors

About the Editor

Dr. Viktor Wang, a globally recognized professor in the Department of Educational Leadership & Technology at California State University, San Bernardino, USA, stands as a trailblazer in the field of Education. With an extensive body of work that includes over 240 peer-reviewed publications, he has made significant contributions to academic scholarship while fostering the growth of students and colleagues alike. His leadership in academic publishing has inspired peers to contribute more than 200 articles to his journals and over 1,500 chapters to his books, with collaborations from prominent scholars around the world. These publications are widely respected and cataloged by esteemed institutions, including the JOHN M. PFAU LIBRARY and other top-tier university libraries globally. Dr. Wang's achievements have earned him numerous accolades, including the prestigious 2016 Presidential Award for Exceptional and Innovative Leadership from the American Association for Adult and Continuing Education, alongside several institutional honors such as the Distinguished Faculty and Scholarly Achievement Award. As a dedicated mentor, Dr. Wang has guided over 70 doctoral students through their dissertations, leaving an indelible mark on the future of education through his commitment to research, leadership, and innovation.

About the Contributors

Dr. Zuzana Buzzell currently serves as an Associate Dean for Business Programs at Southern New Hampshire University's Global Campus. Dr. Buzzell has over 20 years of experience teaching and overseeing successful Finance, Project Management, Economics, and Accounting programs in various academic settings. Having nearly a decade of experience in a leading Top 500 financial services company and collaborating with an international team in India, she specializes in FinTech, digital ethics, predictive forecasting, and real estate. Dr. Buzzell earned her Ph.D. in International Business with a specialization in Finance and FinTech certificate from Hong Kong University.

Michelle I. Caron, PhD, CPC, with 25 years of experience in education, Dr. Michelle Caron has been instrumental in developing and overseeing successful Business, Education, and STEM academic programs across higher education institutions, government agencies, and the private sector. Currently serving as Associate Dean at Southern New Hampshire University's Global Campus, Dr. Caron oversees and innovates Business programs and provides quality assurance across curriculum, governance, and accreditation. In her experience spanning both higher education and the transportation and logistics industries, she has consistently driven teams to exceed strategic goals while fostering cohesion and synergy in diverse environments where a sense of urgency, precision, and safety are paramount. She is also a higher education consultant, international visiting professor, and global speaker for entities in countries such as Kenya, Lebanon, Malawi, Rwanda, South Africa, Sweden, Ukraine, and Vietnam. Dr. Caron's current research focus is university-industry collaboration, the integration of technology and artificial intelligence in business education, and creating service-learning projects that build community resilience.

Praveen K. Dubey, Ph. D., is an Assistant Professor of Education and Director of Clinical Experiences and Partnerships at Montana State University-Northern. His research interest focuses on the areas of Multicultural/Immigrant Education, Diversity, Equity, & Inclusivity, Leadership and Change, Technology in Education (Digital Equity & AI), STEM education, Comparative and International Education, Teacher Quality, and Teacher Choice for diverse classrooms. In his research, he uses the statistical tools of Structural Education Modelling (SEM), Mediation & Moderation, and R programming to address the issues that intersect in improving the learning experiences of diverse student populations, immigrant/refugee students, and minority students. He has presented research papers at several national research conferences such as AERA, UCIE, AEFP, SREE, etc., and is currently working on different projects and grants.

Dr. Linda Ellington

Her link is https://www.linkedin.com/in/lindaellington/

After working in IBM for 23 years, Linda is an Associate Dean of Business at Southern New Hampshire University. She conducted her doctoral research at the University of Oxford and the University of Warwick, United Kingdom. Her research focus is on the intersection of leadership and organizational change, uncovering strategies that explore how effective leaders navigate complex challenges to make impactful strategic choices. Dr. Ellington has published extensively in top-tier journals, scholarly books, and is a member of several university doctoral dissertations, such as at the University of Johannesburg, South Africa. Beyond academia, she has published eight children's books in the genre of bullying and taking care of the planet. She collaborates with community leaders to read stories to local children, fostering a love of literacy and inspiring the next generation of readers. She lives with her two coolest four-legged friends, Max and Riley.

Ted Fleming graduated with a theoretical science degree from Maynooth University in Ireland where he is now Emeritus Professor of Adult Education. He completed his MA and EdD in Adult Education with Jack Mezirow at Teachers College where he is now Adjunct Professor. He received the Jack Mezirow Theory of Transformative Learning Award for 'original contribution to the theory of learning' writing on Axel Honneth and delivered the inaugural Mezirow Memorial Lecture at Teachers College. He is a member of the International Expert Panel advising Aontas and the Irish Government's Further Education and Training Authority (SOLAS) on including student voice in adult education services. Research interests include access for adult students to higher education and critical social theory. He is a member of the Editorial Boards of international journals including American *Journal of Transformative Education;* the Polish *Interdisciplinary Studies in Education & Society; Teraźniejszość - Człowiek – Edukacj;* and the Greek *Adult Education - Critical Issues.* Publications are also available at www.tedfleming.net

Fleming, T. (2024). Experience and sociological imagination: Transforming the researcher's learner identity. *European Journal for Research on the Education and Learning of Adults, 15*(1), 13–26. https://doi.org/10.3384/rela.2000-7426.4841

Kokkos, A. & Fleming, T. (2024). Toward a pedagogy of critical and social imagination: The arts and transformative learning. *Journal of Transformative Education, 00*(0), 1-18. https://doi.org/10.1177/15413446241255908

Fleming, T. (2024). A sociological imagination: The neglected concept in transformation theory. *Adult Education Critical Issues*, *4*(1), 21–25. https://doi.org/10.12681/haea.35922

Sue Kaiser, EdD, is a respected faculty member at California State University, San Bernardino, with a doctorate in Educational Administration from the University of Southern California. With over 40 years of experience in education, Dr. Kaiser has held numerous leadership roles, including teacher, administrator, and consultant. Her expertise lies in leadership development, organizational change, and educational equity, making her a sought-after authority in the field. Dr. Kaiser is deeply committed to mentoring future educational leaders, contributing significantly to both the academic and practical aspects of educational leadership through her teaching, research, and extensive consulting work.

Steve Lambert is an Associate Professor of educational leadership at the University of Chester, UK. His work involves academic leadership programs related to educational leadership within the School of Education. He supervises masters and doctoral students and undertakes research in the areas of educational policy and discourse, the development of sustainable leadership as a leadership concept that secures the future of educational leadership, and the role of emotions in leadership.

James A. Martinez is the Chief Data Officer at DB Legal Support, Inc. | McCune Law Group, where he leads data-driven initiatives to enhance business decision-making through cloud computing and interactive data systems. He ensures data governance and alignment with organizational goals while overseeing a team that strategically utilizes data to achieve business objectives. With a strong foundation in Career Technical Education (CTE), James is committed to preparing the global workforce for the modern economy by emphasizing technological literacy, work-based learning, and cross-cultural competencies. James holds a master's degree in public health with a focus on epidemiology and a doctoral degree from Columbia University. He has earned certifications in project management, Geographic Information Systems (GIS), and modern data science applications. His academic contributions include teaching courses on database design, artificial intelligence, and GIS in public health, all supporting CTE's mission to foster workforce readiness. In addition to his professional roles, James is actively involved in community service. He serves on the boards of several non-profit organizations, mentors students, and volunteers at Morgan STEAM Academy, where he teaches GIS to elementary students. His dedication to education and workforce development highlights his commitment to preparing future generations for success in an interconnected global market.

Dayna Lynn Mitchell, Ed.D. served PK-12 public education for 35 years as a High School Teacher and Administrator, Middle School Principal, Director of Curriculum, Instruction, and Assessment, and Assistant Superintendent. Using an equity lens, Dr. Mitchell developed district-wide professional learning systems focused on continuous cycles of improvement designed to increase student achievement, equity, and engagement to close opportunity gaps and accelerate learning for all students. Dr. Mitchell is an Assistant Professor of Educational Leadership at California State Polytechnic University at Pomona dlmitchell@cpp.edu.

Mattius Rischard is an Assistant Professor of English at Montana State University-Northern. He received his M.A. and PhD at the University of Arizona from the Department of English and Social, Cultural, and Critical Theory Programs, specializing in African American literature of the 20th Century with a focus on the urban novel, as well as digital and cultural studies methods and pedagogy. He has taught grant writing, composition and rhetoric, film, and literature for Montana State, the University of Arizona, Pima Community College, and as a Writing Assessment Specialist for the University of Texas System. He was a graduate teaching associate for the English and Political Science departments, as well as a graduate assistant director conducting pedagogical research for the UA Writing Program. As a PhD Fellow, he was a contributor to the redefining volume on intersectional studies of politics in Anglophone literature, The Routledge Companion to Literature and Class (2021), and recently published the book Street, Text, and Representation in African American Literature (Routledge, 2024). He is the winner of the 2020 International Award for New Directions in the Humanities by the Common Ground Research Network for his article in The International Journal of Critical Cultural Studies. Currently, the author is completing an edited collection on media adaptations and the environmental humanities, and has published widely in journals and edited volumes in the fields of Comparative Urban Literature, Postcolonial Studies, Film Criticism, Digital Humanities, and Humanities pedagogy.

Mona Stephens, CPA, CIA, MSA, MS.DAN, is a distinguished accounting and higher education professional with over 35 years of experience. She currently serves as Associate Dean of Business at Southern New Hampshire University, ensuring curriculum relevancy and promoting learner success through data-driven strategies. Her previous roles in local government include Auditor, and Sr. Administrator for Finance and Accounting. She holds advanced degrees in Accountancy and Data Analytics and maintains multiple certifications. A passionate advocate for continuous improvement, she is an active member of several professional organizations, including the American Accounting Association and the Institute of Management Accountants.

Dr. Gabriele Strohschen is Professor Emerita and a Frédéric Ozanam Fellow at DePaul University. She holds an EdD in Educational Leadership and Policy Studies from Northern Illinois University along with numerous certifications (e.g., Accrediting Council for Independent Colleges and Schools, Langevin Learning Services, the Kentucky Department of Education, the State of New York, Literacy Volunteers of America, and United Way). She served as the inaugural director of the online graduate program in adult education at National Louis University and as director of graduate programs at DPU's School for New Learning In Chicago and Thailand. She taught life skills for adults at the Center for Disabled Student Services with the Chicago City Colleges; graduate courses at the Department of Leadership, Educational Psychology and Foundations of Northern Illinois University; and taught in the cohort-based Adult, Continuing & Literacy Education doctoral program and the interdisciplinary, field-based baccalaureate program in the College of Arts and Sciences at National-Louis University. Consulting with the Mayor's Office of Employment and Training, she developed an award-winning workforce education program within a public-private sector partnership. As a Visiting Professor, she taught at universities in China, Germany, Kenya, Mexico, and Thailand. In Japan, India, and the USA, she supported dissertation development for doctoral students. Her action research, faculty training, and program development and evaluation work is centered in China, the Czech Republic, Germany, Kenya, Mexico, Thailand, and the USA. Based on her work, she presented and published nationally and internationally. During the US occupation, she consulted with UNESCO and the Afghan Ministry of Education to evaluate education programs for women onsite in Afghanistan. She served as a board member and president of professional adult education associations. Locally over the years, she was engaged as a member of the Education Taskforce of Cook County Commissioner Deere and the Chicago Public School Region 1 Community Action Council, as well as on many grass-roots and not-for-profit boards of directors, co-creating education programs for youth and adults. Before working in academia, she was a community organizer, resource developer, and director of youth and adult education and workforce development programs in CBOs in Chicago's Latino immigrant and Black neighborhoods for which she received the Outstanding Educator Award from US Congressman Danny K. Davis, Chicago. After retirement, she returned to her work in community activism, currently working on several civic projects surrounding immigration, poverty, and property tax issues. gstrohsc@depaul.edu

Geraldine Torrisi-Steele is an associate professor/deputy head in the School of Information and Communication Technology at Griffith University, Australia. She is a Senior Fellow of the Higher Education Academy (UK). Her interest in learning and teaching, learning theory, technology for learning, human-computer interaction, and leadership distills from her "pre-academia" experiences in secondary school mathematics and physics teaching, and the design, development, and project management of digital interactive media for learning in higher education.

CHAPTER 1

Work and Its Implications in a Global Society

Dayna Lynn Mitchell, California State Polytechnic University, Pomona, USA

Abstract

Work transcends geographical boundaries in today's interconnected world, emerging as a multifaceted phenomenon with significant global implications. Technological advancements, globalization, and evolving economic landscapes have fundamentally reshaped the nature of work, influencing its perception, organization, and execution across diverse cultures and societies. This chapter delves into the dimensions of work in a global society, examining its economic, social, and ethical implications. We explore the impact of globalization on labor markets, the role of technological advancements in shaping the future of work, and the importance of diversity and inclusion in multicultural workplaces. Additionally, we address the ethical responsibilities of organizations, the significance of ethical leadership, and the role of education in preparing individuals for the global workforce. By understanding these complex interactions, we can navigate the challenges and opportunities presented by work in a global society, fostering more inclusive, productive, and ethical work environments.

Introduction: The Evolution of Work in a Global Context

In today's interconnected world, work is not just an activity confined to a geographical location but a multifaceted phenomenon with global implications. The advent of technology, globalization, and evolving economic landscapes have reshaped the nature of work, bringing profound changes to how work is perceived, organized, and executed across different cultures and societies. This chapter delves into the various dimensions of work in a global society, exploring its implications from economic, social, ethical, and educational perspectives. The concept of work has undergone significant transformation from the industrial age to the information era. Historically, work was primarily labor-intensive, localized, and tied to specific physical locations. With the Industrial Revolution, work began to shift toward mechanization and mass production, leading to the creation of factories, urbanization, and various technologies. The First Industrial Revolution occurred in the 18th and 19th centuries, with the steam engine revolutionizing industrial production and transportation. In the 19th and early 20th centuries, electricity enabled mass production in the Second Industrial Revolution. Starting in the 1960s, the Third Industrial Revolution brought electronic systems and information technologies, such as computers, the Internet, and automated production. The Fourth Industrial Revolution (Industry 4.0) began in 2011, with the advent of smart factories, cyber-physical systems, and integrating technologies from the physical, digital, and biological worlds. Industry 4.0 continues to emerge and varies by location and sector. Requiring new production methods and management strategies to stay competitive, this revolution impacts all industry areas, including supply chain, manufacturing, and management, and demands specialized IT knowledge. While some jobs will be replaced by robots, there will be a growing need for professionals to manage these technologies which will assist them to make informed decisions. The emergence of the information age, characterized by the rise of digital technologies and the internet, has revolutionized the way work is conducted. In the 21st century, globalization has further accelerated the evolution of work, breaking down geographical barriers and creating a global marketplace. This has led to the rise of remote work, cross-border collaborations, and multinational corporations. The global workforce is now more diverse and interconnected than ever, presenting both opportunities and challenges for individuals, organizations, and societies.

Economic Implications of Global Work

GLOBALIZATION AND LABOR MARKETS

Globalization has significantly impacted labor markets worldwide, creating opportunities for economic growth and development leading to job creation and improved living standards for millions of people. In developing countries, globalization has created opportunities for economic growth through access to global markets, foreign investment, and shifting economies, as well as presented challenges impacting wages and labor practices.

ACCESS TO GLOBAL MARKETS

Globalization expands markets for developing countries to export their goods and services. This has led to increased trade, boosting industries like technology, transportation, pharmaceuticals, and textiles. By tapping into global demand, developing nations can grow their economies and reduce poverty. Many developing countries participate in global value chains (GVC) whereby a range of activities and processes involved in the production of goods or services are linked and distributed across multiple countries. Approximately 70% of global trade is driven by GVCs, where services, raw materials, parts, and components often cross borders multiple times before reaching the final consumer (OECD, n.d.). In a GVC, different stages of production are carried out in various countries, leveraging the specific advantages of each region, such as cheaper labor, specialized skills, or access to resources. This can include the initial stages of design, raw material sourcing, manufacturing, assembly, marketing, and distribution. For example, a smartphone might be designed in one country, have components manufactured in several others, assembled in another, and then marketed and sold globally. By spreading production across borders, companies can reduce costs, increase efficiency, and access new markets. GVCs have become a critical component of global trade, accounting for nearly half of all international trade activity. The concept of GVCs highlights the interconnectedness of global economies, where the final product is the result of contributions from multiple countries, emphasizing the importance of international cooperation and policies that support open trade (World Bank, 2020). Global value chains have impacted the economic growth of developing countries over the last 30 years by accelerating growth and raising incomes, lifting nations out of poverty. A 1% increase in GVC participation is estimated to raise per capita income by more than 1%, which is double the effect of conventional trade. However, GVC expansion can plateau during economic recessions and trade reforms, and conflicts, hindering the ability of developing countries to benefit from GVCs, potentially leading to increased poverty and reduced global income.

Kormakova et al.'s (2023) research highlighted the ways globalization positively influences companies by expanding market opportunities. Using data from international corporations such as Apple, Samsung, Toyota, Volkswagon, Ford, Pfizer, Johnson & Johnson, Proctor & Gamble, and Walmart, the study identified the diversification of goods, services, and works as key factors for successful foreign economic activity. The study examined the motivations behind businesses' market development strategies and emphasized the importance of choosing the right strategy when entering international markets, as it shapes future growth. Key strategies include investing in research and development, engaging in joint ventures, mergers, and strategic collaborations, as well as adopting licensing agreements and strategic alliances. Furthermore, companies that leverage consumer insights, localized marketing, and innovation are more likely to succeed. Tailoring products to regional preferences and cultural nuances strengthens a company's position in global markets. Additionally, the study points out the significance of digital technology, robust supply chain networks, and a customer-centric approach to accessing and thriving in international markets.

FOREIGN INVESTMENT

Globalization has impacted broader economic growth in developing countries by facilitating foreign direct investment (FDI), leading to new employment opportunities, particularly in industries like manufacturing, transportation, technology, and energy. FDI fosters innovation and impacts the building of new industries (Ali et al., 2023; Dempere et al., 2023; Qamruzzaman, 2023; Zheng et al., 2024). Supported by external investments, this growth encourages knowledge transfer, enhances technological capabilities, and helps integrate countries into global supply chains. This development improves the business environment and helps attract even more investment, further stimulating economic growth. Tariq et al. (2023) explored the connections between economic globalization, FDI, economic growth, and renewable electricity consumption in the Belt and Road Initiative (BRI) countries from 2000 to 2020. Using the Pooled Mean Group (PMG) autoregressive distributed lag (ARDL) technique, the results show both FDI and economic growth have a positive relationship with renewable electricity consumption. The study suggests that BRI countries promote globalization by enhancing technology and knowledge related to renewable electricity to support long-term sustainability.

SHIFTING ECONOMIES

Countries like China and India have experienced rapid industrialization and economic expansion leading to job creation and improved living standards for millions of people. Both countries implemented significant economic reforms that shifted their economies toward market-based systems. China began its reforms in the late 1970s under Deng Xiaoping, moving from a planned economy to one that embraced foreign investment and privatization (Naughton, 1993). India experienced economic liberalization in the early 1990s, which opened trade, reduced government regulation, and encouraged foreign investment (Rao & Dutt, 2007). Both China and India have large populations, providing an abundant labor force. This has allowed them to become hubs for labor-intensive industries, such as manufacturing and textiles at relatively low cost compared to developed economies (Kroeber, 2020; Mezzadri & Majumder, 2022). Globalization has enabled companies from developed nations to invest in China and India, seeking cheaper production costs (Ikumapayi, et al., 2020). This influx of foreign capital has helped build infrastructure, create jobs, and transfer technology, spurring industrial growth (Alam et al., 2022; Li & Wye, 2023; Yi et al., 2023). Both countries have also heavily invested in technology and infrastructure. China, for instance, has become a leader in high-tech manufacturing, while India has developed a globally competitive IT sector. These advancements have driven economic expansion and increased productivity. Favorable government policies, such as tax incentives for businesses, investment in education, and infrastructure development, have supported industrialization and economic growth. In China, the government played a significant role in directing investment and growth (Wan & Lee, 2023), while in India, reforms facilitated private sector growth and innovation (Manigandan et al., 2024). Both countries have integrated into global supply chains, with China becoming the "world's factory" and India a global center for IT services. This integration has allowed them to benefit from global demand for their products and services, further fueling job creation and economic expansion. As a result, millions of people in both countries have seen improved living standards through better employment opportunities, rising incomes, and access to a growing consumer economy.

GLOBALIZATION CHALLENGES

Globalization has significantly impacted labor markets worldwide. Although it has created opportunities for economic growth and development, particularly in emerging economies, this growth has also come with challenges, such as income inequality and environmental degradation, job displacement, and wage stagnation in certain sectors, particularly in developed countries. The outsourcing of manufacturing and service jobs to countries with lower labor costs has resulted in job losses and economic uncertainty for many workers in advanced economies. This has contributed to rising income inequality and social discontent in some regions.

Globalization has pressured companies and countries to balance economic growth with maintaining fair labor standards. In some regions, globalization has led to improved labor conditions due to international scrutiny and competition. However, in others, it has resulted in poor working conditions, low wages, and labor exploitation as companies seek to minimize costs. Although over the past 40 years, China has lifted nearly 800 million people out of poverty (World Bank, 2022), workers experience unsafe working conditions such as forced labor, child labor, and chemical exposure (Bureau of International Labor Affairs, n.d.).

Globalization has enabled companies to outsource jobs to countries with lower labor costs, particularly in manufacturing and services like customer support or IT. While this has created jobs in developing countries, it has often led to job losses or shifts in more developed nations, where industries relocate to take advantage of cheaper labor. Many businesses in developed countries are moving production to developing countries to reduce costs due to rising labor expenses, taxes, and regulations at home. High-tech companies like Apple are notable examples, of outsourcing manufacturing and assembly to countries with cheaper labor. Apple employs Chinese companies to set up factories in China, where Chinese workers assemble the products. In one example, Apple made a $90 net profit on a $149 product that cost $5 to assemble in China. This practice leads to significant wealth inequality, with outsourcing companies gaining most of the profits and insourcing countries receiving minimal benefits (Liu et al., 2023).

Globalization has contributed to wage disparities both within and between countries. In developing economies, wages may rise due to increased demand for labor, though they often remain low compared to developed nations. In developed countries, wages for lower-skilled jobs may stagnate due to competition from cheaper labor markets abroad. Globalization has also facilitated the movement of workers across borders in search of better employment opportunities. While this benefits migrants and economies needing labor, it can also lead to tensions over immigration and its impact on local labor markets, especially in countries that perceive job competition or wage suppression.

Technological Advancements and the Future of Work

Globalization aids the transfer of technology and knowledge from developed to developing countries, enhancing productivity, efficiency, and innovation. This process accelerates the advancement of industries and infrastructure in developing nations, fostering improved productivity and industrial development. Technological advancements, particularly in automation and artificial intelligence (AI), are reshaping the future of work.

Manufacturing tools such as Computerized Numerical Control (CNC) machines, 3D printing, composite welding, and automation are advancing globalization and outsourcing. CNC machines facilitate the global exchange of products due to standardized industry principles. 3D printing allows manufacturing in diverse locations, reducing the need for factory space and focusing on cost savings. Composite welding is cost-effective and often involves outsourcing specialized skills. Automation significantly cuts production costs by reducing the need for personnel, increasing production capacity, and reducing poor human working conditions. These tools exemplify how globalization and outsourcing are integrated into modern manufacturing (Ikumapayi et al., 2020).

While technology has the potential to increase productivity and create new job opportunities, it poses the risk of job displacement for certain roles. According to a report by the World Economic Forum (2020), automation could displace approximately 85 million jobs by 2025, but it could also create 97 million new roles that require different skills. Generative artificial intelligence (AI) tools create business value by efficiently automating tasks, transforming various aspects of production, labor, and business operations. AI can create content and engineer products without a previously used workforce. Its ability to automate production and labor is redefining human jobs and tasks using synthetic media and data. AI technologies like deep learning, augmented reality, and computer vision enable machines to perform tasks autonomously, which can boost an organization's productivity. AI-driven cognitive, emotional, and social processes are also used to engage customers through personalized marketing. As a result, AI has reconfigured job roles, career paths, and hiring practices, while simultaneously improving organizational productivity and competitive advantage. Although generative AI can positively impact business operations and drive efficiency and growth, AI forecasts an impact on labor market job displacement (Lazaroiu and Rogalska, 2023).

Braxton and Taska (2023) explored the impact of earnings decline and technological change. Key points include:

1. *Impact of Technological Change*: Workers in occupations more exposed to technological change face larger earnings declines and are more likely to switch occupations.
2. *Occupation Switchers*: The biggest earnings losses occur among those who switch occupations due to technological change.
3. *Model Findings*: Their labor market model, which includes technological change, occupation choice, and employment risk, shows that technological change accounts for over 45% of the earnings decline after job loss.
4. *Policy Implications*: Policies encouraging retraining during unemployment could help mitigate these earnings losses.
5. *Earnings Gains and Losses*: Technological change benefits some workers (e.g., those who stay in their occupations) but harms others (e.g., displaced workers).
6. *Recession Link*: Technological change accelerates during recessions, potentially explaining why earnings losses are more severe during these periods.

This study highlights the need for balanced policies that promote technological advancement while supporting displaced workers.

While the integration of AI and machine learning is expected to cause significant job displacement, especially for low-skilled and routine positions, these technologies also have the potential to create new employment opportunities and boost productivity. The impact of AI and machine learning on employment is complex and multifaceted, influenced by factors such as the pace of technological advancement, workers' adaptability to new technologies, and the specific industries and occupations affected (Tiwari, 2023).

The shift toward a knowledge-based economy places a premium on skills such as critical thinking, creativity, and digital literacy. This underscores the importance of education and continuous learning to equip the workforce with the skills needed to thrive in the evolving job market. The global economy supports high-skilled workers who can navigate advanced technologies and international markets. As a result, demand for skilled labor has risen, leading to higher wages for these workers, while lower-skilled labor has faced decreased demand, contributing to a growing skills gap. The term "knowledge-based economy" refers to an economy's reliance on knowledge, information, and highly-skilled labor. This shift has been accompanied by a decline in traditional industrial activities and involves changes in societies' technological, economic, political, and value foundations. The extensive use of information and communication technologies has significantly impacted society, altering how new knowledge is produced and shared, supporting this economic shift. As a result, the importance of human capital has been redefined, emphasizing the value of those who work with their minds over those who work with their hands (Aparicio et al., 2023). To support organizational goals and outcomes, knowledge work requires an employee to have complex skills and competencies such as dynamic decision-making, problem-solving, and analysis rather than a manual task completion (Muzam, 2023).

Social Implications of Global Work

DIVERSITY AND INCLUSION IN THE WORKPLACE

The globalization of work has led to more diverse and multicultural workplaces. Diversity in the workplace brings a wealth of perspectives, ideas, and experiences, which can drive innovation and creativity. However, it also presents challenges in terms of managing cultural differences and fostering an inclusive environment. Effective diversity and inclusion strategies are essential for organizations to leverage the benefits of a diverse workforce. This includes implementing policies and practices that promote equality, respect, and collaboration among employees from different backgrounds. Leaders play a crucial role in modeling inclusive behaviors and creating a culture where everyone feels valued and empowered to contribute.

Effective diversity and inclusion strategies are essential for organizations to leverage the benefits of a diverse workforce. Diversity encompasses various human differences, such as race, gender, and age, while inclusion refers to creating a collaborative environment that fosters belonging and respect. In support of diverse and inclusive practices, organizations can implement practices and policies that promote equality, respect, and collaboration among employees from different backgrounds. A study by Olusanya (2023) surveyed 500 employees across various industries and roles to evaluate diversity, equity, and inclusion in the workplace. The study highlighted several benefits of workplace diversity, including increased innovation, stronger problem-solving abilities, and improved talent attraction.

The study also found that diversity positively influences company culture and helps reduce unconscious bias and discrimination. In some countries, a significant gap exists between male and female workforce participation. To address this gap, companies must ensure female-friendly workplaces to promote gender diversity. Kaur and Arora's, (2020) research highlights the importance of gender diversity and inclusion for business success, emphasizing the benefits in creativity, innovation, reputation, productivity, decision-making, problem-solving, and overall performance, advocating for gender diversity and inclusion as essential organizational policies.

Diversity and inclusion in the workplace bring a wealth of perspectives, ideas, and experiences, which can drive innovation and creativity. Effectively managing an increasingly diverse workforce is an essential component of globalization. To become truly global, companies must leverage the diversity of their human resources. By seeking input from employees with varied backgrounds, educations, and life experiences, companies can enhance their external outputs, such as products and customer service, as well as internal processes like company culture and management policies (Mor Barak, 2022). Parmelee (2020) found that a diverse and inclusive workplace can increase job loyalty.

Companies that embrace the "learning and effectiveness paradigm" (Ely & Thomas, 2020, p. 116) understand the benefit of leveraging a diverse workforce. This approach involves not only recruiting and retaining individuals from underrepresented identity groups but also utilizing their unique knowledge and experiences to enhance the organization's core functions. Research indicates that teams adopting this method are more effective than teams that do not learn from their members' differences. These companies demonstrate that diverse perspectives are valued and do not need to be suppressed for group cohesion. This mindset encourages employees to rethink their work processes and goals. By fostering a learning orientation toward diversity, where individuals draw on their identity-related experiences to reimagine tasks, products, business processes, and organizational norms, companies can significantly boost their effectiveness (Ely & Thomas, 2020). Ashikali et al.'s (2021) study explored how inclusive leadership promotes inclusiveness within diverse teams. Using structural equation modeling, hypotheses were tested on a sample of 293 team members from 45 public sector teams. The findings show that inclusive leadership positively moderates the negative relationship between a team's ethnic-cultural diversity and an inclusive climate. The study reveals that simply having a diverse team does not automatically create an inclusive environment. Inclusive leadership is essential to cultivate a climate where all team members are valued for their contributions.

Muktamar et al. (2023) explore the interplay between globalization, cultural diversity, and innovation within organizations, shedding light on the challenges and opportunities of managing diverse workforces in a globalized business landscape. To successfully foster global innovation and manage culturally diverse teams, organizations must implement strategies for navigating cultural complexities and diversity-related challenges. Thriving in this global environment requires organizations to value cultural differences, develop cross-cultural competence, and adapt management practices to various cultural contexts. Globalization has increased talent mobility and altered workforce dynamics, presenting unique challenges such as differing time zones, languages, and cultural norms. However, it also provides opportunities for organizations to become strategic partners in addressing global business complexities. Scholars emphasize the importance of flexible and culturally sensitive approaches to recruitment, selection, training, and performance management to effectively handle a global workforce.

Cultural diversity within organizations is a key driver of innovation and competitive advantage. Teams composed of individuals from various cultural backgrounds bring a rich array of perspectives, ideas, and approaches, which fosters creativity, enhances problem-solving, and drives innovation. Managing cultural diversity effectively requires a deep understanding of the interplay between organizational culture, individual values, and communication styles. Research emphasizes the importance of inclusive practices that foster an environment where individuals from diverse backgrounds feel valued and empowered to share their unique insights. The literature highlights the need to align diversity strategies with organizational goals for innovation, recognizing that cultural diversity is not just a checkbox but a catalyst for organizational creativity (Muktamar et al., 2023).

WORK-LIFE BALANCE IN A GLOBALIZED WORLD

The blurring of boundaries between work and personal life is a significant social implication of global work. Advances in communication technologies have enabled remote work and flexible schedules, allowing employees to balance work and personal responsibilities more effectively. However, this flexibility can also lead to increased work demands and stress, as employees may feel pressure to be constantly available.

Offering a perspective of remote work dynamics, Buonomo et al. (2024) conducted a study utilizing the Conservation of Resources (COR) theory to examine the impact of various forms of social support on employee outcomes. Their findings indicate that remote work has shifted traditional office environments into more dynamic and diverse settings, influencing employee engagement and organizational structures. When adequately supported, remote work can alleviate stress, burnout, and homework conflict while enhancing engagement and satisfaction. However, it also poses challenges such as social isolation, disconnection from colleagues, and difficulties in maintaining work-life balance. Support from colleagues and supervisors plays a vital role in mitigating work-related stressors, with perceived organizational support significantly preventing strain conditions. Conversely, a lack of perceived support can negatively affect employees' mental health, leading to stress, fatigue, burnout, anxiety, isolation, and a diminished sense of belonging.

Work-life balance (WLB) can create conflict between work and family roles. During the global pandemic, businesses adopted working from home out of necessity, leading to the rise of hybrid working, where employees split their time between home and the office. Flexible working arrangements have been touted as a solution to WLB issues. Recent reviews highlight positive relationships between flexible work and health outcomes, showing improvements in physical health, reduced absenteeism, and fewer somatic symptoms. Additionally, working partly from home has been found to decrease depressive symptoms, stress, and emotional exhaustion, albeit with small but positive effects (McDowall, 2023).

A balance of work and private life can impact workers' well-being. Economic inequality often leads to longer working hours for some people, negatively impacting work-life balance. Inequality, socio-economic status, anxiety, and competitiveness all influence perceptions of working time and work-life balance. Both high and low-wage-earning individuals may experience status anxiety, affecting their work-life balance. Higher-wage individuals face demanding work environments with long hours, high responsibilities, and career expectations, leading to high anxiety levels. Their prestigious positions and financial rewards can blur the lines between work and personal life, driven by the need to maintain their status and the flexibility to overwork. Lower-wage individuals often work longer hours to meet basic needs. They often have less control over their schedules, limited access to benefits, and cannot outsource tasks like childcare. Status anxiety also plays a role, as low-wage individuals may overwork to improve their social standing and alleviate feelings of devaluation. Both high- and low-income individuals sacrifice work-life balance due to status anxiety: the former to maintain their privileged status, and the latter to meet material needs and seek social mobility. Inequality exacerbates financial hardships for low-wage individuals and heightens concerns about social standing and competitiveness (Filippi, et al., 2023).

Achieving work-life balance requires a proactive approach from both employees and employers. Organizations can support work-life balance by implementing policies such as flexible working hours, remote work options, and wellness programs. Employees, on the other hand, need to set boundaries and prioritize self-care to maintain their well-being. Manroop and Petrovski's (2023) study discussed the challenges of remote work and suggested that employers assist workers with developing a realistic preview of the demands they are likely to face while working from home. The study highlights that workers employ one or more coping strategies to navigate the daily stressors of remote work demands such as maintaining a daily schedule to reduce stress; engaging in positive self-talk as a method of self-care to manage their mood, maintaining optimism, boosting confidence and gratitude; or taking breaks to engage in positive, non-work-related activities.

Ethical Implications of Global Work

CORPORATE SOCIAL RESPONSIBILITY

In a globalized world, organizations are increasingly expected to operate ethically and responsibly. Corporate Social Responsibility (CSR) refers to the practices and policies that organizations adopt to have a positive impact on society and the environment. This includes initiatives related to sustainability, fair labor practices, community engagement, and ethical governance. The demand for environmentally and socially sustainable supply chains is growing. A diverse array of trade policies, voluntary standards, and corporate accountability tools is emerging to improve supply chain sustainability. Trade facilitation can significantly contribute to making trade more eco-friendly while minimizing compliance-related trade costs (OECD, 2018). Sustainable development satisfies the needs of the present without jeopardizing the ability of future generations to meet their own needs (Shah, 2008). A major global challenge, sustainable development aims to enhance human lifestyle and well-being while understanding and addressing the impact of climate change and resource demands. Environmental degradation threatens ecosystems and access to natural resources that are vital for societal well-being. Sustainable development encompasses not just material needs but also values, relationships, and freedoms, contributing to moral and spiritual well-being. Transitioning to a knowledge-based service economy is essential for achieving sustainable development (Ortiz-Martínez, et al. 2023).

Le's (2023) quantitative study on corporate social responsibility and sustainable consumption and production patterns discussed the mediating role of a green supply chain management. The importance of security for future generations and the uncertainties and risks in supply chains, will depend on the sustainable development goals that are prioritized by global corporations. Those who benefit from and influence supply chains must contribute to their sustainability. Corporate social responsibility and green supply chain management are crucial in promoting sustainable consumption and production patterns. The study's findings support social cognitive theory, emphasizing the moral responsibility of all stakeholders. For the planet's future, corporations must embed sustainability practices, strategies, and goals into their operations.

Dahan et al., (2023) discusses shared responsibility and labor rights in global supply chains, proposing a minimum threshold shared by most countries around the world (ILO, 2019). The International Labour Organization's four core labor rights are a set of fundamental human rights that include Declaration on Fundamental Principles and Rights at Work: (1) the freedom to organize and the right to collective bargaining; (2) the prohibition of forced labor and compulsory work; (3) the prohibition of child labor; and (4) the prohibition of discrimination in employment and professions (ILO, 1998). Dahan et al.'s research also includes basic working conditions concerning health and safety, working hours, weekly rest, and employee rights concerning overtime regulation, wage deductions, and earning a living wage.

Emphasizing sustainability is not only a moral responsibility but also an effective business strategy to ensure long-term viability and a positive reputation. As companies integrate sustainability into their core strategies, they should consider a reciprocal relationship approach aimed at balancing business and community interests. As an example, extractive industries, such as mining and natural resource extraction, are essential for economic growth but pose significant environmental, social, and economic challenges. Companies in this sector should develop marketing strategies that focus on sustainability and community involvement, as rapid economic growth from these industries often leads to environmental damage, habitat loss, and social issues like poverty and conflict with local communities. Effective communication, community participation in decision-making, and sustainability initiatives can build trust and transparency (Aripin et al., 2023).

Gull et al., (2023) studied ethical corporate governance and the relationship to corporate social responsibility (CSR). The findings show that when the resources of corporate boards and committees are utilized effectively, corporate transparency related to CSR is improved, serving as an effective tool to reduce agency conflicts and align the interests of managers and shareholders. The study suggests that governance boards monitor and disclose CSR-related practices and align performance to mitigate gaps. Opportunistic managers who engage in value-destroying and legitimacy-harming practices to achieve their personal goals, which may not be in line with the interests of investors, can result in agency problems. The study's empirical findings show that CSR governance reduces corporate social irresponsibility and misconduct. CSR is not only a moral obligation but also a strategic imperative. Consumers, investors, and other stakeholders are increasingly holding organizations accountable for their social and environmental impact. Companies that prioritize CSR can enhance their reputation, attract talent, and build stronger relationships with stakeholders.

ETHICAL LEADERSHIP IN A GLOBAL CONTEXT

Ethical leadership is paramount in navigating the complexities of global work. Ethical leaders set the tone for organizational culture and decision-making, ensuring that actions align with core values and principles. In a global context, ethical leadership involves understanding and respecting cultural differences, promoting fairness and transparency, and addressing ethical dilemmas with integrity. Ethical leadership can influence employee ethical behaviors, work environment, corporate social responsibility, economic potential, and global competitive markets (Al Halbusi et al., 2023). Ethical leadership emphasizes moral principles and ethical values in decision-making and daily actions. Acting with integrity, honesty, transparency, and fairness, ethical leaders create an environment that promotes ethical behavior among all members of the organization. They consider the impact of their decisions on all stakeholders, including employees, customers, shareholders, and the broader community. Ethical leaders inspire and support their team to uphold high ethical standards, ensuring these values are embedded in the organization's culture (Mariyani, 2024). Through integrity-based interpersonal skills, ethical leaders model appropriate conduct using strategies such as two-way communication, reinforcement, and decision-making, which promote ethical accountability and employee motivation to engage in behaviors that meet the goals of the organization (Dust et al., 2018). Ethical leadership positively influences employee behavior, enhances a company's reputation, and leads to better overall performance. Unethical leadership is harmful and can negatively affect employees, customers, and other stakeholders, potentially leading to business failure. To combat challenges such as climate change and social injustice, companies need ethical leadership. This type of leadership can help to achieve a sustainable world by balancing profit, people, and the planet (Adamu et al., 2023).

Leadership both drives and reflects cultural change and can shape the moral direction of an organization. A study by Jerab and Mabrouk (2023) highlights the importance of leadership in shaping and changing an organization's culture. Findings show how leaders influence culture and provide strategies for leaders to enhance organizational performance and create a positive work environment. Jerab and Mabrouk (2023) position leaders as **cultural architects** who define and communicate the core values, norms, and behaviors that align with the organization's goals. By fostering a culture of innovation, adaptability, and inclusivity, leaders help organizations thrive in a changing business environment by using strategies to manage resistance to cultural change and encourage collective commitment to transformation to create a culture that embraces sustainability and corporate social responsibility. Ethical leaders have an effect in fostering a culture of accountability and ethical behavior within the organization. This includes implementing robust governance structures, encouraging open dialogue and reporting of unethical conduct, and providing training on ethical issues.

The Role of Education in Shaping the Future of Work

LIFELONG LEARNING AND SKILLS DEVELOPMENT

The dynamic nature of the global job market underscores the importance of lifelong learning and skills development. As industries evolve and new technologies emerge, individuals need to continuously update their skills to remain competitive. This requires a shift from traditional education models to more flexible and accessible learning opportunities. Educational institutions, employers, and policymakers have a shared responsibility to promote lifelong learning. This includes investing in education and training programs that equip individuals with the skills needed for the future of work. It also involves creating pathways for career advancement and reskilling for those whose jobs may be displaced by technological changes (Van der Hijden and Martin, 2023). Van der Hijden and Martin (2023) offer a blueprint for policy development and action regarding the education and training of the workforce. They recommend that employers provide short courses and micro-credentials, create flexible learning pathways, foster learner autonomy, and formally acknowledge competencies as effective tools and strategies for offering up-to-date, quality professional learning.

Digital and AI technologies are rapidly transforming the workforce, necessitating new skills and continuous adaptation. The COVID-19 crisis accelerated this shift. Research by the McKinsey Global Institute (Dondi et al., 2021) defined the skills people will need in the future world of work, highlighting that while manual and basic cognitive skills will decline, there will be a growing demand for technological, social, emotional, and higher cognitive skills. Governments face challenges in defining and teaching these skills. McKinsey's research identified 56 foundational skills across four domains that include a mix of skills and attitudes: cognitive, interpersonal, self-leadership, and digital. Cognitive skills include critical thinking, planning and ways of working, communication, and mental flexibility. These skills are essential for effective problem-solving, efficient work habits, clear communication, and adaptability in various contexts. Interpersonal skills include understanding how to mobilize systems, develop relationships, and promote effective teamwork. These skills are also essential for effective leadership. Self-leadership skills encompass self-awareness and self-management, entrepreneurship, and achievement of goals. These skills encourage personal growth and emotional intelligence. Digital competency such as digital fluency and citizenship, software use and development, and the understanding of digital systems are essential for navigating and leveraging digital environments effectively. These skills are important for adding value beyond automated systems, operating in digital environments, and adapting to new work methods. Higher proficiency in these skills is linked to better employment outcomes, higher incomes, and job satisfaction (Dondi et al., 2021).

The World Economic Forum predicts that by 2025, 50% of employees will need reskilling due to new technologies. Many current job skills will change, with a third of essential skills in 2025 being new technology competencies. AI development has surged due to advancements in sensors, computer chips, algorithms, and big data. AI is seen as a strategic tool to enhance competitiveness, with technologies like natural language processing, machine learning, and deep learning offering advanced data analysis across industries. Examples include AT&T using AI for drone-based base station maintenance and SK Telecom applying machine learning for network traffic analysis. (Li, 2022).

AI is transforming company operations, leading to the replacement of human employees with intelligent machines in sectors like manufacturing, service delivery, recruitment, and finance. This shift is pushing human workers into lower-paid jobs or unemployment. Some predict that by 2040, the workforce will be drastically different and potentially unrecognizable. Although AI excels in speed, accuracy, and rationality, humans are intuitive, emotional, and culturally sensitive, human traits that cannot be automated (De Cremer & Kasparov, 2021).

THE ROLE OF HIGHER EDUCATION

Higher education institutions play a critical role in preparing individuals for the global workforce. This involves not only providing technical and professional skills but also fostering critical thinking, creativity, and intercultural competence. Universities and colleges can also serve as hubs for research and innovation, driving advancements in various fields that contribute to economic and social development.

Waham et al.'s (2023) study explores the challenges and opportunities for international collaboration in higher education in enhancing academic excellence, fostering cultural exchange, and addressing global challenges. Using a mixed-methods approach, including surveys, literature analysis, interviews, and case studies, the research emphasized the need for careful planning, effective communication, and strong institutional commitment to overcome challenges and leverage opportunities. Opportunities include expanding access to global knowledge resources, fostering diverse perspectives, enhancing research productivity, and preparing students for a globally interconnected workforce. Challenges in the work include navigating cultural differences, ensuring academic quality and standards, managing logistical complexities, and addressing funding and resource constraints. Understanding these opportunities and complexities can lead to more successful and impactful international collaborations in higher education.

Saroyan and Frenay (2023) posit that higher education needs to adapt to new global realities by changing its goals and teaching methods. This involves integrating liberal education values across all disciplines and preparing students for 21st-century challenges. Key areas of focus include:

- *Knowledge Areas*: Sciences, mathematics, social sciences, humanities, histories, languages, and the arts.
- *Skills Development*: Critical and creative thinking, communication, quantitative and information literacy, teamwork, and problem-solving.
- *Engagement with Big Questions*: Addressing significant and enduring issues.
- *Personal and Social Responsibility*: Civic knowledge, intercultural competence, ethical reasoning, and lifelong learning.
- *Integrative Learning*: Applying knowledge and skills to new settings and complex problems.

Students must be equipped to make independent judgments and decisions that blend theoretical, practical, professional, and moral foundations (Saroyan and Frenay, 2023).

Collaboration between higher education institutions and industry is essential to ensure that educational programs are aligned with the needs of the job market. This includes partnerships for internships, research projects, and continuing education programs that provide real-world experience and insights. The academic learning environment plays a significant role in shaping students' future experiences and preparing them for industry. Education must evolve to meet current and future industry needs, with universities helping students transition from academia to professional environments. Problem-Based Learning (PBL) is highlighted as an effective approach to engage students and address educational needs. Collaboration between universities and industries can facilitate this by combining theoretical knowledge with practical experience to enhance teaching and learning. The rise of Industry 4.0, marked by significant digitization, requires new skills and greater interdisciplinary collaboration. Higher education must adapt to these changes, focusing on skill-based teaching and preparing students for the job market with both hard and soft skills (Salvador et al., 2023). Collaborations between universities and industries are essential for driving innovation and economic development. These partnerships help firms acquire the technological knowledge needed for product and process innovations. Universities benefit financially and contribute to economic growth through these collaborations. However, success isn't guaranteed due to cultural differences and conflicting goals between academia and industry. Universities focus on long-term knowledge creation, while industries seek quick, practical applications. Trust and frequent interactions are essential to overcoming these challenges (O'Dwyer et al., 2023).

Conclusion

Globalization has reshaped work across cultures and societies by opening labor markets and creating economic growth and job opportunities. The multifaceted nature of work in a global context underscores the importance of adapting to technological advancements, promoting diversity and inclusion in the workforce, and maintaining ethical standards in business practices. Globalization can improve living standards through job creation and economic development. Cultural diversity in workplaces can drive innovation but requires effective management and inclusive strategies. For individuals to stay competitive in the evolving job market, organizations must provide employees with continuous learning and skills development aligned to the dynamic nature of industries and emerging technologies. Corporate Social Responsibility and ethical leadership support responsible and productive business operations. Higher education institutions prepare individuals for the global workforce by fostering critical thinking, creativity, and intercultural competence, equipping individuals with the necessary skills for innovative economic development. Work in a global society is a complex and multifaceted phenomenon with far-reaching implications. Although developing countries benefit from access to global markets, foreign investment, and economic shifts, challenges that include wage and labor inequality persist. The economic, social, and ethical dimensions of global work present both opportunities and challenges that require thoughtful and proactive approaches from individuals, organizations, and policymakers. By embracing diversity, fostering ethical leadership, and promoting lifelong learning, we can navigate the complexities of global work and create a more inclusive and sustainable future for all.

REFERENCES

Adamu, M., Abubakar, N. & Majin, D. (2023). The value of ethical and sustainable leadership to business organization in the 21st century. *International Journal of Advanced Academic Research, 9*(1), 64-85.

Alam, W., Ikram, F., Kumar, P., Haseeb, M., & Ali, N. (2022). Asymmetric effects of foreign direct investment on economic growth: Fresh evidence from India using NARDL simulation. *Millennial Asia, 15*(3). https://doi.org/10.1177/09763996221122

Al Halbusi, H., Ruiz-Palomino, P., & Williams, K. A. (2023). Ethical leadership, subordinates' moral identity and self-control: Two-and three-way interaction effect on subordinates' ethical behavior. *Journal of Business Research, 165*, 114044.

Ali, N., Phoungthong, K., Khan, A., Abbas, S., Dilanchiev, A., Tariq, S., & Sadiq, M. N. (2023). Does FDI foster technological innovations? Empirical evidence from BRICS economies. *Plos One, 18*(3). https://www.ncbi.nlm.nih.gov/pmc/articles/PMC9997950/

Aparicio, G., Iturralde, T., & Rodríguez, A. V. (2023). Developments in the knowledge-based economy research field: A bibliometric literature review. *Management Review Quarterly, 73*(1).

Aripin, Z., Mulyani, S. R., & Haryaman, A. (2023). Marketing strategy in project sustainability management efforts in extractive industries: Building a reciprocity framework for community. *Journal of Development and Community Service, 1*(1).

Ashikali, T., Groeneveld, S., & Kuipers, B. (2021). The role of inclusive leadership in supporting an inclusive climate in diverse public sector teams. *Review of Public Personnel Administration, 41*(3).

Braxton, J. C., & Taska, B. (2023). Technological change and the consequences of job loss. *American Economic Review, 113*(2).

Buonomo, I., De Vincenzi, C., Pansini, M., D'Anna, F., & Benevene, P. (2024). Feeling supported as a remote worker: The role of support from leaders and colleagues and job satisfaction in promoting employees' work–life balance. *International Journal of Environmental Research and Public Health, 21*(6).

Bureau of International Labor Affairs. (n.d.). *List of goods produced by child labor or forced labor*. U.S. Department of Labor. https://www.dol.gov/agencies/ilab/reports/child-labor/list-of-goods-print?items_per_page=10&combine=china

Dahan, Y., Lerner, H., & Milman-Sivan, F. (2023). Shared responsibility and labor rights in global supply chains. *Journal of Business Ethics, 182*(4). https://link.springer.com/article/10.1007/s10551-021-04988-w

De Cremer, D., & Kasparov, G. (2021). AI should augment human intelligence, not replace it. *Harvard Business Review, 18*(1).

Dempere, J., Qamar, M., Allam, H., & Malik, S. (2023). The impact of innovation on economic growth, foreign direct investment, and self-employment: A global perspective. *Economies, 11*(7). https://doi.org/10.3390/economies11070182

Dondi, M., Klier, J., Panier, F., & Schubert, J. (2021). Defining the skills citizens will need in the future world of work. *McKinsey & Company, 25.*

Dust, S. B., Resick, C. J., Margolis, J. A., Mawritz, M. B., & Greenbaum, R. L. (2018). Ethical leadership and employee success: Examining the roles of psychological empowerment and emotional exhaustion. *The Leadership Quarterly, 29*(5).

Ely, R. J., & Thomas, D. A. (2020). Getting serious about diversity. *Harvard Business Review, 98*(6).

Filippi, S., Salvador Casara, B. G., Pirrone, D., Yerkes, M., & Suitner, C. (2023). Economic inequality increases the number of hours worked and decreases work–life balance perceptions: Longitudinal and experimental evidence. *Royal Society Open Science, 10*(10).

Gull, A. A., Hussain, N., Khan, S. A., Khan, Z., & Saeed, A. (2023). Governing corporate social responsibility decoupling: The effect of the governance committee on corporate social responsibility decoupling. *Journal of Business Ethics, 185*(2).

Ikumapayi, O. M., Oyinbo, S. T., Akinlabi, E. T., & Madushele, N. (2020). Overview of recent advancement in globalization and outsourcing initiatives in manufacturing systems. *Materials Today: Proceedings, 26.*

ILO. (1998). Declaration on Fundamental Principles and Rights at Work. https://www.ilo.org/ilo-declaration-fundamental-principles-and-rights-work

ILO. (2019). ILO centenary declaration for the future of work. In *International labour conference 108th session.* International Labour Office.

Jerab, D., & Mabrouk, T. (2023). The role of leadership in changing organizational culture. https://papers.ssrn.com/sol3/papers.cfm?abstract_id=4574324

Kaur, N., & Arora, P. (2020). Acknowledging gender diversity and inclusion as key to organizational growth: A review and trends. *Journal of Critical Reviews, 7*(6).

Kormakova, I., Kruhlyanko, A., Peniuk, V., Ursakii, Y., & Verstiak, O. (2023). Actual strategies for businesses penetrating foreign markets in the modern economy: Globalisation Aspect. *International Journal of Professional Business Review, 8*(5).

Kroeber, A. R. (2020). *China's economy: What everyone needs to know.* Oxford University Press.

Lazaroiu, G., & Rogalska, E. (2023). How generative artificial intelligence technologies shape partial job displacement and labor productivity growth. *Oeconomia Copernicana, 14*(3).

Le, T. T. (2023). The association of corporate social responsibility and sustainable consumption and production patterns: The mediating role of green supply chain management. *Journal of Cleaner Production, 414.*

Li, L. (2022). Reskilling and upskilling the future-ready workforce for industry 4.0 and beyond. *Information Systems Frontiers.*

Li, X., & Wye, C. K. (2023). The effect of investment in education on China's economic growth: The role of financial development. *The Chinese Economy, 56*(1).

Liu, Q., Zhan, J., & Su, D. Y. (2023, February). The effects of outsourcing: Winners and losers. In *International Conference on Business and Policy Studies* (pp. 1667-1682). Springer Nature Singapore.

Manigandan, P., Alam, M. S., Murshed, M., Ozturk, I., Altuntas, S., & Alam, M. M. (2024). Promoting sustainable economic growth through natural resources management, green innovations, environmental policy deployment, and financial development: Fresh evidence from India. *Resources Policy, 90*, 104681.

Manroop, L., & Petrovski, D. (2023). Exploring layers of context-related work-from-home demands during COVID-19. *Personnel Review, 52*(6).

Mariyani, D. (2024). The influence of ethical leadership on the quality of external audits: A business management perspective. *Journal of Contemporary Administration and Management, 2*(2).

McDowall, A. (2023). Work-life balance through a diversity lens: Implications for research and practice. *The Market: International Journal of Business, 4.*

Mezzadri, A., & Majumder, S. (2022). Towards a feminist political economy of time: Labour circulation, social reproduction & the 'afterlife' of cheap labour. *Review of International Political Economy, 29*(6).

Mor Barak, M. E. (2022). *Managing diversity: Toward a globally inclusive workplace* (5th ed.). SAGE Publications, Inc.

Muktamar, A., Wahdiniawati, S. A., Fatmawati, F., & Mardikawati, B. (2023). Challenges and opportunities in HRM research in the era of globalization: A bibliometric analysis of the effects of cultural diversity and innovation in organizations. *West Science Interdisciplinary Studies, 1*(11).

Muzam, J. (2023). The challenges of modern economy on the competencies of knowledge workers. *Journal of the Knowledge Economy, 14*(2).

Naughton, B. (1993). Deng Xiaoping: The Economist. *The China Quarterly, 135.* http://www.jstor.org/stable/654099

O'Dwyer, M., Filieri, R., & O'Malley, L. (2023). Establishing successful university–industry collaborations: Barriers and enablers deconstructed. *The Journal of Technology Transfer, 48*(3).

OECD. (n.d.). *Global value and supply chains.* https://www.oecd.org/en/topics/policy-issues/global-value-and-supply-chains.html

OECD (2018). OECD Due Diligence Guidance for Responsible Business Conduct. https://mneguidelines.oecd.org/due-diligence-guidance-for-responsible-business-conduct.htm

Olusanya, E. O. (2023). Workplace diversity, equity, inclusion. *Journal of Business Diversity, 23*(4).

Ortiz-Martínez, E., Marín-Hernández, S., & Santos-Jaén, J. M. (2023). Sustainability, corporate social responsibility, non-financial reporting and company performance: Relationships and mediating effects in Spanish small and medium sized enterprises. *Sustainable Production and Consumption, 35.*

Parmelee, M. (2020). *Millennial survey.* Deloitte.

Qamruzzaman, M. (2023). Does financial innovation foster financial inclusion in Arab world? Examining the nexus between financial innovation, FDI, remittances, trade openness, and gross capital formation. *Plos One, 18*(6).

Rao, M. J., & Dutt, A. K. (2007). A decade of reforms: The Indian economy in the 1990s. In L. Taylor (Ed.), *External liberalization in Asia, post-socialist Europe, and Brazil* (online ed.). Oxford Academic. https://doi.org/10.1093/acprof:oso/9780195189322.003.0005

Salvador, R., Barros, M. V., Barreto, B., Pontes, J., Yoshino, R. T., Piekarski, C. M., & de Francisco, A. C. (2023). Challenges and opportunities for problem-based learning in higher education: Lessons from a cross-program Industry 4.0 case. *Industry and Higher Education, 37*(1).

Saroyan, A., & Frenay, M. (Eds.). (2023). *Building teaching capacities in higher education: A comprehensive international model.* Taylor & Francis.

Shah, M. M. (2008). Sustainable development. In S. E. Jørgensen & B. D. Fath (Eds.), *Encyclopedia of ecology.* Academic Press.

Tariq, G., Sun, H., Fernandez-Gamiz, U., Mansoor, S., Pasha, A. A., Ali, S., & Khan, M. S. (2023). Effects of globalization, foreign direct investment and economic growth on renewable electricity consumption. *Heliyon*, *9*(3).

Tiwari, R. (2023). The impact of AI and machine learning on job displacement and employment opportunities. *International Journal of Engineering Technologies and Management Research*, *7*(1).

Van der Hijden, P., & Martin, M. (2023). *Short courses, micro-credentials, and flexible learning pathways: A blueprint for policy development and action*. International Institute for Educational Planning.

Waham, J. J., Asfahani, A., & Ulfa, R. A. (2023). International collaboration in higher education: Challenges and opportunities in a globalized world. *International Journal of Educational Research*, *1*(1).

Wan, J., & Lee, C. C. (2023). Corporate investment and the dilemma of the monetary policy: Evidence from China. *Economic Analysis and Policy*, *78*, 106-121.

World Bank. (2020). *World development report 2020: Trading for development in the age of global value chains*. World Bank. https://doi.org/10.1596/978-1-4648-1457-0

World Economic Forum. (2020, October 20). *Recession and automation changes our future of work, but there are jobs coming, report says*. World Economic Forum. https://www.weforum.org/press/2020/10/recession-and-automation-changes-our-future-of-work-but-there-are-jobs-coming-report-says-52c5162fce/

Yi, J., Hou, Y., & Zhang, Z. Z. (2023). The impact of foreign direct investment (FDI) on China's manufacturing carbon emissions. *Innovation and Green Development*, *2*(4), 100086.

Zheng, X., Wang, F., Liu, S., Wang, H., & Zhang, D. (2024). Outward foreign direct investment, dynamic capabilities and radical innovation performance: Empirical evidence from Chinese high-tech companies. *Chinese Management Studies*, *18*(4).

CHAPTER 2

Multicultural Diversity and Its Implications in the Global Workforce

Michelle I. Caron and Zuzana P. Buzzell, Southern New Hampshire University, USAA

Abstract

Multicultural diversity is a vital aspect of the global workforce. Growing interdependence among nations, economies, and cultures drives globalization, which promotes multicultural diversity. This chapter delves into the importance of multicultural diversity, benefits and challenges to the global workforce, and strategies for fostering multicultural diversity to identify unique solutions, increase market competitiveness, attract and retain talent, and build cultural competence. Organizations must acquire these competencies to enable them to effectively lead, collaborate, and communicate with internal and external stakeholders from varied cultural, ethnic, and racial backgrounds. Finding unity in the diversity of the competitive global landscape has the power to build and sustain dynamic capabilities, enhance brand reputation, and attract top talent from every sector of the global workforce.

Introduction

The scale, scope, and speed of digital transformation have permeated every industry, organization, and society at large. Pervasive technology is fueling the global workforce and reshaping economies for better or worse in our rapidly evolving, interconnected world. Diversity and multiculturalism are related concepts, often used interchangeably, that address the recognition and inclusion of various cultural identities within organizations and societies (Alozie, 2020; Beachum, 2020). Diversity encompasses differences in age, gender, race, religion, and nationality, while multiculturalism focuses on creating an inclusive environment that values these differences (Alozie, 2020).

Increased interdependence among nations blurs cultural boundaries, thereby enhancing competition and shifting the distribution of labor. Values and principles such as tolerance, cooperation, and solidarity, help create responsible global citizens where prosperity reigns and social challenges become surmountable through collective effort.

This chapter delves deeply into the nature of multicultural diversity within the global workforce, its benefits, and challenges, and provides effective strategies to leverage culturally diverse teams to spark innovation, inspire creativity, inform sound decision-making, and improve market competitiveness while promoting employee well-being, retention, and inclusivity to build and nurture an inclusive, productive work environment.

The Importance of Multicultural Diversity

Recognizing the implications of multicultural diversity on the global workforce has never been more essential as unprecedented migration creates challenges, heightens tensions, and stimulates cultural hybridization as diverse sub-cultures interact with greater frequency. Finding unity in the diversity of the competitive global landscape has the power to build and sustain the dynamic capabilities of every sector of the global workforce.

Multiculturalism refers to groups from different cultures, ethnic, and racial backgrounds within a society, wherein race represents groups with shared physical characteristics related to one's biological composition, and ethnicity is broadly based on common language, nationality, or religion. Internal and external expressions of cultural norms, beliefs, languages, traditions, values, and practices influence social structures in how others interact with one another, interpret experiences, and make decisions.

Elements of culture are passed down from generation to generation, shaping nations, industries, organizations, leaders, and individuals (Collegenp & Gateway International, 2023):

- Nations rely on multicultural diversity to fill skill gaps and drive economic growth and cultural enrichment to enhance social cohesion, global competitiveness, and exposure to diverse viewpoints to remedy societal challenges. Nations with higher levels of diversity are better equipped to address complex global issues.
- Diversity is recognized as a competitive advantage to industries, as diverse perspectives drive innovative and creative solutions and provide valuable insight to market expansion. Technological advances in industries are made possible by attracting and retaining top talent.

- Organizations find multicultural diversity crucial for strategic insight that resonates with a global customer base and navigating cultural complexities at home and abroad. Leaders who champion diversity and foster a sense of belonging may benefit through enhanced reputation and sphere of influence, while workers may improve their professional experience and development to facilitate career advancement.
- Individuals benefit from interacting with people and groups from diverse backgrounds, as such exposure improves social skills and cultural competence, promotes inclusivity, and further enables individuals to navigate and contribute to a world where global citizenship embraces diversity.

Dimensions of Globalization

Growing interdependence among nations, economies, and cultures drives globalization, which promotes multicultural diversity. Globalization is a broad topic represented by several dimensions: economic, political, technological, and social, where cultural dimensions, such as the spreading of ideas, values, and traditions become interwoven throughout.

Economic globalization has greatly increased the integration of national economies through trade liberalization, global supply chains, foreign direct investment, labor mobility, market competition, and foreign direct investment. Migration and cultural diversity have transformed global economic theory and population demographics. "Migration, free labour movement, and the cultural diversity they generate have all become significant components of current global economic theory and demographic growth. They stress the importance of coexistence and collaboration among different ethnicities, countries, and cultures" (Iriowen, 2023).

Globalization also "poses threats to multicultural societies, potentially eroding local cultures through cultural homogenization" (Sholahudin et al., 2020). However, these challenges may be mitigated by building "diversity immunity", which is propagating collective awareness of the necessity to respect and appreciate differences and preserving and celebrating cultural traditions and practices (Sholahudin, et al, 2020). Cultural identities must be preserved. Korobeynikova and Vodopiyanova, propose_an approach to globalization where diverse cultural identities and languages are valued equally (2020).

Political globalization influencers include global governance institutions (i.e. United Nations (UN) and World Trade Organization (WTO) that set cooperation norms and regional alliances (i.e. European Union (EU) and Association of Southeast Asian Nations (ASEAN)). Setting transnational policies (i.e. human rights, environmental protection, and public health), international laws, and collective security agreements, counterterrorism, and challenges to national sovereignty represent factors that influence political globalization.

Widespread diffusion and integration of technology have catapulted innovation and research, transformed education at every level, provided immersive cultural content exchanges on a global scale (i.e. content creation, Virtual Reality/Augmented Reality), and placed healthcare and medicine firmly on the cutting edge. Technological advances stimulate and accelerate globalization, as they facilitate: a.) the creation of global networks that can address complex global issues, b.) the exchange of ideas, traditions, and practices, and c.) enable "cultural hybridization", which blends cultural elements.

Social globalization refers to the interconnectedness of societies around the world. It dramatically impacts how societies interact and engage, exchange cultural practices traditions, and values, engage in social networks (i.e. transnational migrant communities), and share knowledge and information. Such global influences highlight disparities in opportunities, social stratification, and inequality.

Globalization also "poses threats to multicultural societies, potentially eroding local cultures through cultural homogenization", however, these challenges may be mitigated by building "diversity immunity" (Sholahudin et al., 2020). Cultural identities must be safeguarded by propagating collective awareness of the necessity to respect and appreciate differences and preserving and celebrating them (Sholahudin, et al, 2020). Korobeynikova and Vodopiyanova, propose_a multicultural approach to globalization where diverse cultural identities and languages are valued equally (2020).

These dimensions of globalization create a rich mosaic of multicultural diversity as exposure to different cultures, artistic expressions, and social practices permeate society and the global workforce alike.

Assessing Corporate Culture

Multinational enterprises (MNEs) are considered a driving force of multicultural diversity. "The economic power of these hierarchically and centralistically structured organizations exceeds by far that of many nations" (Moosmüller, 2017). While multicultural diversity can enhance international and domestic business practices, such as engagement and understanding the needs of international clients and partners, it may also lead to cultural clashes in corporate environments. (Iriowen, 2023). Businesses must acquire competencies that enable them to collaborate, manage, and communicate utilizing highly developed interpersonal and technical skills and become culture advocates to build team cohesiveness to best leverage diverse skillsets, experience, innovation, and creativity. This facilitates delivering on the mission and sustaining competitive advantage by leveraging advantages they have acquired from tapping into the multicultural diversity of the global workforce.

Corporate culture refers to the shared values, beliefs, and behaviors demonstrated in the day-to-day cadence of business activities and interactions among internal and external stakeholder groups. Cadence centers around the orchestration and synchronization of process timing and frequency, pacing of the work, smooth transitions of tasks requiring collaborative efforts and shared resources, predictable routines, and agility in response to changing business conditions, and market demands. These elements help businesses run more smoothly and contribute to overall efficiency.

Organizations would want to evaluate multicultural diversity in their corporate culture to foster an inclusive, positive, and innovative workplace for internal gains and to remain competitive in global markets. Corporations must evaluate their culture regularly as the "relative importance of different management approaches can shift over time, and cultural factors play a role in the success of management ideas" (Moosmüller, 2017). Realized improvements from assessing corporate culture include more effective talent attraction and retention, employee engagement, innovative solutions, and creative problem-solving. Optimizing performance, increasing productivity, and fostering inclusivity are additional areas of potential progress and recovery. "Cultural diversity in multinational corporations can provide benefits such as increased creativity, better adaptability, improved productivity, and more talent availability, but also presents challenges that need to be managed" (Moosmüller, 2017).

Key aspects of assessing corporate culture include "mission, governance, personnel practices, service offerings, and outreach approaches" (Capitman et al., 2019). There is no universal approach. A comprehensive framework for managing cultural diversity is crucial, in addressing workforce composition changes due to demographic shifts (Beniflah & Veloz, 2021). Business leaders tend to use a variety of strategies, such as diversity audits and surveys to gather demographic information, customer experience data, leadership commitment to promoting diverse cultures, diversity metric data, and brand perception.

Practical measurement approaches have been developed, focusing on quantifiable dimensions such as ethnicity, language, and belief (Moieni et al., 2017). These can be implemented through digital tools for visual insights into group diversity. Real-time feedback could come from Employee Resource Groups (ERGs), focus groups, and exit interviews. Examination of Diversity, Equity, and Inclusion (DEI) policies and benchmarks should also be reviewed. Custom cultural competence training may improve results over time. Building cultural competence is "viewed as an ongoing developmental process rather than an end state, with organizations and individuals progressing along a continuum from cultural destructiveness to cultural proficiency" (Cross, 2020). Implementing cultural competence initiatives improves the likelihood of better outcomes in multicultural situations with internal and external stakeholders. By implementing a combination of these strategies, organizations are better equipped to identify areas in need of improvement and new areas for potential growth.

Global Workforce

“The global labor market is undergoing significant transformations due to various factors, including technological advancements and globalization. The efficiency of labor markets varies across countries, with multidimensional groupings revealing distinct clusters based on key components” (Dolgikh & Pershina, 2019).

Multicultural diversity is increasingly linked to the global workforce due to globalization, migration, and demographic shifts (Tamunomiebi & John-Eke, 2020). Multicultural diversity is a vital asset for the global workforce and the two are profoundly connected in numerous ways that contribute to innovation, market competitiveness, talent attraction, and enhanced decision-making, in particular. Challenges may be approached from multiple angles, while a broader range of perspectives may provide valuable market insights and improved employee engagement and satisfaction. Collaborative teams leverage varied experiences and diverse groups can foster understanding and respect of cultural differences. Having access to highly skilled global talent and building cultural competence begets better interaction with internal and external stakeholders and a positive brand image as an organization that values inclusivity and social responsibility. Organizations that champion multicultural diversity can navigate complexities within the global workforce to their advantage.

Globalization and digital transformation are creating specific challenges, including increased productivity (i.e., technological advances over human capital), mobility, and inequality (Safronchouk et al., 2021).

> “Several challenges persist in the global labor market, including inequality, decent work deficits, underemployment, structural unemployment, gender asymmetry, and professional segregation. These issues require comprehensive solutions at both national and international levels to achieve strategic goals such as full employment and improved living standards. The ongoing transformations necessitate continued theoretical understanding and empirical assessment to optimize labor utilization in the modern global economy” (Gnevasheva, 2020).

“Inequality and the widespread deficit of decent work lead not only to economic inefficiencies, but also to a decline in social cohesion within countries” (Gnevasheva, 2020). Full employment and increasing the standard of living remain key goals of strategic development of the global workforce. “The emerging global trends of the world labor market pose a number of problematic issues for solving both at the level of national markets and on the world labor market together with international organizations in the framework of the global dialogue” (Gnevasheva, 2020).

As the workforce becomes more diverse, organizations face challenges in managing cultural differences effectively (Kharroubi, 2020). Diversity management initiatives aim to maximize productivity and economic output by leveraging the strengths of a multicultural workforce (Beniflah & Veloz, 2021). However, these efforts can sometimes reproduce workplace inequalities despite claims of inclusivity (Park, 2019).

To address these challenges, companies must adopt comprehensive approaches to transform into truly multicultural organizations (Beniflah & Veloz, 2021). This includes creating learning environments through collaboration, improving inter-functional coordination, and developing frameworks for optimal resource allocation to engage a multicultural workforce (Tamunomiebi & John-Eke, 2020).

Benefits of Multicultural Diversity in the Workforce

Multicultural diversity paves the way for innovation and creativity, market competitiveness, enhanced decision-making, and talent attraction and retention by fostering safe spaces for sharing varied perspectives and cross-cultural exchanges to identify unique solutions through creative collaboration. Organizations implement robust programs and policies to recruit and retain diverse workforces, addressing global challenges through innovative performance (Waghmare, 2021).

INNOVATION AND CREATIVITY

Innovation serves as a key differentiator for multinational enterprises (MNEs). Diversity fuels innovation and creativity in the workplace through sharing new ideas and ways of thinking to solve problems and gain a competitive advantage in the marketplace. "Creativity involves generating new ideas, while innovation encompasses both idea generation and implementation" (Hundeling & Rosing, 2020). "Innovation and creativity significantly benefit the global workforce by enhancing organizational performance, competitiveness, and long-term survival," and they require experienced leadership to unlock their full potential to maximize the benefits of new and enhanced operational approaches" (Klicheva & Klicheva, 2020). These processes can occur at various levels (i.e. individual, team, or organizational) or some combination thereof, resulting in distinct benefits across the organization.

Creativity and innovation at work are the processes, outcomes, and products of attempts to develop and introduce new and improved ways of doing things. The creativity stage of this process refers to idea generation, and innovation to the subsequent stage of implementing ideas toward better procedures, practices, or products" (Hundeling & Rosing, 2020). Every company should have an innovation strategy that serves as a guide to new product development and the approach to achieve the vision. Domestic and global entities are focused on leveraging diversity and innovation at all levels of employment and across all business functions (i.e., Marketing, Finance, Human Resources, Operations, Customer Service, Research & Development, etc.).

Chief Innovation Officer is a C-level position that empowers the organization to innovate at pace and scale and can link innovation efforts to strategic initiatives aligned to the overall mission of the business. Innovation efforts refer to discovering and pursuing creative new opportunities. The Chief Innovation Officer "must find ways to [a] improve the rate at which high-potential new opportunities are spotted, [b] identify the most promising of these opportunities and validate them, [c] drive alignment among the leaders of the organization to make the right investments – to pursue these opportunities further and eventually bring new products and services to the market: real value through novelty" (Krasadakis, 2024). Succeeding in this role relies heavily on a multicultural workforce as customer expectations move at a faster pace than business.

TALENT ATTRACTION AND RETENTION

Attracting and retaining the right talent becomes a critical challenge for organizations unwilling to tap into the global workforce, which significantly broadens the talent pool. "Effective diversity management requires adapting recruitment, retention, and talent management policies to address global workforce challenges" (Khan et al., 2020). "Human resource management efforts to increase diversity and inclusion vary by region, with Europe and North America focusing on gender equality" (Kharroubi, 2020). "Gender and ethnic diversity increase employee skills and talent, positively impacting company performance" (Verma, 2020).

Organizations may enhance their brand by publicizing their commitment to diversity and inclusion and appealing to highly skilled job seekers where an appreciation for differences is valued, respected, and celebrated. Inclusive work environments that foster a sense of belonging and offer career development opportunities that cater to a wide array of cultural perspectives may reduce turnover as employees build stronger connections to the company and grow their professional network. Career development opportunities to attract, promote, and retain talent should cater to various cultural backgrounds and perspectives through providing internships, mentorships, professional development workshops, and leadership training.

Another opportunity to retain talent would be to offer ongoing education and training on diversity, equity, and inclusion practices to promote cultural sensitivity and tolerance to further support building cultural competence. To overcome "challenges and maintain global competitiveness, corporations should focus on cross-cultural communication competence, interpersonal relationships, and equipping managers with cross-cultural negotiation skills" (Okoro, 2019). Global managers should also be trained in interpersonal relationship building and group communication competence (Okoro, 2019).

Navigating cultural differences are essential for everyone, regardless of the organization or industry. Continuing to provide resources and support will further instill the values and cultural norms of the business. Increasingly, corporations recognize the value of preparing global managers as business objectives are not being achieved primarily because of deficiencies in cross-cultural etiquette (Okoro, 2019).

Providing employees opportunities to voice individual and collective concerns and ideas may also pay significant dividends. For example, Employee Resource Groups (ERGs) can prevent costly and potentially embarrassing mistakes when bringing a new innovative product or service to market. Having varied perspectives, experience, and backgrounds helps ensure cultural sensitivity is maintained and these groups may reflect regional and demographic target markets. Such insight into cultural preferences can spark creative collaboration and knowledge-sharing opportunities by leveraging expanded professional networks. Cross-pollination of ideas inspires creative solutions. Encouraging open-mindedness and having a growth mindset, as well as providing psychological safety, where it is acceptable to make mistakes, new ideas are welcomed and challenging existing norms.

Managers also benefit from multicultural diversity through improved team cohesion and performance. "Diverse and inclusive organizations foster innovation and outperform homogeneous workforces, although integrating diversity can be challenging" (Kriw, 2021). Diverse teams often exhibit higher levels of collaboration and adaptability, as team members learn to navigate and integrate different viewpoints and approaches. This adaptability can lead to more effective project execution and problem resolution. Additionally, managing a diverse team equips leaders with enhanced skills in communication and conflict resolution, as they must address and harmonize varying perspectives and cultural nuances, ultimately strengthening their leadership capabilities.

These approaches facilitate attracting and retaining talent, long-term employee satisfaction, increased motivation, improved team dynamics and performance, reduced turnover, and brand loyalty, thereby creating a more dynamic, engaged workforce that feels appreciated for their unique contributions. Overall, embracing workforce diversity is crucial for companies to remain competitive in the globalized business environment.

MARKET COMPETITIVENESS

"Multicultural diversity in the global workforce significantly benefits market competitiveness by enhancing organizational performance and innovation" (Okoro, 2019). Multicultural diversity can significantly impact market competitiveness, offering both advantages and challenges. Understanding these effects helps businesses leverage diversity effectively while addressing potential drawbacks. To succeed in the global marketplace, companies must demonstrate cultural sensitivity and effectively manage workforce diversity (Okoro, 2019). Workplace diversity directly correlates with organizational competitiveness, resulting in stronger brand identity, improved collaboration, and enhanced problem-solving abilities (Soriano, 2022).

"Recent studies indicate that while some corporations compete successfully in the global marketplace, others have failed to sustain their competitive advantage because of cultural imperialism or inadequate acculturation of their managers on international assignment" (Okoro, 2019). By fostering a culture where opposing viewpoints and a wide array of perspectives are encouraged, leaders can provide informed decision-making processes and strategy development.

A diverse workforce can better understand and serve diverse markets. Employees with different cultural backgrounds can provide valuable insight into the preferences and needs of various customer segments. This cultural competence enables companies to develop products and services that resonate with a broader audience, enhancing market competitiveness. Cultural diversity in the workforce leads to higher creativity, better market understanding, improved access to international markets, and efficient innovation management (Kraus et al., 2019).

"The concept of global economy has expanded consumer awareness, defined new standards and rules of operations, and increased the need for national and corporate interdependence" (Okoro, 2019). Multinationals are exploring opportunities "demonstrating sensitivity towards cultural differences in order to gain from the proliferation and growth of international enterprise" (Okoro, 2019).

Challenges of Multicultural Diversity in the Workforce

Multicultural diversity in the workforce brings numerous benefits, however, it also presents various challenges. Organizations are proactively addressing these challenges to lessen the impact on employee interaction, satisfaction, and job retention. The section below examines some effective tools to support employees through these challenges.

COMMUNICATION BARRIERS

In the current global economy, multinational enterprises (MNEs) must stay competitive by leveraging international markets and diverse global teams to achieve financial success. Interaction and communication among employees are vital in global corporations, yet they often pose significant challenges in multicultural workplaces. Employees encounter several barriers in their diverse communication daily. Recognizing these barriers and understanding why they exist will help craft strategies for overcoming them and effectively supporting employees.

Language is one of the most important communication tools and at the same time could represent a significant barrier to effective communication. Every organization needs to determine, what official language should be used in oral and written communication. Very few organizations chose more than one official internal language. United Nations is one of the few organizations that employs more than one official language. “There are six official languages of the UN. These are Arabic, Chinese, English, French, Russian and Spanish” (UN.org). In the global economy, most of MNCs adopted as the main language. One of the primary reasons is the widespread use of the internet, which has significantly increased global knowledge of the English language. In 2024, there were 5.45 billion internet users worldwide and the number is predicted to increase to 7.9 billion in 2029 (Statista, 2024)

Common language is crucial to organizational success. Leadership should keep inclusion in mind and approach mandated common language with caution and careful preparation. According to Neeley, leadership should (2012):

- Involve all employees in advance and provide ample time for the transition to the new language to ensure non-speaking employees are not left behind.
- managers have to take full responsibility, set norms, help with the transition, and even coach in the mandated language
- native speakers should help non-native speakers and allow the employees transitioning to a new language period to learn, speak up, and correct them with positive feedback
- as this is a mandate, non-native speakers must comply and transition to the language in the organization.

Mandated common language reduces differences among multinational teams. It can initially lead to resistance from non-native speakers, which might affect job retention. To address this, MNEs should equip employees with the necessary tools for the transition, including language training programs and translation tools. In the long run, a common language leads to greater interpersonal understanding and higher and equal participation from all team members. It also leads to a greater knowledge transfer since the team communicates in the same language.

The majority of communication occurs electronically, and teams from different cultural backgrounds write business emails in different tones. In organizations that have presence and employees in countries from high-context and low-context cultures, communication guidelines should be developed and followed to avoid culturally insensitive correspondence. "High-context cultures generally prefer the circular method, which involves jumping back and forth on the given topic, while the linear way that goes from one point to another suits low-context cultures better" (Yang, et al, 2021). MNEs should provide formal training on email writing for all employees, native speakers, and non-native speakers as written communication could present a challenge for everyone.

Multinational enterprises employ teams spread across the globe and operate in various time zones. This is defined as time distance, which "is considered to be a targeted measurement of the time shift experienced by two associates who want to communicate with each other. Time distance can be caused by both time shifts in work patterns and differences in time zones" (Petreska, 2022). Communication can be challenging due to delays in response, especially when decisions are needed quickly. Organizations need to adopt asynchronous tools that allow teams to share projects and allow for time-zone flexibility. To support a global workforce, key leadership meetings should be recorded and made accessible on a shared platform, ensuring all employees have equal access to information.

CULTURAL MISUNDERSTANDINGS

In multicultural organizations, employees working on the same team from different countries might struggle with communication due to their different cultural norms and upbringings. Edward T. Hall (1976) developed the "iceberg" model of culture to illustrate the external and internal culture. According to his research, only 10% of the culture is visible to others at any given time, the so-called external or surface culture, and 90% of culture is the deep culture below the surface (Hall, 1976). External culture is learned and can be observed through sight, sounds, touch, and smell. It includes objective knowledge that is consciously learned and can be influenced and changed. Internal is difficult to observe and provides core values individuals were raised in such as beliefs, priorities, assumptions, and perceptions. It includes subjective knowledge, it was implicitly learned, unconscious, and difficult to change.

Initial interactions among employees often occur at a surface level, which can lead to misunderstandings later on as the working relationship becomes more established communication increases and the deep culture becomes more prevalent. The two most common differences are between a.) direct cultures which prefer simple and precise communication and indirect cultures, where the message is implied, and b.) task-oriented cultures which don't require personal relationships to accomplish a task, and relationship-oriented cultures where before working together, trust must be developed (Barille, 2020).

Instead of considering these as differences and barriers organizations should leverage cultural misunderstandings to bring employees closer and promote organizational growth. "The primary focus of an organization with this intercultural communication training should be on raising cultural awareness, aligning behaviors, a sense of equity, improving communication skills, and diversity and sensitivity among its employees" (Shahid, 2022)

BIAS AND DISCRIMINATION

Biases can influence how we communicate and perceive others' communication, a phenomenon known as cognitive bias. "Cognitive biases are significant because they can influence how individuals perceive and interpret information, which may or may not lead to judgment and decision-making errors" (DaSilva et al., 2023). Employees often gravitate toward team members who share similar communication styles. This defeats the organizational diversity strategy and discourages diverse perspectives in decision-making. Implementing inclusive leadership practices, encouraging open dialogue, and supporting employees from underrepresented groups can help mitigate this bias and promote diverse communication.

Strategies for Fostering Multicultural Diversity

Fostering multicultural diversity means creating an inclusive environment that recognizes, respects, and values diverse cultural backgrounds. Equipping employees with essential tools and training, while adhering to current organizational and national policies, is crucial for the success of multicultural diversity. The following section explores Diversity, Equity, and Inclusion and organizational policies that support multicultural diversity.

DIVERSITY AND INCLUSION POLICIES

Diversity and Inclusion policies (D&I) are formal guidelines organizations implement to foster a diverse and inclusive workplace. These policies aim to ensure that all employees, regardless of their background, feel valued, and respected, and have equal opportunities for advancement. As organizations must address various aspects of these new policies to promote retention and recruitment, many organizations developed or started offering targeted DEI (Diversity, Equity, and Inclusion) training. We have also seen a shift in organizational workplace cultures.

Setting the right policies begins by understanding of what Diversity, Equity, and Inclusion stand for. According to the International Institute for Management Development (IMD):

- Diversity: is about representing and appreciating individuals of different backgrounds, identities, and experiences, including varied races, sexual orientations, and religions.
- Equity involves recognizing that certain groups are disadvantaged due to historical and systematic patterns of oppression. It's about supporting and promoting these groups in the interest of creating a fair playing field.
- Inclusion is a state of belonging where all types of people are made to feel valued and welcomed, regardless of sexual orientation, ethnicity, race, etc." (2023)

As the definition above demonstrates, diversity and inclusion policies should be multifaceted and not concentrate solely on race or gender. According to the PEW Research group, most workers (56%) see DEI as a positive thing, and thus dedicating time and resources to developing, promoting, and maintaining these policies should be part of the leadership strategy of every organization (Pew, 2023). A successful DEI strategy should be embedded in the strategic planning and assist the overall vision of the company rather than a separate department within the organization making decisions apart from other departments.

All organizations with 15 or more employees are required to follow the recruitment policies outlined in the U.S. Equal Employment Opportunity (EEO), which ensures that "everyone is treated fairly in employment decisions, including hiring, promotion, and compensation." It prohibits discrimination based on characteristics like race, gender, age, religion, and disability, ensuring that all individuals have an equal chance for employment. In addition to this universally adopted federal policy, organizations have made great progress in ensuring employees are treated equitably in the workplace. Several new policies expanded on the EEO Act, and additional policies were developed to respond to the new way of conducting business in our new diverse global environment.

First is the Zero-Tolerance Policy for Discrimination and Harassment which is closest to EEO Act and prohibits any form of discrimination, harassment, or inappropriate behavior based on race, gender, age, religion, and disability, just like EEO, but also prohibits discrimination based on with sexual orientation and other protected characteristic. This policy also includes a process for confidential reporting and complaints and immediate investigation. A growing number of US states require organizations to have a formal written harassment policy in the workplace. It is up to each organization to verify the laws of the state the organization operates in and ensure that they are followed. Most multinational organizations follow the same strict Zero-Tolerance Policy for Discrimination and Harassment in their global subsidiaries as in their United States-based operations, even though some global cultures might not require these policies to be in place.

The second policy that many employees don't realize is a policy is Diversity, Equity, and Inclusion Training. In a world where employees work with diverse teams, accepting ideas, and embracing a positive organizational culture where all employees feel valued is essential to drive corporate innovation and success. Many DEI trainings are ineffective, and face resistance from employees. According to a comprehensive study from WebMd Health Organization, 62% of employees find the programs ineffective and 46% of employees even claimed that it personally failed them (2023). Organizations that are seeking better ways to incorporate their DEI training into their overall strategy should start by changing the name to face less resistance. Any professional development should promote a sense of belonging as the same survey indicated that to 57% of employees "feeling valued" matters and this feeling should not be ignored (2023).

The third policy is Flexible Work Arrangements that support hybrid work models, such as fully remote work, and flexible hours to accommodate different employee lifestyle needs. This type of policy is not addressed by the Fair Labor Standard Act (FLSA) as this act can't mandate the number of hours. This policy can promote psychological and physical employee well-being, lead to increased productivity, and have a positive impact on work-life balance. Deloitte research has shown that 90% of employees value flexibility, and 82% of employees have taken advantage of flexible work options. This policy also leads to a 29% increase in efficiency at work (Deloitte, 2020).

CULTURAL COMPETENCE TRAINING

Cultural competence training is replacing the diversity, equity, and inclusion training in the workplace. These learning and development opportunities help employees in the organization navigate the complex interactions with team members from different cultural backgrounds. "Cultural competence is about understanding yourself as a cultural being, and the impact that you have on other cultural beings in a variety of spaces and contexts" (Calkins, 2020). Effective cultural competence training should be provided to employees in stages or modules to address the following cultural competencies a.) *cultural awareness* to introduce employees to different cultures b.) *bias and stereotype reduction* to help employees recognize their own biases c.) *communication skills training* to improve verbal and non-verbal communication styles d.) *continuous learning development* to provide ongoing opportunities for learning diversity competence.

Cultural awareness starts by recognizing that employees from dominant cultures interact with colleagues from underrepresented groups and understanding the differences. MNCs are often faced with these issues when employees from the headquarters interact with employees in subsidiaries. This first step should provide a path for employees to find common ground and priorities and help align everyone within the organization toward the same goal. Bias and stereotype reduction training should create an environment where employees can explore their unconscious biases and engage in practical scenarios to overcome challenging biases in the workplace. The class should be based on the official definition of bias based on Senate Bill 5/House Bill 28, which states that "A bias in judgment that results from subtle cognitive processes, including the following prejudices and stereotypes that often operate at a level below conscious awareness and without control" (Pena-Melnyk, et al, 2021).

Communication skills should encompass visual, verbal, and non-verbal communication in inclusive language. The language used in organizations should include people of all ethnicities, gender identities, ages, etc. Offering continuous learning opportunities for employees to grow in their cultural competence should be an integral part of organizational culture. Training should be incorporated into the organizational calendar and diverse facets of learning should be utilized, such as webinars, workshops, podcasts, and videos.

INCLUSIVE LEADERSHIP

Organizations recognize that to attract diverse talent, retain employees, and be competitive in the industry, leadership needs to be fully committed to inclusion. Inclusive leaders foster a culture of multicultural diversity, and openness, and promote diverse perspectives. It is crucial to involve leaders in diversity goals from the outset. If the overall goals differ from how the leaders and employees currently operate, they should be involved in the goals from the start to ensure smooth implementation and transition of any changes. Their early and full engagement ensures they can effectively bridge the overall strategy with the employees, fostering a cohesive and inclusive environment. Some examples of effective traits that inclusive leaders share are: a.) encouraging open dialogue b.) providing equitable opportunities c.) supporting inclusive decision-making d.) commitment to diversity by measuring and tracking diversity goals.

Encouraging open conversation starts with appropriate space that offers an equal opportunity to be engaged and present. Inclusive leaders should be mindful of what conversation will be taking place, select participants, and where the meeting will take place based on the type of anticipated dialogue. Inclusive leaders should walk into any conversation aware of their own biases and practice self-reflection when change is needed. They should strive to provide psychological safety, particularly for marginalized groups, by creating spaces where everyone can express themselves without fear of repercussions. Promoting active listening and the use of appropriate language should be integral parts of this open dialogue.

Inclusive leaders invite feedback and are "not afraid to challenge well-established practices that had outlived their relevance" (Zheng et al., 2023). Diverse teams offer opportunities for rich opinions and experiences. Adopting an inclusive decision-making process allows organizations to develop more comprehensive strategies that support employee engagement, and creativity and drive innovation. This strategy is supported by inclusive leaders' commitment to tracking diversity goals and promoting an equitable working environment for all team members and the organization as a whole.

Employees across every organization should be offered equal opportunities to participate in training and be offered highly visible projects that will progress their career path. Inclusive leaders encourage and value diverse work styles and contributions, avoiding the bias of assigning projects to the same employees. Recognizing the completed work, acknowledging the challenges faced by the individual team members, and appreciating diverse talents fosters a more cohesive team atmosphere. This approach encourages team members to speak up, participate actively, and seek opportunities for additional projects.

Leaders at the top of the organization should model the expected behavior and support initiatives that promote an inclusive environment. Effective inclusive leaders create an environment where employees feel valued, and their opinions heard. "Practicing inclusive leadership requires both a mindset and behaviors to create experiences of inclusion which ensure that everyone feels like they are part of the group, they can participate fully, and are valued for their contributions" (Robertson & Perry, 2022).

EMPLOYEE RESOURCE GROUPS

Employee Resource Groups (ERGs) play a vital role in supporting and advancing the organizational DEI strategy, and the overall culture within the organization. ERGs are non-profit, voluntary employee organizations formed to support, but not limited to, employees with shared interests and common identities, comparable cultural backgrounds, disability status, sexual orientation, military status, or religious beliefs. ERGs could be effective in fostering deeper inclusion, improving diversity, and driving social impact outside of the organization.

There are 5 dimensions of ERG activity (Catalino, et al, 2022):

- External engagement – volunteering outside of the organization
- Allyship – leveraging allies to help members of the ERG
- Leadership connection – channel to engage with leadership
- Employee community building – effective networking
- Career advancement – career mentoring for ERG members

ERGs help organizations by bringing workers together to exchange ideas freely, which leads to improved work conditions for some alienated workers. The provides people with the power to make cohesive decisions about issues that matter to them and have a common voice to provide feedback to leadership about issues that matter. ERGs and the organization's leadership share common values and benefit from each other support and presence.

INCLUSIVE HIRING PRACTICES

Building and promoting a diverse and equitable workforce begins with inclusive hiring practices. Organizations should ensure that their hiring processes are fair, and unbiased and actively promote recruitment of a diverse workforce. Reducing bias at the start of the recruitment process and attracting a diverse pool of candidates will lead to more creative and better decision-making teams.

The first step in the inclusive hiring process is to write and advertise a job with an unbiased job description. The description should be gender-neutral; for example, use "chairperson" instead of "chairman" and replace exclusionary terms like "grandfathered" with "legacy." The language used in the job description needs to be inclusive and ADA-compliant, ensuring that descriptor words are not prejudicial to potential employees with disabilities. This might include substituting the word "walk" with "traverse" or "move," as not all potential candidates may be able to walk. The ADA does not place requirements on job descriptions; however, it recommends that a "job description will be most helpful if it focuses on the results or outcome of a job function, not solely on the way it customarily is performed. A reasonable accommodation may enable a person with a disability to accomplish a job function in a manner that is different from the way an employee who does not have a disability may accomplish the same function" (ADA.org).

The second step is blind hiring or blind recruitment, where any identifying markers, such as name, gender, and address, are removed from the candidate's application during the initial screening process. This approach allows talent acquisition managers and human resource specialists to focus solely on the candidate's qualifications, experience, and skills, eliminating potential biases. Blind hiring only helps organizations trying to increase their pool of diverse employees. According to Fath "blind hiring boosts interview rates for members of traditionally disadvantaged groups when used by companies that typically under-select applicants from these groups" (Fath, 2023). On the other hand, blind hiring should not be used in organizations that have succeeded in diversifying their employee pool.

The third step is to adopt a standardized structured interview technique, ensuring that each candidate receives the same job-related questions. Their responses are then scored and evaluated consistently. Since structuring these questions can be challenging, they should be tested in a pilot with current employees performing the same job. If any assessment tools are needed for a particular position, equitable assessment tools must be provided to each candidate to reduce bias.

The fourth and one of the most crucial steps is to provide comprehensive DEI hiring training for all managers involved in the hiring process. This training should include implicit bias training specifically related to hiring, instruction on using structured interview tools, guidance on candidate matrix scoring, and selecting the most suitable current managers or employees to participate in panel interviews.

Inclusive hiring practices, such as bias-neutral job descriptions, blind hiring, and structured interviews should all lead to a more diversified employee pool while ensuring new hires meet the qualifications and skills to effectively contribute to the organization

MENTORSHIP AND SPONSORSHIP PROGRAMS

Mentorship and sponsorship programs are effective strategies to promote employee growth and career development within an organization. Career advancement could be challenging, especially for employees from minority groups, and mentorship and sponsorship are particularly effective in fostering and propelling an individual's talent. There is a distinct difference between a mentor and a sponsor. A mentor is a guide who shares their knowledge and provides support and advice. The sponsor arranges direct access to opportunities for advancement and serves as an advocate. Summarizes in one sentence, "A sponsor opens the door to opportunities for another employee, while a mentor supports and guides an employee so that they can open the door for themselves" (Den Houter, et al 2023).

According to the 2023 Gallup survey, only 40% of employees have a mentor in the workplace, and the sponsorship rate is even lower at 23%. Employees participating in formal mentorship or sponsorship programs are significantly more likely—75% and 97%, respectively—to strongly agree that their organization provides a clear plan for their career development (Den Houter, et al, 2023). Pizzoni recommends finding both an internal and an external mentor, as an internal mentor can guide and promote career growth within the organization, while an external mentor can assist with effective networking (2024).

Large organizations started implementing reverse and cross-cultural mentorship programs where junior workers provide experienced workers with informal cultural and technology training. This approach helps bridge intergenerational gaps and enhances employee retention across all experience levels. It empowers younger employees to develop leadership skills and management to gain new perspectives.

Given the increasing diversity within organizations, mentorship programs should be expanded to include diversity-focused initiatives. Some organizations may find it challenging to pair mentors with diverse mentees internally, but they can overcome this by offering virtual mentoring programs in partnership with other organizations. This proved especially beneficial in the medical field which is facing a scarcity of diverse mentors and led to the creation virtual Diversity Mentoring Initiative (DMI) for trainees underrepresented in medicine (URiM) "to increase residency programs' ability to recruit Black, Latinx, and Native American residents and increased graduation rates among URiM students" (Carillo, et al, 2023).

Mentorship and sponsorship programs are crucial for advancing the careers of diverse employees. They provide essential guidance, access to key opportunities, and advocate for diverse employees. These programs not only aid in retaining diverse talent but also help promote more inclusive leadership.

Conclusion

Multicultural Diversity in the global workforce presents both opportunities and challenges. Embracing diversity can enhance innovation, decision-making, and market competitiveness while fostering an inclusive environment that improves employee satisfaction and retention. Multinational corporations need to incorporate their diversity, equity, and inclusion policies as part of their strategic goals and reinforce with their employees the need for innovative and continuous training. Team members should be supported by inclusive leaders who appreciate and value their opinions. Above all, "the DEI strategy should be continually refined as pilot projects deliver results, lessons are learned, leaders and employees develop new skills and awareness, and the business's overarching strategy evolves" (Brown et al., 2023). Through training and continuous employee support, organizations can reduce the bias still festering in the workplace. Adopting a systematic approach to DEI strategy is the only way to ensure that changes will be effective. Diverse teams are a key driver of organizational success. They bring a wealth of knowledge and unlock the full potential of the global workforce.

REFERENCES

ADA National Network. (n.d.). Does the ADA require employers to develop written job descriptions? https://adata.org/faq/does-ada-require-employers-develop-written-job-descriptions

Alozie, O. E. (2020). Diversity V multiculturalism: Advantages and disadvantages of workplace diversity. *International Journal of Scientific and Research Publications (IJSRP), 10*(1), 135–140. https://doi.org/10.29322/ijsrp.10.01.2020.p9720

Barile, N. (2020, September 20). *Understanding cultural differences to communicate in a global world.* Business Acumen. https://archive.catalyst.iabc.com/Articles/understanding-cultural-differences-to-communicate-in-a-global-world

Beachum, F. D. (2020). Diversity and multiculturalism. *Oxford Research Encyclopedia of Education*. https://doi.org/10.1093/acrefore/9780190264093.013.643

Beniflah, J., & Veloz, J. (2021). Building a multicultural organisation: A conceptual model for organisational change in the 21st century. *Journal of Cultural Marketing Strategy*. https://doi.org/10.69554/neox8833

Boyles, M. (2023, October 3). DEI: What it is & how to champion it in the workplace. Harvard Business Review.

Brown, J. S., Ellsworth, D., Katen-Narvell, A., & Maor, D. (2023, May 10). *It's (past) time to get strategic about DEI*. McKinsey & Company. https://www.mckinsey.com/capabilities/people-and-organizational-performance/our-insights/its-past-time-to-get-strategic-about-dei

Calkins, H. (2020). How you can be more culturally competent. *Good Practice*. https://www.apaservices.org/practice/good-practice/becoming-culturally-competent.pdf

Capitman, J. A., Hernandez-Gallegos, W., & Yee, D. L. (2019). Diversity assessments in aging services. In *Diversity and aging services* (pp. 143–150). Routledge. https://doi.org/10.4324/9781315227566-17

Carrillo, T., Rodriguez, L. M., Landry, A., Alvarez, A., Ceniza, A., Gay, R., Green, A., & Faiz, J. (2023). A virtual national diversity mentoring initiative to promote inclusion in emergency medicine. *Western Journal of Emergency Medicine: Integrating Emergency Care with Population Health, 24*(4), 662–667. https://doi.org/10.5811/westjem.59666

Catalino, N., Gardner, N., Goldstein, D., & Wong, J. (2022). Effective employee resource groups are key to inclusion at work: Here's how to get them right. *McKinsey & Company*. https://www.mckinsey.com/capabilities/people-and-organizational-performance/our-insights/effective-employee-resource-groups-are-key-to-inclusion-at-work-heres-how-to-get-them-right

Cross, T. (2020). Cultural competence continuum. *Journal of Child and Youth Care Work, 24*, 83–85. https://doi.org/10.5195/jcycw.2012.48

Da Silva, S., Gupta, R., & Monzani, D. (2023). Editorial: Highlights in psychology: Cognitive bias. *Frontiers in Psychology, 14*, 1242809. https://doi.org/10.3389/fpsyg.2023.1242809

Deloitte. (2020). Workplace flexibility survey: A deeper dive into flexible work options. https://www2.deloitte.com/us/en/pages/about-deloitte/articles/workplace-flexibility-survey.html

Den Houter, K., & Maese, K. (2023, April). Mentors and sponsors make the difference. *Gallup*. https://www.gallup.com/workplace/473999/mentors-sponsors-difference.aspx

Dolgikh, E., & Pershina, T. (2019). Statistical analysis of labor market efficiency in the world countries. *Vestnik Universiteta, 6*, 100–104. https://doi.org/10.26425/1816-4277-2019-6-100-104

Fath, S. (2023). *When blind hiring advances DEI – and when it doesn't*. Harvard Business Review. https://doi.org/H07NT2-PDF-ENG

Gnevasheva, V. A. (2020). Global trends of labor market transformation. *Алма матер, 11*, 84–91. https://doi.org/10.20339/am.11-20.084

Hall, E. T. (1976). *Beyond culture*. Anchor.

Hundeling, M., & Rosing, K. (2020). The role of affect and its regulation for creativity and innovation. In N. Ashkanasy & W. Zerbe (Eds.), *The Cambridge handbook of workplace affect* (pp. 131–145). Cambridge University Press. https://doi.org/10.1017/9781108573887.011

Iriowen, C. (2023). The impact of multi-culture on international business. *Vilnius University Proceedings, 37*, 28–33. https://doi.org/10.15388/vgisc.2023.4

Khan, M. D. R., Shobikah, N., & Kaium, M. A. (2020). Managing workforce diversity in organization: A case study on Aetna health care service. *Khatulistiwa, 10*(1), 62–94. https://doi.org/10.24260/khatulistiwa.v10i1.1693

Kharroubi, D. (2021). Global workforce diversity management: Challenges across the world. *SHS Web of Conferences: Globalization and Its Socio-Economic Consequences, 92*, 1–10. https://doi.org/10.1051/shsconf/20219202026

Klicheva, K., & Gavkhar, K. (n.d.). *Team creativity and innovation psychosocial factors affecting organizational performance. European Journal of Research and Reflection in Educational Sciences, 8*(12), 15. https://www.idpublications.org/wp-content/uploads/2020/12/Full-Paper-TEAM-CREATIVITY-AND-INNOVATION-PSYCHOSOCIAL-FACTORS-AFFECTING-ORGANIZATIONAL.pdf

Korobeynikova, L. A., & Vodopiyanova, E. V. (2020). Cultural diversity and globality. *Vestnik Tomskogo Gosudarstvennogo Universiteta. Kul'turologiya i Iskusstvovedenie, 40*, 80–91. https://doi.org/10.17223/22220836/40/7

Krasadakis, G. (2024, March 3). Chief innovation officer: Mission and responsibilities. *The Innovation Mode.* https://www.theinnovationmode.com/the-innovation-blog/chief-innovation-officer-mission-and-responsibilities

Kraus, S., Schleich, M., Tröster, A., & Roig-Tierno, N. (2019). Cultural diversity in large enterprises: A qualitative analysis from the alpine Rhine valley. *Journal of Promotion Management, 25*(5), 640–663. https://doi.org/10.1080/10496491.2019.1585570

Kriw, A. M. (2021). Integration of diversity in multinational companies. *International Journal of Scientific and Research Publications (IJSRP), 11*(8), 691–694. https://doi.org/10.29322/ijsrp.11.08.2021.p11683

McKeogh, M. I. (2011). Chapter 5: Influence of globalization of education on labor market efficiency: Effect of higher education and training on efficient use of talent. In *Education Policy in the Twenty-First Century* (pp. 81–96). Nova Publishing.

Moosmüller, A. (2017). Intercultural challenges in multinational corporations. In A. Moosmüller (Ed.), *Conflict challenges in multinational corporations.* Routledge. https://www.taylorfrancis.com/chapters/edit/10.4324/9781315266916-18/intercultural-challenges-multinational-corporations-alois-moosm%C3%BCller

N.A. (2023, May 21). Exploring the benefits and challenges of multicultural society. *Collegenp.com.* https://www.collegenp.com/article/exploring-the-benefits-and-challenges-of-multicultural-society/

N.A. (2023, October 27). The role of international education in promoting global citizenship. *Gateway International.* https://gateway-international.in/blogs/international-education-in-promoting-global-citizenship/

Neeley, T. (2012). *Global business speaks English: Why you need a language strategy now.* Harvard Business Review.

Okoro, E. (2019). Intercultural communication competence in multinational competitiveness: Literature review and synthesis. *Journal of Business & Economic Policy, 6*(2). https://doi.org/10.30845/jbep.v6n2a1

Pena-Melnyk, J., & Lewis, R. (2021, March 3). Public health – Implicit bias training and the Office of Minority Health and Health Disparities, House Bill 28. *Maryland General Assembly.* https://mgaleg.maryland.gov/2021RS/bills/hb/hb0028F.pdf

Petreska, E. (2022). Managing virtual teams. *Economic Development / Ekonomiski Razvoj, 24*(4), 160–173.

Pew Research Center. (2023, May). Diversity, equity and inclusion in the workplace: A survey report. https://www.pewresearch.org/social-trends/2023/05/17/diversity-equity-and-inclusion-in-the-workplace/

Pizzoni, V. (2024). Mentoring, reverse mentoring, sponsorship. *TCE: The Chemical Engineer, 999*, 30–31.

Rezza Moieni, Mousaferiadis, P., & Carlos Oscar Sorezano. (2017). A practical approach to measuring cultural diversity on Australian organizations and schools. *International Journal of Social Science and Humanity*, 735–739. https://doi.org/10.18178/ijssh.2017.v7.917

Rizy, C., Feil, S., Sniderman, B., & Egan, M. E. (2011, July). *Diversity V multiculturalism advantages and ...* Forbes Insights: Global Diversity and Inclusion. https://www.ijsrp.org/research-paper-0120/ijsrp-p9720.pdf

Roberson, Q., & Perry, J. L. (2022). Inclusive leadership in thought and action: A thematic analysis. *Group & Organization Management*, 47(4), 755–778. https://doi.org/10.1177/10596011211013161

Safronchouk, M., Ivanitskaya, N. V., & Baibulov, A. (2021). Global Labor Market and challenges of digitalization. *Social Science Research Network*, 1–5. https://doi.org/10.2139/ssrn.3846506

Shahid, D. (2022). Importance of intercultural communication in an organization. *Journal of Business & Management Studies (2709-0876)*, *4*(2), 459–463. https://doi.org/10.32996/jbms.2022.4.2.33

Sholahudin, U., Wahyudi, M. H., & Hariri, A. (2018). IbPE USAHA MEUBEL KARDULUK SUMENEP MADURA JAWA TIMUR. *Jurnal Dedikasi*, *15*(Mei), 55–61. https://garuda.kemdikbud.go.id/documents/detail/1330846

Schlachter, S., Rolf, S., & Welbourne, T. M. (2024). Dynamics of employee resource groups: Leader experiences driving mutual benefits for employees and employers. *Compensation & Benefits Review*, *56*(3), 119–137. https://doi.org/10.1177/08863687231192179

Soriano, W. C. (2022). Workplace diversity: A key to organizational competitiveness. *International Journal of Research Studies in Education*, *11*(14). https://doi.org/10.5861/ijrse.2022.b055

Statista. (2024). Number of internet and social media users worldwide as of July 2024. https://www.statista.com/statistics/617136/digital-population-worldwide/

Tamunomiebi, M. D., & John-Eke, E. C. (2020). Workplace diversity: Emerging issues in contemporary reviews. *International Journal of Academic Research in Business and Social Sciences*, *10*(2). https://doi.org/10.6007/ijarbss/v10-i2/6926

United Nations. (n.d.). *Official languages*. https://www.un.org/en/our-work/official-languages

U.S. Equal Employment Opportunity Commission. (n.d.). U.S. Equal Employment Opportunity Commission. https://www.eeoc.gov/

Verma, A. (2020). Critical Review of literature of the impact of workforce diversity (specifically age, gender, and ethnic diversity) on organizational competitiveness. *Asian Journal of Management*, *11*(1), 125. https://doi.org/10.5958/2321-5763.2020.00020.7

Waghmare, R. B. (2021). Workforce diversity to foster an innovation. *Advances in Human Resources Management and Organizational Development*, 109–120. https://doi.org/10.4018/978-1-7998-3515-8.ch006

WebMD Health Services. (2023, February). Why your program may be failing employees. https://www.webmdhealthservices.com/resources/webinars/how-well-being-programs-are-failing-women-and-millennials/

What is diversity, equity & inclusion (DE&I) & why is it important? (2023, September). https://www.imd.org/blog/leadership/what-is-dei/

Yang, X., Hou, J., & Arth, Z. W. (2021). Communicating in a proper way: How people from high-/low-context culture choose their media for communication. *INTERNATIONAL COMMUNICATION GAZETTE*, *83*(3), 238–259. https://doi.org/10.1177/1748048520902617

Zheng, W., Kim, J., Kark, R., & Mascolo, L. (2023, September). *What makes an inclusive leader*? Harvard Business Review. https://hbr.org/2023/09/what-makes-an-inclusive-leader

CHAPTER 3

The Cultural and Social Status of Jobs

Steve Lambert, University of Chester, United Kingdom

Abstract

This chapter, "The Cultural and Social Status of Jobs," explores the intricate relationship between employment, cultural perceptions, and social status. Employment plays a crucial role in determining an individual's social position, heavily influenced by education, income, occupational prestige, and social networks. The chapter examines how education facilitates access to higher-paying jobs, contributing to elevated social status. It delves into the conceptualization of social status within society, emphasizing how certain professions, such as medicine and law, are highly regarded due to their cultural significance and occupational prestige.

The discussion extends to how modern society is reconceptualizing essential jobs that are vital to societal function but may not hold equivalent social status. The chapter also explores the concepts of cultural capital and social networks, demonstrating how these factors shape career advancement and social mobility. Additionally, it highlights persistent disparities in employment based on gender and race, underscoring the need for policies to promote equity and inclusiveness in the workforce. Ultimately, the chapter provides a comprehensive analysis of how employment, cultural constructs, and social status intertwine to shape occupational value and societal hierarchies.

Introduction

Employment is a fundamental aspect of modern society that significantly influences an individual's social status and position within the societal hierarchy. Social status is often perceived as one's societal position, which comprises notions of employment intertwined with factors such as income, education, occupational prestige, and social networks.

This chapter examines the interaction between employment, culture, and social status. The chapter starts by exploring the role that education has in facilitating access to higher-paid employment and thus increased social status. After which the way in which social status is typically conceptualised in society is discussed. This is achieved by looking at how society values specific occupations, such as medicine and the judiciary, and how occupational values contribute to society's perception and understanding of these. Finally, consideration is given to how society is reconceptualizing jobs particularly when they are key to the normal function of society.

Historically, certain professions have been highly regarded, conferring substantial social status upon those who held them. Turner (2010) reminds us that in medieval times, roles within the clergy, medicine, and the judiciary were considered prestigious due to their functions within society and the extensive training required to enter these occupations. The onset of the Industrial Revolution from 1760 (until – 1840) marked a significant shift, introducing a broader range of occupations and altering perceptions of employment status. This period saw the rise of factory workers and industrialists, whose economic contributions began to redefine social hierarchies (Harvey, 2018).

One of the primary ways employment influences social status is through income. Higher-paying jobs not only provide better living standards but also afford individuals the means to participate in social activities often seen as the preserve of those who are more affluent, Breen (2005), such as game-shooting or attending theatre and opera performances. The economic capital gained from high-income employment enables individuals to invest in what those without financial contracts might refer to as luxuries but to who invest in such services would consider to be essentials, this includes accessing private education, private healthcare, and larger more opulent homes, all of which are markers of higher social status.

A key determinant of higher social status is educational attainment, which remains a key factor in accessing high-income employment and improved social status. Jobs requiring higher education levels tend to be more prestigious and better-remunerated, thus elevating the social status of individuals in these roles (Collins, 1979). There is a direct correlation between education and income with the Institute of Fiscal Studies (IFS) stating that individuals with a university degree often occupy positions of authority and influence within organizations and can expect to earn (after tax) £130,000 more over their working life than those without. This increases to almost £500,000 for degrees from prestigious institutions (Britton et al., 2020). However, research from Davern et al. (2024) suggests that the proportion of the population in America obtaining degrees is declining (Figure 1) which could have an impact on social status.

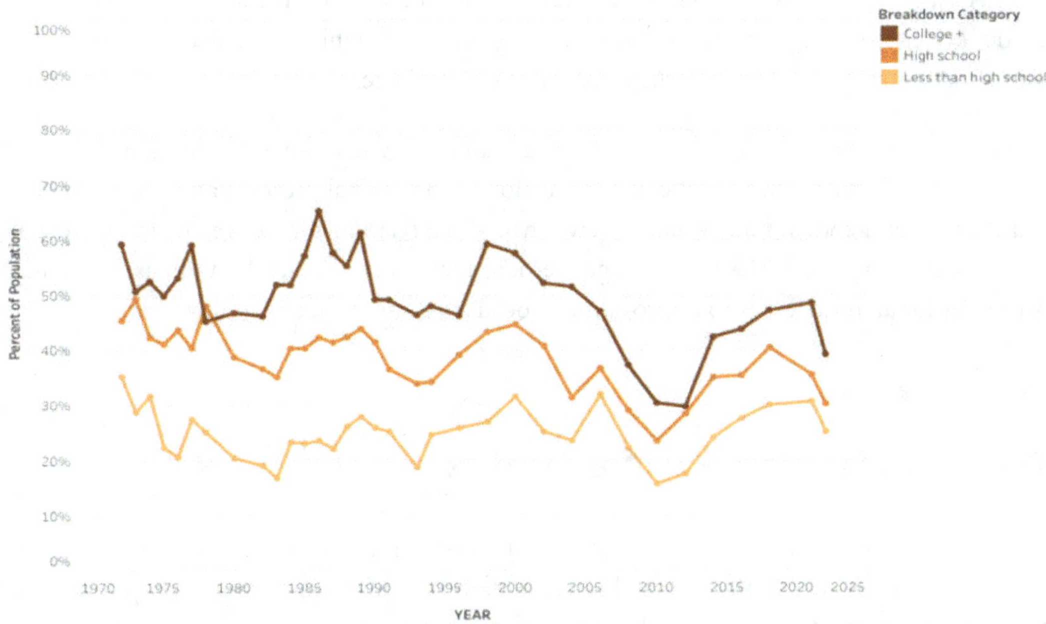

FIGURE 1: Proportion of individuals obtaining a degree (Davern et al., (2024).

The concept of occupational prestige refers to the collective perception of the value and importance of different jobs within society. Sociologists have long studied occupational prestige to understand how various jobs are ranked in terms of social status. The National Opinion Research Centre (NORC) has developed the General Social Survey, which ranks occupations based on public perceptions of their prestige Extracts by Smith and Son (2014) and Davern et al. (2024) continuously highlight professions such as doctors, lawyers, and university professors consistently rank high in occupational prestige due to the perceived societal importance and the extensive education required for these roles.

The connections and relationships formed through an individual's job can provide opportunities for social mobility through career advancement and social recognition (Granovetter, 1973, 2018; Kim & Fernandez, 2023). These social networks often help individuals gain access to better job opportunities and resources that can further enhance their social status. Moreover, professional associations and workplace environments facilitate the development of social capital, which is essential for navigating and ascending the social hierarchy (Bourdieu, 1986).

While employment significantly influences social status, it is also important to recognize the disparities that exist. Gender and racial inequalities in the workplace remain a hindrance to certain groups in achieving higher social status through employment. Women and minority groups often face barriers such as wage gaps, underrepresentation in high-status occupations, and discriminatory practices (Hegewisch & Hartmann, 2014). These disparities highlight the need for policies and initiatives that promote equity and inclusiveness in the workforce.

Thus, employment is a pivotal determinant of social status, influencing an individual's position within the hierarchy of society through income, education, occupational prestige, and social networks. While historical and contemporary factors have shaped the relationship between employment and social status, ongoing disparities based on gender and race must be addressed to ensure equitable opportunities for all individuals to improve their social standing through employment.

Defining Cultural and Social Status in Employment

Cultural and social status are pivotal constructs in understanding how societies value different occupations. These constructs influence the hierarchy of jobs, determining which professions are esteemed and which are marginalized. This section explores the definitions of cultural and social status, their relevance in the valuation of occupations, and how societal norms, beliefs, and perceptions shape these valuations. The key factors involved in shaping societal beliefs include educational attainment, socioeconomic background, cultural capital, and social networks, which collectively shape the opportunities and constraints individuals face in their professional lives.

Having touched upon the role that educational attainment has in providing social mobility through access to higher-paid jobs, educational attainment is also a critical determinant of cultural and social status in employment. According to Bourdieu (1986), education serves as a form of cultural capital, providing individuals with the knowledge and skills valued by employers. This capital is not only instrumental in securing employment but also in climbing the social and professional ladder. For instance, graduates from respected institutions often have access to prestigious job networks and are perceived as more competent and capable, reinforcing their higher status in the workplace (DiMaggio, 1982; Dumais, 2002; Mikus, Tieben, & Schober, 2020).

Socioeconomic background also plays a significant role in defining cultural and social status in employment. Individuals from affluent families more readily have access to better educational resources, professional networks, and career guidance, which can facilitate their entry into high-status occupations. Conversely, Lareau (2003) and Manstead, (2018) argue that individuals from lower socioeconomic backgrounds may (but not always) face barriers such as limited access to quality education and fewer professional connections, which can hinder their career advancement. These disparities contribute to the perpetuation of social inequalities within the labor market.

It is important to note that cultural capital extends beyond formal education to include non-credentialed forms of knowledge, skills, and cultural competencies. Indeed, Bourdieu (1986), argues that it encompasses a range of non-financial social assets, including education, intellect, style of speech, dress, and physical appearance, which promote social mobility beyond economic means. While cultural capital is widely recognized for its impact on educational attainment, its influence extends significantly beyond the realm of education.

In the world of work, cultural capital plays a critical role in career advancement. It manifests through professional demeanor, communication skills, and the ability to navigate social networks within corporate settings (Lamont & Lareau, 1988). It may also include language proficiency, which helps an organization navigate cultural norms and practices. Lareau (2003) states that employers often favor individuals who possess cultural capital that aligns with the organizational culture, as it is perceived to enhance productivity and workplace harmony. Individuals who possess cultural capital that aligns with the dominant corporate culture often experience greater career success and mobility. For instance, knowledge of business etiquette and the ability to engage in culturally relevant conversations can lead to better networking opportunities, career progression, and leadership positions. Moreover, cultural capital can influence social inclusion and exclusion mechanisms in various social contexts. It affects access to elite social circles, participation in high-status activities, and the ability to influence others (Bourdieu, 1984). Cultural capital can also enhance an individual's credibility and authority, enabling them to effectively advocate for policies and mobilize support. Thus, cultural capital extends beyond education by shaping social interactions, career trajectories, and broader socio-political engagement, thereby perpetuating social stratification and influencing overall life outcomes.

As alluded to already, social networks form another critical factor in defining cultural and social status in employment. The concept of social capital, as articulated by Coleman (1988), highlights the importance of social relationships in providing access to job opportunities and career advancement. Networks can offer valuable information about job openings, recommendations, and mentorship, which can be pivotal in securing desirable positions. Studies have shown that individuals with extensive and high-status networks are more likely to be employed in prestigious and well-paying jobs (Granovetter, 2018).

The interplay of these factors creates a complex landscape where cultural and social status in employment is continuously negotiated and reproduced. Intersectionality, a framework developed by Crenshaw (1989), emphasizes the need to consider multiple, overlapping social identities and how they interact to create unique experiences of privilege and disadvantage (Coaston, 2019). For example, race, gender, and class intersect to shape an individual's access to educational and employment opportunities, and subsequently, their cultural and social status within the workplace. Defining cultural and social status in employment involves understanding the multifaceted influences of educational attainment, socioeconomic background, cultural capital, and social networks. These factors interact in complex ways to shape an individual's career trajectory and their standing within the organization and professional hierarchy.

The Importance of Cultural and Social Status in Defining Occupational Value

Cultural and social status plays a pivotal role in shaping occupational value within contemporary labor markets. These factors influence how different professions are perceived, the social prestige associated with various occupations, and the economic rewards tied to specific jobs. Understanding the interplay between cultural capital, social status, and occupational value is crucial for comprehending labor market dynamics and the persistence of social inequalities.

Occupational value refers to the perceived worth of a job in terms of social prestige, economic rewards, and cultural significance. It encompasses both intrinsic and extrinsic values associated with different professions.

- Intrinsic values relate to the personal satisfaction and sense of fulfillment derived from a job.
- Extrinsic values pertain to material rewards such as salary, benefits, and job security.

The societal perception of occupational value is often influenced by historical, cultural, and economic contexts, which shape how different professions are viewed and valued.

Pierre Bourdieu's (1986) concept of cultural capital is instrumental in understanding how cultural factors influence occupational value. As previously discussed, cultural capital comprises non-financial social assets, including education, intellect, style of speech, dress, and physical appearance, which can enhance an individual's social mobility. In the context of employment, cultural capital affects both the acquisition and valuation of different occupations. Individuals possessing high levels of cultural capital are more likely to access prestigious jobs that are highly valued within society. For instance, professions requiring advanced education and specialized skills, such as medicine, law, and academia, are often held in high esteem due to the cultural capital associated with extensive education and professional training (Bourdieu, 1986). These jobs do not offer the substantial economic rewards that entrepreneurs or business owners are afforded, they do however confer significant social prestige. Moreover, cultural capital influences the professional trajectories of individuals within their chosen fields. Professionals who can navigate social norms, display appropriate cultural knowledge, and engage in effective communication are more likely to ascend to higher positions and gain recognition. This dynamic underscores the importance of cultural capital in enhancing occupational value and professional success.

The association between social status and occupational value is evident in the differential valuation of jobs across various social groups. For example, blue-collar and service-sector jobs, often associated with lower social status, tend to be undervalued in terms of both social prestige and economic rewards. These occupations are typically characterized by lower wages, limited job security, and fewer opportunities for advancement, reflecting broader societal biases and structural inequalities (Lamont & Lareau, 1988). However, the labor market has been significantly reshaped through what has become commonly referred to as the gig economy. Characterized by short-term contracts and freelance work, it offers flexibility and autonomy to workers but also introduces challenges such as job insecurity, lack of benefits, and income volatility. De Stefano (2016) highlights that gig workers often experience precarious working conditions and limited access to social protections. Despite its rapid growth, Kässi and Lehdonvirta, (2018) argue that the gig economy raises important questions about the future of work and the need for regulatory frameworks to protect gig workers' rights and ensure fair labor standards. Conversely, white-collar and professional occupations, which are often linked to higher social status, are generally more highly valued. These jobs offer better pay, greater job security, and enhanced social prestige, contributing to a reinforcing cycle where high social status and high occupational value are mutually sustaining.

The interplay between cultural and social status in defining occupational value is complex and multifaceted. Cultural capital can enhance social status, as educational achievements and professional success contribute to an individual's overall standing within society. Conversely, high social status can provide individuals with the resources and opportunities to acquire cultural capital, facilitating access to valued occupations. This dynamic interaction perpetuates social stratification, as those who possess both high cultural and social status are more likely to attain and maintain positions in high-value occupations. This phenomenon is evident in elite professions, where entry often requires a combination of advanced education, professional networks, and cultural knowledge (Lareau, 2003).

The significance of cultural and social status in defining occupational value has profound implications for social inequality. The differential valuation of occupations contributes to the perpetuation of income disparities, occupational segregation, and unequal access to opportunities. Addressing these issues requires a multifaceted approach that considers both cultural and social dimensions of inequality.

Policy interventions aimed at reducing educational disparities, promoting social mobility, and ensuring equitable access to high-value occupations are essential. Additionally, efforts to challenge and transform societal perceptions of occupational value can help mitigate the biases that devalue certain professions and perpetuate social inequalities.

Cultural and social status are integral to understanding the valuation of occupations within society. Cultural capital and social status shape the opportunities available to individuals, influence the perceived worth of different professions, and contribute to the persistence of social inequalities. Addressing these issues requires a comprehensive approach that considers the complex interplay between cultural and social factors, intending to foster a more equitable labor market and society.

Societal Norms, Beliefs, and Perceptions in Shaping Occupational Status

Societal norms, beliefs, and perceptions significantly influence the status attributed to various jobs. These factors shape collective attitudes toward different professions, determining their social prestige, desirability, and the value accorded to them. Understanding how these cultural and social constructs impact occupational status provides insight into labor market dynamics and the perpetuation of social hierarchies.

Societal norms encompass the shared expectations and rules that guide behaviors within a community. These norms are deeply ingrained in the social fabric and influence how different occupations are perceived and valued. For example, in many cultures, jobs that involve intellectual labor, such as medicine, law, and academia, are highly esteemed due to the societal norm that values cognitive skills and advanced education (Bourdieu, 1984). Conversely, occupations involving manual labor, despite being essential, often receive lower social status due to prevailing norms that devalue physical work. These societal norms are not static; they evolve with changes in economic conditions, technological advancements, and cultural shifts. For instance, the rise of the technology sector has elevated the status of jobs related to information technology and digital innovation, reflecting a societal shift toward valuing technical expertise and innovation (Florida, 2002). This dynamic nature of societal norms underscores their crucial role in shaping and reshaping occupational status over time.

Beliefs, which Lortie (2002) describes as deeply held convictions about the world and human nature, also play a vital role in determining the status of various jobs. These beliefs are often rooted in cultural, religious, and historical contexts, influencing how different occupations are viewed. For example, the belief in the inherent dignity of certain professions can elevate their status. In many societies, teaching is regarded as a noble profession because it is believed to shape future generations and contribute to societal progress (Lortie, 2002). Moreover, beliefs about gender roles significantly impact the status attributed to jobs. Traditionally, jobs dominated by men, such as engineering and finance, have been accorded higher status compared to those dominated by women, such as nursing and teaching, reflecting gendered beliefs about work and value (England, 2010). While these gendered perceptions are changing, they do still contribute significantly to occupational segregation and the differential status of professions based on gender. An example of this is the role of women in the military. For over 100 years women have been allowed to serve in the military, however, only since 2018 have they been allowed to serve in frontline roles alongside men (British Army, 2018).

Perceptions, or how individuals interpret and understand their surroundings, further influence occupational status. These perceptions are shaped by media representations, personal experiences, and societal discourse. Media plays a crucial role in shaping public perceptions of different jobs by highlighting certain professions as glamorous, lucrative, or impactful. For example, the portrayal of doctors and lawyers in television and film often emphasizes their intelligence, success, and importance, thereby enhancing the perceived status of these professions (Fiske, 1993).

Conversely, jobs that are less visible or stereotyped negatively in media, such as waste disposal work or domestic labor, often suffer from lower status. These perceptions can perpetuate stigma and devaluation of essential but less celebrated occupations. Efforts to challenge and change these perceptions through positive representation and public awareness can help elevate the status of undervalued jobs. Without such roles, many of the functions of society would not operate correctly (Figure 2).

FIGURE 2: by Mike Birdy via Pexels.

The interplay of societal norms, beliefs, and perceptions in shaping occupational status has profound implications for social inequality. High-status occupations typically offer better pay, job security, and career advancement opportunities, contributing to economic and social mobility. Conversely, low-status jobs are often associated with lower wages, job insecurity, and limited upward mobility, reinforcing social and economic disparities (Tilly & Tilly, 1998).

Addressing these disparities requires a multifaceted approach that includes challenging societal norms and beliefs that devalue certain occupations and fostering positive perceptions of all forms of work. Policy interventions aimed at improving working conditions, ensuring fair wages, and promoting equitable access to high-status professions are essential. Additionally, efforts to recognize and valorize the contributions of all workers, regardless of their occupation, can help in mitigating the effects of occupational status hierarchies.

Societal norms, beliefs, and perceptions are fundamental in shaping the status attributed to various jobs. These cultural and social constructs influence how different professions are valued, impacting economic rewards, social prestige, and career opportunities. Understanding and addressing the factors that shape occupational status is crucial for promoting social equity and recognizing the diverse contributions of all workers within society.

Case Study 1: The Prestige of STEM Careers

In many Western societies, the prestige of STEM (Science, Technology, Engineering, and Mathematics) careers is a reflection of their significant societal impact and the high level of expertise required. STEM professions are often perceived as prestigious due to their contributions to innovation, economic development, and addressing critical global challenges such as climate change, healthcare, and technological advancement (Xie & Killewald, 2012).

STEM careers are typically associated with high educational attainment, specialized skills, and rigorous training, which contribute to their elevated status. This perception is reinforced by the substantial economic rewards, job security, and career advancement opportunities these fields offer (Fayer, Lacey, & Watson, 2017). Furthermore, the cultural capital inherent in STEM careers—marked by intellectual prowess and problem-solving capabilities—aligns with societal values that prioritize scientific progress and technological innovation.

Media representations and public discourse also play crucial roles in enhancing the prestige of STEM careers. Scientists, engineers, and tech innovators are often depicted as pioneers and heroes in popular culture, further cementing the high status of these professions (McAlpine & Emmioğlu, 2014). Consequently, STEM careers continue to attract individuals seeking both personal fulfillment and societal recognition.

Case Study 2: The Evolving Status of Trades

In contrast, skilled trades such as plumbing, electrical work, and carpentry have traditionally been undervalued despite their essential nature. However, there is a growing recognition of the importance of these trades, driven by labor shortages and the increasing complexity of modern infrastructure. Efforts to promote vocational training and change societal perceptions are gradually enhancing the status of these occupations (Morrison, 2020).

The status of occupational trades has evolved significantly over recent decades, reflecting changes in societal values, economic demands, and labor market dynamics. Traditionally, trades such as plumbing, electrical work, and carpentry were often perceived as less prestigious compared to white-collar professions. This perception was largely due to societal norms that prioritized academic education over vocational training and undervalued manual labor (Bourdieu, 1984).

However, the evolving economic landscape has prompted a re-evaluation of these trades. The growing recognition of the essential role that skilled tradespeople play in infrastructure development, maintenance, and innovation has elevated their status. As economies face shortages of skilled labor, trades have become increasingly lucrative, offering competitive salaries, job stability, and opportunities for entrepreneurship (Hoffman, 2011).

Moreover, the push for sustainability and green technologies has further enhanced the prestige of trades. Electricians, heating and ventilation technicians, and construction workers are now at the forefront of implementing energy-efficient solutions and sustainable practices, aligning their work with contemporary environmental values (Gould, 2015).

Efforts to integrate vocational training with modern education systems have also contributed to this shift, providing pathways that combine technical skills with academic knowledge, thereby broadening the appeal and recognition of occupational trades.

Cultural and social status are crucial in defining the value of different occupations. Historical context, economic implications, educational attainment, occupational prestige, and social networks all contribute to the status of various jobs. Societal norms, beliefs, and perceptions, shaped by cultural traditions, media representation, and economic changes, further influence these valuations. Recognizing and addressing the disparities in occupational status is essential for creating a more equitable society where all jobs are valued for their contributions.

Historical Perspectives on Job Status

The cultural and social status of different professions has been shaped by a multitude of historical factors, reflecting the evolving economic, social, and political contexts. This section explores these factors, analyzing how societal changes over time have influenced the perceived value of certain jobs. The status attributed to various professions has historically been influenced by several key factors, including economic structures, technological advancements, and prevailing cultural and social norms, each of which will be looked at in turn.

ECONOMIC STRUCTURES

Economic structures play a critical role in determining the status of different professions. In agrarian societies, occupations related to agriculture, such as farming and animal husbandry, held high status due to their direct connection to survival and sustenance. Land ownership, in particular, was a significant determinant of social status, with landowners enjoying higher prestige and influence (Marx, 1867).

The Industrial Revolution marked a significant shift, as industrial and manufacturing jobs became more prominent. The rise of factories and mass production created new labor demands, leading to the emergence of a working class. Industrialists and entrepreneurs, who drove economic growth and innovation, gained high social status and economic power (Weber, 1905). Conversely, manual laborers, despite being essential to industrial production, were often viewed as low-status due to the harsh working conditions and lack of autonomy.

TECHNOLOGICAL ADVANCEMENTS

Technological advancements have continually reshaped the job market and the status of different professions. During the Renaissance, advancements in science and art elevated the status of scholars, artists, and scientists. Figures like Leonardo da Vinci and Galileo Galilei were celebrated for their contributions to knowledge and culture, reflecting a societal shift towards valuing intellectual and creative pursuits (Burke, 1972).

In the 20th century, the advent of information technology revolutionized the job market once again. Professions related to computer science, engineering, and information technology gained high status due to their association with innovation and economic growth. The tech industry, in particular, has produced some of the most influential and wealthy individuals in contemporary society, further enhancing the prestige of these professions (Florida, 2002).

CULTURAL AND SOCIAL NORMS

Cultural and social norms also play a significant role in shaping the status of professions. These norms are deeply embedded in societal values and influence perceptions of different types of work. For example, during the Victorian era, professions such as law, medicine, and the clergy were highly respected, reflecting the era's emphasis on education, morality, and public service (Davidoff & Hall, 1987).

Gender norms have historically influenced the status of professions. Traditionally male-dominated fields, such as engineering and finance, have been accorded higher status compared to female-dominated fields, such as nursing and teaching. These gendered perceptions are rooted in societal beliefs about gender roles and the value of different types of work (England, 2010).

Societal Changes and Perceived Job Value

Societal changes over time, including economic shifts, social movements, and cultural transformations, have significantly affected the perceived value of certain jobs.

ECONOMIC SHIFTS

Economic shifts, such as the transition from manufacturing to service-based economies, have altered the job market and the status of different professions. In post-industrial societies, service-oriented jobs, particularly in finance, healthcare, and education, have gained prominence. The rise of the knowledge economy has elevated the status of professions that require advanced education and specialized skills (Bell, 1973).

Globalization has also influenced job status, with professions related to international trade, finance, and technology gaining higher status due to their global impact. Conversely, jobs in traditional manufacturing sectors have declined in status as these industries have moved to regions with lower labor costs (Sassen, 2001).

SOCIAL MOVEMENTS

Social movements have played a crucial role in challenging and reshaping the status of various professions. The labor movement in the late 19th and early 20th centuries advocated for workers' rights, leading to improved working conditions, higher wages, and greater recognition of the contributions of manual laborers. These changes helped elevate the status of blue-collar jobs and emphasized the importance of fair labor practices (Hobsbawm, 1964).

The feminist movement has also had a profound impact on job status, particularly in challenging gendered perceptions of work. Efforts to achieve gender equality in the workplace have highlighted the value of traditionally female-dominated professions and advocated for equal pay and opportunities. This has led to a gradual increase in the status of professions such as nursing, teaching, and social work (Freeman, 1975).

CULTURAL TRANSFORMATIONS

Cultural transformations, including shifts in societal values and technological advancements, have influenced the perceived value of different jobs. The increasing importance of sustainability and environmental consciousness has elevated the status of professions related to renewable energy, environmental science, and conservation. These jobs are now seen as crucial for addressing global challenges such as climate change and resource depletion (Gould, 2015).

The rise of the digital age has transformed the job market, with new professions emerging in areas such as digital marketing, data science, and cybersecurity. These jobs are highly valued for their role in driving technological innovation and economic growth. The cultural emphasis on technological proficiency and digital literacy has further enhanced the status of these professions (McAfee & Brynjolfsson, 2014).

The historical and evolving status of different professions is shaped by a complex interplay of economic structures, technological advancements, and cultural and social norms. As societies change, so too do the perceptions of various jobs and the value attributed to them. Understanding these historical factors and societal changes is crucial for comprehending contemporary labor market dynamics and addressing social inequalities. By recognizing and valuing the diverse contributions of all professions, societies can foster a more inclusive and equitable workforce.

Challenges and Controversies

The cultural and social status of jobs is a complex and multifaceted issue, influenced by historical, economic, social, and political factors. This discussion explores some of the key challenges and controversies surrounding job status, focusing on gender and racial disparities in occupational prestige, the impact of globalization and technological advancements on job status, and the stigma associated with certain types of work.

DEMOGRAPHICS AND OCCUPATIONAL PRESTIGE

Gender and racial disparities in occupational prestige are deeply rooted in historical and cultural contexts. These disparities manifest in various ways, including wage gaps, underrepresentation in certain fields, and differential valuation of jobs predominantly held by women and minorities.

Historically, gender roles have significantly influenced the status of various occupations. Traditionally male-dominated fields such as engineering, finance, and technology often command higher prestige and pay compared to female-dominated fields like nursing, teaching, and social work. This disparity is partly due to societal norms that have historically undervalued work performed by women (England, 2010).

The gender pay gap is a persistent issue, with women earning significantly less than men for comparable work. According to the World Economic Forum's Global Gender Gap Report 2020, the global gender pay gap is estimated to be 16%, with women earning, on average, 84% of what men earn (World Economic Forum, 2020). This pay gap is more pronounced in certain professions and industries, reflecting broader societal biases and structural inequalities.

Additionally, women are underrepresented in leadership positions across many industries, which further perpetuates gender disparities in occupational prestige. The "glass ceiling" phenomenon, where women face barriers to advancement into higher-level positions, is a significant challenge. Studies have shown that women often encounter biases in promotion decisions, lack of mentorship opportunities, and work-life balance challenges that hinder their career progression (Eagly & Carli, 2007).

Racial disparities in occupational prestige are similarly pervasive, with minorities often experiencing lower status and fewer opportunities for advancement in many professions. Historical and systemic racism has resulted in unequal access to education, professional networks, and job opportunities for minority groups.

Racial wage gaps persist, with minority workers generally earning less than their white counterparts. For example, in the United States, African American and Hispanic workers earn significantly less than white workers, even when controlling for education and experience (BLS, 2020). These disparities reflect broader societal issues, including discrimination in hiring, promotion, and pay practices.

Moreover, minority workers are often concentrated in lower-status, lower-paying jobs, which reinforces occupational segregation and limits upward mobility. This segregation is partly due to historical patterns of discrimination and exclusion, as well as ongoing biases and stereotypes that influence employment decisions (Pager & Shepherd, 2008).

Globalization and technological advancements have profoundly reshaped the job market, influencing the status and value of various occupations. While these changes have created new opportunities, they have also introduced significant challenges and controversies.

Globalization has facilitated the movement of goods, services, and labor across borders, creating a more interconnected global economy. This interconnectedness has had both positive and negative effects on job status.

On the positive side, globalization has created new opportunities for high-skilled workers, particularly in industries such as technology, finance, and consulting. These professions often benefit from global markets, cross-border collaboration, and access to a broader talent pool, enhancing their prestige and economic rewards (Sassen, 2001).

However, globalization has also led to the outsourcing and offshoring of many low- and mid-skilled jobs, particularly in the manufacturing and service sectors. Workers in developed countries have seen a decline in job security and wages in these industries as companies seek to reduce costs by relocating operations to countries with lower labor costs. This shift has devalued certain jobs and contributed to economic instability and social dislocation in affected communities (Blinder, 2006).

TECHNOLOGY AND OCCUPATIONAL PRESTIGE

Technological advancements, particularly in automation and artificial intelligence, are transforming the nature of work and job status. While technology has the potential to increase productivity and create new industries, it also poses significant challenges for workers in certain occupations.

Automation and AI are displacing jobs in various sectors, particularly those involving routine, repetitive tasks. For example, manufacturing, retail, and administrative jobs are increasingly being automated, leading to job losses and reduced job security for workers in these fields (Autor, 2015). This displacement often affects low- and mid-skilled workers the most, exacerbating existing inequalities and reducing the status of these occupations.

Conversely, technology has elevated the status of jobs that require advanced technical skills and expertise. Professions in software development, data science, and cybersecurity, for example, have seen a significant increase in demand and prestige due to their critical role in driving technological innovation and economic growth. These jobs often offer higher salaries, better job security, and greater career advancement opportunities (Brynjolfsson & McAfee, 2014).

Certain types of work carry social stigma, which affects the perceived status and desirability of these occupations. This stigma is often rooted in cultural norms, stereotypes, and societal values that devalue specific forms of labor.

MANUAL AND LOW-SKILLED LABOR

Manual and low-skilled labor, despite being essential to the functioning of society, is often stigmatized and viewed as low-status. Jobs such as sanitation work, domestic labor, and agricultural work are frequently associated with low pay, poor working conditions, and limited opportunities for advancement. This stigma reflects broader societal biases that devalue physical labor and prioritize cognitive and technical skills (Lamont, 2000).

The stigma associated with these jobs can have significant negative effects on workers' self-esteem and social identity. It can also contribute to social and economic marginalization, limiting workers' access to social protections, professional development opportunities, and upward mobility. This can be seen in the following examples.

CARE WORK

Care work, including jobs in childcare, eldercare, and healthcare support, is another area that is often stigmatized despite its critical importance. These jobs are predominantly performed by women and are frequently undervalued both socially and economically. The low status of care work is partly due to gendered perceptions that view caregiving as a natural extension of women's domestic roles, rather than as skilled, professional work (Folbre, 2006).

This stigma not only affects the status and pay of care workers but also has broader societal implications. The undervaluation of care work can lead to inadequate investment in these essential services, affecting the quality and availability of care for vulnerable populations.

GIG AND PRECARIOUS WORK

The rise of the gig economy has introduced new forms of work that are often stigmatized and associated with precarity. Gig workers, such as Uber drivers, delivery couriers, and freelance platform workers, often face job insecurity, lack of benefits, and unpredictable income. These conditions contribute to the perception of gig work as low-status and undesirable (De Stefano, 2016). However, in 2021 the UK Supreme Court ruled that Uber drivers qualified for the national minimum wage, paid vacation, and the same rights as other workers (Uber BV and others (Appellants) v Aslam and others (Respondents), 2021) This is one step towards providing some form of equity for those in the gig economy and their permanent counterparts.

Moreover, the gig economy has highlighted issues of labor rights and protections, as many gig workers are classified as independent contractors rather than employees. This classification limits their access to social protections, such as health insurance, unemployment benefits, and retirement savings, further exacerbating the stigma and challenges associated with gig work.

The cultural and social status of jobs is influenced by a complex interplay of historical, economic, social, and cultural factors. Gender and racial disparities, the impact of globalization and technological advancements, and the stigma associated with certain types of work all contribute to the challenges and controversies surrounding job status.

Addressing these issues requires a multifaceted approach that includes challenging societal norms and biases, implementing policies to promote equity and inclusion, and recognizing the diverse contributions of all workers. By valuing all forms of labor and ensuring fair treatment and opportunities for all workers, societies can work towards a more inclusive and equitable labor market.

Conclusion

The landscape of employment is evolving rapidly, driven by technological advancements, globalization, and shifting societal values. This transformation is not just about the nature of work but also encompasses the cultural and social status of various jobs. Children who are in school are being taught skills for a society that most of us cannot imagine and for jobs that have not yet been invented.

The increasing awareness of mental health and the importance of work-life balance is reshaping how job status is perceived. Traditionally, high-status jobs were often associated with long hours and high stress, symbolizing dedication and success. However, there is a growing shift towards valuing jobs that offer flexibility, mental well-being, and personal fulfillment.

Research by the Harvard Business Review (Schwartz, 2010) suggests that companies promoting work-life balance are viewed more favorably, attracting top talent who prioritize holistic well-being over mere financial rewards. This trend is likely to continue, with organizations that support flexible work arrangements and employee well-being gaining cultural prestige. At the same time, the rising importance of the impact society is having on the environment is gaining increased recognition. A survey by Deloitte (2021) found that younger generations, particularly Millennials and Gen Z, place a higher value on jobs that have a positive social impact. This shift is reflected in the growing prestige of roles in renewable energy, non-profit organizations, and social enterprises. Companies and jobs that align with sustainable practices and corporate social responsibility are likely to enjoy higher social status in the future.

According to the International Labour Organization (2019), the demand for skills such as multilingualism, cultural awareness, and global strategic thinking is also on the rise. Professionals who can navigate and lead in a multicultural environment are likely to see their social and cultural status elevated, reflecting the interconnected nature of the modern world in which we live and operate.

The future of the cultural and social status of jobs is shaped by a complex interplay of technological advancements, societal values, and global dynamics. As the nature of work transforms, jobs requiring uniquely human skills are gaining prominence. The gig economy is redefining professional identity, while the emphasis on work-life balance, social impact, and sustainability is reshaping what constitutes a prestigious job. Globalization and the need for lifelong learning further influence the evolving landscape of job status. Understanding these trends is essential for navigating the future workforce and fostering a society that values diverse contributions and holistic well-being.

REFERENCES

Autor, D. H. (2015). Why are there still so many jobs? The history and future of workplace automation. *Journal of Economic Perspectives*, *29*(3), 3-30.

Bell, D. (1973). *The coming of post-industrial society: A venture in social forecasting*. Basic Books.

Blinder, A. S. (2006). Offshoring: The next industrial revolution? *Foreign Affairs*, *85*(2), 113-128.

Bourdieu, P. (1984). *Distinction: A social critique of the judgement of taste*. Harvard University Press.

Bourdieu, P. (1986). The forms of capital. In J. Richardson, (Ed.), *Handbook of theory and research for the sociology of education* (pp. 241-258). Greenwood.

Breen, R. (2005). *Social mobility in Europe*. Oxford University Press.

British Army. (2018, October 25). All British Armed Forces Roles Now Open to Women. Army.mod.uk. https://www.army.mod.uk/news-and-events/news/2018/10/women-in-ground-close-combat-roles/

Britton, J., Dearden, L., Waltmann, B., & van der Erve, L. (2020). The impact of undergraduate degrees on lifetime earnings. Institute for Fiscal Studies. https://ifs.org.uk/publications/impact-undergraduate-degrees-lifetime-earnings

Brynjolfsson, E., & McAfee, A. (2014). *The second machine age: Work, progress, and prosperity in a time of brilliant technologies.* W.W. Norton & Company.

Burke, P. (1972). *The Renaissance sense of the past.* Edward Arnold.

Coaston, J. (2019, May 28). The Intersectionality Wars. Vox; Vox Media. https://www.vox.com/the-highlight/2019/5/20/18542843/intersectionality-conservatism-law-race-gender-discrimination

Coleman, J.S. (1988). Social capital in the creation of human capital. *American Journal of Sociology, 94*(1), 95-120.

Collins, R. (1979). *The credential society: An historical sociology of education and stratification.* Academic Press.

Crenshaw, K. (1989). Demarginalizing the intersection of race and sex: A black feminist critique of antidiscrimination doctrine, feminist theory, and antiracist politics. *University of Chicago Legal Forum, 1989* (1), 139-167.

Davern, M., Bautista, R., Freese, J., Herd, P., & Morgan, S. (2024) Current Affairs: Has financial situation changed? General Social Survey 1972-2024. National Opinion Research Center.

Davidoff, L., & Hall, C. (1987). *Family fortunes: Men and women of the English middle class, 1780–1850.* University of Chicago Press.

[The] Deloitte Global 2021 Millennial and Gen Z Survey | Deloitte Global. (n.d.). www.deloitte.com. Retrieved July 31, 2024, from https://www.deloitte.com/za/en/about/people/social-responsibility/millennialsurvey-2021.html

De Stefano, V. (2016). The rise of the "just-in-time workforce": On-demand work, crowdwork, and labor protection in the gig-economy. *Comparative Labor Law & Policy Journal, 37*(3), 471-504.

DiMaggio, P. (1982). Cultural capital and school success: The impact of status culture participation on the grades of US high school students. *American Sociological Review, 47*(2), 189-201.

Dumais, S. A. (2002). Cultural capital, gender, and school success: The role of Habitus. s*Sociology of education, 75*(1), 44–68. https://doi.org/10.2307/3090253

Eagly, A. H., & Carli, L. L. (2007). *Through the labyrinth: The truth about how women become leaders.* Harvard Business School Press.

England, P. (2010). The gender revolution: Uneven and stalled. *Gender & Society, 24*(2), 149-166.

Fayer, S., Lacey, A., & Watson, A. (2017). *STEM occupations: Past, present, and future.* U.S. Bureau of Labor Statistics.

Fiske, S. T., & Taylor, S. E. (2013). *Social Cognition: From Brains to Culture.* Sage Publications.

Fiske, J. (1993). *Media matters: Race and gender in U.S. politics.* University of Minnesota Press.

Florida, R. (2002). *The rise of the creative class: And how it's transforming work, leisure, community and everyday life.* Basic Books.

Folbre, N. (2006). *Valuing children: Rethinking the economics of the family.* Harvard University Press.

Freeman, J. (1975). *The politics of women's liberation: A case study of an emerging social movement and its relation to the policy process.* David McKay Company.

Friedman, T. L. (2015). *Thank You for Being Late: An Optimist's Guide to Thriving in the Age of Accelerations.* Farrar, Straus and Giroux.

Global Commission on the Future of Work | International Labour Organization. (2017, August 14). www.ilo.org. https://www.ilo.org/resource/global-commission-future-work.

Gould, K. A. (2015). Green collar jobs: Occupational trades and sustainability. *Sociological Perspectives, 58* (1), 159-168.

Granovetter, M. S. (1973). The strength of weak ties. *American Journal of Sociology, 78*(6), 1360-1380.

Granovetter, M. (2018). The impact of social structure on economic outcomes. In *The sociology of economic life* (pp. 46-61). Routledge.

Harvey, D. (2018). *The condition of postmodernity: An enquiry into the origins of cultural change.* Blackwell.

Hegewisch, A., & Hartmann, H. (2014). *Occupational segregation and the gender wage gap: A job half done.* Institute for Women's Policy Research.

Hobsbawm, E. J. (1964). *Labouring men: Studies in the history of labour.* Weidenfeld & Nicolson.

Hoffman, N. (2011). *Schooling in the workplace: How six of the world's best vocational education systems prepare young people for jobs and life.* Harvard Education Press.

Kässi, O., & Lehdonvirta, V. (2018). Online labour index: Measuring the online gig economy for policy and research. *Technological Forecasting and Social Change, 137,* 241-248.

Kim, M., & Fernandez, R. M. (2023). What makes weak ties strong? *Annual Review of Sociology, 49*(1). https://doi.org/10.1146/annurev-soc-030921-034152

Koo, H. (2007). The Korean Stratification System: Continuity and Change. In C.K. Armstrong (Ed.), *The Korean society: Civil society, democracy, and the state* (pp. 39-64). Cornell University Press.

Lamont, M. (2000). *The dignity of working men: Morality and the boundaries of race, class, and immigration.* Harvard University Press.

Lamont, M., & Lareau, A. (1988). Cultural capital: Allusions, gaps and glissandos in recent theoretical developments. *Sociological Theory, 6*(2), 153-168.

Lareau, A. (2003). *Unequal childhoods: Class, race, and family life.* University of California Press.

Lortie, D. C. (2002). *Schoolteacher: A sociological study.* University of Chicago Press.

Manstead, A. S. (2018). The psychology of social class: How socioeconomic status impacts thought, feelings, and behaviour. *British Journal of Social Psychology, 57*(2), 267-291.

Marx, K. (1867). *Capital: Critique of political economy.* Progress Publishers.

McAlpine, L., & Emmioğlu, E. (2014). Navigating careers: Perceptions of sciences doctoral students, post-PhD researchers and pre-tenure academics. *Studies in Higher Education, 39*(4), 743-759.

Mikus, K., Tieben, N., & Schober, P. S. (2020). Children's conversion of cultural capital into educational success: the symbolic and skill-generating functions of cultural capital. *British Journal of Sociology of Education, 41*(2), 197–217. https://doi.org/10.1080/01425692.2019.1677454

Morrison, T. (2020). The Skills Gap and the Changing Perception of Skilled Trades. *Labor Market Trends Journal, 45*(2), 112-130.

Pager, D., & Shepherd, H. (2008). The sociology of discrimination: Racial discrimination in employment, housing, credit, and consumer markets. *Annual Review of Sociology, 34,* 181-209.

Sassen, S. (2001). *The global city: New York, London, Tokyo.* Princeton University Press.

Schwartz, T. (2010, June). *The Productivity Paradox: How Sony Pictures Gets More Out of People by Demanding Less.* Harvard Business Review. https://hbr.org/2010/06/the-productivity-paradox-how-sony-pictures-gets-more-out-of-people-by-demanding-less

Smith, T. W., & Son, J. (2014). *Measuring occupational prestige on the 2012 general social survey*. National Opinion Research Center.

Tilly, C., & Tilly, C. (1998). *Work under capitalism*. Routledge.

Turner, B. S. (2010). *Theories of modernity and postmodernity*. Sage Publications.

Uber BV and others (Appellants) v Aslam and others (Respondents), (UK Supreme Court February 19, 2021). https://www.supremecourt.uk/cases/docs/uksc-2019-0029-judgment.pdf#page=7.77

Weber, M. (1905). *The Protestant ethic and the spirit of capitalism*. Scribner.

Weber, M. (1946). *From Max Weber: Essays in sociology*. Oxford University Press.

Wilson, W. J. (2012). *The truly disadvantaged: The inner city, the underclass, and public policy*. University of Chicago Press.

World Economic Forum. (2020). Global Gender Gap Report 2020. World Economic Forum. https://www.weforum.org/publications/gender-gap-2020-report-100-years-pay-equality/

Xie, Y., & Killewald, A. (2012). *Is American science in decline?* Harvard University Press.

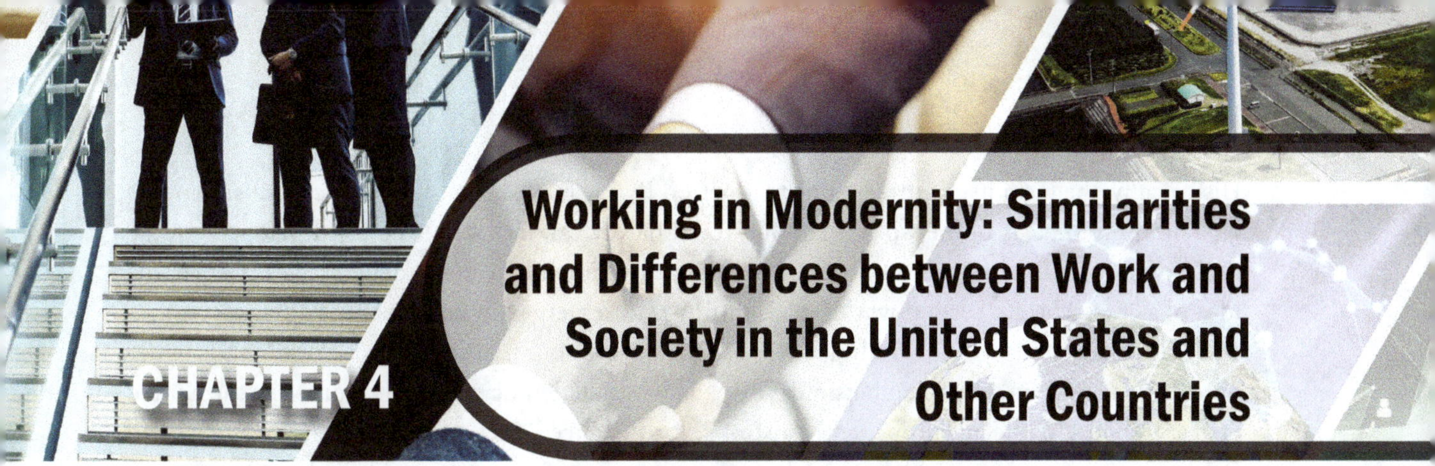

CHAPTER 4

Working in Modernity: Similarities and Differences between Work and Society in the United States and Other Countries

Mattius Rischard, Montana State University-Northern, USA

Abstract

This chapter explores the concept of Modernity and its profound impact on global labor markets, focusing on comparing workplace cultures in the United States and other nations. Rooted in the rise of capitalism, Modernity represents a shift away from traditional, agrarian lifestyles toward urban, industrialized societies. This transition brought about significant changes in labor practices, economic structures, and societal norms worldwide. The chapter highlights distinctions between First, Second, and Third-World countries, examining how each region adapted to capitalist labor markets. In First-World nations, like the U.S., work culture is heavily influenced by individualism and neoliberal democracy, while Second- and Third-World countries exhibit varying levels of industrialization and market integration. Through a discussion of workplace psychology and the role of identity in modern labor, the chapter considers how Modernity has shaped not only economic systems but also personal and societal experiences. Psychological phenomena like Japan's "Smile Mask Syndrome" and the Western concept of the "false self" illustrate the fragmentation of individual identity in the face of modern work demands. Ultimately, the chapter offers a comparative analysis of how modernization has affected labor across cultures, focusing on the tension between traditional values and modern economic imperatives.

Introduction

What does the word "modern" mean to you? Is it merely the latest appliance or style of architecture? A fad or a hashtag for current events? What does "modernity" actually entail, as a lifestyle? For the future of global labor markets? For the work cultures of those markets?

Historically, the term itself corresponds to a period that is marked by the rise of capitalism and its globalization to parts of the world that one would hardly call industrialized or "developed" in the sense of laws and infrastructure that are normalized in liberal, Western democracies. Hence, the idea of a "first world," "second world," and "third world" emerged in terms of how different regions and nations adapted to the institution of capitalism and its labor markets. "First World" tends to denote those nations in which capitalism developed alongside democratic institutions, like the United States, Canada, Western Europe, and Australia, for instance. "Second World" became shorthand for those countries that quickly rose to develop their economies for the world market, but often via the counter-forces of communism and socialist economics, like the Soviet Union and China, while "Third World" came to refer to those nations who still struggle to exert dominance on global trade due to infrastructural or postcolonial roadblocks to industrial development, including most of the African, South Asian, and Latin American states (Ikenberry, 2024).

But in essence, what sets global capitalism apart is the way it creates a sense of distance from art, politics, food sources, community ties, and the products of one's labor. This distance is a hallmark of Modernity—a system where cultural expression and sensory experiences are institutionalized and commodified. Within the framework of Western capitalism, global imperialism, and neoliberal democracy, Modernity represents a dominant worldview. Historically, it is marked by material changes in social relations and a cultural shift away from tradition in favor of more efficient and disciplined forms of power. This period of industrialization, driven by Modernity, emphasizes individualism, freedom, and formal equality. It places faith in secular progress—social, scientific, and technological—and encourages a move from rural, agrarian life to urban, capitalist environments focused on market economies (Sharma, 2024). Modernity also sees the rise of the nation-state, representative democracy, and various public institutions like schools, prisons, hospitals, and police forces, to varying degrees, around the world (Inglehart, 2020).

This worldview creates a "semiotic economy," where meaning and value are detached from political realities or material production. Instead, the worth of objects is tied to their symbolic significance, often conveyed through media, equating the consumption of goods with happiness. In this way, Modernity sustains a global market by embedding cultural and mythic values into commodities, making their representation in media a key factor in their perceived value.

So, when it comes to the topic of labor and workplace culture, there emerged a distinct problem during the 18th Century with the rise of capitalism that is still prevalent to this day in differing forms in First, Second, and Third-World countries: what kind of worker culture is required for investors and employers get maximal use-value out of the labor they pay for? And, conversely, what kind of culture do laborers want or need in order to remain healthy, happy, and productive members or their society and workplace?

In order to get laborers into cities where invested employers sought to create hubs of industry and manufacturing, they had to first incite laborers to accept a modest wage for maximal time spent at work, and to forgo the liberties of laboring on their own time to reap a harvest or hone a craft in their own homes and workshops, which were often situated in rural and village-type environments. Industrialists sought to do away with subsistence farming and peasant lifestyles that supported a local economy in exchange for engaging laborers in currency that would owe itself to purchasing goods on a global market. First, Second, and Third-World countries are, in many ways, merely designations meant to denote how far nations have come in achieving this kind of social relationship between workers, proprietors, governments, and the land or natural resources of a region. In today's urbanized environments, where workers themselves are wholly dependent on a market economy, people have become so controlled by the obligations of wage work and exchange that their individual identities seem irrelevant. According to philosopher Michel Foucault (2012b), this is because of the influence of modern "micro-power," which aims to create self-policing individuals with little sense of personal identity. The soul, in this context, becomes a tool for political control, trapping the body in a specific job market or industrial purpose.

Even if one were to consider the effects of Modernity on the state of this individual subject before thinking through the radical schism between its compelled bodily gestures at work and at home, look no further than the psychological studies of smile mask syndrome (SMS) or *honne/tatemae,* which were coined in the post-war period in East Asian countries as a product of globalized Western sociocultural and economic influence on the individual. SMS was coined as an explanation for the symptoms that university students exhibited during counselling in Makoto Natsume's practice, who noticed that a number of them had spent so much time faking their smiles that they were unaware that they were smiling even while relating stressful or upsetting experiences to him (Shin, 2014, p. 87). Japanese author Tomomi Fujiwara notes that the demand for a common smile in the workplace emerged in Japan by the 1980s, and blames the cultural changes wrought by the Tokyo Disneyland, opened in 1983, for popularizing the demand for an obligatory grin for the customer (Lewis 2008). In South Korea, a similar phenomenon was observed when Yoon-Do-Rahm compared the current society, which is full of "smile-masks," to a clown show: both are characterized by plentiful, yet empty and fake significations of happiness (Lee, 2012, pp. 8-9). *Honne* and *tatemae* (Japanese for "true sound" and "public façade") entered the lexicon after WWII as a result of the conflict of these imported corporate practices of bodily signification (Doi, 1986, p.35). Similar concepts exist in the Arabic terms *zahir* (ظاهر(and *batin* (باطن(—the latter being an inner private self that interprets the world through desire and the former a social self that "manifests" in a public face (see *The Oxford Dictionary of Islam*). In Western psychoanalysis, where the repression of anti-social desires into the unconscious is a concept at least as old as Freud, Donald Winnicott used "true self" to describe a subjectivity based on spontaneous authentic experience and a feeling of being alive, i.e., having a real self. The "false self," by contrast, Winnicott (1960) saw as a defensive façade, which, in extreme cases, could leave its holders lacking spontaneity and feeling emptied-out behind a mere appearance of being real, which becomes the basis for a narcissistic personality (see pp. 140-57).

It seems that across the nations with ways of articulating a self-discipline to culturally accommodate the mythology and ethics of Modernity, they share the common characteristic of a collectively imposed social relation that leads to the production of subjects who cannot reconcile the demands of a public face with their interior experiences and desires, nor can they accept the imposition of a strict ideological divide between private and public ways of being. These schizoid subjects are products of the repeated psychological splitting of the ideal self-image as soon as it encounters a discrepancy between real and ideal conditions created by modern technologies of power. Fredric Jameson (1991) has demonstrated how our hypermediated representations of reality construct this schizophrenic experience, smashing our sense of time and place in the process of interpreting and ordering what we see: "both in our relationship to public History and in the new forms of our private temporality, whose 'schizophrenic' structure will determine new types of syntax or syntagmatic relationships in the more temporal arts" such as cinema (p. 6). With the loss of historicity, the present is experienced by the schizophrenic subject "with heightened intensity, bearing a mysterious charge of affect" (p. 28), which can be "described in the negative terms of anxiety and loss of reality, but which one could just as well imagine in the positive terms of euphoria, a high, an intoxicatory or hallucinogenic intensity" (pp. 28-9). Being lost in the multitude of alienating fictions of contemporary photography and imagery, the modern subject has no space to critique the construction of representation, only to conform their interpretations of that which they look at with the mythology (i.e. the collection of beliefs and values bound up in narrative) that co-constructs the media in the never-ending search for emotional "intensities" compensating for the depthlessness of image-worlds. The cultural logic of late capitalism leads to an aesthetic regime demanding ego-dystonic and schizoid responses at every turn to understand what is demanded by the status quo.

As a result, many critics argue that the modern worker becomes trapped in a cycle of constantly conforming to societal expectations while feeling disconnected from their true self. This leads to a loss of historical context and a heightened, often disorienting, experience of the present. However, beyond the subjective experience of work cultures in the Eastern versus Western or Northern versus Southern hemispheres of the world, there are substantial and concrete comparisons and contrasts that can be made between society and work in First, Second, and Third-World regions of development under the common denominator of Modernity. This chapter shall explain how Modernization affected and affects workplace culture in different societies, and some distinctions that can be made between the culture of the United States and other First World nations relative to the developments in work-society relationships in states labeled as Second and Third World nations according to the Western worldview of modernization.

Workerism and Modernity: Labor-as-Essence in Creating Industrialized Societies

Many Western philosophers and scientists of the Industrial Revolution, from Karl Marx to Adam Smith, have tried to emphasize the centrality of work as a core purpose of human society and the primary source of an individual's sense of meaning and motivation in the world. However, critics of Modernity, from Max Weber to the late Michel Foucault, have argued that this emphasis is a discursive construction of the industrial political economy and Protestant Reformation that emerged by the end of the 17th century. According to Weber (2021), where Catholic Europe of the Middle Ages praised hard work among peasants and craftsmen as a means of living, Industrialization and the rise of Protestantism brought about a reversal in the meaning of work in relation to society: where Medieval folk worked to live and support the holiest vocations, such as the priesthood, the nobility, and the monastic centers, the new modern individual lived to work. Thus, immense wealth was not a sign of greed and other sins, but a symbol of God's approval of one's work ethic. Idleness and sloth were now condemned as primary sins, which manifested in harsher punishments for unemployment and vagrancy (Weber, 2021; Lynn 2023). Thus, societies in Northern and Western Europe and their colonies became oriented around maximum productivity and trading power, rather than glorification of religious or landowning powers and interests.

According to Foucault (2008), in the 18th century, "work discipline" and the rising emphasis on the control and management of workers' time had become a chief focus of the emerging social sciences. The new techniques of power that Foucault identifies as part of the deployment of discipline are applied as much to the experience of work as they are to the other fields, such as education, medicine, or the military. In his 1973-1974 lectures at the Collège de France on Psychiatric Power, Foucault applies this logic to work directly, for instance in focusing on the imposition of the "livret", the employment record, on laborers:

> in the [18th century], the great instrument of worker discipline, the employment document, the livret, is imposed on every worker. No worker can or has the right to move without a livret recording the name of his previous employer and the conditions under which and reasons why he left him... (2008, p. 70)

Work then was much more central as an explanatory factor behind the rise of disciplines. In a modern disciplinary society, supervision and punishment are essential tools used to control individuals, ensuring they are integrated into the production system. This power relationship is necessary to enforce ethical and political norms, making people conform to the demands of labor and productivity, according to Foucault (2015, p. 196).

Thus, new sciences, techniques, and regulations, new architectural designs, and modulations of time are constantly invented and refined to observe, train, control, shape, surveil, and punish workers. As industrial production expanded and became more complex, continuous and intense supervision of workers became essential. This supervision focused on workers' skills, behavior, and efficiency, becoming a crucial part of the production process. Specialized personnel were needed to oversee this, separate from the workers themselves. Although workers preferred a guild-like system in the Middle Ages (because they set their own hours and standards of work), employers recognized that surveillance was essential for maintaining industrial production, private property, and profit. Thus, surveillance became a key economic tool and a fundamental part of disciplinary power (Foucault, 2012b, p. 174).

Foucault also highlights how work became the central, guiding principle in every social realm (notably the family and education), and for every person in how she conceives of her life goals and values. Modern capitalism, he argued in 1975, works through a disciplining of people's times, seeking to make every moment of workers' time functionally useful to production:

> the modern society that formed at the beginning of the nineteenth century was basically indifferent or relatively indifferent to individuals' spatial ties: it was not interested in the spatial control of individuals insofar as they belonged to an estate, a locale, but only insofar as it needed people to place their time at its disposal. (Foucault, 2001, p. 80)

A whole set of new social policies and institutional procedures, some of which seemingly remote from the world of production and apparently serving welfare ends, were put in place to make the whole of workers' time functionally welded to capitalist interests. In the 19th century, measures were taken to reduce workers' time off and control their savings (Foucault, 2001, p. 81). Employers needed workers to have savings to survive periods of unemployment, leading to wage increases in England and France. However, to prevent workers from using their savings for strikes or leisure, savings banks and relief funds were created to control how savings were used. These institutions, appearing protective, actually ensured that workers' entire lifespans were subordinated to labor market demands. This mechanism extended control over workers' time beyond the workday, using consumption and advertising to enforce it.

Today this impact persists—even though most Westerners may not work in mines or factories anymore, this method of bringing a society in line with the demands of modernized work culture is imposed across the world to bring about similar kinds of socioeconomic and political development, often with the aim of exploiting new sources of labor, raw materials, and natural resources to the global market. However, even in the changing context of work settings caused by COVID-19 and the digitization of the Fourth Industrial Revolution, modern forms of power exert themselves through distant control, cybersecurity, and surveillance mechanisms in new ways (Bonin, 2020).

The full impact of COVID-19 on work is still unclear and will take time to understand. However, some changes are already visible, particularly in where work is done. Many people have shifted to working from home, a trend that has been growing thanks to technology and may continue after the pandemic due to lower costs, reduced commuting, and environmental benefits (Mirakyan & Berezka, 2022). While working from home offers employees more freedom, it also means employers have less direct control over their workers.

This loss of control worries businesses because it can be harder to supervise employees remotely. However, technology allows for remote monitoring, which helps companies manage this challenge. The idea of worker surveillance isn't new—it started with industrialization. Despite advancements in technology, it may not fully replace the oversight possible in a traditional office setting. As a result, some experts suggest tying employees' pay to their output instead of hours worked (Tursunbayeva et al., 2022). For workers, the psychological impact of being monitored might be more significant than the actual technology used. The "panopticon effect," where people behave as if they are constantly being watched, could continue to influence how workers perform, even if they're not being closely monitored (Foucault, 2012b, p. 202).

While managerial oversight may increase and become more internalized, this isn't a one-sided story. Critical management studies have long explored the idea, inspired by Foucault, that "where there is power, there is also resistance" (Foucault, 2012a, p. 95). Resistance at work is a key area of study in these fields. Foucault even suggested that resistance comes before power, emphasizing the importance of understanding work from the perspective of the worker. What does work mean to them, and how do they make choices and rationalize their actions? How do they organize and unionize to demand better pay, protection, and benefits? This focus on the worker as a site of resistance encourages us to closely examine the specific actions individuals and worker groups take to resist surveillance, control, and exploitation.

Western v. Eastern Divergence in Development

While both the Western/Capitalist and the Eastern/Communist world orders sought to implement the project of modernization through a prioritization of labor in everyday life, the ways in which they developed work cultures reflected distinct approaches to the spiritual and material needs and wants of the workers themselves. Protestant ethics and socialist labor morality helped motivate labor during the early stages of capital accumulation in First and Second world societies, with the Protestant-capitalist model accentuating personal efforts on the basis of private property and the socialist model stressing individual efforts on the basis of state ownership as the surest path towards rapid industrialization in the Soviet Union, for instance (Inglehart, 2020; Levada, 2018; Magun, 2018; Rajković, 2021; Sharma, 2024). However, if the Protestant work ethic gave rise to the "spirit of capitalism" and spurred economic growth in the West, secular socialist ideology has largely failed to generate the "spirit of communism" and to furnish the foundation for sustained economic growth in the socialist East (Raiković, 2021).

Under the First World order, we find that businesses are mostly privately owned, and profit is the primary motivation of social investment in work. Individuals and companies seek to maximize profits and shareholder value. Competition (as well as a pool of unemployed or underemployed workers to draw upon) drives innovation, efficiency, and keeps wages stable. Companies compete for customers, resources, and market share, leading to a dynamic and often rapidly changing work environment. There is a cultural emphasis on individual achievement and success, where employees are often rewarded based on performance, with incentives such as bonuses, raises, and promotions. As a result, income and wealth disparities are common. Some individuals and companies can accumulate significant wealth, while others may struggle economically. Unemployment, poverty, market volatility or collapse, and company bankruptcy are thus viewed as natural consequences of the capitalist economy and seen as acceptable, or even desirable outcomes, given that competition is prioritized over economic stability in the job market (Korotayev et al., 2020; Rajković, 2021).

Job mobility is higher than in socialist countries, and career advancement often involves changing companies or roles. Thus, employees may face job insecurity but also have opportunities for upward mobility, as opposed to being rewarded for loyalty or seniority within an industry in Eastern countries (Inglehart, 2020). Decisions are typically made by business owners or managers at various levels, allowing for flexibility and responsiveness to market conditions, but also a relative lack of accountability to the workers themselves and their communities or families. Unions are typically in an antagonistic relationship with business owners and managers or outlawed completely by the governments that mediate between them (Korotayev et al., 2020).

By contrast, many Second World nations have attempted to modernize their economies on the notion of collective ownership in the wake of social, political, and cultural revolutions in the 20th Century, where the means of production are owned collectively, often by the state. The focus of production is on the common good rather than individual profit. Economic activity and production are centrally planned and controlled by the government. The aim is to meet the needs of the population rather than respond to market demands. These societies, at least in theory and public policy, support ideas of collective achievement and equality as a way to circumvent the shortcomings of capitalist political economies in the project of modernization and industrial development (Levada, 2018; Magun, 2018).

Thus, the work environment is often designed to foster a sense of community and shared purpose, with rewards often distributed more evenly. Wealth and resources are intended to be distributed more equally among the population (though this is not always the case in reality), and basic needs are typically provided for by the state. In contrast to the unemployment and market volatility of First World countries, jobs are usually guaranteed, and there is less emphasis on competition and job mobility; employees are rewarded for seniority and years of service in a position, rather than leveraging better job offers at competing firms or companies, or re-skilling themselves for other industries. Employees may have less opportunity for rapid career advancement but benefit from greater job stability and unionization that provides wage and benefit guarantees and increases (Inglehart, 2020; Levada, 2018; Magun, 2018).

In many Second World economies, decisions about productivity and market supply chains are made by central political authorities and trade union leadership, which can lead to less flexibility and slower responses to changing conditions, but aims to ensure that resources are used efficiently for the collective good. But this social ideal and the reality of work were often two different things. Soviet society, for instance, could never overcome the gap between the official labor ethics that touted public good along with job content as normative labor motives and the real motivation that propelled Soviet workers, most of whom saw their labor as a means of furthering their personal and family well-being (Levada, 2018; Magun, 2018). The breakdown of totalitarianism effectively eliminates this contradiction. In the late 80s and early 90s, the fundamental cultural shift took place, which legitimized personal interests and private life. Similarly, the economic reforms of Communist China in the 1990s allowed for the integration of foreign and domestic companies and privatization, though the markets were still subject to the approval of the state (Dutta, 2019).

Case Study: What Do Western and Eastern Workers Really Want from Society?

It should come as no surprise that in both capitalist and communist states, private, material interests drive workers' job motivation as a psychological fact. This phenomenon is proven in the process of Second World nations opening their markets to global trade and capitalism: two Russian surveys conducted in 1989 and 1990 revealed that workers, both in capitalist and communist states, prioritize personal and family interests in their job choices (Cook 1995). The most valued job characteristic was "good earnings," with 70% of respondents highlighting it as important, compared to only 43-44% who valued an "interesting job." This reflects a desire to maximize job rewards and minimize personal costs, such as poor working conditions and workplace tension.

A 1991 Russian survey showed similar trends, with 80% of respondents emphasizing "good earnings" as crucial, consistent with values observed since 1976. This focus on earnings reflects an increasing desire for material goods and services, paralleling Western consumption expectations. However, there has been a noticeable decline in the willingness of young people to endure labor hardships.

Yuri Levada's studies from 1988 to 1992 also found a drop in the value placed on "hard and deliberate work" as a key to success, from 45% to 32% (Levada, 2018). This shift is interpreted not as a breakdown in moral values but as a reaction to the Soviet labor ethic, which demanded hard work for minimal rewards. Despite this, the growth in secondary employment suggests that workers are not reducing their overall labor efforts but are instead seeking to reduce the personal effort required for each unit of pay.

Socialism created its own labor culture, which included specific labor values and labor morality. This labor morality successfully functioned as a mobilizing device during the period of forced modernization industrialization but gradually lost its legitimacy and yielded to unofficial norms that markedly differed from the orthodox doctrine (Dutta, 2019; Levada, 2018; Rajković, 2021; Sharma, 2024). These changes laid a motivational groundwork for a market economy, which appeared on the micro level way before the macro-social framework for a market economy was in place. What this means, among other things, is that the transformation of the socialist system into a market economy has deep roots in the consciousness of Eastern peoples and is not something artificially imposed on it from without, though it may manifest in different forms depending on the culture.

The anti-totalitarian revolutions in the East brought in its wake a new labor culture which is based on private property on the production assets and, even more importantly, on the real ownership of the individual over his labor force, including his freedom to dispose of it as he sees fit. At the head of the new labor culture is the consumer interests of the worker and their family. Its other relevant component is the close attention that salaried workers pay to the cost-benefit ratio of their work (Levada, 2018; Murin, 2018; Rajković, 2021). This norm, which is now being extended to other economic resources besides labor, is akin to personal thriftiness that played such a central role at the dawn of Western capitalism as an element of the Protestant ethic.

Case Study: Second World Work Values Still Remain in Eastern Societies

Despite the shift towards a market economy in the 1990s, Russian workers showed a strong preference for collective forms of enterprise ownership and management. This indicates a lingering belief in collective control over production, even as the broader economic system moved towards privatization. At the end of the Soviet Union, workers had a growing awareness of their collective interests and formed independent labor organizations like trade unions and strike committees that were not appointed by the government. A significant turning point was the 1989 mass strikes by Soviet miners, which shattered the communist myths of labor as a spiritual need and harmony in labor-management relations. These events marked a shift in Russian workers' willingness to assert their group interests.

Studies show that Russian workers are highly conscious of their interests and prefer collective ownership and management of enterprises (Magun, 2018). More than half of Russian respondents in a survey preferred to own their enterprise collectively and elect their managers, a preference stronger than in any other country surveyed. This inclination is particularly strong in ex-socialist countries, where workers are committed to employee participation in property ownership and management relative to Western nations.

The "insubordination index" from another survey reveals that Russian workers are the most likely to question and defy managerial decisions (Magun, 2018). This finding aligns with studies of socialist economies, where workers often engaged in market-style negotiations with managers despite centralized national planning. The lack of managerial control observed in these enterprises contrasts sharply with capitalist practices, leading to a unique form of workplace autonomy under socialism.

After years of mistreatment by communist bosses, Russian workers are eager to assert their dignity and human rights. They are disillusioned with past political and union leaders, resent being asked to work hard for minimal pay, and hold their incompetent managers in contempt. As they embrace democratic freedoms, they face the challenge of reconciling these ideals with the autocratic management practices common in capitalist economies.

The new labor morality of a free market for labor being integrated into the Second World nations relative to the United States requires new ideologies to back it up. Fully legitimized labor norms, in turn, could help mobilize labor in the post-Soviet market place. Whether Russia can pull from its present economic crisis and evolve into a prosperous society depends in large measure on the success of this process (Rajković, 2021). This shift is also detectable in China, for instance, since it opened up to the free market (Dutta, 2019).

Northern v. Southern Divergence in Work and Social Developments

The Global South and the Global North are terms used to distinguish between different regions of the world based on various economic, political, social, and historical factors. These terms are often preferred over the more traditional "developed" and "developing" countries, as they acknowledge the complex dynamics and inequalities that exist between these regions. However, most nations typically termed "First World" and "Second World" reside in the Global North, while those grouped as "Third World" are located in the Global South. Typically, the Global North includes countries with advanced economies, high levels of industrialization, and significant wealth that may itself be derived from an exploitative economic relationship with the Global South (Ikenberry, 2024). "Northern" countries usually have a high GDP per capita, robust infrastructure, and diversified economies. Examples include Western nations like the United States, Canada, and most of Europe, but also Eastern nations like Japan, and South Korea. The Global South includes countries with lower levels of industrialization, often with economies that are less diversified and more dependent on agriculture or extractive industries. Many of these countries have lower GDP per capita and face challenges like poverty, inadequate infrastructure, and economic instability. Examples include most of Africa, Latin America, parts of Asia, and the Middle East.

The First and Second World countries were often colonial powers that benefited economically and politically from the exploitation of regions in the Global South. Their historical development is marked by early industrialization, accumulation of capital, and global influence. Third World countries are defined as those subjected to colonization, which has had lasting impacts on their political, social, and economic structures. The legacies of colonialism, including economic exploitation and artificial borders, continue to influence their development (Ikenberry, 2024).

As a result, Third World countries have less influence in global political and economic systems. These countries are often more vulnerable to external pressures from international organizations like the IMF and the World Bank, and their interests can be underrepresented in global decision-making (Inglehart, 2020; Munro, 2023; Sharma, 2024). These nations often face challenges like lower levels of education, poorer healthcare, and higher rates of infant mortality and disease. Social inequality tends to be more pronounced, and access to basic services can be limited, particularly in rural areas.

First world countries like the United States have highly diversified economies supported by large levels of industrialization and infrastructure. Their work culture benefits from technological advancements and efficient systems. Generally, work environments are regulated, ensuring safe and healthy conditions, fair wages, and benefits such as healthcare, retirement plans, and paid leave. Higher levels of education and skill development are prevalent. Employees often have access to continuous training and development opportunities. A large proportion of the workforce is employed in service-oriented and high-tech industries, such as finance, healthcare, IT, and education. There is a growing emphasis on work-life balance, with policies supporting flexible working hours, remote work, and family leave (Inglehart, 2020; Sharma, 2024). Strong labor laws and regulations protect workers' rights, ensuring fair treatment, nondiscrimination, and mechanisms to resolve disputes and negotiate wages.

In contrast, Third World countries often have postcolonial, subsistence, and industrial economies, with limited infrastructure. Work culture can be heavily influenced by economic instability, wars, and limited skilled labor. This is no accident—work environments may be less regulated, leading to unsafe or unhealthy conditions that provide the raw materials and basic elements of economic activity in the North at little cost (Ikenberry, 2024; Inglehart, 2020; Munro, 2023; Waweru et al., 2019). Wages can be low, and benefits such as healthcare and retirement plans are often minimal or nonexistent, despite new demands on employees' time in modernizing states from the Middle East (Abduljaber, 2018).) to Kenya (Waweru et al., 2019). As a result, access to education and skills training can be limited, yielding a workforce with varying levels of education and fewer opportunities for professional development. Many of the skilled laborers and professionals must obtain their credentials and training overseas. A significant portion of the workforce is employed in agriculture, manufacturing, and informal sectors, with many relying on subsistence farming or small-scale enterprises. Those that have a strong export/import economy, such as Venezuela or Nigeria, largely rely on the proceeds of global markets for oil or other natural resources shipped to/from their ex-colonial dependencies like the UK, the USA, or the EU to import goods and fund public services and infrastructure, rendering their entire industrial sector dependent on the global prices and availability of their major export (Munro, 2023).

There is often less emphasis on work-life balance, with longer working hours and fewer opportunities for flexible work arrangements. Labor laws and regulations may be weak or poorly enforced, leaving workers vulnerable to exploitation, discrimination, and lack of job security. As such, there are more complaints about worker abuse, corruption in management and regulatory agencies, and compensation for injuries and accidents (Sharma, 2024).

However, it must be acknowledged that this "Three Worlds" system of East, West, and South has been complicated by modern events. Russia's war on Ukraine is accelerating a global conflict highlighted by the "Three Worlds" system (Ikenberry, 2024). This emerging structure divides the world into the global West (led by the U.S. and Europe), the global East (dominated by China and Russia), and the global South (comprising non-Western developing nations). While these factions are not formal blocs, they represent evolving global power dynamics. This system will drive a competitive and creative politics of order-building, with the West and East vying for the cooperation of the global South. For the global West to maintain leadership, it must accommodate the East and South while promoting a more pluralistic world. The West has an advantage in its competition with the East over their race to develop economic ties and dependencies with the "Third World" because the global South criticizes the West not for its model of modernity, but for failing to live up to its promises and equitably sharing the benefits of liberal modernization. Thus, there is still a chance that liberal, Western-style economics and work-society models may prevail in the modernization of the global South, if less exploitative models of wealth distribution and economic mobility are made available.

Conclusion

To be clear, the reliance on subsistence farming or small-scale enterprises, collective land ownership, family work arrangements, traditional craft-making, and homemade goods in the Global South is not in itself a bad thing (though the lack of coordinated political and work protections for these arrangements leaves many vulnerable to expropriation by foreign and domestic industrial developers and modernization). Indeed, there is no reason that a social group has to become "modern" to develop sustainable livelihoods.

The entire concept of "First," "Second," and "Third" World economies and work-society arrangements is predicated on a capitalist worldview in which nations are ranked by their relative degree of "development" towards Western standards of modernization and social organization around industrial processes and technologies. Thus, even if a society is labeled with the pejorative of a "developing" nation-state that is somehow "behind the curve" of modernization according to capitalist-industrial standards, it may indeed have far more complex language, culture, and social arrangements or responsibilities than a "modern" society. It is not as if the indigenous peoples of the Amazon or the tribes of the Nigerian interior are inherently lacking social cohesion or personal well-being simply because they have not developed Western models of industrial-scale infrastructures. The mere ability of modernization to upend their local economies and colonize them in the network of global trade does not mean that modernization is an inherently "better" kind of system for work and society; much in the same way that a schoolboy being larger and stronger than his classmates does not make him a superior being, regardless of his ability to force his peers into yielding up their lunch money.

Case Study: USING AI to Visualize Differences in Work-Society Cultural Assumptions

Ekphrasis refers to the literary and rhetorical trope of summoning up—through words—an impression of a visual stimulus, object, or scene. As critical trope, the word ekphrasis (ἔκφρασις) is attested from the first century CE onwards: it is discussed in the Imperial Greek Progymnasmata, where it is defined as a "descriptive speech which brings the subject shown before the eyes with visual vividness."

What if we were to use an AI image generator to perform "ekphrasis" on the abstract differences in the imaginings of work, labor, architecture of work, capitalism, and management, using big data? What happens if we resort to DALL-E (not truly an AI data processor, but an accumulator of aggregated images) "AI image generator" that data mines Big Data to see what quantified VISUAL associations pop up when I type in "First World Workplace," "Second World Workplace," and "Third World Workplace?"

This kind of analysis—of course—directly relates to the work that the General Semantics scholars such as S. I. Hayakawa were doing to uncover those associations hidden from our own minds, feelings that are stirred when certain high-level abstractions are used. Words do not have a mere dictionary definition. Words also carry vivid somatic responses. Hayakawa said that there were words that would make him "clench his fists." This kind of trigger response might be detectable when using terms like First and Third-World to describe the general "rankings" of countries according to their process of modernization.

How does the DALL-E graphic image generating program "see" the phrase "workplace," in different nations when described in this way? Well, it could demonstrate the differences in cultural assumptions—harvested from thousands of images tagged with these descriptors—in the varying economic, social, and regulatory environments that shape work cultures in first world, second world, and third world countries.

IMAGE 1: "First World Workplace" in DALL-E

For the “First World” prompt, the image depicts a sleek, open-concept office space with large floor-to-ceiling windows offering a view of a city skyline. The space is brightly lit with natural light and modern light fixtures. There will be several workstations with ergonomic chairs and desks, each equipped with large monitors, laptops, and other tech gadgets. A few employees are seen collaborating in a small meeting area, while others are focused on their work at their desks. There are plants scattered throughout the space, adding a touch of greenery. In the background, a glass-walled conference room will be visible, along with a break area featuring a coffee machine and comfortable seating.

IMAGE 2: “Second World Workplace” in DALL-E

In the “Second World” prompt, the image shows a modest office space with a mix of old and new furniture. The walls may have a slightly aged look, with some signs of wear. The office has a few modern computers and equipment, but also some older technology, such as bulky monitors or outdated printers. The lighting is a combination of natural light from small windows and fluorescent lights. A few employees are working at their desks, some using older office supplies like paper files. The overall atmosphere will reflect a work environment that is functional but not as advanced or high-tech as those in developed countries.

IMAGE 3: “Third World Workplace” in DALL-E

The “Third World” image shows a small, crowded office space with minimal and worn-out furniture. The walls are unpainted or have peeling paint, and the lighting is dim, with only a few fluorescents providing illumination. The desks are old and mismatched, with outdated computers or no computers at all. Employees may be using paper files, old typewriters, or other manual equipment in addition to mismatched computers. The floor appears to be bare concrete or simple tiles, and the overall atmosphere reflects a lack of resources.

This image generating DALL-E and other tools like Craiyon are tools for understanding how we create clichés and words that by-pass our temporal analytical neuro-functions in the brain’s frontal lobe in favor of what “everybody” (the aggregate of many minds) visualize in real time. This machine-learning aggregate image generator has learned from a corpus of lexical data to associate things like “First World” with white people, the most up-to-date tech, and modern architecture, while “Third World” is associated with black people, obsolete information technologies, and mismatched furniture in repurposed buildings. These are pre-conscious elements in minds that connect abstractions with something concrete—like race, technology, and environment.

Advertisers and all kinds of propagandists are masters of amplifying simple two-valued classifications. These two-valued appeals go directly to the fight or flight part of the brain, the Amygdala. In political posters, videos, or ads to sell products these visual elements can work on the mind’s basic phobias (such as racial minorities or hygiene) to make a large group sway this way or that. What is very neat and effective about this image generation is that these elements are the most common associations. It used to cost advertising agencies thousands to run focus groups to see what the most common “like” and “dislike” factors were, but now these can be located via the elements of a single image or an image pair, such as two-valued and simplistic rhetoric involved in the “First World” and “Second/Third World” images of work.

Why should our new rhetorical analysis tool, machine-learned image generation, be studied? I should like to think it is because now we can understand how a neutral object like an office space can be transformed and weaponized into something negative because of ingrained mental associations in the vast majority of Internet users causes them to place many, many images that are of something called “Third World” as having defects. Our human discourse communities’ collective mental associations are driving the visual elements that are associated with the simplistic two-valued logic of modernization and colonialism, those who profit from conflict and globalization can pop in the visual elements in subtle or unsubtle ways in what we see, hear, and read.

We can now accomplish, even in this brief case study, the kinds of data visualization that S. I. Hayakawa could only demonstrate in exemplary quotes of the time. For instance, he said in his 1940 text *Language in Action* that he didn’t understand why Hitler and his “Aryan” concept for all manner of physical objects, stating

> If Hitler approves, it is "Aryan." If he disapproves, it is "non-Aryan" or "Jewish dominated." The absurdity of classifying the Japanese as "Aryan," just because Japan and Germany have friendly understandings, and President Roosevelt as "Jewish," of classifying pointed roofs as "Aryan" and flat roofs as "inter-national" and therefore "Jewish," or of classifying one branch of physics as "Aryan" and another as "Jewish," does not in the least deter Hitler or his propaganda minister. (130)

Both Hitler and Stalin crafted *two-valued rhetoric* to make their movements appear a "natural outgrowth" of the cultural traditions in their respective countries. In 1940, Stalinist Ukrainian biologist Trofim Lysenko became director of the Institute of Genetics within the USSR's Academy of Sciences, and he used his political influence and power to suppress dissenting opinions and discredit, marginalize, and imprison his critics, elevating his anti-Mendelian theories to state-sanctioned doctrine Lysenko forced farmers to plant seeds very close together since, according to his "law of the life of species", plants from the same "class" never compete with one another. Lysenko played an active role in the famines that killed millions of Soviet people and his practices prolonged and exacerbated the food shortages, as noted in a December 19th 2017 article in *The Atlantic*

In much the same way, DALL-E was developed in the West by programmers with certain biases and rhetorical assumptions about the meaning of terms, and was designed for English language input (and that means less other language users). However, DALL-E must have many non-English speakers using it because when I searched with a number of languages, I did get results. Large linguistic communities give more result. When CRAIYON generates images, it gives nine squares. When it is lacking an image for one of those squares, CRAIYON uses a photo of a camera lens to fill that blank. Longitudinal searches over time will be needed to support the validity or not of what these searches show.

We need to ask *what are we testing* when we run CRAIYON or DALL-E searches? What is the rate of CRAIYON or DALL-E's data sampling? How stable are the "conditioned cultural biases" in CRAIYON images or DALL-E over days and weeks? What if there were a tool, one that resembles a Pew Research Poll, that let us leap across political and cultural borders, not depending upon biased leaders and their media? We formerly had to travel to a place, live there for years, to get a feeling for what its people were thinking at ground level because all we get in English has been filtered out and various spins applied to information. We can never totally depend upon what our own leadership or other countries' leaders say that their people think. This is highly filtered.

"Big Data" mining image generators show the biases ingrained in linguistic discourse communities, but these are generated from aggregate data, much like a very comprehensive survey. But, better than a survey, this data comes with no wish to deceive and ingratiate. A next phase of comparing images of high-level abstract metaphors such as "First World" or "Third World" as visualized across linguistic communities would be to use the image generating software now coming online in countries like China and Russia, for instance. Russia now has a few competing AI generators, for example, the beta version of Shedevrum (Шедеврум). And China has a front runner machine-learned image generator called Tongyi Wanxiang which translates roughly as "truth from tens of thousands of pictures."

Throughout this chapter, the differences and similarities in work and society have been outlined in the United States and other Western nations in terms of economic context, cultural foundations of modernization, and work-life balance. These were then triangulated against Eastern work-society factors, and those of the Global South. The chapter concluded with a deconstruction of modernization in the context of global economic development and trade relations that affect the work-society realities of these countries. Further, we look at case studies highlighting how work is constructed and contested in Eastern as opposed to Western industrial societies, and how the Global South is "imagined" versus the Global North in terms of workspace culture and architecture via Big Data image visualization.

In sum, the modernization of work has brought with it certain advantages and challenges unique to the industrial and post-industrial epochs that impact global societies differently, depending on their position in the system of global exchange and international cultures. Only time will tell if modernization can resolve the self-same issues that it brings about in this global system, but it also bears with it the promise that greater levels of individual freedom, technological progress, and governmental democratization will increase the quality of life for workers and their respective societies.

REFERENCES

Abduljaber, M. (2018). Effects of modernization and globalization on values change in the Arab world. *Changing Societies & Personalities, 2*(2), 161-182.

Bonin, B. (2020). Pandemic driven remote working and risk management strategies. *ISACA Journal, 5*, 20-25.

Cook, L. (1995). Workers in the Russian Federation: Responses to the post-communist transition, 1989–1993. *Communist and Post-Communist Studies, 28*(1), 13-42 https://doi.org/10.1016/0967-067X(95)00003-D.

Doi, T. (1986). *The Anatomy of Self: The Individual Versus Society*. Trans. Mark A. Harbison, Kodansha International Foucault, M. (2008). *Psychiatric Power: Lectures at the College de France, 1973--1974*. Edited by Jacques Lagrange. Palgrave Macmillan.

Dutta, M. J. (2019). What is alternative modernity? Decolonizing culture as hybridity in the Asian turn. *Asia Pacific Media Educator, 29*(2), 178-194.

Foucault, M (2015). *The punitive society. Lectures at the Collège de France 1972-1973.* Edited by Bernard Harcourt. Palgrave Macmillan.

Foucault, M. (2001). Truth and Juridical Forms. In J.D. Faubion (Ed.), *Essential works of Foucault, 1954-1984: Power.* Penguin.

Foucault, M (2012a). *Discipline and Punish: The Birth of the Prison.* Translated by Alan Sheridan. Vintage Books.

Foucault, M (2012b). *The history of sexuality: An introduction, volume I.* Edited by Translated by Robert Hurley. Vintage Books.

Hayakawa, S. I. (1990). *Language in thought and action.* Random House.

Ikenberry, G. J. (2024). Three Worlds: the West, East and South and the competition to shape global order. *International Affairs, 100*(1), 121–138.

Inglehart, R. (2020). *Modernization and postmodernization: Cultural, economic, and political change in 43 societies.* Princeton University Press.

Jameson, F. (1991). *Postmodernism, or, the cultural logic of late capitalism.* Duke University Press.

Korotayev, A., Slinko, E., Meshcherina, K., & Zinkina, J. (2020). Variation of human values and modernization: Preliminary results. *Cross-Cultural Research, 54*(2-3), 238-272.

Lee, S. (2012). The Depressing Truth Behind a Smile." *The Hanyang Journal, 316,* 8–9.

Levada, Y.A. (2018). Civic culture. In *Russian culture at the crossroads* (pp. 299-312). Routledge.

Lewis, L. (9 Feb. 2008). Smiling can seriously damage your health. *The Times.*

Lynn, A. (2023). *Saving the protestant ethic.* Oxford University Press.

Magun, V. S. (2018). Labor culture. In *Russian culture at the crossroads* (pp. 279-297). Routledge.

Mirakyan, A., Berezka, S. (2022). Management and COVID-19: Digital Shift to Remote Work and Remote Management. In: Alexandrov, D.A., *et al. Digital Transformation and Global Society.* DTGS 2021. *Communications in Computer and Information Science* 1503. Springer.

Munro, P. (2023). Energy justice, modernity and transitions: more-than-modern energy for all in the Global South. In *Handbook on energy justice* (pp. 213-225). Edward Elgar Publishing.

Rajković, I. (2021). From freedom to loaf to freedom to work. *Work, Society, and the Ethical Self: Chimeras of Freedom in the Neoliberal Era, 7,* 158.

Sharma, J. (2024). Forms of modernization and its impact on economy. *Journal of APF Command and Staff College, 7*(1), 199-218.

Shin, D.C. (2014). Emotional labor and human rights protection in the case of airlines. *The Korean Journal of Air & Space Law and Policy, 29*(2), 87-108.

Tursunbayeva, A., Di Lauro, S., & Antonelli, G. (2022). Remote work at the time of COVID-19 pandemic and beyond: A scoping review. In S.R. Mondal, F. Di Virgilio, & S. Das (Eds), *HR analytics and digital HR practices.* Palgrave Macmillan.

Waweru, C., Koome, P., & Gichuhi, D. (2019). Influence of cultural modernisation on employee performance: A case of Nakuru lands offices in Nakuru County, Kenya. *Editon Consortium Journal of Arts, Humanities and Social Studies, 1*(2), 41-54.

Weber, M. (2021). *The Protestant ethic and the spirit of capitalism.* Routledge Classics.

Winnicott, D. (1960). Ego distortion in terms of true and false self. In *The maturational process and the facilitating environment: Studies in the theory of emotional development* (pp. 140-157). International Universities Press.

CHAPTER 5

Work Under Democratic Capitalism, Dictatorship, Islamic Fundamentalism, and Socialism: Working Toward a Peaceful Global Society

Gabriele Strohschen, DePaul University, USA
with contributions by Brigitte Bartsch, PiChi Han, Kenneth Elazier, Zaya Khananu, and Vincent Wiggins[1]

Abstract

This chapter explores the multifaceted concept of work across various political and economic systems, focusing on democratic capitalism, dictatorship, Islamic fundamentalism, and socialism. Through personal narratives and theoretical insights, the chapter provides an examination of how work is defined, valued, and practiced within these contrasting systems. By presenting firsthand accounts from individuals living under different regimes, the chapter uncovers the relationship between political ideologies, economic structures, and workplace dynamics.

The narratives reflect a range of experiences shaped by each system's approach to freedom, education, labor rights, and the distribution of resources. These experiences offer insight into the inherent challenges and opportunities workers face globally, revealing how socio-cultural, religious, and political factors influence one's understanding of work. The chapter emphasizes the importance of understanding these perspectives as essential to fostering international dialogue, lifelong learning, and preparing for a 21st-century global workforce.

Ultimately, this chapter aims to stimulate critical thinking about how diverse political-economic systems impact not only individual lives but also the possibility of achieving a peaceful, interconnected global society. By examining these varied contexts, it urges readers to engage in further research and reflection on the evolving nature of work in a globalizing world.

1. Several other individual chose to contribute anonymously; one individual chose not to contribute due to fear of retributions to relatives in their home country. The authors respect the request for anonymity and appreciate the contributions of Margrit, Max, and Eva.

Introduction

The word *work* is rooted in a prolific history with a varied range of meanings and implications that reflect its importance in individual and societal life. At first glance, asking anyone what the simple word *work* means seems an uncomplicated question to answer. After all, *work* by any definition is something we all *do,* because, in its simplest definition in our dictionaries, *work* is any activity involving effort or exertion to achieve a specific purpose or goal.

Yet, we pose the question to adults of different economic systems and political structures and cultures from one's own, it becomes a more deeply complicated concept to grasp. In a snap, the question conjures a concept that is as multifarious as the questioner's and the respondent's experiences, values, attitudes, class, religious beliefs, language, gender, age ... you get the point. Untangling such kind of sociocultural factors, within the context of economic systems and political structures to boot, adds another dimension to clarifying what *work* means in different cultures, and how attitudes towards *work* around the world are said to be related to economic growth, productivity, and leisure.

The premise in this chapter is that, fundamentally, our stated differences, the kind of *othering* in which we engage when comparing *us with them*, or *our system with theirs,* and so on, presents a two-pronged conundrum as we explore implications for a global workforce. One, it could lead us to deeper unity in world society as we face the future; and two, it can continue to divide us in warring, exploiting human and material resources from other nations, colonizing land and minds, and with that reinforces the many *~isms* we uphold. The given title of this book, *Work and Society,* and the one given to the chapter, *Work under Democratic Capitalism, Dictatorship, Islamic Fundamentalism, and Socialism*, implies that we are categorizing and therewith *otherizing* individuals and systems even around the simple notion of *work,* subsumed with labels that are a mix of political and economic aspects. Without waxing philosophically and psychologically about these challenges, suffice it to emphasize that we have a choice of which path for learning to pursue in our quest to understand ourselves and others within our world society. This choice may well be the first step in acquiring a needed global perspective on *work and society*, and I posit it ought to be based on further dialogue and research.

Our deep-seated need to *understand* our own and others' reality is rooted, perhaps, in our desire to belong to a community (Tönnies, 1887). The values and norms of the society in which we live become a sort of scaffold that assures a sense of belonging. Clarity about our identity, knowledge, and skills, and the desire to connect to a community is important for self-efficacy (Bandura, 1986; Bandura & Wessels, 1997), and to be an accepted member of society. Why am I suggesting this human need also plays a role in our topic on *work and society*? It is because one's surrounding ideology and positionality define a good deal of our beliefs and actions. If we are looking toward increasing our awareness of self and others, i.e., the totality of humans with whom we shall be working or with whom we are in contact in a globalizing world, then our examined and clarified sense of self, including our values and beliefs, our commitments, and our goals, is essential for purposefully and authentically engaging with *others.*

Toward that end, this chapter presents *facts from the ground by means of narratives.* It offers insights directly from individuals hailing from countries categorized in this textbook as Democratic Capitalism, Dictatorship, Islamic Fundamentalism, and Socialism. The descriptions and analyses are intended to ascertain how *work* differs (or not) from the norms and values about *work* among the given systems for this chapter. This chapter can in no way delve into the depths of clarification through deep cross-analyses needed to grasp the complexities of economic systems and political structures and the respective entanglement of theorems between them. Nor can one chapter tackle the many issues inherent in the concept of *work and society* in our rapidly changing world. Yet, given the continuous evolution and advancement of technologies, in an era of ethnic conflicts, infectious diseases, climate change, food insecurity, and other pressing threats, the need for educated and highly skilled denizens is crucial. And this need is of an international nature, workers of any country ought to be informed to function effectively in this increasingly interconnected global workforce.

My intention here is to arouse curiosity about the complexity of what *work* means in a world society by way of learning about work in the context of a few particular countries. Analysis of the personal narratives provides us with sufficient fodder to instigate *further* problem-posing, questioning, and study on essential assumptions we make about the topic. Such investigation includes learning about the history of economic structures and political ideologies in our respective countries and those *abroad* to lead us to realizing the interrelatedness and even interdependence in our world. Understanding such connections holds the possibility of appropriate preparation for a 21st-century global workforce and lifelong learning, essential to the security and stability to exist as a peaceful world community.

Economic Systems and Political Philosophy: Some Food for Thought

Political systems have generally been defined as the relationship between politics and economics and how this impacts upon denizens' freedom and equality. A *political-economic system*, then, can be said to be seen as the relationship between political and economic institutions in any given country, which determines its policies. Schiffbauer (n.d., para 1), introduces the economic-political system within a context of four prevailing economic systems, i.e., command/planned, market, mixed, and traditional, by stating:

> An economic system can be defined as any method a nation uses to allocate and manage its resources among its population. The three aspects of any economic system involve production, distribution, and consumption. Political systems are defined as the organized set of laws, common values, and institutions that make up a nation's government; in this definition is included the method in which a state is actually run and is *not only limited to how it is supposed to run* [chapter author's emphasis]. Political and economic systems are deeply interwoven, and changes that affect one usually impact the other.

An Ever-So-Brief Synopsis

The given focus of this chapter is on the systems denoted as *Democratic Capitalism, Dictatorship, Islamic Fundamentalism, and Socialism,* with a generalized brief description of the indicated categories applied to political systems and economic structures. These general descriptions are juxtaposed to experiences on the ground of denizens by way of their narratives. The brief generalities of core principles, workplace dynamics, and social implications below suffice to get a cursory grasp of what is written and accessible in the literature. However, the narratives from individuals in selected nations corresponding to these categories provide insights for learning and analyzing facts, as experienced by workers there. I suggest that the combination of authentic voices and the analysis in the conclusion ought to provide a foundation for dialogue, further research, and critical analysis.

THE FOUR CATEGORIES AND CORRESPONDING NATIONS[2]

United States of America - federal democratic republic capitalist democracy with a mixed economy incorporating both aspects of capitalism and socialism

Federal Republic of Germany - a democratic and federal parliamentary republic with a social market economy

Core Principles: Democratic capitalism is characterized by a free-market economy where the means of production are privately owned, and political power is exercised through democratic institutions. The system promotes individual entrepreneurship, competition, and the pursuit of profit, underpinned by the rule of law and protections for private property.

2. The descriptions of all noted Core Principles, Workplace Dynamics, and Social Implications are provided by. Professor Dr. Viktor Wang via personal communication. On September 2, 2024.

Workplace Dynamics: In democratic capitalist societies, work is largely shaped by market forces. Employers and employees engage in contracts that define the terms of employment, including wages, benefits, and working conditions. Workers have the right to unionize, strike, and bargain collectively, although the strength and influence of labor unions vary significantly from one country to another. The labor market is dynamic, with a focus on productivity, innovation, and efficiency.

Social Implications: The emphasis on individual success and economic growth often leads to significant disparities in income and wealth. However, democratic institutions provide mechanisms for addressing these inequalities, such as progressive taxation, social welfare programs, and regulations that protect workers' rights. Despite these measures, the tension between economic freedom and social equity remains a central challenge in democratic capitalist societies.

Third Empire of Germany (1933 -1945) - autocratic dictatorship with a mixed economy with some free market central planning

Core Principles: In a dictatorship, political power is concentrated in the hands of a single leader or a small group, with limited or no accountability to the public. Economic policies under dictatorships can vary widely, ranging from state-controlled economies to crony capitalism, where the ruling elite controls significant economic resources.

Workplace Dynamics: Work under dictatorship is often characterized by limited freedom and autonomy for workers. The state or ruling elite may directly control key industries, and workers are expected to comply with directives without question. Labor unions, if they exist, are typically co-opted by the state and serve as tools for enforcing compliance rather than advocating for workers' rights.

Social Implications: The suppression of political freedoms often extends to the workplace, where dissent and demands for better working conditions are harshly punished. Economic inequality is often pronounced, with wealth concentrated among the ruling elite and their supporters. Workers may face poor working conditions, low wages, and limited opportunities for advancement. In some cases, forced labor or exploitative practices are used to maintain control and sustain the economy.

Federal Parliamentary Republic of Iraq - a democratic parliamentary republic with a mixed economic system with some private freedom, combined with weak centralized economic planning and government regulation

Core Principles: Islamic fundamentalism refers to a movement that seeks to return to what is perceived as the original teachings and practices of Islam, often with a focus on implementing Sharia (Islamic law) in all aspects of life, including work. The interpretation and application of Islamic principles can vary significantly across different contexts and cultures.

Workplace Dynamics: In societies governed by Islamic fundamentalist principles, work is often viewed through a religious lens. Islamic law influences labor practices, business ethics, and the rights of workers. For example, the concept of Zakat (charitable giving) is an essential aspect of Islamic economics, and it impacts how wealth and income are distributed. Employment laws may enforce gender segregation, restrict women's participation in the workforce, and limit the types of work deemed acceptable.

Social Implications: The influence of religious principles on work can lead to a focus on ethical business practices and a strong sense of community responsibility. However, the strict interpretation of Islamic law can also result in limited personal freedoms, especially for women and religious minorities. The balance between economic development and adherence to religious principles is a significant issue in these societies, with varying degrees of success in achieving both.

People's Republic of China - unitary one-party communist/socialist with a mixed economy

Core Principles: Socialism advocates for collective or state ownership of the means of production, with the goal of achieving greater economic equality and reducing the disparities that characterize capitalist systems. In a socialist system, the government plays a central role in managing the economy and ensuring that resources are distributed equitably.

Workplace Dynamics: In socialist societies, work is often organized by the state, with a focus on meeting collective needs rather than maximizing individual profit. Employment is generally guaranteed by the state, and workers may have access to a range of social benefits, including healthcare, education, and pensions. The role of labor unions is typically integrated into the state apparatus, with the goal of fostering collaboration rather than conflict between workers and management.

Social Implications: While socialism aims to reduce inequality and ensure that all citizens have access to basic necessities, the system can also lead to inefficiencies and a lack of innovation. The emphasis on collective welfare sometimes results in lower incentives for individual effort and creativity. Additionally, the concentration of economic power in the hands of the state can lead to bureaucratic inefficiencies and limit personal freedoms.

Narratives: The Facts from the Ground

CAPITALISM AND DEMOCRACY – MEMBERS OF TWO USA GENERATIONAL COHORTS SPEAK

Generally, a capitalist democracy is defined within concepts of its three co-equal branches of government, i.e., the (Executive, Legislature, and Judiciary), universal suffrage, and a mostly market-driven economic systems. Although there is a strongly held belief that in a democracy one abides by the rule of law and private property rights, Fiss (1992) also states,

> Capitalism permits of many definitions, but at its core it is a system designed to tap the motivational force of self-interest. It assumes that individuals are autonomous actors who advance their own self-interest. Capitalism encourages efficiency and productivity by forcing individuals to compete with one another and then differentially rewarding those who are most productive, a standard that is defined in terms of consumer satisfaction. (p. 908).

One of the two voices to speak to the topic at hand comes from Vincent. He details his opportunities gained through an expansive learning journey and his successful work trajectory in the field of education. He is assigned to the Gen X cohort, defined as a member of the generation born between 1965 to 1980.

> Generation X is known as the *middle child* generation because of its small size in comparison with the Baby Boomers and millennial generations. They were the first generation to grow up with personal computers. Gen Xers tend to have liberal views on social issues. They are more ethnically diverse than boomers. (McKenna, 2024).

Vincent excelled in academic achievement with several advanced degrees in education and telecommunications, certifications, and further training in leadership, technology, and administration. In his narrative, he credits the impact of early educational opportunities and mentorship for his successful career in higher education.

Max is a Baby Boomer. They make up as much as 40% of the American population. Said to "have exerted a strong pull on the American culture at large, particularly during the social movements of the 1960s" (The Investopedia Team, 2024), they remain economically and politically influential. Max is a highly-educated USA-born Black male from the South. His work experiences span a broad array, ranging from manual labor to a professorship. His work in education, community, and civic engagement along with international consulting had him experience perceptions by non-USA denizens of his status in society as significantly different from those by his landsmen. His insights align with the origin and influences of how the USA-brand of capitalism and democracy evolved from mercantilism and continues to develop, built on the foundations of slavery and colonialism, and that these systems continue to define a hierarchy of color in the workforce.

VINCENT: A GEN XER DETAILS THE POWER OF EDUCATION

The meaning of work to me is a dedication to lifelong learning, the advancement of education through innovative approaches and the empowerment of others through professional development. My educational background includes a Doctor of Education in Curriculum Studies, where I focused on curriculum studies, instructional technology, and supporting at-risk students. I also hold a Master of Arts in Adult Education and a Master of Science in Telecommunication. In addition to my degrees, I have earned several certifications (e.g., Quality Matters Peer Reviewer, Certified Online Learning Administrator, Six Sigma Green Belt). During my post-secondary education, I found my true calling in education – to dedicate my career to improving educational practices and supporting both students and educators in higher education. My roles in higher education allowed me to develop advanced skills in leadership, project management, instructional technology, and curriculum development. My experience as a faculty member, technology integration specialist, and academic advisor has also provided me with deep insights into student support and success, making me well-versed in both the theoretical and practical aspects of education and technology.

Reflecting on my journey through primary, secondary, and post-secondary education in the United States, however, the foundation for my career path was laid early on. I was introduced to the power of education through supportive teachers who nurtured curiosity and creativity in primary school and taught me that acquiring knowledge was also for applying it in meaningful ways. I sharpened my focus in middle school where I sharpened my focus on technology in education. I noticed how technology could enhance learning experiences, making them more interactive and accessible. This realization stayed with me and later became a cornerstone of my career, particularly in my work with instructional technology and self-directed learning. High school was where I truly began to see the connection between leadership, technology, and education. Through my involvement in activities like the Marching Band, Honor Society, and Science Club, I developed organizational and leadership skills. Each stage of my educational journey contributed to my decision to focus on the intersection of technology, pedagogy, and student support services. These experiences have guided me toward a career where I can make a meaningful impact on educational practices, ensuring that diverse learners have the tools and support they need to succeed.

I have a deep commitment to societal impact and personal fulfillment through professional excellence. I view work as a vehicle for both self-actualization and societal contribution and belief in the transformative power of education and technology to uplift individuals and communities. Work isn't just about personal advancement but is a means to shape a more equitable and informed society, particularly through empowering at-risk and marginalized students. In society, I see work as a crucial tool for driving change, fostering innovation, and creating opportunities for others. My role in academic leadership is vital to promoting inclusive and student-centered learning environments, aligning with my dedication to supporting diverse learners. My involvement in professional development, curriculum design, and mentoring showcases my belief in the importance of continuous learning and adaptation, not just for individual success, but for the betterment of society as a whole.

MAX: BORN A SOUTHERN BLACK MALE BABY BOOMER

In order to speak of work in the 21st century USA and its relationship to capitalism, one ought to consider how the USA was formed and the systems leading up to the present economic arrangement. Ironically, the origins of capitalism go back to Muslim Spain, the Orient, and the Far East (Meiksins Wood, 2002). The quest for a shorter route to the East, by way of Columbus, resulted in the eventual settlement of the English colony in Virginia. It is a long history to unpack (Elazier, in press).

One's identity in our country is largely defined by the type of work one does. Work determines one's class status in the USA, within certain boundaries and exceptions of race and gender. Often the first question asked upon meeting is the type of work one performs, which determines how that person will be perceived henceforth. High-status work typically equals high-status personhood and vice-versa.

Industrial workers, farm workers, and other categories of manual labor had to fight, strike, or revolt against harsh conditions and maltreatment by organized capital institutions and organizations. These efforts at reform resulted in *collective* bargaining for wages and benefits, work rules, etc., all of which were admonished by the capitalists as undemocratic, socialist, and communist. Throughout this dark period of labor-capital adjustment, many workers lost their lives. Settlements included restrictive work covenants, discriminatory hiring and employment practices, closed guilds and unions; all sanctioned, undemocratic practices against the *other*. The organizational man emerged during the rapid industrialization and consolidation of industrial and governmental powers fueled by two world wars (Spector, 2008; Whyte, 2002). The Man in the Gray Flannel Suit in the executive suite: American corporate movies in the 1950s.

As caricatured in the satire novel by Lewis (1922), the new worker, the soulless, vapid *Babbitts,* entered the soulless corporations to exploit the manual ranks of workers. These new *organization men* in gray-flannel suits cloned by the suburbs replaced the overtly undemocratic foreman of the shop floor. His god of status-seekers was worshiped at the altar of conformity and he basked in the anonymity of the corporate conglomerate management structure. The nature of his work was as bland, vacuous, and soulless, as he.

In the USA, Man is defined by his work, and his status in the work organization provides for him the intrinsic and the outward symbols of success. Even working in a high-prestige company alone provides increased status though performing the same work tasks as those in a less prestigious firm. I don't envision that equation changing any time soon. I don't know what the future holds in store for workers and the nature of work within the coming decades, but there seems to be a trend toward eliminating work, altogether.

Islam – Religion at the Crux of Systems

In Iraq, Islam is the official religion anchored in the constitution and laws cannot be enacted if they contradict the established provisions of Islam (Ottaway (2023). While other religious practices are afforded some freedom (e.g., Muslims, Christians, Yezidis, and Sabean-Mandeans) the laws do not allow such explicitly. Zaya delineates the impact of social systems on the economic structures by way of the opportunities afforded scholars and workers in Iraq.

In present-day Afghanistan, the Taliban instituted Sharia law as well with Islam as the official religion. This resulted in "[...] *an increasingly tightly interwoven patchwork of written and verbal decrees, policies, and systematized practices with gender discrimination and mass oppression of women at their core*" (UNWomen, 2024, para 6). Only one individual, however, felt sufficiently comfortable to share a narrative about the theme of Islamic Fundamentalism in work and society; therefore, no current Afghani voice is included in these narratives.

At the time of his work in the USA, Zaya defines work as all efforts and experiences "put together to produce and accomplish tasks to serve and benefit department, institution, and community." His story, however, started in his native Iraq, where he came of age during the Iran–Iraq War that lasted from September 1980 to August 1988. (Wael Al-Sallami, 2014; Wael Al-Sallami, n.d.). Once he emigrated to the USA, his opportunities and experiences changed.

ZAYA: ASSYRIAN – A CHRISTIAN MALE FROM IRAQ

The work I dreamed of becoming was always that of a physician throughout my elementary, secondary, and high school; and even after receiving my BS degree in Agricultural Science and Engineering, which I completed in Iraq in 1988 with four years of study at Mosul University-Iraq. I also completed academic projects and internships. However, the education system did not allow me to go to medical school after I successfully graduated from high school with the required 90% average passing grade in a science major. The reason was that the priority for students to study in the science field was for Islamic students and for those who were active members of the Arab Baath Party (government party). I was born Christian and had never been active in any government party because my singular focus was on education. So, I lost my future dream of being a doctor in Iraq.

The education system enrolled me. The only choice of studying was in the Agricultural Engineering field. Had I accepted otherwise, I would have been thrown out altogether from studying or placed into a military service. That was in 1983, at the time Iraq was at war with Iran. So, I did my best and graduated as an Agricultural Engineer and my feeling fully productive as educator and professional engineer, and I was so happy to start a job. I applied for a government scholarship to start my own agriculture project in the same city where I lived. However, my application was rejected because I was not an active member in the government political party. Moreover, my ethnicity is Assyrian and by that time in 1987 the government investigated me and found that my sister was living in USA, which made me completely ineligible to work. I was so disappointed, and all my professional dreams were destroyed. I ended up being forced to serve in the military.

My dream job was to be a doctor serving my community and support poor people who cannot afford the medical expenses, but the government and education system blocked me to be a professional even though I was a good citizen with high education in my country.

After emigrating to the USA, I first attended City Colleges of Chicago (CCC) and took courses in computer science and then completed my graduate program at DePaul University, School of Computer Science in 2005. I worked as an IT professional at DePaul University's School for New Learning applying my prior knowledge and experience, and in 2018, worked as an IT Director, managing hardware, software, and information cybersecurity. In 2021 I started a position at CCC as a Computer Science instructor and in 2024, I earned my tenured, full-time position to become Assistant Professor of Computer Science. I have attended three Cybersecurity Education conferences sponsored by Florida Internation University (FIU) and earned my Certificate in Digital Forensic in 2022. I am in the process of completing my second master's degree in data science at DePaul University.

I enjoy learning and serving communities. My early learning during my primary, secondary, and post-secondary schooling in my native country Iraq was in general education and sciences. Yet, I was very close to my classmates in terms of helping them learning math and problem solving. It was in the US that I have developed and built solid communication and professional teaching skills, based primarily on my many adjustments throughout my life, which resulted in a commitment to my own lifelong learning style.

Assisting faculty, administrators, and students in a very diverse educational systems motivates me to grow in my work and build a network with others. My international experience in training and lecturing in Information Technology and System security in Nairobi, Kenya (2009 - 2016), has helped me to expand my learning and teaching skills beyond academic institutions. I will continue my role as an educator, scholar, and leader to provide the best services for people in needs in our communities.

I love my job and what I am doing for my CCC – Truman College, as assistant professor. I now teach computer science courses based on recent knowledge in information technology and cybersecurity. I encourage students to engage in collaboration and focus on their career path and development. I am committed to serving college students and make them market-ready experts in the field of information and cybersecurity to serve and protect our society from cyber threats.

Dictatorship: Life Before and During The 3rd Empire

THE WAR COHORT DURING THE 3RD EMPIRE

Assumptions about dictatorships abound in the literature, both in scholarly writing and fiction. The evolution of a country's system from an aristocracy to a dictatorship to a democratic and federal parliamentary republic in the short span of 16 years is significant, as at least three if not four generations experienced these transformations in their lifetime. Life in Germany during WWII to the present day, therefore, lends itself to analysis of commonly seen aspects and attitudes about work and society in the context of understanding *work* in the social systems and economic structures which rapidly changed, nonetheless maintaining traditional values.

The offspring of the WWI generation came of age during WWII. Two members of the war generation tell their story during these eras. Rudolf and Gretchen experienced the Weimarer Republic and the National Socialist regime as children; WWII and the fall of the 3rd Empire as adolescents; and the post war years and the transformation to present day Germany as adults. Both only haltingly described life during and after the war. They broke eye contact during some questions, with pauses, indicating they remembered, perhaps…

RUDOLF AND GRETCHEN: SOLDIER AND VICTIM

(Synopsis based on interviews with the chapter author)

He was the first-born son, born in 1926. His parents had been through WWI. His father was an accountant. His mother raised the children. After WWI, their previous upper-middle-class life had vanished and advancement opportunities were severely limited during the new regime unless one joined the party. During WWII, Rudolf's father served in the supply corps for combat missions in Russia. His mother was a member of the Communist Party of Germany (*Kommunistische Partei Deutschlands*) and eventually divorced her husband.

Gretchen was born in 1928, to parents who had been driven out of their large farm in West Prussia, which was given back to Poland after WWI. Seeking to make a living, her father worked as a horse coach driver in Berlin and as a janitor of a condominium complex owned by members of the German-Jewish elite, while her mother served as a maid for the families in that mansion. They lived a modest lifestyle, with her father mourning the forced abdication of Kaiser Wilhelm II.

As children, Rudolf and Gretchen participated in the National Socialist government-run youth programs, where different activities for boys and girls taught traditional values with an emphasis on the goals of the new regime. And yes, indoctrination of the goals of the regime was part of the learning, with slogans like Arbeit Macht Frei (*Work Sets You Free*) and Seid Bereit (*Be Prepared*).

In 1942, Rudolph volunteered to join the Waffen-SS, and joined the elite panzer division, a highly trained combat unit of the military. He was sent to fight in Russia, got wounded several times, lost a limb, and survived the Battle of Stalingrad before being taken prisoner of war by the US in 1945.

By then, Gretchen had survived the bombings; been gang-raped by 12 Allied soldiers; lost all of her belongings and apartment that collapsed one night, while huddled in a bunker during an aircraft alarm in Berlin.

Both survived the war and the first few years after 1945; weathered starvation, diseases, and violence, making them two of the 2.8 million of the city's original population of 4.3 million still alive in their city.

By 1948, she began an apprenticeship as a baker. The same year, Rudolf was sprung out of American prison camp by his father, returned to Berlin, and unloaded airplanes during the air lift which provided him with meager funds to barter for food on the black market.

They met, married, and bore children. Then, in 1949, under their occupying governments, the Allieds established two Germanys. In the west, a Federal Republic of Germany was allied with the

U.S., the U.K. and France and adopted a provisional constitution for a democratic country with a capitalist market economy. In the east, the German Democratic Republic was allied by the Soviet Union under a centralized communist rule with a planned economy structure. In the West, within a soon burgeoning capitalist economic system, people eagerly rebuilt their communities. In the East, rebuilding and economic development lagged behind the west (Henderson, n.d.).

The unspoken experiences and unresolved memories of their childhood and adolescence became their children's burden to carry, to uncover, to soften, and to overcome. Their children, the Post-War Generation, continued the rebuilding.

LIFE AFTER THE FALL OF THE 3RD REICH (3RD EMPIRE)

Allied air forces had dropped nearly two million tons of bombs on Germany, destroying some 60 cities, killing more than half a million German citizens, and leaving 80,000 pilots dead (Duggan et al., 2024). The country lay in shambles. Farm animals were destroyed and land lay barren. People starved, died, and became ill.

The Economic Recovery Act of 1948 signed by President Truman provided economic assistance to restore the economic infrastructure of postwar Europe (The U.S. National Archives and Records Administration, n.d.), early life meant shortages of shelter, food, clothing, energy, and more. Those who been youngsters and adolescents before WWII, now became the parents of the Post War generational cohort. This generation's members tell us how *they* rebuilt the city - brick by brick, side-by-side with returning soldiers and women who were adolescents and adults during the war. Work to all of them meant survival. Many of the elder survivors stoically dulled memories, repressed pain, worked hard, and maintained hope. Mass suicides in the face of atrocities during the armistice and fear of more during the occupation resulted in thousands of deaths in addition to the over 500,000,000 who died from starvation and diseases (Jacinto, 2022, Huber, 2020).

Eva was born at the very beginning of the NS regime. She lived through WWII as a young child and entered her adolescence after the fall of the 3rd Reich. Eva does not share many details of her childhood, which she survived during the bombings in a city in Northeast Germany. She tells of the hardships during the country's new beginning. Eva has lived long enough to speak to life in present-day Germany as a senior. She is a supporter of social-democrat ideals. At age 91, she has a keen memory of life during the few years right after the war. Eva avoided discussing details of her experiences during the war. She answered questions somewhat superficially, focusing on positive aspects with a smile.

EVA: A CHILD DURING THE WAR

I was born in 1933. My relatives had a small farm in Silesia, which somewhat sustained us with food during the war. No one had enough to eat but we were among the lucky few with whom family shared what little they had. Sometimes, in the dark of the night, we would sneak to fields which had already been harvested. How happy we were to find some tiny potatoes or other vegetable left behind. Oh, how I remember the soups mother made; stretched every which way with any plant, left over potato peel, or animal bone to be had. The pigeons weren't safe in our town.

Mother worked in a factory for only women (*Frauenfabrik;* Owings, 1995), obliged to serve by the government. Father was a bus driver. I was sixteen when I left school. I had started Gymnasium (college preparation high school) but felt uncomfortable with attitudes of teachers and many students. Everyone was poor after the war; but some kept up the old classist behavior – and I didn't like to be shamed. We also had to pay eight German Mark (about $2[3]) each month to the school, and it put a bit of a strain on my parents.

I completed a three-year apprenticeship in tailoring and liked it very much. Each month, we got paid about $8 the first year, $10 the second year, and $14 the third year. After graduation, my first job as a tailor paid about $2.70 an hour and I worked as a tailor until I retired. Although the wages went up, it was bad the first few years. Due to the low income during the first ten years of my employment, my current monthly social security income, for which I also have to pay income tax and incur deductions for health insurance and a home care allowance, is leaving many of the seniors of my generation living in poverty today. I hope we can stop the wars. I only hope we have learned and the world will change after I die.

The Post-War Generation Living in the Present

Born approximately during the ten-year period after the end of World War II in 1945, the *Nachkriegskinder* (post-war children) are called the Post-War Cohort in Germany. Unlike the Baby Boomers in the USA, early life for them meant growing up among the ruins or in partially bombed-out buildings after the military campaigns by the Allied Forces had razed entire cities (Hansen, 2010). The humanitarian crisis of post-war Germany impacted everyone with different levels of severity.

Born to adults who came of age during the war, the post-war children witnessed the impact of a war-torn country and they carried the guilt for their parents that had been projected upon their parents.

3. Conversion of 1950 Deutsche Mark (DM) value is also noted here in 1950 USA Dollar (US$) value.

"For a long time, the collective fog that hung over the National Socialist past irritated our perception and unsettled our attitude to life (Bode, 2012, p.12).

From the vantage points of growing up in a city and small-town life respectively, the two women share a glimpse into their view on work and society. Most of the parents of her generation, who were the war children, were strict, pushed children toward independence early, and taught and expected absolute respect and obedience from their children. Being of the same age, their experiences differ primarily in their very early memories.

Margrit grew up in the original capital of Germany in the early 1950s by elders who had fought in the war or had lived under bombing attacks as civilians in the city, and who later navigated the harrowing years after the end of WWII.

Brigitte grew in small towns in the Southwest of Germany which saw heavy bombing during the last two years of the war. In a span of 4.5 years of bombings, the loss of life and materials was significant. Military records indicate that 1.5million cubic meters of rubble, 4,590 civilian causalities, and 39,125 buildings were damaged or destroyed in the nearest city to the surrounding rural towns (Military Wikipedia, n.d.).

MARGRIT: WE JUMPED FROM BOMBED-OUT BUILDINGS...

We are not called *Baby Boomers*; in Germany, we are called the *Nachkriegskinder*. We grew up amidst bombed-out buildings, raised by traumatized elders; and we were impacted by significant social, economic, and political transformations during our early years. Before we experienced the *Wirtschaftswunder* (economic miracle) of the 1960s, we grew up in a city that lay in ruins. Mothers and fathers worked to rebuild homes and lives from the rubble. I remember our apartment where one outside wall was missing. We lived in and played among ruins. Food and resources were still scarce. Many times, we went hungry. In the streets, we walked past heavily armed soldiers guarding the then-still *invisible walls* between the Allied Forces' sectors until *that* wall was built and divided my home city, Berlin, in 1961 Carmichael, n.d.).

Mine was a child's world that saw the aftermath of violence and hate. I saw parents, grandparents, uncles, and aunts struggle with physical and psychological damage; saw them struggle with the impact imposed upon them by ethnocentric and expansionist goals during their adolescence. In my childhood, I did not know one adult male who did not bear some physical damage: not to even mention the adults' PTSD-induced maladaptiveness. Now, however, they were silent and stoically worked diligently for long hours and little money until their tenacity began to drive the economy and foreign investment saw the opportunities.

We did not have a preschool or nursery to attend; we were left alone while parents worked with strict orders to behave; at times, we did with someone's neighboring grandma checking on us. We learned early that work and steadfastness are important, to follow rules or at least not get caught too far away from expectations of behaviors. We became independent early in life. We explored our world. We relied on ourselves and one another as we roamed in the city in little collaborative bands, each contributing some skills or piece of knowledge necessary during our forbidden excursions. In first grade at age seven, we lined up for government-sponsored hot cocoa, a roll, and cod liver oil in the mornings to hold us over till supper. We sat at desks for two and learned to read and write; we actually still had an ink quill and inkpot for utensils at first. There were no playgrounds; but for fun we would jump from bombed out buildings onto mattresses we had piled up below.

We continued our elders' tradition of working hard; we learned to make do and survive - silently - daily. They kept silent about the unresolved trauma of the horrors of war, the subsequent imprisonment in war camps, the rapes and violence they endured during the war and the Allieds' systematic starvation and degrading of Germans during the occupation (Nizer, 1944). There are many versions of *facts* that emerged after the fall of the Third Reich. Not all have been shown. We knew few then.

We had learned early to observe our adults very carefully so that we could gauge our next action – a skill that underscored the development of self-efficacy in our work life. We had learned that work was to be taken very seriously, and we still adhered to the maxim *work to live but don't live to work.* Aside from creating music genres, participating in peace protests, and challenging social norms that ushered in social changes, even if not sufficient or long-lasting, our cohort consists of an ingenious, innovating, industrious bunch. Alongside with our parents, we rebuild the country, largely contributing to the economic miracle of the Federal Republic of Germany.

BRIGITTE: WORK IS THE BASIS FOR LIVING

I am a member of the post war cohort. Born the middle child, a girl between two brothers: one 6 years older, and the other one 7 years younger, I lived in a small village in the Southwest of Germany. I was very well taken care of and protected, being raised by my grandmother and mother. When I was of six, my grandfather died, which prompted my father to become an entrepreneur. We moved to another village and my father established a gas station and an auto mechanic shop, right behind our home.

At age 11, I took the public schools' mandatory assessment test to determine for which secondary education I would be eligible. The school system in Germany has three secondary level tracks: *Gymnasium*, completion of which is mandatory to enroll for study at a public University, *Realschule*, which is a middle track for those seeking to work after graduation or complete an apprenticeship for a particular business mid-career, and *Hauptschule*, which leads to the required secondary school completion. Although I did very well in primary school, my parents' expectations for advanced schooling for girls still followed more traditional roles. I was lucky, however, to be allowed to seek a different field of work than my brothers, who joined the family business after graduating from the Hauptschule and completing their apprenticeship to become certified automotive mechanics.

Like many of my girlfriends at the time, my parents did not see the benefit of a girl attending university. Therefore, my choice was to select the middle track of secondary schooling, the *Realschule*, which included four years of study in two modern languages, mathematics, biology, chemistry, physics, practical arts, and commercial business subjects. After graduation, I completed a Commercial Education apprenticeship, and later also took certification courses in Electronic Data Processing and Accounting.

One of the key experiences that guided my eventual professional trajectory was my home environment and upbringing. Running your own business was not only a value in my family but a requirement for success that was instilled in me. Until retirement, the advanced secondary education competently prepared me to freelance as an accountant under Germany's small business regulations.

I see work as a basis for life, but work also needs to be an enjoyable task. Work is an important aspect of being a member of society, it defines you to a large extent. We were taught early in the family and school to earnestly and diligently give our best as good citizens. Looking back, I can say that I combined a dedicated and steady work ethic interspersed with relaxing vacations, enjoyed an enjoyable dance hobby, and partook in local and international travel excursions and adventures.

With the work culture and employment and business regulations, the working conditions in Germany supported fair pay, paid vacations, national healthcare, and decent working conditions for a well-educated workforce in large part due to the heavy involvement of unions. However, there are changes underway since the days of the economic miracle. Worldwide trends, migration, German employment law changes, political system fluctuations, and job vacancies in large part due to the retirement of members of mine and my parents' cohort make for current challenges that cast doubt on the sustainability of our internationally hailed workforce and economic status (GTAI, 2024; Rizvi, 2024).

People's Republic of China

From the imperial system to the communist take-over in 1949 to the creation of The *Zhonghua Renmin Gong He Guo* (People's Republic of China) in 1966 under Mao ZeDong who launched the Great

Proletarian Cultural Revolution, China has seen clashes for decades as political leaders finetune and redefine her social systems and economic structures. Although the long-time ruling Chinese Communist Party is identified as running a unitary one-party communist political system, the constitution defines China as a socialist democracy and a people's democratic dictatorship with a socialist market economy (Keping, 2009).

The republic's stated goal was to preserve Chinese socialism by purging remnants of capitalist and traditional elements from Chinese society. Perspectives by Chinese nationals about work and society and the impact of the Cultural Revolution in1949 and the economic reform under Deng Xiaoping (1978/1980) vary by age, the latter of which ushered in a dominant state-owned enterprises sector that exists parallel with market capitalism and private ownership (AsiaLink, n.d).

Pi Chi grew up in China and completed extensive graduate study in the field of education in the USA. She explores the nature of work from the viewpoint of the purported values and the lived experience of maneuvering workplace hierarchies and inequitable treatment of individuals based on gender and class.

PI CHI – IT'S NOT WHAT YOU KNOW BUT WHO YOU KNOW

It is challenging to describe the meaning of work in today's social and economic system in China to a Western audience, I think. Generally, China is known as a communist country, defined by Marxism-Leninism; or the country is seen as a series of dynasties that go back to 2070 BCE. For millennia, China's deep cultural roots in its traditions and rituals are informed by several philosophers, of which Confucius remains rather prominent. I believe these teachings and values still inform the behaviors of the Chinese today; they may well be part of our DNA.

The Confucian Work Ethic centers on the values of hard work, loyalty to the organization, thrift, dedication, social harmony, a love of education and wisdom, and a concern for social propriety (Baumann & Winzar, 2017). Perhaps primary in our social system is the concept of *guangxi*. This refers to the relationship building across job positions and the status in the social hierarchy one holds. *Guangxi* is crucial in creating a kind of long-term collective network that reduces uncertainty in your daily tasks. It means to accept one's station in life, remain outwardly humble, establish interpersonal trust, exchange gifts to show respect and provide favors freely to maintain mutually beneficial social, personal, and business relationships.

At the same time, one's position, defined within strict hierarchies of class belonging and gender, cannot be easily transcended like in the West. The national cultural dimension prevails in keeping boundaries. While the Cultural Revolution sought to eliminate the class system, class barriers are still intact. So, one cannot openly outperform the boss even if one is superior in skills; credit ought to belong to the higher-ups. Great value is also given to education and we have a highly competitive society. From childhood on, excellence in school is demanded by parents and teachers; and this pressure continues in job training and higher education.

This leads to a paradox, however, in that workers do not truly develop collaboration. It is the recognition of you by your boss that counts whether you are competent or not, which basically stifles developing and maintaining a competent, accountable workforce.

Overall, I think there are three key aspects to how achieving success and some upward mobility in your profession and jobs are acquired: belonging to the ruling party; money; and strong *guangxi* behavior. This means if you have groomed a network of people who support you, you succeed although not necessarily because of capacity and capability.

Conclusion

In this conclusion, I confess that I merely present a cliff-noted account of what work and society mean within the context of the four social systems and economic structures in discussion. I augmented the descriptions of the social systems and economic structures with narratives given by native-born denizens in the countries that had been labeled into categories by generalized definitions. We tend to prefer to categorize systems within set values and goals, grounded in the beliefs of cultures, which hold some accuracy but also many generalizations. Within any such pigeon-holed category, there are myriad nuances. The *categorical definitions* we give the systems, become culture-bound approaches to cross-cultural understanding These systems, however, are held together by the people who build them. And the *builders'* values, goals, perspectives, and experiences may differ across many aspects. In addition to belonging to a culture, it seems nearly indisputably evident that class, race, gender, and age are aspects that play a significant role for the builders in actualizing the systems they built.

This holds true when analyzing *work* and *society* within the categories of social structures and economic systems. It remains important to determine how different individuals experience their immediate surroundings and how it molds them, in addition to relying on predefined definitions. Experiences and perceptions differ vastly for individuals and groupings.

Hence is it difficult, if not faulty altogether, to gauge a culture, a system, or a structure based on generalized categorical descriptions. Furthermore, we need to move beyond our respective paradigmatic assumptions (Brookfield, 1995) to grasp how we and others see work and society with the goal of cross-cultural understanding and working together. As noted in the introduction, my intention for this chapter was to offer food for thought and critical analysis through which we could strengthen a sense of interconnectedness, because that holds the possibility of appropriately preparing for a global workforce and equitable societies and engaging in lifelong learning, so essential to the security and stability to live in a peaceful world community.

Insights About Mutual Understanding Within and Across Cultures and Systems

Speaking to a USA readership, our experiences may not concur with other countries' readers and do not necessarily coincide across individuals in the USA. At the same time, there are sameness and similarities between one's experiences and those of *others* as noted by the voices in the narratives; and yet even these stories and facts will be viewed and interpreted differently in Western and in what we term non-Western countries. We each have a particular lens of which we ought to become aware.

The list below identifies the commonalities and differences extracted through *my* analysis of the narratives. These **both-and** short statements are indicative of how an ideology, i.e., the system of ideas and ideals, especially one that forms the basis of economic, social, and political theory and policy can have a positive **and** a negative impact upon an individual and its community, within a system and across and between systems.

Commonalities and Differences

- Academic achievement is valued and defines one's social status

and

does not secure access to a higher class despite better economic positioning such education affords

- School-based social activities prepare youngsters to gain self-worth and skills

and

are highly competitive, often elitist and costly, and therefore not accessible across classes

- Commitment to popular values and ethical and moral ideals is motivating

and

can be detrimental if such values and beliefs are not accepted by individuals

- Adherence to the prevalently popular ideology supports success in the mainstream

and

not *going along to get along* with the ideology can hinder professional advancement or create unsafe living conditions

- Meritocracy can serve those adhering to prevailing systems' edicts

and

can prevent maximizing the talents of individuals with respect to class, gender, and political orientation

- Wars can be fought to drive out a particular *evil*

and

it can be used to expand one's country's territory and riches

- Religiosity can support cohesiveness in values and behavior and remove fear and uncertainty

and

it can lead to human rights violations

- Accepting one's station in life and role in society can mean physical and emotional survival

and

it can harm one's mental well-being.

Common Values and Desires

In any society and culture, *work* has always been associated with activities to achieve a specific goal. Effort, energy, and often strenuous endeavors are fundamental for survival and progress. We contribute to society through established systems as much as we support ourselves and our families and create value for the community/country. The many forms of work, e.g., physical labor, intellectual contributions, and creative pursuits, are essential aspects of human existence throughout history. Work is tied to concepts of productivity, achievement, self-worth, and fulfillment. In short, *work* defines individual identities as much as it plays a significant role in social structures and relationships.

The assumption that we need to define how *they* work without clarifying how *we* work already sets us up to fail at learning to work together. The same can be said about comparing social systems and economic structures. Consider the famous line in the poem by Mary T. Lathrap (1895), *Take the time to walk a mile in his moccasins.* While we cannot walk in someone else's shoes, we can certainly examine and clarify our own experiences and find common ground when examining those of others. In the narratives here, we have heard of opportunities, successes, and support by societies' systems. We have read about wars, famines, and oppression throughout the world that occurred during our lifetime alone. We were told how social systems can transform rapidly, and economic structures and our role as members and workers can fluctuate along with the changes. At the time of this writing, some say we are on the verge of a third world war.

This is an essential point to make in this chapter as it underscores the global nations' actions based on economic and social ideologies. We have been embarking increasingly on developing technological and other means, that connect our respective nations in positive endeavors that serve the world population, as much as potentially harming it through territorial expansionism and economic exploitation. Basic needs and desires are essentially alike across different societies as much as opportunities to fulfill these differ in our respective countries or within our hierarchies. When reading about war and its aftermath in but one country, i.e., Germany 79 years ago, one cannot help but acknowledge that such scenarios have repeatedly been true in the world since then and rage at the time of this writing. When reading about corruptive and discriminatory behaviors by the powers that be, may that be a boss a political leader, or an oligarch, one cannot help but acknowledge that such scenarios are repeatedly true in our experiences. And when reading about the manipulation of man-made religious systems for expansionism how can one not acknowledge that we have many commonly shared experiences among our world's countries? We have been so well trained in *feeling* our way through arguments instead of using reason to address the criticality of these issues ... and age-old prejudices prevail, cemented in the paradigmatic assumptions with which we gauge our world. Our world as *we* see it.

Final Food for Thought

A goal of this volume on *Work and Society* was to identify what work means in different cultures, and how attitudes towards work around the world are related to economic growth, productivity, and leisure. This chapter sought to explore how different social systems and economic structures can relate to creating a globally connected workforce that is essential to the security and stability to exist as a peaceful world community. I provide no solution to that. However, the examinations and narratives beckon us to acknowledge that in our interdependence we can find possibilities to create a peaceful sustainable world. Were we to adopt an attitude of critical inquisitiveness about ourselves and *others,* our and their different religions, our and their different traditions, and our and their different political systems and economic structures, then, despite the assumed differences, we might be able to uncover that fertile common ground in our connections. It is when ideology trumps truth-seeking, that we shall not be able to engage in further dialogue toward such possibilities. When we open our minds and hearts to anything *other than self and our subjective reality*, we can begin to learn and work together in a global context.

REFERENCES

AsiaLink (n.d.). China's Economy. https://asialinkbusiness.com.au/china/getting-started-in-china/chinas-economy?doNothing=1

Bandura, A., & Wessels, S. (1997). *Self-efficacy* (pp. 4-6). Cambridge University Press.

Bandura, A. (1986). The explanatory and predictive scope of self-efficacy theory. *Journal of Social and Clinical Psychology, 4*(3), 359–373. https://doi.org/10.1521/jscp.1986.4.3.359

Brookfield, S. (1995). *Becoming a critically reflective teacher*. Jossey-Bass.

Carmichael, N. (n.d.). A Brief History of the Berlin Crisis of 1961. National Declassification Center/ National Records and Archives Administration. https://www.archives.gov/files/research/foreign-policy/cold-war/1961-berlin-crisis/overview/berlin-wall-overview.pdf

Baumann, C., &Winzar, H. (2017). Confucianism and Work Ethic. In I. Oh and G.-S. Park (Eds.), *The political economy of business ethics in East Asia: A historical and comparative perspective* (pp. 33-60). Chandor Publishing.

Duggan, L.G., Berentsen, W.H., Hall Kirby, G., Elkins, T.H., Geary, P. J., Sheehan, J.J.,

Heather, P.J., Leyser, K.J., Wallace-Hadrill, J.M., Hamerow, T.S., Strauss, G., & The Editors of Encyclopaedia Britannica. (2024). *Germany.* Encyclopedia Britannica. Encyclopaedia Britannica. https://www.britannica.com/place/Germany#ref189083

Fiss, O.M. (1992). Capitalism and Democracy. 13 Michigan Journal of International Law, *13*(14, 908). https://repository.law.umich.edu/mjil/vol13/iss4/6

Elazier, K. (in press). A brief history of capitalism and free enterprise. *International Forum of Teaching and Study.* American Scholars Press.

GTAI – Germany Trade and Invest. We've Got Talents- Germany's Skilled Workforce. *Federal* Ministry for Economic Affairs and Climate Actions. https://www.gtai.de/en/invest/hot-topics/skilled-workforce-germany-got-talents

Hansen, Randall. (2010). *Fire and fury: The allied bombing of Germany 1942-1945.* Dutton Caliber.

Henderson, D.R. (n.d.). German Economic Miracle. *The Library of Economics and Liberty*. https://www.econlib.org/library/Enc/GermanEconomicMiracle.html

Huber, F. (2020). *Promise me you'll shoot yourself: The downfall of ordinary Germans.* Little, Brown Spark.

Jacinto, A. (2022, October 31). The Mass Suicides by Ordinary Citizens in the Last Days of Nazi Germany. [Newsletter]. *El Pais.* https://english.elpais.com/culture/2022-10-31/the-mass-suicides-by-ordinary-citizens-in-the-last-days-of-nazi-germany.html.

Keping, Y. (2009). *Democracy is a good thing: Essays on politics, society, and culture in contemporary China.* Brookings Institution Press. https://www.jstor.org/stable/10.7864/j.ctt6wph96

Lewis, S. (1922) Babbitt, *Empire Books* https://www.britannica.com/topic/Babbitt-novel-by-Lewis.

McKenna, A. (2024, September 28). Generation X. *Encyclopedia Britannica.* https://www.britannica.com/topic/Generation-X

Meiksins Wood, E. (2002). *The origins of capitalism: A longer view*. Verso.
Military Wikipedia (n.d.) Bombing of Stuttgart in World War II. https://military-history.fandom.com/wiki/Bombing_of_Stuttgart_in_World_War_II
Nizer, L. (1944). *What to do with Germany*. Forgotten Books. [Classic Reprint Series].
Ottaway, M. (2023, January 13). Iraq and the Problem of Democracy. *Insight and Analysis*, Wilson Center. https://www.wilsoncenter.org/article/iraq-and-problem-democracy
Rizvi, Osama (12/01/2024). What Are the Biggest Challenges Facing the German Economy in 2024? https://www.euronews.com/business/2024/01/12/what-are-the-biggest-challenges-facing-the-german-economy-in-2024
The Investopedia Team. (2024, June 8) Baby Boomer: Definition, Age Range, Characteristics, and Impact. *Part of Dotdash Meredith publishing family*. Reviewed by Caitlin Clarke and fact checked by Vikki Velasquez. https://www.investopedia.com/terms/b/baby_boomer.asp
Tönnies, (1887), *Gemeinschaft und Gesellschaft, Abhandlung des Communismus und des Socialismus als empirischer Culturformen*. Hachette Livre Bnf. (*for English summary see*: Ferdinand Tönnies, Community and Civil Society (1887), published in: German History Intersections, https://germanhistory-intersections.org/en/knowledge-and-education/ghis:document-163 [November 29, 2023]).
Schiffbauer,L. PhD. (n.d.). *International Business*. Pressbook. https://pressbooks.pub/internationalbusiness/chapter/chapter-4-political-and-economic-systems/
Spector, B. (2008). The Man in the Gray Flannel Suit in the executive suite: American corporate movies in the 1950s. *Journal of Management History*, *14*(1), 87-104.
Owings, A. (1995). *Frauen: German women recall the Third Reich*. Rutgers University Press https://www.goodreads.com/book/show/708735.Frauen
UNWomen. (2024). Afghanistan Gender Country Profile 2024 [Executive Summary]. European Union. https://www.unwomen.org/sites/default/files/2024-06/Gender-country-profile-Afghanistan-Executive-summary-en.pdf
The U.S. National Archives and Records Administration. (n.d.). *Milestone Documents: Marshall Plan (1948)*. https://www.archives.gov/milestone-documents/marshall-plan
Wael Al-Sallami (2014, July 2) I Grew Up In Iraq During Saddam's Worst Days - Here's What Life Was Like. *Business Insider*. https://www.businessinsider.com/heres-what-life-in-iraq-was-like-under-saddam-hussein-2014-7
Wael Al-Sallami (n.d.) Why So Some Iraqis Say Iraq Is Secular When It Has State Religion, War, and Sharia Law? *Quora* [Blog]. https://www.quora.com/Why-do-some-Iraqis-say-Iraq-is-secular-when-it-has-state-religion-war-and-Sharia-law
Whyte, W. H. (2002). *The organization man*. University of Pennsylvania Press. http://www.jstor.org/stable/j.ctt3fh9tq.4

CHAPTER 6

The Effects of Immigration and Migration On Work In the United States, Mexico, China, India, Africa, and Vietnam

James A. Martinez, Loma Linda University, USA

Abstract

This chapter examines the multifaceted effects of immigration and migration on work in the United States, Mexico, China, India, Africa, and Vietnam. It explores how internal and international migration shape labor markets, influences economic development and impact socio-political dynamics in these regions. The analysis highlights the economic contributions of migrants, including filling labor shortages, driving innovation, and providing remittances. It also addresses the challenges migrants face, such as social integration, discrimination, and access to services. The chapter further discusses the policy responses necessary to maximize the benefits of migration while mitigating its adverse effects. A comparative analysis provides insights into the unique contexts and common themes of migration across these diverse regions, emphasizing the need for comprehensive and inclusive migration policies to foster sustainable development and social cohesion.

Introduction

Immigration and migration have profoundly shaped the socio-economic landscapes of countries across the globe. As individuals move within their country (internal migration) or across national borders (immigration), they bring diverse skill sets, cultural practices, and economic demands that redefine the labor markets of their destination regions. This chapter explores the effects of immigration and migration on work in the United States, Mexico, China, India, Africa, and Vietnam, examining how these movements have impacted employment trends, labor market dynamics, and economic development.

In the modern era, work has transcended its traditional boundaries, evolving beyond specific tasks or industries. From the early days of agrarian societies to the Industrial Revolution, and now in the Information Era, the concept of work has been continuously redefined by technological advancements, economic shifts, and cultural transformations (De Stephano, 2016). Today, work encompasses a complex system of various sub-systems, each influenced by the broader forces of globalization, technological innovation, and cultural change (Allen & Shockley, 2012).

This chapter aims to explore the multifaceted impacts of immigration and migration on labor markets, economic development, and socio-political dynamics across different regions. It examines how the concept of work has evolved in various countries since the Industrial Revolution and how these changes are being influenced by the rapid technological advancements of the Information Era. Furthermore, it delves into migration policies and the globalized nature of work, and seeks to provide a comprehensive understanding of how work is viewed differently across cultures and how these perceptions relate to economic growth, productivity, and leisure.

United States

The United States has a long and complex history of immigration dating back to the colonial era. Successive waves of immigrants from different regions have shaped the country's demographic landscape over centuries. The Industrial Revolution, spanning from the late 18th to the 19th century, transformed labor practices and attracted millions of immigrants seeking economic opportunities. The post-World War II economic boom further solidified America's position as a prime destination for both skilled and unskilled immigrants from around the world.

MIGRATION PATTERNS

Historically, the United States primarily received immigrants from Europe. However, the late 20th century saw a significant shift in immigration patterns, with increasing diversity in the origin of immigrants, particularly from Latin America and Asia. Internal migration patterns have also played a crucial role in shaping the country's demographic and economic landscape, with notable movements such as the migration from the Rust Belt to the Sun Belt in search of economic opportunities.

IMPACT ON LABOR MARKETS

Immigrants have consistently filled labor shortages in various sectors of the U.S. economy, including agriculture, construction, healthcare, and technology. While there is ongoing debate about the impact of immigration on wages for low-skilled native workers, research generally indicates that the overall economic impact is positive. High-skilled immigrants, in particular, have made significant contributions to innovation and entrepreneurship, especially in sectors like technology and healthcare.

ECONOMIC DEVELOPMENT

Immigrants have been crucial in developing key industries in the United States. A prime example is the pivotal role of immigrant entrepreneurs and workers in shaping Silicon Valley's tech sector. Beyond direct economic contributions, remittances from immigrants to their countries of origin represent a significant flow of capital that supports economies worldwide. Moreover, immigrant-owned businesses contribute substantially to job creation and economic growth across various sectors of the U.S. economy.

SOCIAL AND POLITICAL IMPLICATIONS

Immigration remains a contentious issue in U.S. politics, with ongoing debates about immigration policy and border control. While immigrant communities have enriched the country's cultural diversity, challenges persist in social integration and addressing xenophobia. The political landscape has become increasingly polarized around immigration issues, influencing policy decisions and public discourse.

CHALLENGES AND OPPORTUNITIES

The United States faces several challenges related to immigration, including addressing illegal immigration, integrating diverse populations, and addressing skill mismatches in the labor market. However, immigration also presents significant opportunities. It helps balance demographics in an aging population, boosts innovation across various sectors, and contributes to cultural enrichment. The diverse perspectives brought by immigrants often spark creativity and drive economic growth.

POLICY INITIATIVES AND REFORM

The United States has undergone periodic reforms of its immigration laws, with the Immigration and Nationality Act of 1965 marking a significant shift towards a more equitable system. More recent initiatives, such as the Deferred Action for Childhood Arrivals (DACA) program, have aimed to address the status of undocumented youth. However, comprehensive immigration reform remains a topic of intense debate, with various stakeholders advocating for different approaches to managing immigration and its impacts.

FUTURE PROSPECTS

Looking ahead, the United States is likely to continue attracting global talent, given its economic opportunities and quality of life. However, the country will need to develop policies that address its aging workforce and maintain economic competitiveness in a global market. Immigration has the potential to offset declining birth rates and contribute to economic growth, but this will require carefully crafted policies that balance economic needs with social cohesion and national security concerns (Congressional Research Service, 2020; Pew Research Center, 2015).

EVOLUTION OF WORK

The concept of work in the United States has been historically intertwined with the "American Dream," a cultural ethos promoting the idea that hard work, determination, and ambition are keys to achieving success and upward mobility (Cullen, 2003; Rumbaut, 2014). The Industrial Revolution was a critical period in shaping this work ethic, fundamentally transforming the nature of labor and production. The advent of mass production, mechanization, and the rise of factories revolutionized the economy, creating vast employment opportunities and accelerating economic growth. However, these advancements also introduced significant challenges, such as labor exploitation, poor working conditions, and widening income inequality (Schminke, Arnaud & Taylor, 2015; Greenhaus & Allen, 2011).

During the Industrial Revolution, work became more regimented and hierarchical, with factory workers subjected to long hours, strict supervision, and often dangerous conditions. This shift not only altered the nature of work but also reshaped social structures, as the working class grew in numbers and began to demand better wages, safer working conditions, and greater rights. These demands eventually led to the rise of labor unions and the enactment of labor laws aimed at protecting workers (Allen, 2013).

The Information Era has introduced new complexities to the American work model, further challenging traditional notions of work. With the rapid advancement of automation, digitalization, and the gig economy, traditional employment structures have been disrupted, leading to a redefinition of what it means to work in the modern era. These changes have created unprecedented opportunities for innovation, entrepreneurship, and flexible work arrangements, but have also led to significant challenges such as job displacement, wage stagnation, and increased economic insecurity (Lund et al., 2020).

However, these changes have also led to significant challenges. Automation and artificial intelligence have displaced many jobs, particularly in manufacturing and routine-based sectors, contributing to job losses and the decline of stable, middle-class employment. Wage stagnation and increased economic insecurity have become pressing issues for many American workers, as the benefits of technological progress have not been evenly distributed. The gig economy, while offering flexibility and autonomy, has also been criticized for its lack of job security, benefits, and protections for workers, leading to a rise in precarious employment (Katz & Krueger, 2016).

As the United States navigates these challenges, there is an ongoing debate about how to balance technological progress with the need to protect workers' rights and ensure social equity. Policymakers, business leaders, and labor advocates are grappling with questions about the future of work, including workforce preparation for the digital economy, addressing growing income inequality, and ensuring access to decent wages, benefits, and working conditions for all workers (Autor, 2015).

The evolution of work in the United States, from the Industrial Revolution to the Information Era, underscores the dynamic nature of labor and the need for adaptive policies and practices that can respond to changing economic and technological landscapes. As the country continues to grapple with the challenges and opportunities presented by the digital age, the concept of work will likely continue to evolve, with new forms of employment, new expectations for workers, and new frameworks for understanding the relationship between work, economic growth, and social well-being.

Mexico

Mexico has a long history of emigration, particularly to the United States, driven by economic factors and social networks established over generations. In recent decades, Mexico has also become an important transit country and, increasingly, a destination for migrants, particularly from Central America. The country's work culture is strongly influenced by family and community values, which shapes both internal and international migration patterns.

MIGRATION PATTERNS

Mexico experiences significant emigration to the United States, often driven by economic factors and family reunification. Simultaneously, the country has seen an increase in immigration from Central America, with many migrants intending to transit through Mexico to reach the United States. Internally, there is substantial migration from rural to urban areas as people seek better economic opportunities.

IMPACT ON THE LABOR MARKET

Emigration has led to labor shortages in certain sectors of the Mexican economy, particularly in agriculture. However, remittances sent back by Mexican workers abroad play a crucial role in supporting local economies and families. The phenomenon of return migration brings back individuals with new skills and experiences, potentially benefiting local labor markets. The Industrial Revolution, while not as transformative in Mexico as it was in the United States, still had a notable impact on the country's economic landscape. The introduction of manufacturing industries, particularly in urban areas, marked a shift from predominantly agricultural work to industrial and urban employment. This period saw the growth of factory-based work and a gradual move away from traditional crafts and agriculture. The rise of manufacturing industries contributed to Mexico's economic development and helped to modernize its economy (Fajnzylber & López, 2017). However, the benefits of industrialization were unevenly distributed, and many rural areas continued to rely on traditional agricultural practices.

The Information Era has brought new complexities and opportunities to the Mexican workforce, presenting both challenges and potential for growth. One of the most pressing issues facing Mexico today is the digital divide. Despite advancements in technology, a significant portion of the Mexican population still lacks access to the education and digital resources necessary to thrive in a modern, technology-driven economy. This divide affects workers' ability to acquire new skills and adapt to the demands of the Information Era, creating disparities in employment opportunities and economic outcomes (World Economic Forum, 2020).

ECONOMIC DEVELOPMENT

The dual role of Mexico as a sender and receiver of migrants has led to unique economic dynamics. Remittances have contributed significantly to the national GDP, while the return of migrants brings back skills and experiences that benefit the local labor market. The development of industries catering to returning migrants has emerged as a niche economic sector. Additionally, the growth in outsourcing and manufacturing sectors, particularly in border regions, has attracted internal migrants and created new economic hubs. Mexico's geographical proximity to the United States and its integration into global supply chains have positioned it as a key player in the global technology and service sectors. The country's role as a major manufacturing hub and its growing involvement in technology-driven industries highlight its potential for economic growth in the digital age. Mexico has increasingly become a center for technology outsourcing, software development, and e-commerce, leveraging its strategic location and competitive labor costs to attract international business (World Economic Forum, 2020).

CHALLENGES AND OPPORTUNITIES

Mexico grapples with the challenges of brain drain and economic dependence on remittances. The integration of transit migrants, particularly from Central America, poses both humanitarian and logistical challenges. However, opportunities exist in leveraging the skills of returning migrants and developing a more diverse economy that can retain skilled workers and attract foreign investment.

POLICY INITIATIVES AND REFORM

The Mexican government has implemented programs to support returning migrants, aiming to reintegrate them into the local economy and society. Efforts have also been made to improve conditions for Central American migrants in transit, though this remains a complex issue. Bilateral agreements with the United States on migration management have been a key feature of Mexico's migration policy.

As Mexico continues to adapt to the evolving demands of the Information Era, there is a critical need for policies that address the digital divide and promote workforce development. Investing in life-long learning and skills development is essential for preparing workers for the challenges of a rapidly changing job market. This includes expanding access to education and training programs, improving digital literacy, and supporting initiatives that enhance workers' ability to compete in a globalized economy. By addressing these issues, Mexico can better harness the opportunities presented by the digital age and build a more inclusive and resilient workforce.

Additionally, Mexico's workforce development strategy must consider the diverse needs of its population, including those in rural and underserved areas. Ensuring equitable access to digital resources and training programs will be crucial for bridging the gap between different regions and fostering a more balanced economic growth. As Mexico navigates the complexities of the Information Era, a comprehensive approach to workforce development will be key to sustaining its economic growth and enhancing its role in the global economy.

FUTURE PROSPECTS

Mexico may see an increased role as a destination country for migrants as its economy develops. There is a growing need for policies to retain skilled workers and attract investment to create more domestic opportunities (International Organization for Migration, 2020; World Bank, 2021). The diversification of Mexico's economy, particularly in technology and service sectors, could reshape migration patterns and the country's position in regional and global labor markets.

China

China's migration patterns have been heavily influenced by its political and economic policies and its approach to work has been profoundly shaped by Confucian values, which stress discipline, respect for hierarchy, and collective achievement (Li & Wang, 2016). These traditional values have long influenced Chinese work ethics and organizational culture, emphasizing the importance of social harmony and the role of individuals within a broader societal context. Historically, international migration was limited due to restrictive policies. However, the late 20th century saw massive internal migration following economic reforms. The country's work culture is strongly influenced by Confucian values, emphasizing hierarchy, collective achievement, and social harmony.

INTERNAL MIGRATION

China's dominant migration pattern is internal, with large-scale movement from rural to urban areas driving rapid urbanization. In recent years, there has been an increase in the emigration of skilled workers and students seeking opportunities abroad. While the number of international immigrants to China is growing, it remains relatively small compared to other major economies.

The Industrial Revolution in China, while not as early or as intense as in Western countries, began in earnest with the country's economic reforms in the late 20th century. These state-led policies and reforms were instrumental in transforming China into a global manufacturing powerhouse. The government's focus on massive infrastructure projects, rapid urbanization, and the development of export-oriented industries created millions of jobs and significantly boosted the country's economic growth. The expansion of manufacturing industries, particularly in cities like Shenzhen and Dongguan, helped lift hundreds of millions of people out of poverty and facilitated China's rise as a major player in the global economy (Zhang, 2018).

During this period, China's work model was characterized by a focus on large-scale industrial production, often involving low-skilled labor in labor-intensive factories. This model enabled the country to become the "world's factory," producing a vast array of goods for international markets. The economic growth driven by this model led to significant improvements in living standards and economic development. However, it also resulted in challenges such as environmental degradation, labor exploitation, and regional disparities in economic development.

IMPACT ON LABOR MARKETS

Internal migrants have been crucial for urban development and the growth of China's manufacturing sector. This large-scale movement has led to labor shortages in some rural areas, changing the dynamics of agricultural production. As China's economy evolves, there is an increasing demand for high-skilled workers, particularly in technology sectors, influencing both internal migration and policies to attract international talent.

ECONOMIC DEVELOPMENT

Internal migration has been a key driver of China's rapid urbanization and industrialization, contributing significantly to its position as a global manufacturing hub. A growing focus on developing high-tech and service industries has been reshaping the demand for different types of labor and skills. As China has transitioned into the Information Era, it has faced new challenges and opportunities that require significant adjustments to its workforce and economic strategies. The rise of automation, digitalization, and the shift from low-skilled manufacturing jobs to high-skilled technology and service-oriented roles has created pressures on the workforce. The country is now striving to move up the value chain, focusing on innovation, high-tech industries, and service sectors to maintain its economic competitiveness (Wu & Zhou, 1996; Cheng & Duran, 2021). This transition involves re-skilling and up-skilling workers to meet the demands of a modern, technology-driven economy.

SOCIAL AND POLITICAL IMPLICATIONS

The integration of rural migrants in urban areas remains a challenge, particularly due to the hukou (household registration) system, which can limit access to social services for migrants. Migration has also led to changing family dynamics, with many families split between rural and urban areas. There is increasing pressure for social reforms and workers' rights as the migrant population becomes more established in cities.

The Chinese government has recognized the importance of life-long learning and skills development as critical components of maintaining the country's economic edge. Significant investments have been made in education and training programs to enhance the capabilities of the workforce and support the shift toward higher-value industries. Initiatives such as the "Made in China 2025" plan and the promotion of technology hubs and innovation clusters reflect China's commitment to fostering a skilled and adaptable workforce (Wu & Zhou, 1996; Cheng & Duran, 2021).

CHALLENGES AND OPPORTUNITIES

China faces challenges in addressing the rural-urban divide and the aging population in rural areas left behind by younger migrants. Environmental concerns related to rapid urbanization also pose significant challenges. However, opportunities exist for continued economic growth and potential for innovation, particularly in high-tech sectors leveraging the skills of a more educated workforce. Despite their contributions, migrant workers in China often face challenges such as a lack of access to social services, housing, and education due to the household registration system (hukou). Addressing these challenges is essential for sustainable economic development. However, the transition to a more advanced economy also presents several challenges. Income inequality remains a significant issue, with disparities between urban and rural areas exacerbating social and economic divides. The integration of rural migrants into urban workforce settings continues to be a complex issue, as these workers often face barriers to accessing social services, quality education, and equal job opportunities. The government has introduced policies aimed at addressing these challenges, such as improving social security systems and promoting urban-rural integration, but progress remains uneven (Zhang, 2018).

POLICY AND REFORM

The Chinese government has been gradually reforming the hukou system to provide better support and integration for migrant workers in cities. There are also initiatives to develop inland cities to balance migration flows and reduce pressure on coastal urban centers. Policies have been implemented to attract high-skilled overseas Chinese back to China, aiming to reverse brain drain and boost innovation. These reforms aim to ensure that the benefits of economic growth are more evenly distributed among the population. China's approach to work has evolved from a focus on traditional Confucian values and industrial labor to addressing the demands of the Information Era. The country's rapid industrialization has lifted millions out of poverty and established it as a global economic powerhouse. As China navigates the complexities of a digital economy, it faces challenges related to workforce re-skilling, income inequality, and social integration. The government's ongoing investments in education and training, along with efforts to address regional disparities, will be crucial for sustaining economic growth and ensuring a smooth transition to a more advanced, technology-driven economy.

FUTURE PROSPECTS

China is likely to see continued urbanization and internal migration as it further develops its economy. There is potential for increased international immigration as the economy evolves and demands more diverse skills. Policies will need to address demographic challenges, including an aging population, and potential skill shortages in key sectors (McKinsey Global Institute, 2021; OECD, 2022; United Nations Department of Economic and Social Affairs, 2022).

India

In India, the concept of work has been historically shaped by the caste system, which rigidly dictated the type of work individuals could perform based on their social status and hereditary occupation (Singh, 2015). This deeply entrenched social hierarchy influenced labor practices and economic opportunities for centuries, with certain castes being associated with specific types of work, often relegating lower castes to manual and menial tasks. The post-independence era saw large-scale internal and international migration, driven by economic opportunities and social factors. The rapid economic liberalization since the 1990s has further accelerated migration trends and reshaped the labor market.

MIGRATION PATTERNS

India experiences significant internal migration, with millions moving from rural to urban areas in search of better employment opportunities. Internationally, India has a large diaspora spread across the globe, with particular concentrations in the Gulf countries, the United States, and the United Kingdom. The Industrial Revolution brought about transformative changes in India, particularly in urban areas, where the emergence of new industries such as textiles and steel production created new employment opportunities and facilitated some degree of social mobility. The growth of industrial centers, such as Mumbai (formerly Bombay) and Kolkata (formerly Calcutta), marked a shift from a primarily agrarian economy to one increasingly characterized by industrial production and urbanization. This period saw the development of infrastructure, including railways and factories, which contributed to economic growth and the expansion of the labor market (Da Haas, 2012).

IMPACT ON LABOR MARKETS

Internal migrants play a crucial role in India's urban development and construction sectors, often filling labor shortages in rapidly growing cities. International migration has helped alleviate unemployment pressures in certain regions and skill categories. Remittances from international migrants play a significant role in supporting rural economies and driving local development. In recent years, there has been an increasing trend of return migration, especially among skilled professionals.

ECONOMIC DEVELOPMENT

The growth of India's IT and services sector has been partly driven by returning skilled migrants who bring back expertise and international connections. Remittances contribute significantly to India's foreign exchange earnings and support household incomes in many regions. There's also notable development in migrant-sending regions through investments made possible by remittances. Internal migration in India contributes to the development of urban economies, with migrants providing essential labor for various industries. International migration, on the other hand, brings in substantial remittances that support the Indian economy. However, the benefits of industrialization were unevenly distributed. While urban areas experienced significant economic and social advancements, many rural regions remained largely agrarian and underdeveloped. The disparities between urban and rural areas were pronounced, with rural areas often lacking access to the same opportunities for education, infrastructure, and economic development as their urban counterparts. This uneven distribution of industrial benefits contributed to persistent regional disparities and socio-economic challenges (Da Haas, 2012).

The advent of the Information Era has further transformed India's economy, introducing new dynamics and opportunities that have reshaped the workforce. The rise of the IT and service sectors has been particularly pivotal, positioning India as a global leader in information technology and business process outsourcing. Major cities such as Bengaluru, Hyderabad, and Pune have emerged as prominent tech hubs, attracting international investment and fostering a vibrant entrepreneurial ecosystem (Bala, 2017). The growth of these sectors has been driven by a young, educated population and the increasing demand for digital services, enabling India to compete on the global stage.

SOCIAL AND POLITICAL IMPLICATIONS

Migration in India affects social dynamics, including issues of caste, class, and regional identity. Migrants often face challenges related to social integration and access to resources in their destination areas. The expansion of the IT and service sectors has contributed to the emergence of a growing middle class, which has fueled consumer demand and supported economic growth. This shift has also led to the creation of new job opportunities and a more dynamic labor market. The transition to a knowledge-based economy presents several challenges. The Indian diaspora has gained significant political influence, affecting relations between India and host countries. One of the most pressing issues is the digital divide, which remains a significant barrier to equitable participation in the modern economy. However, challenges persist in protecting the rights of low-skilled international migrants, particularly in Gulf countries, lack access to digital resources and training, hindering their ability to benefit from new economic opportunities (Tumbe, 2018; Bhagat, 2011).

CHALLENGES AND OPPORTUNITIES

India faces challenges related to brain drain, the exploitation of low-skilled migrants abroad, and strain on urban infrastructure due to rapid internal migration. However, opportunities exist in leveraging diaspora networks for economic and diplomatic gains, and in harnessing the knowledge transfer from return migrants to boost domestic industries.

POLICY INITIATIVES AND REFORM

The Indian government has launched several initiatives to support migrants, including housing schemes, skill development programs, and legal protections to enhance the employability of potential migrants. Bilateral labor agreements have been established with major destination countries to protect workers' rights. There are also initiatives to engage with the diaspora for investment and knowledge transfer, recognizing their potential contribution to India's development. These efforts aim to enhance the economic and social well-being of migrants. Income inequality is another critical challenge facing India. While the rise of the IT and service sectors has created substantial wealth, the benefits have not been evenly distributed across the population. There remains a stark contrast between the affluent urban centers and the underdeveloped rural areas. Addressing these disparities requires targeted policies and investments aimed at improving access to education, digital skills training, and economic opportunities for marginalized communities (Tumbe, 2018).

Additionally, the need for life-long learning opportunities is crucial for ensuring that all workers can adapt to the rapidly changing demands of the knowledge-based economy. Continuous skill development and education are essential for maintaining competitiveness and addressing the evolving needs of the labor market. The Indian government and private sector are increasingly focusing on initiatives to promote skill development, enhance educational opportunities, and support entrepreneurship, but further efforts are needed to bridge the gaps and support a more inclusive economic growth model (Bala, 2017).

India's approach to work has evolved from being influenced by the caste system and agrarian traditions to adapting to the demands of the Information Era. The rise of the IT and service sectors has transformed the economy and created new opportunities, but significant challenges remain, including addressing the digital divide, income inequality, and the need for ongoing skill development. As India continues to navigate these complexities, a comprehensive approach to workforce development and social equity will be essential for sustaining economic growth and fostering a more inclusive and resilient economy.

FUTURE PROSPECTS

India is likely to see continued growth in both internal and international migration. There's potential for increased return migration as domestic economic opportunities grow, particularly in the technology and start-up sectors. The country will need to develop comprehensive migration management policies to maximize the benefits of migration while mitigating its challenges (Dhar & Bhagat 2020; World Bank, 2021).

Africa

Africa's migration patterns have been significantly influenced by its colonial legacy, including arbitrary borders that often split ethnic groups. The post-independence era has been marked by conflict-induced displacements in various regions. Traditionally, many African societies emphasized communal labor and agricultural production, which continues to influence work cultures across the continent.

MIGRATION PATTERNS

Africa is characterized by significant internal and international migration. Africa experiences significant intra-continental migration, with many people moving to neighboring countries for work or safety. Many Africans migrate within the continent, while others seek opportunities in Europe, the Americas, and the Middle East, driven by economic opportunities and sometimes by conflict or environmental factors. Forced displacement due to conflicts and climate change remains a significant issue in several regions. In Africa, the concept of work has historically been closely intertwined with cultural and traditional practices, with a strong emphasis on communal labor and agricultural production. Traditional African societies have long relied on communal efforts for agricultural activities, where work is often organized around collective tasks such as planting, harvesting, and maintaining crops. This communal approach reflects deep-rooted values of cooperation, shared responsibility, and mutual support within communities (Lucas, 2006).

The impact of the Industrial Revolution on Africa was uneven, with varying degrees of industrialization across the continent. In some regions, particularly those with more developed colonial infrastructures, there was a degree of industrial growth. For example, South Africa saw the development of mining industries and manufacturing sectors. However, in many parts of Africa, the Industrial Revolution had limited impact, and the continent remained predominantly agrarian. The colonial legacy significantly influenced this disparity, as colonial powers often focused on resource extraction and the exploitation of local labor, rather than fostering broad-based industrial development (Bakewell, 2008; Lucas, 2006).

IMPACT ON LABOR MARKETS

Migration has led to a brain drain in critical sectors like healthcare and education in many African countries. Migration has both positive and negative effects on labor markets in Africa. However, remittances from migrants working abroad have become a crucial support for local economies and entrepreneurship. While emigration can lead to brain drain, it also results in remittances that support local economies. Internal migration supports urbanization and economic development. Intra-African migration often fills labor shortages in more economically developed African countries, contributing to regional economic integration. The colonial era left a lasting imprint on Africa's economic structures and labor markets. Colonial administrations often disrupted traditional economic practices and imposed new economic systems that served the interests of the colonizers. This included the development of infrastructure primarily for resource extraction and export, rather than for fostering local economic development. The legacy of these colonial policies contributed to ongoing economic challenges, such as limited industrialization, inadequate infrastructure, and economic dependence on former colonial powers (Stahl, Maznevski, Voight & Jonsen, 2010).

ECONOMIC DEVELOPMENT

Remittances serve as a crucial source of external financing for many African countries, often exceeding foreign direct investment. Diaspora investments contribute to infrastructure development and business growth in their countries of origin. The phenomenon of 'brain circulation' is emerging, as some migrants return with new skills, capital, and international networks, potentially boosting local economies.

SOCIAL AND POLITICAL IMPLICATIONS

Rapid urbanization, partly driven by internal migration, presents challenges in managing diverse ethnic and cultural groups in African cities. Political tensions over migration issues exist both within Africa and with destination countries, particularly in Europe. However, migration also facilitates positive cultural exchanges and contributes to regional integration efforts. However, realizing this potential requires addressing the underlying challenges. Political stability is essential for creating an environment conducive to investment and development. Improving access to quality education and training is crucial for equipping the workforce with the skills needed for the digital economy. Infrastructure development, particularly in areas such as internet connectivity and energy, is also vital for supporting technological growth and economic development (Adepoju, 2000).

Life-long learning and skill development play a key role in this transition. By investing in educational programs that emphasize digital skills and entrepreneurship, African countries can better prepare their workforce for the demands of the modern economy. Supporting initiatives that promote innovation, facilitate access to technology, and encourage entrepreneurial ventures will be important for driving sustainable economic growth and creating a more inclusive labor market.

Africa's approach to work has been shaped by a blend of traditional practices and the impacts of historical events, such as colonialism and uneven industrialization. The Information Era presents both significant challenges and opportunities for the continent. While Africa faces barriers such as political instability, limited access to education, and inadequate infrastructure, there is also substantial potential for growth through technology and innovation. By addressing these challenges and investing in life-long learning and digital skills, Africa can position itself to take advantage of the opportunities presented by the digital economy and drive sustainable economic development.

CHALLENGES AND OPPORTUNITIES

Africa faces challenges related to brain drain, irregular migration, and refugee crises that strain resources in host countries. However, there are opportunities in harnessing diaspora resources for development and furthering regional economic integration through managed migration. It also provides opportunities for skill development, cultural exchange, and economic growth. African migrants often face challenges such as exploitation, discrimination, and lack of legal protection. Entering the Information Era, Africa faces both significant challenges and promising opportunities. The continent is endowed with abundant natural resources and a young, rapidly growing population, which presents potential advantages for economic development. However, Africa also contends with substantial barriers to growth, including political instability, limited access to education and technology, and inadequate infrastructure. These challenges hinder the ability of many African countries to fully capitalize on the opportunities presented by the digital economy (Adepoju, 2020).

Despite these obstacles, there is considerable potential for Africa to leapfrog into the digital economy. Investments in technology and innovation are beginning to shape the future of work on the continent. Mobile technology, for instance, has already demonstrated its transformative potential in areas such as financial inclusion and access to information. Initiatives like mobile banking and digital health services have shown how technology can address specific local needs and drive economic development.

REGIONAL COOPERATION

African countries are increasingly collaborating on migration policies, focusing on enhancing the benefits of migration while addressing its challenges. Regional agreements aim to facilitate safe and legal migration.

The growth of technology hubs and innovation centers in cities like Nairobi, Lagos, and Accra underscores the continent's capacity for digital advancement. These hubs are fostering entrepreneurial ecosystems, creating new job opportunities, and attracting international investment. Additionally, initiatives to improve digital literacy and expand access to technology are critical for enabling a broader segment of the population to participate in the digital economy (Lucas, 2006).

POLICY INITIATIVES AND REFORM

The African Union has been working towards facilitating the free movement of people within the continent, aiming to boost intra-African trade and economic growth. Many countries have developed national policies to engage their diasporas in development efforts. There's also an increasing focus on bilateral and multilateral agreements for better migration management.

FUTURE PROSPECTS

Africa is likely to see a continued increase in both intra-continental and international migration. As African economies develop, there's potential for 'brain gain' through return migration and circular migration patterns. Future policies will need to address the root causes of forced migration, enhance regular migration channels, and maximize the developmental impact of migration (International Organization for Migration, 2021; McKinsey Global Institute, 2023; United Nations Economic Commission for Africa, 2023).

Vietnam

Vietnam's migration history in the 20th century was significantly shaped by conflicts, including the Vietnam War, which led to large-scale displacements. The economic reforms (Đổi Mới) initiated in 1986 have been a major driver of both internal and international migration in recent decades. Traditional emphasis on family ties continues to influence migration decisions and patterns

MIGRATION PATTERNS

Vietnam has a significant internal migration flow, with many people moving from rural areas to urban centers. Additionally, Vietnam has a growing number of international migrants, predominantly from rural to urban areas, driven by industrialization and urbanization. International labor migration, particularly to East Asian countries and the Middle East, has become increasingly common. There's also a growing trend of student migration for higher education, mainly to developed countries. Vietnam's approach to work has been profoundly shaped by its historical experiences of colonization, war, and economic reform. The colonial period, which included French rule from the mid-19th century to the mid-20th century, had a limited impact on Vietnam's industrial development. During this time, the focus was primarily on resource extraction and agricultural production, with little emphasis on industrialization or workforce development (Le & Pham, 2020). The subsequent wars, including the First Indochina War and the Vietnam War, further disrupted economic activities and development, leaving the country in a state of economic and infrastructural disarray.

IMPACT ON LABOR MARKETS

Internal migration has been crucial for the growth of Vietnam's manufacturing and construction sectors, supporting the country's rapid economic development. Overseas workers help alleviate domestic unemployment pressures, particularly in rural areas. Returning migrants often bring back new skills and knowledge, potentially benefiting local industries.

ECONOMIC DEVELOPMENT

Migrants from rural areas have been essential to Vietnam's economic development, particularly in manufacturing and services. Remittances from overseas workers contribute significantly to poverty reduction and local development in Vietnam. The growth of export-oriented industries has been partly driven by returned migrants' investments and skills. There's also been development in the vocational training sector to meet international labor demand, indirectly contributing to skill development domestically. International migrants contribute through remittances and the transfer of skills and knowledge. The turning point for Vietnam's economic development came with the adoption of market-oriented reforms known as Đổi Mới (Renovation) in the late 1980s. These reforms marked a shift from a centrally planned economy to a socialist-oriented market economy. The Đổi Mới policies were instrumental in initiating rapid industrialization and urbanization, facilitating the integration of Vietnam into global manufacturing networks. This period saw significant economic growth, as the country began to attract foreign direct investment and develop its industrial base (Le & Pham, 2020). The expansion of industries such as textiles, electronics, and consumer goods created new employment opportunities and contributed to a significant reduction in poverty.

SOCIAL AND POLITICAL IMPLICATIONS

Migration in Vietnam has social implications, including changes in family structures and community dynamics, with many families separated due to rural-urban or international migration. The government has implemented policies to support migrants, focusing on improving living conditions and social integration. Despite these advancements, the transition to the Information Era has introduced new challenges for Vietnam. Rapid urbanization, fueled by internal migration, presents challenges in urban planning and service provision. As the global economy increasingly values high-skilled technology and service-oriented roles, Vietnam's workforce faces pressures to move beyond low-skilled manufacturing jobs. The need for workers to acquire new skills in technology and services has become paramount, as the country seeks to maintain its competitive edge in a rapidly evolving global market (Tran, 2019). Rapid urbanization, fueled by internal migration, presents challenges in urban planning and service provision. Vietnam's efforts to protect the rights of its migrant workers abroad have become an important aspect of its foreign relations, particularly with major destination countries.

CHALLENGES AND OPPORTUNITIES

Vietnam faces challenges related to brain drain in certain sectors and social issues arising from rapid urbanization. The exploitation of migrant workers abroad remains a concern. However, opportunities exist in leveraging the skills acquired through international migration and channeling remittances into productive investments.

POLICY INITIATIVES AND REFORM

The Vietnamese government has implemented programs to support and protect overseas workers, including pre-departure training and support services in destination countries. Domestically, there are policies aimed at managing urbanization and supporting internal migrants' integration. Initiatives to engage with the diaspora for knowledge transfer and investment have also been developed.

FUTURE PROSPECTS

Vietnam is likely to see continued growth in both internal and international migration as its economy further develops. There's potential for increased high-skilled migration as the country moves up the value chain in global production networks. As Vietnam continues to develop, migration is expected to play a crucial role in shaping its economic and social landscape. Comprehensive policies will be needed to maximize the development impacts of migration, including measures to protect workers' rights, facilitate skill transfers, and support returnee reintegration (Mori, & Stroud, 2021; Bank, 2018).

However, there are still significant issues that need to be addressed. Income inequality remains a concern, with disparities between urban and rural areas contributing to uneven economic development. Rural workers, who have historically been reliant on agriculture, face challenges in transitioning to urban industries and technology-driven sectors. Social mobility also poses a challenge, as access to quality education and training is not evenly distributed, potentially perpetuating existing inequalities.

To address these issues, Vietnam must focus on several key areas. First, efforts to improve the integration of rural workers into the urban workforce are essential. This includes enhancing access to vocational training programs and providing support for migration and resettlement. Second, addressing income inequality through targeted policies and investments in rural development can help to ensure more balanced economic growth. Finally, expanding life-long learning opportunities and improving educational infrastructure will be crucial for preparing the workforce for the demands of the Information Era and fostering a more inclusive economic environment (Tran, 2019).

Vietnam's approach to work has evolved from a historical context of colonization and war to a period of rapid industrialization and economic reform. The Information Era presents new challenges as the country navigates the transition from low-skilled manufacturing to high-skilled technology and service roles. Investments in education and skills development are crucial for addressing these challenges, but issues related to income inequality, social mobility, and rural-urban integration remain significant. By addressing these challenges and focusing on inclusive growth strategies, Vietnam can continue to build on its economic successes and adapt to the demands of the modern global economy.

ECONOMIC CONTRIBUTIONS

Across all regions, migration contributes significantly to economic development. Migrants fill labor shortages, drive innovation, and contribute to economic growth through remittances and skills transfer. However, the extent and nature of these contributions vary depending on the specific context of each country. Table 1 highlights the key industries and migration patterns across various countries, revealing how economic opportunities drive both emigration and immigration. The United States continues to attract immigrants, especially from Latin America, Asia, and Africa, due to its robust industries in technology, finance, healthcare, and engineering. Mexico, while experiencing significant emigration to the U.S., also sees return migration and immigration from Central America as economic conditions evolve. China's internal migration fuels its industrial and technological growth, with a growing number of students and professionals moving abroad. India is a major exporter of skilled workers, especially in IT and healthcare, while countries like Nigeria, South Africa, and Kenya experience both emigration for education and employment and immigration from neighboring countries. Vietnam is seeing increased immigration alongside emigration for education and skilled work, driven by its growing manufacturing and technology sectors (Le & Pham, 2020). The dynamic relationships between economic sectors and migration patterns, with each country's migration flows influenced by their industrial needs and global economic integration.

TABLE 1: PROMINENT INDUSTRIES AND MIGRATION PATTERNS

Country/Region	Prominent Industries	Migration Patterns
United States	Technology & Innovation, Finance & Business, Healthcare & Medicine, Creative Industries, Engineering & Manufacturing	The U.S. remains a top destination for immigrants, especially from Latin America, Asia, and Africa, due to economic opportunities and education.
Mexico	Manufacturing & Automotive, Agriculture, Tourism & Hospitality, Logistics & Supply Chain, Craftsmanship	Mexico sees significant emigration to the U.S. for work opportunities, but in recent years, return migration and immigration from Central America have increased.
China	Manufacturing & Industrial Production, Technology & Innovation, Engineering & Construction, Finance & Trade, Cultural Industries	Chinese migration includes students seeking education abroad, skilled professionals moving for jobs, and retirees, especially to North America and Europe.

India	Information Technology & Software Development, Pharmaceuticals & Biotechnology, Education & Research, Business Process Outsourcing, Agriculture	India is a major source of global migrants, particularly for skilled workers in IT, healthcare, and engineering, with significant diaspora in the U.S., UK, and Gulf countries.
Nigeria	Natural Resources & Mining, Agriculture, Tourism & Wildlife Conservation, Renewable Energy, Entrepreneurship	Many Nigerians migrate for economic opportunities, education, and healthcare, with significant migration to Europe, North America, and other African countries.
South Africa	Natural Resources & Mining, Agriculture, Tourism & Wildlife Conservation, Renewable Energy, Entrepreneurship	South Africa experiences both emigration (skilled professionals to Europe and Australia) and immigration, particularly from neighboring African countries.
Kenya	Natural Resources & Mining, Agriculture, Tourism & Wildlife Conservation, Renewable Energy, Entrepreneurship	Many Kenyans migrate for education and employment opportunities, especially to North America, Europe, and the Gulf, while some African migrants move to Kenya.
Vietnam	Manufacturing & Textiles, Agriculture, Technology, Tourism & Hospitality, Craftsmanship	Vietnam sees emigration for education, skilled work, and family reunification, particularly to the U.S., Australia, and Europe, but it has increasing immigration due to economic growth.

The future prospects for each region depend largely on these intersections, and on their ability to integrate migrants effectively, invest in skill development, and implement inclusive policies. The potential for economic growth and innovation is significant, but it requires overcoming existing challenges such as brain drain, social integration, and skill mismatches. Table 2 shows that the economic growth of each country is strongly linked to specific skill sets. The U.S. continues to lead in sectors like technology and healthcare, driving its projected GDP growth. Mexico's economy is fueled by manufacturing and agriculture, while China's growth is powered by advancements in technology and manufacturing. India's emphasis on IT and services underpins its high growth rate, while African countries like Nigeria and South Africa rely on natural resources and renewable energy. Vietnam's manufacturing and tech industries contribute to its strong growth projections.

TABLE 2: PROMINENT SKILLS AND ECONOMIC GROWTH RATE

Country	Prominent Industries	GDP (2023)	Growth Rate (2023)	GDP Projection (2024)
United States	- **Technology**: Software development, AI, cybersecurity - **Finance**: Financial analysis, consulting - **Healthcare**: Medical research, pharmaceuticals - **Creative Industries**: Film, digital media - **Engineering**: Aerospace, automotive	$26.7 trillion	2.1%	$27.5 trillion
Mexico	- **Manufacturing**: Automotive, electronics - **Agriculture**: Maize, fruits, vegetables - **Tourism**: Hospitality, cultural preservation - **Logistics**: Supply chain management - **Craftsmanship**: Traditional arts	$1.55 trillion	3.0%	$1.61 trillion
China	- **Manufacturing**: Mass production, electronics - **Technology**: AI, robotics, e-commerce - **Construction**: Infrastructure projects - **Finance**: Trade, fintech - **Cultural Industries**: Film, animation	$18.5 trillion	5.0%	$19.3 trillion
India	- **IT & Software**: Software development, IT services - **Pharmaceuticals**: Drug production, biotechnology - **Education & Research**: STEM fields - **BPO**: Customer service, data processing - **Agriculture**: Diverse farming practices	$3.85 trillion	6.3%	$4.1 trillion
Nigeria	- **Natural Resources**: Oil, minerals - **Agriculture**: Crops like cocoa, maize - **Tourism**: Wildlife conservation - **Renewable Energy**: Solar, wind - **Entrepreneurship**: Small business development	$477 billion	3.2%	$493 billion
South Africa	- **Natural Resources**: Mining, minerals - **Agriculture**: Commercial farming - **Tourism**: Wildlife, ecotourism - **Renewable Energy**: Solar, wind - **Entrepreneurship**: Business development	$399 billion	1.1%	$404 billion
Kenya	- **Natural Resources**: Mining - **Agriculture**: Coffee, tea, horticulture - **Tourism**: Wildlife conservation, ecotourism - **Renewable Energy**: Geothermal, wind - **Entrepreneurship**: Small business	$118 billion	5.0%	$124 billion

Vietnam	- **Manufacturing**: Textiles, electronics - **Agriculture**: Rice, aquaculture - **Technology**: Software, digital technologies - **Tourism**: Cultural tourism - **Craftsmanship**: Traditional arts	$435 billion	5.8%	$455 billion

Table 3 highlights the intersection of economies, policies, and challenges faced by different countries. The U.S. benefits from a diversified economy but struggles with immigration policy debates and labor mismatches. Mexico's reliance on remittances poses challenges, but return migration offers opportunities for local industries. China faces issues of urban-rural integration amid rapid growth, while India must address inequality and brain drain, despite opportunities in tech. African countries grapple with migration management and political instability but have the potential to leverage diaspora resources. Vietnam's rapid urbanization and economic integration create challenges but offer high-tech expansion opportunities (Lucas, 2006).

TABLE 3: INTERSECTION OF COUNTRIES WITH ECONOMIES, POLICIES, CHALLENGES, AND OPPORTUNITIES

Country	Economies	Policies	Challenges	Opportunities
United States	- Diversified economy driven by innovation, tech, and services. - Immigrants fuel key sectors like technology and healthcare.	- Immigration policies focus on managing labor market needs. - Ongoing debates on reforms like DACA and comprehensive immigration laws.	- Social and political contention over immigration. - Skill mismatches in the labor market.	- Leveraging immigrant talent to sustain tech leadership. - Policies that integrate immigrants could enhance innovation.
Mexico	- Economy reliant on remittances and manufacturing. - Challenges with labor shortages in agriculture.	- Focus on cross-border migration management. - Supporting returning migrants and improving conditions for transit migrants.	- Brain drain and labor shortages in key sectors. - Economic dependence on remittances.	- Harnessing returning migrants' skills to boost local industries. - Expanding digital economy could reduce dependence on remittances.

China	- Rapid industrial growth fueled by internal migration. - Transitioning from manufacturing to high-tech industries.	- Hukou system reforms to improve migrant integration. - Policies to attract high-skilled talent and manage urbanization.	- Urban-rural divide and social integration of migrants. - Environmental and resource management issues.	- Moving up the value chain in global production networks. - Leveraging tech advancements to sustain economic growth.
India	- Economy driven by IT, services, and remittances. - High unemployment in rural areas managed through migration.	- Policies support internal and international migration. - Focus on diaspora engagement and protecting migrant workers.	- Brain drain and inequality between urban and rural areas. - Digital divide impacting workforce readiness.	- Engaging with the diaspora to boost domestic industry. - Expanding IT and tech sectors to enhance global competitiveness.
Africa	- Economies supported by remittances and natural resources. - High potential in technology and innovation hubs.	- Regional policies focus on managing migration and brain drain. - Efforts to harness diaspora resources for development.	- High levels of irregular migration and refugee crises. - Political instability and infrastructure deficits.	- Developing technology hubs and innovation centers. - Leveraging diaspora for investment and knowledge transfer.
Vietnam	- Economy driven by manufacturing and export-oriented industries. - Significant contribution from remittances.	- Policies manage rapid urbanization and internal migration. - Protection and support for overseas workers, including returnees.	- Social issues from rapid urbanization. - Brain drain in certain sectors.	- Expanding high-tech manufacturing and services. - Engaging the diaspora for skills and investment.

LABOR MARKET DYNAMICS

Migration significantly impacts labor markets, influencing employment rates, wage levels, and the distribution of occupations. While migration can lead to competition for jobs, it often complements the native workforce by filling essential labor roles in various sectors. Migrants, by bringing different skills and perspectives, contribute to economic diversity and innovation, yet their presence can also lead to challenges in integration, particularly when social and political tensions arise due to perceptions of job competition and cultural differences (Scheja, Mohapatra & Ratha, 2011). These labor market dynamics underscore the need for policies that balance the contributions of migrants with the protection of local labor markets.

The social and political implications of migration are profound, with issues of integration, discrimination, and political responses varying across regions. In many cases, migration leads to demographic shifts that require countries to address challenges related to social cohesion, cultural integration, and political stability. Managing migration flows and ensuring that migrants are integrated into society without facing discrimination are crucial tasks for governments worldwide (Lucas, 2006). Effective migration management requires policies that facilitate the integration of migrants into the labor market and ensure their rights are protected, thus promoting both economic growth and social stability (Lucas, 2006).

Migration policies are essential in maximizing the benefits of migration while mitigating its challenges. These policies must provide legal protections for migrants, promote their social integration, and enhance economic opportunities for both migrants and native workers. Comprehensive migration policies address issues such as discrimination, access to healthcare, and education, while also fostering an environment where migrants can contribute to economic development. By focusing on these aspects, migration policies can help countries harness the full potential of migration for both economic and social advancement.

In the United States, immigration has had a significant impact on the labor market, contributing to various sectors such as agriculture, manufacturing, technology, and services (Cullen, 2003; Rumbaut, 2014). Immigrants have historically driven economic growth and innovation, though debates over immigration policy remain contentious, particularly regarding border control and labor market integration. The Information Era has introduced additional complexity, as the U.S. economy increasingly depends on knowledge-based industries. Policies that support life-long learning and skills development, especially for immigrants, are critical for enabling them to adapt to new economic demands. Comprehensive immigration policies that promote social cohesion and provide access to education and vocational training are necessary to ensure that immigrants can effectively contribute to and benefit from the evolving economy.

Mexico's labor market has been shaped by migration, particularly by the movement of workers to the United States. While remittances from abroad provide essential financial support for many Mexican families, the country faces challenges such as labor shortages due to the emigration of skilled workers (Massey & Parrado, 1994; Hansen, 2006). Mexico's migration policies have historically focused on managing cross-border flows, but there is an increasing need for domestic policies that address the rights of migrants within Mexico, ensuring they have access to education, healthcare, and protections against exploitation (Fajnzylber & López, 2008). Developing comprehensive policies that support both emigrants and immigrants will be critical for sustaining Mexico's economic growth and social stability.

China's labor market is shaped by one of the largest internal migration movements in modern history, with millions of rural workers relocating to urban centers for better economic opportunities. This internal migration has been a key driver of China's industrialization and economic development, though it has also raised issues of social integration and the protection of migrant workers' rights (Chan, 2013). China's migration policies have traditionally focused on regulating rural-to-urban migration but are now shifting towards improving access to social services such as healthcare, housing, and education for internal migrants (Wu & Zhou, 1996; Cheng & Duran, 2021). Addressing these challenges will be essential for China to maintain social stability and continue its economic growth.

India has experienced significant internal migration, particularly from rural to urban areas, as workers seek better employment opportunities. India's globalizing economy, especially in the IT and services sectors, has also driven international migration, with Indian workers contributing to labor markets abroad (World Economic Forum, 2020). India's migration policies must balance the needs of both domestic and international migrants, addressing issues such as income inequality, the digital divide, and equitable access to social services (Tumbe, 2018; Bhagat, 2011). By ensuring that policies facilitate workers' transition into high-skilled roles, India can continue to leverage migration for economic development.

Migration within Africa is driven by economic, social, and political factors, with millions of people moving across borders in search of improved opportunities (Lucas, 2006). Migration contributes to economic growth and innovation but also presents challenges related to social cohesion, political stability, and the protection of migrants' rights. Effective migration policies in Africa must address the diverse needs of migrants, including access to education, healthcare, and legal protections against exploitation. Addressing these challenges is crucial for promoting social and economic development, while fostering a stable environment for migrants and their host communities (Lucas, 2006).

Vietnam's migration dynamics have traditionally focused on internal migration, with millions of people moving from rural to urban areas. However, as Vietnam integrates further into the global economy, there is a growing need to address the challenges faced by international migrants as well (Le & Pham, 2020). Vietnam's participation in global supply chains, particularly in manufacturing and technology, necessitates migration policies that support both domestic and international workers. Ensuring access to social services, protections against discrimination, and policies that promote social cohesion are essential for fostering equitable growth and integration in the labor market (Le

& Pham, 2020). As Vietnam's economy evolves, continued investment in education and skills development will be crucial for maintaining competitiveness in a globalized world.

The global landscape of migration and labor markets reveals the profound influence migration has on economic development, social cohesion, and political stability. While migration offers immense potential for innovation and growth, it also requires comprehensive policy responses that address its complexities. By implementing effective migration policies that protect migrants' rights, promote social integration, and enhance economic opportunities, countries can better manage migration flows and harness its benefits for sustainable development.

Migration Policies in Fostering Sustainable Development

Migration policies play a crucial role in shaping the future of work, ensuring that labor markets are inclusive, equitable, and sustainable. As globalization drives the movement of people across borders, these policies must address the complex challenges and opportunities associated with migration, while promoting sustainable development and social cohesion. The importance of comprehensive, inclusive, and ethically grounded migration policies has been widely recognized, particularly in the context of promoting social and economic development in both sending and receiving countries.

Comprehensive migration policies are essential to fostering sustainable development and creating labor markets that are both inclusive and equitable (World Economic Forum, 2020). Such policies must address the wide-ranging needs of migrants, ensuring access to education, healthcare, social services, and protections against discrimination and exploitation (Lucas, 2006). By facilitating the integration of migrants into the labor market, these policies enable migrants to access decent work opportunities and contribute productively to economic growth. Moreover, comprehensive policies tackle social and cultural challenges, such as discrimination, social exclusion, and cultural adaptation, helping to build social cohesion. When migrants are economically integrated and socially included in their new communities, they can make valuable contributions to both the local economy and society (Lucas, 2006).

Inclusive migration policies further enhance social and economic development by ensuring that migrants have access to the resources and opportunities they need to succeed in the labor market. These policies foster social cohesion and cultural integration by combating discrimination and promoting cultural understanding. For instance, policies that support the development of skills and knowledge among migrants can strengthen their ability to contribute to the economic competitiveness of host countries (Da Haas, 2012). Additionally, inclusive policies help create a more cohesive and productive society by ensuring that migrants are equipped to thrive economically and socially, thus benefiting both the migrants themselves and their host communities.

Migration policies must also align with the Sustainable Development Goals (SDGs) to ensure that migration contributes to sustainable development and social equity (Adepoju, 2020). The SDGs emphasize the importance of inclusive and equitable labor markets, social protection, and access to essential services, such as education and healthcare, for all individuals, including migrants (Lucas, 2006). Migration policies aligned with these goals facilitate the integration of migrants into the economy and help ensure that their presence contributes to sustainable development while addressing the social and economic challenges they face (Lucas, 2006).

Global cooperation and governance are essential for addressing the challenges and opportunities presented by migration in a globalized economy (Le & Pham, 2020). International organizations, governments, and civil society must collaborate to develop and implement migration policies that promote sustainable development, social cohesion, and cultural integration. Through global cooperation, key issues such as irregular migration, human trafficking, and labor exploitation can be addressed, while skill development among migrants can be promoted (World Migration Report, 2022). Effective global governance ensures that migration policies adhere to international human rights standards and principles of social justice and equity (De Haas, 2012). By fostering collaboration and adhering to international norms, global stakeholders can work towards creating a more just and sustainable migration framework that benefits all parties involved.

Ethical considerations are central to the development and implementation of migration policies. These policies should be designed to respect the rights and dignity of migrants, promote social justice and equity, and ensure that migration contributes positively to sustainable development (Gibney, 2014). Ethical migration policies address the root causes of migration, such as poverty, inequality, and conflict, while also ensuring the protection of migrants' rights (De Haas, 2010). Additionally, such policies provide migrants with the resources and opportunities needed to succeed in the labor market, enabling them to contribute to the economic growth and development of their host countries (Lucas, 2006). By embedding ethical principles into migration policies, governments and organizations can create a more humane and effective migration system that supports both individual migrants and broader societal goals.

Migration policies are vital for fostering sustainable development and creating inclusive, equitable, and effective labor markets. Comprehensive and inclusive policies that address the needs of migrants, align with the SDGs, and incorporate ethical considerations are essential for ensuring that migration contributes positively to both economic and social development. Global cooperation and governance play a crucial role in developing and implementing these policies, helping to address the complex challenges of migration while promoting social cohesion and cultural integration. By prioritizing ethical principles and fostering collaboration, stakeholders can create a migration framework that supports sustainable development and enhances the well-being of both migrants and host communities.

Global Economies, Skills, and Resources

Diversity initiatives and policy approaches to managing global workforce mobility have become increasingly crucial in the evolving landscape of international labor markets. Successful diversity and inclusion initiatives provide valuable insights into how various entities can effectively promote innovation and competitiveness in the global economy (Lucas, 2006).

The Global Diversity and Inclusion Benchmarks (GDIB) framework stands out as a comprehensive tool, offering organizations resources to enhance diversity and inclusion. By providing a structured approach, GDIB has guided companies toward creating more inclusive and innovative workplaces, fostering environments where diverse perspectives can thrive (Olsen & Martins, 2012). In the corporate world, tech giants like Google have implemented wide-ranging diversity programs that serve as models for other organizations. These initiatives include unconscious bias training and diversity-focused hiring practices. Such efforts have contributed to a more innovative and inclusive work environment, demonstrating the tangible benefits of prioritizing diversity in the workplace (Hossain & Sial, 2018; Google, 2020).

On a broader scale, governmental bodies like the European Union have established policies to promote diversity and inclusion across member states. These policies include support for anti-discrimination measures and initiatives to integrate minority groups into the workforce. The EU's approach highlights the importance of supranational efforts in creating a more inclusive global labor market (World Economic Forum, 2020). These case studies underscore the significance of collaboration between governments, companies, and educational institutions in advancing diversity and inclusion. By working together, these entities can create more comprehensive and effective strategies for fostering inclusive workplaces and leveraging the benefits of a diverse workforce (Schminke, Arnaud & Taylor, 2015).

Turning to policy approaches for managing global workforce mobility, it's clear that effective management requires a nuanced understanding of the complex dynamics at play. Policies must balance the benefits of global workforce mobility with the need to address challenges such as brain drain and social integration (World Economic Forum, 2020). One key policy approach involves facilitating skills transfer across borders. This can be achieved through programs that encourage knowledge sharing between migrant workers and local employees, fostering innovation and economic growth. Such policies help bridge skills gaps and enhance global collaboration, benefiting both sending and receiving countries (World Bank, 2018; OECD, 2017).

Countries experiencing a loss of skilled workers can implement policies to incentivize return migration, such as offering research grants or tax benefits to returning professionals. Simultaneously, policies that focus on developing local talent and creating attractive work opportunities can help mitigate the long-term impacts of brain drain (Le & Pham, 2020).

The global economy is characterized by intricate and interdependent structures that shape how work, skills, and resources are distributed worldwide (Le & Pham, 2020). Trade agreements between countries, for instance, play a significant role in facilitating the flow of goods, services, and labor across borders. These agreements can lead to increased market access, economic growth, and job creation in participating countries. However, they can also create economic dependencies and vulnerabilities, particularly for countries that become reliant on external markets. In addition to trade agreements, foreign direct investment (FDI) plays a critical role in economic development by providing capital, technology, and managerial expertise. This investment often leads to the creation of new jobs and industries but can also exacerbate economic disparities and negatively impact local industries (Da Haas, 2012).

Another key component of the global economic structure is the expansion of global supply chains, which have integrated economies and created opportunities for employment and economic growth, particularly in developing countries. While global supply chains offer opportunities for economic advancement, they also present significant challenges, including income inequality, labor exploitation, and job displacement (Scheja, 2011). Addressing these dynamics is crucial for designing policies that promote equitable and sustainable workforce development. For instance, tackling labor exploitation and ensuring fair labor practices within global supply chains are essential for creating fair employment opportunities and protecting workers' rights (World Economic Forum, 2020).

Skills development is also a cornerstone of global competitiveness in the Information Era. As economies increasingly transition towards knowledge-based industries, investing in both technical and soft skills is crucial for maintaining a competitive edge. In terms of technical skills, countries must focus on developing digital literacy and technological expertise, including proficiency in areas such as data analysis, programming, and cybersecurity. These skills are critical for thriving in the modern labor market and ensuring that countries remain competitive in a rapidly evolving technological landscape. Equally important are soft skills, such as communication, leadership, and cultural sensitivity, which enhance workers' ability to navigate diverse and collaborative work environments. These skills are increasingly valued by employers and are essential for global workforce mobility

(Freeman & Huang, 2015). Countries that emphasize both technical and soft skills development are better positioned to compete globally, with nations investing in STEM (science, technology, engineering, and mathematics) education often experiencing increased innovation and economic growth (Marginson, Tytler, Freeman, & Roberts, 2013).

Effective resource allocation is vital for fostering equitable and sustainable workforce development. This involves the strategic investment of financial resources, technological infrastructure, and human capital. Countries that allocate financial resources to support skill development, particularly in emerging fields, are more likely to achieve sustainable economic growth. Technological resources also play a significant role, as access to technology and digital tools enhances learning opportunities and improves workforce productivity (Lucas, 2006). Furthermore, investing in human capital through education, healthcare, and social services is critical for building a skilled and healthy workforce capable of contributing to economic development (World Economic Forum, 2020). Countries that prioritize these aspects are better equipped to promote equitable workforce development and economic competitiveness. For example, nations that provide robust support for STEM education and health services often see improved labor market outcomes and increased innovation (Le & Pham, 2020).

Global workforce mobility and skills exchange are increasingly prominent in shaping the global labor market. Workers moving across borders bring diverse skills and knowledge, contributing to innovation and economic growth. This exchange can help bridge skills gaps and enhance global collaboration. However, workforce mobility also presents challenges, such as brain drain, where skilled workers leave their home countries for better opportunities abroad, often weakening the labor markets of their home nations. Conversely, brain gain can occur in host countries that benefit from the influx of skilled talent. Social integration is another challenge for migrant workers, who often face difficulties related to cultural adaptation and integration into new work environments. Effective policies that support migrant workers and facilitate their successful integration are essential for enhancing their contributions to host economies while addressing the negative impacts of migration.

The role of global economies, skills, and resources in shaping workforce development is multifaceted and interconnected. Effective management of global economic structures, investment in skills development, strategic resource allocation, and support for global workforce mobility are essential for promoting equitable and sustainable workforce development. By addressing these areas, countries can enhance their competitiveness, foster innovation, and contribute to global economic growth.

Diversity and inclusion have become critical elements in workforce development, particularly in the Information Era, where innovation, creativity, and competitiveness are highly valued. Cultural diversity, gender equality, and social inclusion play pivotal roles in driving workforce development, fostering innovation, and enhancing global competitiveness (Lucas, 2006). Cultural diversity, in particular, is a significant driver of innovation and creativity. When teams are composed of individuals from diverse cultural backgrounds, they bring varied perspectives, experiences, and ideas that can lead to the development of innovative products, services, and business models. Culturally diverse teams are also better equipped to approach problems from multiple angles, leading to more creative and effective solutions. Furthermore, companies with culturally diverse teams are better positioned to understand and cater to the needs of a global customer base, increasing market reach and customer satisfaction. Embracing cultural diversity fosters cross-cultural understanding and collaboration, which is essential in a globalized labor market (Taras, 2021). For example, multinational corporations that prioritize cultural diversity in their workforce can leverage a wide range of cultural insights to drive innovation and remain competitive in the global market (Freeman & Huang, 2015; World Economic Forum, 2020).

Gender equality is also essential for a competitive and innovative workforce. Ensuring equal opportunities for all genders promotes fairness and enhances organizational performance. Organizations that promote gender equality are more likely to attract and retain top talent, leading to higher employee satisfaction and retention (Freeman & Huang, 2015). Gender-diverse teams bring different viewpoints and problem-solving approaches, which can lead to enhanced creativity and innovation. Research has shown that gender-diverse teams are more likely to develop innovative solutions and achieve better financial performance (Dixon-Fyle, Dolan, Hunt & Prince, (2020). Moreover, promoting gender equality in the workplace contributes to broader economic growth, as economies benefit from the full potential of their workforce when all individuals have equal opportunities to contribute (Olsen & Martins, 2012; Levine, 2024). Countries and companies that advance gender equality are better equipped to address global labor market challenges and leverage opportunities for growth.

Social inclusion is another critical factor for equitable and sustainable workforce development. Ensuring that all individuals, regardless of background, have access to education, training, and employment opportunities is essential for reducing disparities and promoting a more balanced workforce (Le & Pham, 2020). Inclusive workplaces foster social cohesion and cultural integration, which are particularly important in a globalized labor market. By embracing diversity, organizations can create more harmonious and productive work environments, which ultimately lead to better labor market outcomes. Social inclusion also contributes to broader economic and social benefits, including reduced poverty and increased social mobility. Companies that implement inclusive hiring practices and support diverse talent pools are better positioned to attract and retain top talent, enhance innovation, and remain competitive in the global economy.

Examining successful diversity and inclusion initiatives provides valuable insights into how various entities can effectively promote these values. For instance, the Global Diversity and Inclusion

Benchmarks (GDIB) framework offers organizations tools and resources to enhance diversity and inclusion, guiding companies toward creating more inclusive and innovative workplaces (McKinsey Global Institute, 2015). Similarly, Google has implemented diversity programs such as unconscious bias training and diversity-focused hiring practices, contributing to a more inclusive work environment that fosters innovation (Google, n.d.). These case studies highlight the importance of collaboration between governments, companies, and educational institutions in advancing diversity and inclusion.

Despite the recognized benefits of diversity and inclusion, challenges remain. Cultural barriers and discrimination continue to hinder progress, particularly in regions where traditional norms and prejudices persist (Page, 2017). There is also a need for more effective diversity and inclusion policies that address the unique needs of various workers, including access to education, training, and career development opportunities (Da Haas, 2012). However, opportunities for enhancing diversity and inclusion are also emerging. Technology, for example, can facilitate diversity and inclusion by providing platforms for remote work and virtual collaboration, helping to integrate diverse talent into the workforce. Moreover, developing comprehensive diversity and inclusion policies and promoting collaboration between stakeholders can drive progress and create more equitable workplaces (Da Haas, 2012).

Diversity and inclusion are integral to workforce development in the Information Era. Embracing cultural diversity, promoting gender equality, and ensuring social inclusion contribute to innovation, creativity, and competitiveness. Addressing the challenges and leveraging the opportunities in these areas can lead to more equitable and sustainable workforce development, enhancing organizational performance and contributing to global economic growth.

Conclusion

The global landscape of work is undergoing a profound transformation, shaped by a complex interplay of historical legacies, technological advancements, migration trends, and the imperative of life-long learning. As countries and organizations navigate this evolving terrain, workforce preparedness, ethical considerations, and the pursuit of inclusive and equitable policies are increasingly recognized as central to addressing the complexities of labor markets and economic development in regions such as the United States, Mexico, China, India, Africa, and Vietnam.

The importance of workplace ethics in global contexts has been underscored by researchers like Brown & Treviño (2006), who stress the need to recognize diverse cultural norms and apply ethical principles in navigating cultural differences. These perspectives align with the broader understanding that historical legacies continue to shape how work is organized, valued, and rewarded in different societies. The influence of past economic systems, cultural values, and societal structures remains evident in the current labor markets, affecting work dynamics and contributing to the challenges of social and economic inequality.

Technological advancements are rapidly reshaping job roles and skill requirements, with automation and artificial intelligence (AI) leading both to the displacement of certain jobs and the creation of new opportunities. Understanding these technological changes is crucial for preparing the workforce for future demands. AI, for instance, is transforming industries by automating repetitive tasks while simultaneously creating demand for high-skilled positions in fields such as technology, data analysis, and machine learning. Workers must be prepared to continuously adapt, as automation necessitates not only technical skills but also critical thinking, problem-solving, and digital literacy (Santiago et. al., 2021). In this context, life-long learning emerges as a vital strategy for maintaining workforce competitiveness. Life-long learning involves the continuous acquisition of skills and knowledge throughout an individual's career, enabling workers to stay relevant and competitive in a dynamic global labor market.

Moreover, work-life balance plays a critical role in workforce goals and the ability to engage in life-long learning. Reports by the OECD (2020, 2023) emphasize the positive relationship between effective work-life balance policies, employee satisfaction, and productivity. Balanced work environments not only foster employee well-being but also facilitate continuous professional development. Kolb (2014) further highlights that environments conducive to work-life balance enable individuals to engage in life-long learning, enhancing both personal and organizational performance. These findings illustrate how adapting to the evolving demands of the Information Era requires not only skill development but also a work environment that supports ongoing learning and adaptability.

Migration policies also play a pivotal role in shaping workforce development and contributing to sustainable economic growth. Brown & Treviño (2006), stress the importance of comprehensive migration policies that address the diverse needs of migrants while aligning with global standards and the Sustainable Development Goals (SDGs). Such policies are crucial for fostering inclusive labor markets, where migrants are equipped to contribute to economic competitiveness. Research by Le and Pham (2020) highlights how inclusive migration policies can promote social and economic development in both sending and receiving countries, supporting migrants' integration and enhancing their ability to contribute meaningfully to their new communities.

Diversity, inclusion, and social cohesion are essential components of fostering innovation and creativity in the workforce. Cultural diversity, in particular, brings together varied perspectives and ideas, which can lead to the development of new products, services, and business models. Gender equality and social inclusion further ensure that all individuals have equal opportunities to succeed, creating a more competitive and innovative labor market. By fostering diverse work environments, companies and organizations can harness a range of experiences and approaches, driving creativity and improving problem-solving capabilities (Lucas, 2006).

Social inclusion is equally critical for workforce development. Ensuring that all individuals, regardless of background, have access to education, training, and employment opportunities is fundamental to promoting equitable and sustainable workforce growth. Social inclusion fosters social cohesion and cultural integration, which are vital in a globalized labor market. Companies that prioritize social inclusion are better equipped to attract and retain diverse talent and foster an innovative, dynamic workforce. This approach not only benefits organizations but also contributes to broader societal well-being, as inclusive policies help reduce disparities and promote equal opportunities for all.

Ethical leadership and cultural ethics are crucial in shaping fair and just labor practices. They advocate for policies that respect the rights and dignity of migrants, promote social justice and equity, and ensure that migration contributes to sustainable development. Ethical migration policies should address the root causes of migration, such as poverty, inequality, and conflict, while also protecting the rights of migrants and ensuring that they have the resources and opportunities needed to succeed in the labor market (De Haas, 2010). By embedding ethical principles into migration policies, governments and organizations can create a more humane and effective migration system that supports both individual migrants and broader societal goals.

In confronting the challenges of the modern labor market, several key strategies emerge. These include fostering collaboration among stakeholders, investing in education and training, promoting diversity and inclusion, and aligning policies with international standards and the SDGs. By adopting these strategies, countries and organizations can build a workforce that is prepared for the challenges and opportunities of the Information Era. Investing in education and training is particularly critical for equipping individuals with the skills needed to thrive in an increasingly technology-driven world. Prioritizing access to education and continuous skill development enhances workforce adaptability and resilience.

Promoting diversity and inclusion is equally fundamental. Organizations and countries must actively create environments where all individuals can contribute and succeed, regardless of gender, race, or socio-economic background. Inclusive practices not only enhance creativity and innovation but also strengthen global competitiveness (Treviño, Brown & Hartman, 2003). Aligning workforce policies with international standards and the SDGs further ensures that migration and labor strategies are designed to address global challenges and promote sustainable development. This alignment helps create a workforce that is innovative, competitive, and also fair, just, and sustainable.

This chapter provides a comprehensive overview of the effects of immigration and migration on work in various regions. Each section highlights the unique context of migration in the United States, Mexico, China, India, Africa, and Vietnam, offering insights into the economic, social, and policy implications. The future of work is shaped by a blend of historical context, technological progress, migration trends, and life-long learning. Embracing ethical leadership, investing in continuous education, promoting diversity and inclusion, and aligning policies with global standards are essential for navigating the evolving global labor market. This comprehensive approach, supported by research and international cooperation, paves the way for a more inclusive, innovative, and sustainable workforce in the face of ongoing global challenges and opportunities.

REFERENCES

Allen, T. D., Johnson, R. C., Kiburz, K. M., & Shockley, K. M. (2013). Work–family conflict and flexible work arrangements: Deconstructing flexibility. *Personnel Psychology, 66*(2), 345–376. https://doi.org/10.1111/peps.12012

Autor, D. H. (2015). Why are there still so many jobs? The history and future of workplace automation. *The Journal of Economic Perspectives, 29*(3), 3–30. https://www.jstor.org/stable/43550118

Avolio, B. J., & Gardner, W. L. (2005). Authentic leadership development: Getting to the root of positive forms of leadership. *The Leadership Quarterly, 16*(3), 315–338. https://doi.org/10.1016/j.leaqua.2005.03.001

Bakewell, O. (2008). 'Keeping them in their place': The ambivalent relationship between development and migration in Africa. *Third World Quarterly, 29*(7), 1341–1358.

Bal, P. M., & De Lange, A. H. (2015). From flexibility human resource management to employee engagement and perceived job performance across the lifespan: A multisample study. *Journal of Occupational and Organizational Psychology, 88*(1), 126–154. https://doi.org/10.1111/joop.12082

Bala Subrahmanya, M. (2017). How did Bangalore emerge as a global hub of tech start-ups in India? Entrepreneurial ecosystem – evolution, structure, and role. *Journal of Developmental Entrepreneurship, 22*(01), 1750006. https://doi.org/10.1142/s1084946717500066

Bank, A. D. (2018). Strategy 2030: Achieving a prosperous, inclusive, resilient, and sustainable Asia and the Pacific. In www.adb.org. *Asian Development Bank.* https://www.adb.org/documents/strategy-2030-prosperous-inclusive-resilient-sustainable-asia-pacific

Bhagat, R. (2011). Emerging pattern of urbanisation in India. *Economic and Political Weekly, 46*(10), 10–12.

Borjas, G. J. (2014). *Immigration economics.* Harvard University Press. https://www.hup.harvard.edu/books/9780674049772

Brousseau, K., & Dorr, E. (2021). The future of work: Skills for a changing world. *McKinsey & Company.* https://www.mckinsey.com/business-functions/mckinsey-digital/our-insights/the-future-of-work-skills-for-a-changing-world

Brown, M. E., & Treviño, L. K. (2006). Ethical leadership: A review and future directions. *The Leadership Quarterly, 17*(6), 595–616. https://doi.org/10.1016/j.leaqua.2006.10.004

Brynjolfsson, E., & McAfee, A. (2014). *The second machine age: Work, progress, and prosperity in a time of brilliant technologies.* W.W. Norton & Company. https://psycnet.apa.org/record/2014-07087-000

Cappelli, P. (2008). *Talent on demand: Managing talent in the age of uncertainty*. Harvard Business Review Press.

Castles, S., de Haas, H., & Miller, M. J. (2014). *The age of migration: International population movements in the modern world* (5th ed.). Guilford Press.

Chan, K. W. (2013). China: Internal migration. *The Encyclopedia of Global Human Migration*. https://doi.org/10.1002/9781444351071.wbeghm124

Cheng, M., & Duan, C. (2021). The changing trends of internal migration and urbanization in China: New evidence from the seventh National Population Census. *China Population and Development Studies, 5*(3), 275–295. https://doi.org/10.1007/s42379-021-00093-7

Congressional Research Service. (n.d.). U.S. immigration policy: Chart book of key trends. *https://crsreports.congress.gov/product/pdf/R/R42988*

Criollo-C, S., Guerrero-Arias, A., Jaramillo-Alcázar, Á., & Luján-Mora, S. (2021). Mobile learning technologies for education: Benefits and pending issues. *Applied Sciences, 11*(9), 4111. https://www.mdpi.com/1093816

Cullen, J. M. (2003). *The American dream: A short history of an idea that shaped a nation*. Oxford University Press. https://doi.org/10.1093/oso/9780195158212.001.0001

De Haas, H. (2010). Migration and development: A theoretical perspective. *International Migration Review, 44*(1), 227–264.

De Stefano, V. (2016). The rise of the "just-in-time workforce": On-demand work, crowd work, and labour protection in the "gig-economy." *SSRN Electronic Journal, 71*(3). https://doi.org/10.2139/ssrn.2682602

Dhar, B., & Bhagat, R. B. (2020). Return migration in India: Internal and international dimensions. *Migration and Development, 10*(1), 107–121. https://doi.org/10.1080/21632324.2020.1809263

Dixon-Fyle, S., Dolan, K., Hunt, V., & Prince, S. (2020, May 19). Diversity wins: How inclusion matters. *McKinsey & Company*. https://www.mckinsey.com/featured-insights/diversity-and-inclusion/diversity-wins-how-inclusion-matters

Fajnzylber, P., & López, J. H. (2008). *Remittances and development: Lessons from Latin America*. World Bank Publications.

Flahaux, M.-L., & De Haas, H. (2016). African migration: Trends, patterns, drivers. *Comparative Migration Studies, 4*(1). https://doi.org/10.1186/s40878-015-0015-6

Freeman, R. B., & Huang, W. (2015). Collaborating with people like me: Ethnic coauthorship within the United States. *Journal of Labor Economics, 33*(S1), S289–S318. https://doi.org/10.1086/678973

Frey, C. B., & Osborne, M. A. (2017). The future of employment: How susceptible are jobs to computerisation? *Technological Forecasting and Social Change, 114*(1), 254–280. https://doi.org/10.1016/j.techfore.2016.08.019

Gibney, M. J. (2014). The ethics of immigration by Joseph H. Carens. *Migration Studies, 3*(2), 292–294. https://doi.org/10.1093/migration/mnu046

Goler, L., Gale, J., Harrington, B., & Grant, A. (2018). Why people really quit their jobs. *Harvard Business Review*. https://hbr.org/2018/01/why-people-really-quit-their-jobs

Goldin, I., Cameron, G., & Balarajan, M. (2011). *Exceptional people: How migration shaped our world and will define our future*. Princeton University Press. https://www.jstor.org/stable/j.ctt7rk89

Greenhaus, J. H., & Allen, T. D. (2011). Work-family balance: A review and extension of the literature. In J. C. Quick & L. E. Tetrick (Eds.), *Handbook of occupational health psychology* (2nd ed., pp. 165–183). American Psychological Association.

Hanson, G. H. (2006). Illegal migration from Mexico to the United States. *Journal of Economic Literature, 44*(4), 869–924. http://www.jstor.org/stable/30032389

Hollifield, J., Martin, P., & Orrenius, P. (2022). *Controlling immigration: A global perspective*. Stanford University Press. https://www.sup.org/books/title/?id=35326

Hossain, M., & Sial, M. (2018). The other diversity dividend. *Harvard Business Review*. https://hbr.org/2018/07/the-other-diversity-dividend

Hunt, D. V., Yee, L., Prince, S., & Dixon-Fyle, S. (2018). Delivering growth through diversity in the workplace. *McKinsey & Company*. https://www.mckinsey.com/capabilities/people-and-organizational-performance/our-insights/delivering-through-diversity

International Labour Organization. (2019). *Work for a brighter future – Global Commission on the Future of Work*. Geneva: ILO.

International Organization for Migration. (2020). *World Migration Report 2020*. Iom.int. https://worldmigrationreport.iom.int/wmr-2020-interactive/

International Organization for Migration. (2021). *Global Migration Indicators 2021*. https://www.iom.int

International Organization for Migration. (2022). *World migration report 2022: Chapter 10 - Human trafficking in migration pathways: Trends, challenges and new forms of cooperation*. https://publications.iom.int/books/world-migration-report-2022-chapter-10

Katz, L. F., & Krueger, A. B. (2016). The rise and nature of alternative work arrangements in the United States, 1995–2015. *National Bureau of Economic Research Working Paper Series*. https://www.nber.org/papers/w22667

Kelliher, C., & Anderson, D. (2010). Doing more with less? Flexible working practices and the intensification of work. *Human Relations, 63*(1), 83–106. https://doi.org/10.1177/0018726709349199

Kolb, D. A. (2014). *Experiential learning: Experience as the source of learning and development* (2nd ed.). Pearson Education. https://www.pearson.com/en-us/subject-catalog/p/experiential-learning-experience-as-the-source-of-learning-and-development/P200000000384/9780133892406

Kapur, D. (2010). *Diaspora, development, and democracy: The domestic impact of international migration from India*. Princeton University Press. https://press.princeton.edu/books/hardcover/9780691125381/diaspora-development-and-democracy

Le, T. K., & Pham, D. M. (2020). Migration policies and economic development in Vietnam. *International Journal of Migration Studies, 18*(3), 30–50.

Levine, E. (2024). Toward a critical social work ethics of immigration, migration, and human rights. *International Journal of Social Work Values and Ethics, 21*(1), 98–136. https://doi.org/10.55521/10-021-109

Lucas, R. E. B. (2006). Migration and economic development in Africa: A review of evidence. *Journal of African Economies, 15*(2), 337–395. https://doi.org/10.1093/jafeco/ejl032

Lund, S., Madgavkar, A., Manyika, J., Smit, S., Ellingrud, K., & Robinson, O. (2021, February 18). The future of work after COVID-19. *McKinsey & Company*. https://www.mckinsey.com/featured-insights/future-of-work/the-future-of-work-after-covid-19

Marginson, S., Tytler, R., Freeman, B., & Roberts, K. (2013). *STEM: Country comparisons*. Australian Council of Learned Academies.

Massey, D. S., & Parrado, E. (1994). Migradollars: The remittances and savings of Mexican migrants to the USA. *Population Research and Policy Review, 13*(1), 3–30. http://www.jstor.org/stable/40229687

McKinsey Global Institute. (2015). How advancing women's equality can add $12 trillion to global growth. *McKinsey & Company*. https://www.mckinsey.com/featured-insights/employment-and-growth/how-advancing-womens-equality-can-add-12-trillion-to-global-growth

McKinsey Global Institute. (2021). Reskilling China: Transforming the world's largest workforce into lifelong learners. *McKinsey & Company*. https://www.mckinsey.com/featured-insights/china/reskilling-china-transforming-the-worlds-largest-workforce-into-lifelong-learners

McKinsey Global Institute. (2023). Reimagining economic growth in Africa: Turning diversity into opportunity. *McKinsey & Company*. https://www.mckinsey.com/mgi/our-research/reimagining-economic-growth-in-africa-turning-diversity-into-opportunity

Mori, J., & Stroud, D. (2021). Skills policy for growth and development: The merits of local approaches in Vietnam. *International Journal of Educational Development, 83*, 102386. https://doi.org/10.1016/j.ijedudev.2021.102386

OECD. (2017). The contributions of migrants to innovation and economic growth. *OECD*. https://www.oecd.org/migration/contributions-of-migrants-to-innovation-and-economic-growth.htm

OECD. (2018). The future of education and skills: Education 2030. *OECD Education Policy Perspectives*. https://doi.org/10.1787/54ac7020-en

OECD. (2020a). *OECD Employment Outlook 2020: Worker security and the COVID-19 crisis*. OECD Publishing. https://doi.org/10.1787/1686c758-en

OECD. (2020b). "Work-life balance". In *How's life? 2020: Measuring well-being*. OECD Publishing. https://doi.org/10.1787/e6597da1-en

OECD. (2022). "China". In *International Migration Outlook 2022*. OECD Publishing, Paris. https://doi.org/10.1787/dbbad992-en

OECD. (2023). *OECD Employment Outlook 2023: Artificial intelligence and the labour market*. OECD Publishing. https://doi.org/10.1787/08785bba-en

Olsen, J. E., & Martins, L. L. (2012). Understanding organizational diversity management programs: A theoretical framework and directions for future research. *Journal of Organizational Behavior, 33*(8), 1168–1187. https://doi.org/10.1002/job.1792

Page, S. E. (2017). *The diversity bonus: How great teams pay off in the knowledge economy*. Princeton University Press. https://doi.org/10.2307/j.ctvc77c0h

Pew Research Center. (2015). *The Future of World Religions: Population Growth Projections, 2010-2050*. Pew Research Center's Religion & Public Life Project. https://www.pewresearch.org/religion/2015/04/02/religious-projections-2010-2050

Piketty, T. (2014). *Capital in the twenty-first century* (A. Goldhammer, Trans.). The Belknap Press of Harvard University Press. https://www.jstor.org/stable/j.ctt6wpqbc

Rigaud, K. K., Jones, B., Bergmann, J., Clement, V., Ober, K., Schewe, J., Adamo, S. B., McCusker, B., Heuser, S., & Midgley, A. (2018). *Groundswell: Preparing for internal climate migration*. Academic Commons. https://doi.org/10.7916/D8Z33FNS

Rumbaut, R. G. (2014). *Immigrant America: A portrait* (4th ed.). University of California Press. https://www.academia.edu/13968411/Immigrant_America_A_Portrait_new_4th_edition_

Santiago, C., Leah, M., Ulanday, P., Zarah, J., Centeno, M., Cristina, D., Bayla, J., & Callanta. (2021). Flexible learning adaptabilities in the new normal: E-learning resources, digital meeting platforms, online learning systems, and learning engagement. *Asian Journal of Distance Education, 16*(2), 38–55. https://files.eric.ed.gov/fulltext/EJ1332615.pdf

Schein, E. H. (2010). *Organizational culture and leadership* (4th ed.). Jossey-Bass.

Scheja, E., Mohapatra, S., & Ratha, D. (2014). How does migration shape economic and social development? *World Bank Blogs*. https://blogs.worldbank.org/en/peoplemove/how-does-migration-shape-economic-and-social-development?_gl=1

Schminke, M., Arnaud, A., & Taylor, R. (2015). Ethics in the workplace: Review and research agenda. *Journal of Management, 41*(1), 267–292.

Taras, V., Baack, D., Caprar, D., Jimenez, A., & Froese, F. (2021, June 9). Research: How cultural differences can impact global teams. *Harvard Business Review*. https://hbr.org/2021/06/research-how-cultural-differences-can-impact-global-teams

Tumbe, C. (2018). *India moving: A history of migration*. Penguin India.

United Nations. (2015). *Transforming our world: The 2030 agenda for sustainable development*. United Nations. https://sdgs.un.org/publications/transforming-our-world-2030-agenda-sustainable

United Nations Department of Economic and Social Affairs. (2022). *World population prospects 2022: Summary of results*. https://www.un.org/development/desa/pd/content/World-Population-Prospects-2022

United Nations Economic Commission for Africa. (2023). *Economic Report on Africa 2023*. https://www.uneca.org/economic-report-on-africa-2023

United Nations Population Division. *World Population Prospects 2022*. https://population.un.org/wpp/

World Bank. (2012). *World development report 2012: Gender equality and development*. World Bank Publications.

World Bank. (2018). *Global knowledge partnership on migration and development: Skills transfer and migration*. World Bank. https://www.worldbank.org/en/topic/migrationremittancesdiasporaissues/brief/global-knowledge-partnership-on-migration-and-development

World Bank. (2021). *Mexico Economic Prospects*. https://data.worldbank.org/country/mexico

World Bank. (2021). *India's Migration and Remittances Update 2021*. https://data.worldbank.org/country/india

World Economic Forum. (2020). *The future of jobs report 2020*. https://www3.weforum.org/docs/WEF_Future_of_Jobs_2020.pdf

Wu, H. X., & Zhou, L. (1996). Rural-to-urban migration in China. *Asian-Pacific Economic Literature, 10*(2), 54–67. https://doi.org/10.1111/j.1467-8411.1996.tb00016.x

CHAPTER 7

The Effects of Climate on People's Attitudes Toward Work

Sue Kaiser, California State University, San Bernardino, USA

Abstract

This chapter examines the multifaceted impacts of climate on work-related attitudes and behaviors, drawing on interdisciplinary insights from psychology, sociology, and environmental studies. The exploration begins by debunking early deterministic views, such as environmental determinism, and transitions to a nuanced understanding of how climatic factors interact with psychological and sociocultural dynamics to influence work attitudes. Psychological factors like perception, cognition, and emotional responses significantly determine individual reactions to climatic variations, while social psychology factors emphasize the role of social norms and cultural contexts. Additionally, the chapter delves into the direct effects of climate on job satisfaction, organizational commitment, and work motivation, illustrating how temperature and seasonal changes affect employee performance and well-being. The indirect impacts through economic and environmental stressors are also discussed, linking job security, mental health, and organizational support with climatic conditions. Organizational strategies for fostering supportive cultures and implementing flexible work arrangements are proposed to mitigate climate-related impacts on work attitudes. Through comprehensive theoretical frameworks and empirical research, this chapter provides a deeper understanding of the complex interplay between climate and work, proposing strategies to enhance productivity and employee well-being in varying climatic scenarios.

Introduction

Climate, encompassing both the immediate atmospheric conditions and broader patterns of weather over time, plays a significant role in shaping human behavior, including attitudes toward work. This chapter explores the intricate ways in which climate affects people's work-related attitudes and behaviors, integrating insights from psychology, sociology, and environmental studies. By examining the interplay between climate and work attitudes, we can gain a more in-depth understanding of how to foster productive and satisfying work environments across different climatic conditions.

Theoretical Framework

CLIMATE AND HUMAN BEHAVIOR

The relationship between climate and human behavior has been a subject of interest for centuries. Early theories, such as environmental determinism prominently discussed in the late 19th and early 20th centuries suggested that societies in tropical climates were less developed due to the oppressive heat, while those in temperate climates were more advanced due to the more favorable weather conditions (Meyer & Guss, 2017). However, this theory has been widely criticized and largely discredited for its oversimplification and failure to account for human agency and cultural factors, suggesting that climate directly determines human behavior and societal development (Hume, 2011). While such deterministic views have been largely discredited, contemporary research acknowledges that climate can influence behavior through more complex mechanisms (Doe, 2021).

Current theories about the relationship between climate and human behavior recognize that the effects of climate on behavior are not solely direct and deterministic (American Psychological Association, 2009). Instead, these theories incorporate the role of psychological and social factors in mediating these effects. This nuanced understanding reflects an integration of psychology and social psychology emphasizing the complexity of human-environment interactions.

Psychological Factors. Psychological factors significantly influence how individuals respond to climate-related events. Perception and cognition play a critical role. For example, two people experiencing the same heatwave might react differently based on their previous experiences, knowledge about climate change, and personal coping mechanisms (Gifford, 2014). Emotional responses such as fear, anxiety, and hope are also crucial in determining reactions to climate threats. These emotions can drive changes in behavior, leading individuals to adopt more sustainable practices or advocate for policy changes ~~(Clayton, Manning, & Hodge, 2014)~~ (Clayton, et al., 2024).

Social Psychology Factors. Social factors are instrumental in shaping how individuals respond to climate-related challenges. Social norms and influences often determine individual behaviors. For instance, if sustainable practices are widely accepted and promoted within a community, individuals are more likely to adopt similar behaviors (Cialdini & Goldstein, 2004). Additionally, the cultural context, including values and practices, can shape community perceptions and responses to climate-related issues. Cultural beliefs can either facilitate or hinder the adoption of adaptive behaviors (Adgar, et al., 2023)

WORK ATTITUDES

Work attitudes encompass a range of affective, cognitive, and behavioral responses to work and the work environment. Key components include job satisfaction, organizational commitment, work motivation, and occupational stress. These attitudes are influenced by various factors, including individual characteristics, job characteristics, and broader environmental conditions.

Job Satisfaction. Job satisfaction represents the degree to which employees find fulfillment and contentment in their roles, influenced by various elements such as job characteristics, the work environment, and their personal expectations. Determinants of job satisfaction include job characteristics such as autonomy, task variety, and opportunities for skill utilization, which are positively associated with job satisfaction (Hackman & Oldham, 1980). Furthermore, job satisfaction can be increased by supportive management, positive relationships with coworkers, and a safe and healthy work environment (Judge et al., 2017).

Personal expectations also play a crucial role, as alignment between job expectations and actual job experiences enhances job satisfaction (Locke, 1976). The impact of job satisfaction is significant; satisfied employees are more productive, creative, and likely to engage in organizational citizenship behaviors (OCBs) (Demerouti et al., 2020). Moreover, higher job satisfaction reduces employee turnover and absenteeism (Hom et al., 2019).

Job satisfaction significantly impacts not only the individual employee's performance but also the overall organizational climate. According to Spector (1997), job satisfaction is influenced by factors such as compensation, work-life balance, and the extent of involvement in decision-making processes, all of which can contribute to an employee's overall feeling of satisfaction or dissatisfaction at work. Satisfied employees tend to exhibit a higher commitment to the organization, which in turn can foster a positive work culture and lower turnover rates (Spector, 1997).

The psychological contract between employer and employee—comprising mutual expectations and perceived obligations—also plays a critical role in shaping job satisfaction. Rousseau (1995) argues that when employees perceive that their employer is fulfilling promises, whether regarding career development opportunities or fair management practices, satisfaction is likely to increase. This fulfillment not only boosts morale but also enhances trust and loyalty towards the organization (Rousseau, 1995).

Moreover, advancements in technology and changes in work patterns, such as remote work and flexible hours, have introduced new dimensions to job satisfaction. These changes often affect job satisfaction by altering work dynamics and relationships. As found in a study by Kossek, Roberts, Fisher, and Demarr (1998), flexible working arrangements can significantly enhance job satisfaction by providing employees with more control over their work and personal life balance, thus leading to reduced stress and increased job performance (Kossek et al.).

Organizational Commitment. Organizational commitment is the psychological attachment an employee feels towards their organization, influencing their willingness to remain and contribute to its success. Employees who have strong organizational commitment tend to demonstrate higher job performance and exhibit lower intentions to leave the organization (Meyer et al., 2002). Meyer and Allen (1991) categorized three types of organizational commitment: affective commitment (emotional attachment), continuance commitment (perceived cost of leaving), and normative commitment (sense of obligation). Several factors that influence organizational commitment include job satisfaction, perceived support from the organization, and the quality of interactions between leaders and members.

Organizational commitment is a multifaceted construct that significantly impacts employee behavior and organizational success. By understanding and fostering the different dimensions of commitment, organizations can cultivate a loyal, motivated, and high-performing workforce.

Affective Commitment. Affective commitment involves an employee's emotional connection and alignment with their organization. Employees with high affective commitment stay with the organization because they want to, deriving satisfaction from their work and aligning closely with the organization's goals and values. Meyer and Allen (1991) emphasize that affective commitment is associated with positive workplace behaviors, including increased job performance, lower turnover intentions, and higher levels of organizational citizenship behaviors (OCBs).

Continuance Commitment. Continuance commitment involves the perceived cost of leaving the organization. Employees with high continuance commitment stay because they feel they have to, often due to the financial, social, or professional costs associated with leaving. This type of commitment can be influenced by factors such as tenure, accumulated benefits, and lack of alternative job opportunities. While it can reduce turnover, it may not always translate to high job performance or engagement, as the primary motivation is the perceived cost rather than genuine attachment (Allen & Meyer, 1996).

Normative Commitment. Normative commitment involves a sense of duty or obligation to stay with the organization. Employees with high normative commitment stay because they believe it is the right thing to do, often due to personal values or social norms. This sense of obligation can arise from cultural or familial expectations, or from the belief that loyalty to the organization is a moral duty. Normative commitment can enhance organizational stability and cohesion, but like continuance commitment, it may not always lead to high performance or job satisfaction if not accompanied by affective commitment (Wiener, 1982)

Work motivation. Work motivation involves the internal and external forces that initiate work-related behaviors and determine their form, direction, intensity, and duration. Several theories provide frameworks for understanding work motivation. Self-Determination Theory (SDT) emphasizes the role of intrinsic and extrinsic motivation and the fulfillment of basic psychological needs, including autonomy, competence, and relatedness (Deci & Ryan, 2000).

Expectancy Theory contends that motivation is driven by the belief that effort will result in performance, which will in turn produce outcomes, and these outcomes are deemed valuable (Vroom, 1964). Key determinants of work motivation include goal setting, where specific, challenging, and achievable goals enhance motivation and performance (Locke & Latham, 2002); feedback, where constructive feedback facilitates employees understand how to improve and motivates them to achieve goals (Kluger & DeNisi, 1996); and recognition, where acknowledgment of achievements boosts motivation by fulfilling needs for competence and relatedness (Deci & Ryan, 2000). The influence of work motivation is considerable, as motivated employees are more likely to be more productive, creative, and dedicated to maintaining high-quality standards (Grant, 2008). Furthermore, high levels of motivation lead to greater work engagement and job satisfaction (Schaufeli et al., 2002).

Occupational Stress. Occupational stress elicits a range of affective, cognitive, and behavioral responses in employees. Affective responses to occupational stress often include feelings of anxiety, depression, and irritability. These emotional reactions can undermine job satisfaction and overall well-being (Lazarus & Folkman, 1984; Kelloway & Day, 2005). Cognitive responses involve changes in thought processes, such as increased worry, difficulty concentrating, and negative attitudes towards work. These cognitive shifts can impair decision-making and problem-solving abilities, leading to decreased job performance (LePine, Podsakoff, & LePine, 2005). Behavioral responses to occupational stress may manifest as changes in work behavior, including increased absenteeism, reduced productivity, and withdrawal from work-related activities (Quick et al., 2003). Additionally, coping mechanisms, such as seeking social support or engaging in stress-relief activities, play a critical role in managing these responses (Ganster & Rosen, 2013). Understanding these multidimensional responses to occupational stress is crucial for developing effective interventions to enhance employee well-being and organizational performance.

Worker Attitude Summary. Work attitudes significantly influence worker well-being and productivity, encompassing a range of affective, cognitive, and behavioral responses to work and the work environment. Key components of work attitudes include job satisfaction, organizational commitment, work motivation, and occupational stress. Job satisfaction is crucial as it affects overall happiness and contentment with one's job, influencing productivity and the likelihood of engaging in positive work behaviors (Judge et al., 2017). Organizational commitment, which involves the psychological attachment to the organization, impacts retention rates and employee performance (Meyer & Allen, 1991). Work motivation drives the intensity and persistence of work-related behaviors, directly affecting productivity and quality of work (Deci & Ryan, 2000). Occupational stress, conversely, can undermine well-being and performance by causing anxiety, depression, and other negative outcomes (Lazarus & Folkman, 1984). These attitudes are shaped by individual characteristics, job characteristics, and broader environmental conditions, highlighting the complex interplay between personal and organizational factors in determining worker well-being and productivity (Hackman & Oldham, 1980; Ganster & Rosen, 2013).

Direct Effects of Climate on Work Attitudes

TEMPERATURE AND WORK PERFORMANCE

Temperature is one of the most studied climatic variables in relation to work attitudes and performance and a critical environmental factor that affects human performance in various ways (Lan, Wargocki, & Lian, 2011). Both extreme heat and cold can impair cognitive and physical functions, leading to decreased productivity and increased health risks. Recent studies on the impact of temperature on work performance, providing insights into the mechanisms involved and suggesting strategies for optimizing workplace temperature.

Temperature affects human physiology through various pathways, influencing both cognitive and physical performance. High temperatures can lead to heat stress, resulting in dehydration and fatigue, while low temperatures can cause cold stress, affecting muscle coordination and strength. High temperatures have been shown to impair cognitive functions such as attention, memory, and executive functioning. For instance, a study by Lan et al. (2019) found that high temperatures reduced the accuracy and speed of cognitive tasks, particularly those requiring sustained attention and complex problem-solving. On the other hand, exposure to cold environments can impair physical performance by reducing muscle strength and coordination. Research by Wiboonchutikul et al. (2020) demonstrated that prolonged exposure to cold temperatures negatively affected cognitive and physical capabilities, emphasizing the need for maintaining optimal thermal conditions.

SEASONAL AFFECTIVE DISORDER (SAD)

Seasonal Affective Disorder (SAD) is a depression condition that occurs at specific periods of the year, usually during the fall and winter months when there is a decrease in natural sunlight (Magnusson & Boivin, 2003). It is marked by recurring episodes of depression that align with a seasonal pattern, most commonly starting in late autumn and early winter and subsiding during the spring and summer. Individuals living in higher latitudes with less sunlight exposure are at greater risk of developing SAD, as prevalence rates vary significantly based on geographic location (Rohan & Rough, 2013).

Seasonal Affective Disorder (SAD) can significantly impact employees, leading to increased absenteeism and lower productivity during the winter months. Employees suffering from SAD often experience a range of symptoms such as persistent low mood, fatigue, difficulty concentrating, a general decline in job satisfaction, and loss of interest in daily activities, which can hinder their job performance and overall workplace engagement (Melrose, 2015). Addressing these challenges requires proactive measures from employers, such as providing access to light therapy lamps, promoting outdoor breaks to maximize exposure to natural light, and encouraging regular physical activity to help mitigate symptoms (Corporate Wellness Magazine, 2020; Spill, 2022).

Indirect Effects of Climate on Work Attitudes

ECONOMIC IMPACTS OF CLIMATE

The indirect impact of climate conditions on work attitudes through economic conditions can be understood through several mechanisms. Climate-induced economic disruptions can lead to job losses and reduced job security. Job insecurity is closely linked to negative work attitudes, including lower job satisfaction and decreased organizational commitment. Employees facing job insecurity due to economic instability caused by adverse climate events may exhibit increased stress and reduced motivation (Sverke et al., 2002). Economic instability resulting from climate events can contribute to financial stress among employees. Financial stress negatively impacts mental health, leading to anxiety, depression, and burnout. Poor mental health, in turn, affects work attitudes by reducing job satisfaction and increasing turnover intentions (Wilson et al., 2004). Additionally, climate-related economic challenges can strain organizational resources, limiting the support provided to employees. Reduced organizational support during economic downturns can lead to feelings of undervaluation and decreased organizational commitment. Employees may perceive a lack of investment in their well-being, leading to disengagement and decreased job satisfaction (Eisenberger et al., 2002).

ENVIRONMENTAL STRESSORS

Environmental conditions can play a crucial role in shaping work attitudes and overall employee well-being. Creating healthy work environments that minimize exposure to environmental stressors is crucial for maintaining positive work attitudes. Adverse conditions such as extreme temperatures, air pollution, and noise can have detrimental effects on employees' job satisfaction, organizational commitment, work motivation, and occupational stress levels. Extended exposure to extreme temperatures, whether hot or cold, can result in discomfort, fatigue, and various health issues, all of which potentially negatively impact job satisfaction. Lan et al. (2019) found that employees working in non-optimal thermal environments reported lower job satisfaction and higher levels of frustration. Poor air quality, marked by elevated levels of pollutants, can potentially lead to respiratory problems and other health issues. Workers exposed to poor air quality over long periods report decreased job satisfaction due to health concerns and discomfort (Zivin & Neidell, 2014). Prolonged exposure to high noise levels can produce hearing loss, emotional stress, and decreased concentration, adversely affecting job satisfaction. Basner et al. (2014) found that noise pollution in the workplace is associated with lower job satisfaction and higher irritation levels.

Psychological Mechanisms Linking Climate and Work Attitudes

STRESS AND COPING

Climate-related stressors can trigger psychological stress responses that affect work attitudes. The transactional model of stress and coping (Lazarus & Folkman, 1984) provides a useful framework for understanding this process. This transactional model of stress and coping suggests that stress arises from an individual's perception of an event and their evaluation of their ability to handle it.

The model highlights cognitive appraisal's significance in determining whether an event is perceived as stressful. in determining if an event is seen as stressful and differentiates between problem-focused and emotion-focused coping strategies. It highlights the dynamic and interactive nature of the stress response, stressing that effective coping depends on the individual's capacity to evaluate and manage both the demands of the situation and their emotional reactions.

Specifically, the Lazarus and Folkman's model first involves two key cognitive appraisal stages: primary and secondary appraisal. During the primary appraisal stage, individuals evaluate whether an event is irrelevant, benign-positive, or stressful. If deemed stressful, the event is further assessed to determine whether it poses a threat, harm, or challenge. In the secondary appraisal stage, individuals evaluate the resources and options available to cope with the stressor. This involves assessing their ability to manage the situation and considering potential strategies for dealing with the stress. Together, these appraisal processes help individuals understand and respond to stressful events effectively. Secondly, problem-focused coping strategies aim to address the problem causing the stress by taking actions such as seeking information, planning, and implementing direct steps to change the situation. In contrast, emotion-focused coping strategies are designed to manage the emotional response to the stressor. These strategies can involve seeking emotional support, engaging in relaxation techniques, or reframing the situation in a more positive light. Together, these coping mechanisms enable individuals to manage stress effectively by either addressing the root cause of the stress or mitigating its emotional effects.

AFFECT AND MOOD

The effects of weather and climate conditions on mood can significantly influence work attitudes and productivity. Positive mood enhancements from favorable weather conditions can lead to increased job satisfaction, higher organizational commitment, and improved performance, resulting in better performance and lower turnover rates (Lan et al., 2019; Isen & Baron, 1991). Ulrich et al. (1991) observed that exposure to natural environments and favorable weather conditions is associated with positive affect and enhanced mood. Conversely, adverse weather conditions, such as prolonged rain or extreme temperatures, can lead to negative affect and mood. Negative mood states, such as irritability and depression, can reduce job satisfaction and increase turnover intentions (Judge & Larsen, 2001). Mental health issues arising from adverse weather conditions, such as psychological distress from heat or depression from lack of sunlight, can significantly reduce productivity. Addressing these mental health issues through interventions such as light therapy or improved workplace conditions can help mitigate their negative impact on work performance (Rohan et al., 2016).

Sociocultural Factors Mediating Climate Effects on Work Attitudes

CULTURAL ATTITUDES TOWARD CLIMATE

Cultural attitudes toward climate can significantly shape how individuals perceive and respond to climatic conditions. These attitudes are influenced by a combination of historical experiences, social narratives, economic factors, and cultural values, which together determine the collective and individual approaches to climate-related issues (Adger, et al., 2013).

Historical Experiences. Historical experiences with climate events play a crucial role in shaping cultural attitudes. Societies that have faced severe climate-related disasters may develop a heightened sensitivity to climate change and a proactive stance toward mitigation and adaptation efforts. For example, European countries like Germany, which have a history of severe weather events, have a strong cultural narrative around climate catastrophe ("Klimakatastrophe"), leading to robust public support for environmental policies and actions (Nieman Foundation, n.d.). Another study on climate change in rural Pakistan found that communities facing recurrent extreme weather events, such as droughts and floods, developed stronger adaptive strategies and community resilience (Sambrook, et al., 2021).

Social Narratives. Social narratives constructed around climate events influence public perception and response. In the United States, the term "global warming" is commonly used, which may lead to a perception of climate change as a distant, gradual process, influencing a more complacent attitude toward immediate action. Conversely, German media underscore the disastrous potential of climate change, instilling a sense of urgency and shared responsibility (Nieman Foundation, n.d.).

Economic Dependence. Economic reliance on climate-sensitive sectors, like agriculture, significantly shapes perceptions of climate change. In areas where agriculture is the main economic activity, like Nepal's Terai, climate change is seen as an immediate threat to livelihoods, driving higher awareness and adaptive behaviors (Poudel & Duex, 2017). Conversely, in regions with diversified economies, climate change may not be perceived as an immediate threat, leading to less proactive responses (Lee, et al., 2015).

Resource Availability. The availability of resources for climate change mitigation and adaptation also shapes cultural attitudes. Wealthier nations or regions with more resources can invest in sustainable practices and technologies, fostering a culture of environmental responsibility. On the other hand, economically disadvantaged regions might prioritize immediate economic benefits over long-term environmental sustainability (Lee et al., 2015).

Collectivist vs. Individualist Cultures. Cultural orientation towards collectivism or individualism plays a significant role in shaping climate attitudes. Collectivist cultures, which prioritize group harmony and community well-being, are more likely to perceive climate change as a significant threat and take collective action against it (Dai, & Zheng, 2019, Mehta & Ticku, 2021). In contrast, individualist cultures, which emphasize personal freedom and individual responsibility, may have varied responses to climate change. Individuals in such cultures may prioritize personal convenience and economic benefits over collective environmental actions, leading to higher levels of climate inaction (Gifford & Chen, 2017).

A study by Dai and Zheng (2019) concluded that people from collectivist cultures, which emphasize group harmony and community, are more likely to perceive climate change as a significant threat and take collective action against it. Conversely, individualist cultures may focus more on personal impacts and immediate benefits, leading to different climate actions. Research by Mehta and Ticku (20210 showed that collectivist cultures tend to have higher environmental concerns and prioritize sustainability, while individualist cultures may focus more on immediate economic benefits. Other studies have shown that in collectivist societies, there is a stronger sense of responsibility towards environmental sustainability and communal efforts to combat climate change (Shi et al., 2015; Xue et al., 2016).

SOCIAL SUPPORT AND COMMUNITY

Social support and community networks play a crucial role in buffering the negative effects of climate on work attitudes. These networks provide emotional, informational, and instrumental support, and community resilience and collective efficacy, which can enhance individuals' resilience to climate-induced stressors, thereby maintaining positive work attitudes even in adverse climate conditions.

Emotional Support. Emotional support from peers, family, and community members can significantly alleviate the stress and anxiety associated with climate-related challenges. When individuals feel supported and understood by their social networks, they are better able to manage the emotional strain of climate impacts on their work environment (Cohen & Wills, 1985). This support helps mitigate feelings of isolation and helplessness, promoting a more positive outlook on their work and personal lives.

Informational Support. Community networks often serve as valuable sources of information during climate crises. Having access to timely and precise information about climate conditions, coping strategies, and available resources can empower individuals to make better informed decisions and take active measures to safeguard their well-being and maintain work productivity (Kaniasty & Norris, 2000). This informational support helps reduce uncertainty and enhances individuals' sense of control over their circumstances.

Instrumental Support. Instrumental support, which includes tangible assistance such as financial aid, transportation, and physical help, is crucial during climate-related disruptions. Communities that band together to provide such support can significantly ease the burden on affected individuals, allowing them to maintain their work commitments and attitudes despite challenging conditions (Gurung, 1989). This collective approach fosters a sense of solidarity and shared purpose, reinforcing positive work attitudes.

Community Resilience and Collective Efficacy. The concept of collective efficacy, or the shared belief in the community's ability to manage and overcome challenges, is particularly relevant in the context of climate impacts. Communities with high collective efficacy are more likely to engage in coordinated efforts to address climate-related issues, providing a strong support network for individuals. This communal resilience boosts individuals' confidence and optimism about their work environment, even in the face of adverse climatic conditions (Bandura, 2000).

ORGANIZATIONAL STRATEGIES FOR ADDRESSING CLIMATE-RELATED WORK ATTITUDES

Organizational strategies for addressing climate-related work attitudes are essential for maintaining employee morale, productivity, and overall well-being in the face of climate change. These strategies can include fostering a supportive organizational culture, implementing flexible work arrangements, providing training and resources, and promoting sustainability initiatives. These organizational strategies supported by research are described below.

FOSTERING A SUPPORTIVE ORGANIZATIONAL CULTURE.

Cultivating Environmental Values. Embedding environmental values into the core mission and vision of the organization can enhance employee identification with and commitment to sustainability goals (Schein, 2010). This can be achieved through leadership that prioritizes climate action and by integrating sustainability into the company's value system. Leaders who are visibly committed to environmental sustainability can inspire similar values among employees. This commitment can be demonstrated through public statements, strategic priorities, and personal involvement in sustainability initiatives (Schein). Leaders who practice sustainable behaviors and make environmentally conscious decisions set a powerful example for employees (Brown, Treviño & Harrison,

2005). By doing so, they can reinforce the importance of sustainability and encourage employees to adopt similar practices.

Encouraging Employee Participation. Involving employees in the development and implementation of sustainability initiatives can increase their engagement and sense of ownership over climate-related actions (Robertson & Barling, 2015). Implementing systems where employees can submit ideas for sustainability initiatives encourages active participation (Amabile & Kramer, 2011). These platforms can be online suggestion boxes, intranet portals, or dedicated meetings. Acknowledging and rewarding employees for their suggestions can motivate continued participation and foster a culture of continuous improvement (Deci & Ryan, 2000).

FLEXIBLE WORK ARRANGEMENTS.

Remote Work. Remote work significantly reduces the need for daily commuting, thereby lowering greenhouse gas emissions and reducing employees' exposure to adverse weather conditions. This reduction in commuting contributes to decreased overall traffic congestion and pollution (Bloom, Liang, Roberts, & Ying, 2015). Furthermore, permitting employees to work from home can improve their work-life balance by allowing them greater control over their work environment and schedules. This increased flexibility can result in greater job satisfaction and lower stress levels (Hill, Hawkins, Ferris, & Weitzman, 2001).

Flexible Scheduling. Flexible scheduling allows employees to adjust their work hours to avoid the worst impacts of adverse weather conditions, such as choosing to work earlier or later in the day to escape extreme heat or severe storms (Christensen & Schneider, 2010). This adaptability can lead to increased productivity, as employees can work during their most productive times of the day, thereby reducing the stress and health issues associated with rigid work schedules (Golden, 2006).

Support for Families and Communities. Flexible work arrangements can help employees manage family responsibilities, such as childcare and eldercare, particularly during extreme weather events when schools or care facilities may be closed (Kossek & Lautsch, 2018). Additionally, employees with flexible work schedules may have more time to engage in community activities, including local climate action initiatives, which can strengthen community resilience to climate impacts (Putnam, 2000).

Organizational Resilience. Flexible work arrangements can enhance an organization's resilience by ensuring business continuity during extreme weather events. Employees can continue to work from home or adjust their schedules to maintain operations despite adverse conditions (De Smet, et al., 2021). Additionally, providing flexible work arrangements can enhance an organization's appeal to potential employees and aid in retaining current staff, especially those who prioritize work-life balance and the ability to adjust to varying environmental conditions (Kossek et al., 2015).

Environmental Sustainability Initiatives. Organizations can also address climate-related work attitudes by implementing environmental sustainability initiatives.

These initiatives not only minimize the environmental impact of business operations but also reflect a commitment to social responsibility, which can boost employees' sense of purpose and job satisfaction (Ramus & Steger, 2000). Sustainability initiatives may include reducing energy consumption, minimizing waste, promoting green commuting options, and supporting environmental conservation projects. Engaging employees in these initiatives can also foster a sense of collective effort and pride in contributing to a larger cause.

Case Studies: Climate and Work Attitudes in Different Regions

CASE STUDY 1: EXTREME HEAT IN THE MIDDLE EAST

Employers in the region have implemented various strategies to mitigate these risks of the harsh climate in the Middle East. The article titled "Climate Change and Heat Stress Resilient Outdoor Workers: Findings from Systematic Literature Review" examines the impact of climate change on outdoor workers who are particularly vulnerable to heat stress. The review synthesizes findings from numerous studies to identify effective strategies for enhancing the resilience of these workers. Key strategies discussed include scheduled rest breaks in shaded or air-conditioned areas to help workers recover from heat exposure, providing shaded areas and cool drinking water enhanced with electrolytes to maintain hydration and prevent heat stress, implementing heat acclimatization programs to help workers' bodies gradually adapt to high temperatures, adjusting work schedules to avoid the hottest parts of the day, and educating workers on the risks of heat stress, as well as the importance of hydration and rest, ensures they can identify and effectively respond to heat-related symptoms.

Despite the measures summarized above, extreme heat continues to affect work attitudes, leading to lower job satisfaction and higher turnover rates in some sectors. Addressing these issues requires ongoing efforts to improve working conditions and promote awareness of heat-related health risks. Employers can implement several strategies to mitigate the adverse effects of extreme heat. Providing adequate hydration stations, ensuring access to shaded or air-conditioned rest areas, and scheduling regular breaks can help employees manage heat stress (Bates et al., 2020). Additionally, modifying work schedules to avoid the peak heat periods and implementing flexible work arrangements. can significantly reduce heat exposure and its associated risks (Christensen & Schneider, 2010).

Promoting awareness of heat-related health risks is also crucial. Training programs that educate employees on recognizing the symptoms of heat stress and implementing preventive measures can empower individuals to implement proactive measures in managing their health (Clayton et al., 2014). Employers should also consider investing in heat acclimatization programs to help workers gradually adapt to high temperatures, enhancing their resilience to heat stress (Basner et al., 2014).

Overall, a comprehensive approach that combines improved working conditions, flexible arrangements, and educational programs can help minimize the adverse effects of extreme heat on work attitudes, ensuring a healthier and more productive workforce.

CASE STUDY 2: SEASONAL AFFECTIVE DISORDER IN NORTHERN EUROPE

In Norway, public health campaigns actively raise awareness about Seasonal Affective Disorder (SAD) and promote the use of light therapy (Life in Norway, 2020; HealthLink BC, 202; VA Research, 2015). These campaigns aim to mitigate the impact of long, dark winters, which are known to exacerbate SAD symptoms. As part of these efforts, schools and workplaces are encouraged to provide access to light therapy lamps, which simulate natural sunlight and help alleviate the symptoms of SAD. For example, public health guidelines recommend the use of light therapy boxes emitting 10,000 lux for about 30 minutes to 2 hours daily, typically in the early morning, to improve mood and energy levels among individuals affected by SAD (HealthLink BC, 2022).

Cognitive-behavioral therapy (CBT) has been shown to equally as effective as light therapy in treating Seasonal Affective Disorder (SAD) (VA Research, 2015). This makes CBT a viable alternative treatment for individuals who either do not respond to light therapy or prefer a different approach. Research by Rohan et al. (2016) indicates that CBT can help individuals with SAD by teaching them coping strategies to manage their symptoms, such as scheduling pleasant activities, engaging in regular physical exercise, and practicing relaxation techniques (Rohan et al., 2016). Comparing the effectiveness of CBT and light therapy, Rohan et al. found that both treatments were equally effective in reducing the symptoms of SAD. However, the study noted that the benefits of CBT were more enduring, with patients showing fewer recurrences of depressive episodes in subsequent winters compared to those who received only light therapy. This suggests that while light therapy is effective in the short term, CBT offers more sustained benefits by equipping patients with tools to manage their condition proactively.

Conclusions

From this chapter, several action-oriented conclusions can be drawn to address the impact of climate on work-related behaviors and attitudes:

1. **Adapt Workplace Environments**: Modify work environments to accommodate different climatic conditions. This includes adjusting office temperatures, utilizing ergonomic designs that adapt to weather variations, and providing access to natural light to combat effects like Seasonal Affective Disorder (SAD).
2. **Promote Psychological Well-being**: Implement strategies to manage the psychological impact of climate on employees. This could involve stress management programs, mental health days, and resources like counseling and support groups, particularly in regions prone to extreme weather conditions or where SAD is prevalent.
3. **Enhance Organizational Culture**: Develop a workplace culture that supports sustainability and acknowledges the psychological and physical needs of employees in different climates. This might include promoting and rewarding sustainable practices, and integrating climate considerations into corporate policies and goals.
4. **Flexible Work Arrangements**: Encourage flexible working conditions that allow employees to work during hours that suit their productivity peaks and weather conditions. For instance, avoiding work during the hottest part of the day in warmer climates or providing remote work options during severe weather periods.
5. **Employee Training and Awareness**: Educate employees on the impact of climate on their health and work performance, and train them in adaptive behaviors and resilience strategies. This education could cover how to recognize symptoms of heat stress or cold impact, and effective coping mechanisms.
6. **Community and Social Support**: Strengthen social support networks within the workplace to provide emotional and practical support during climate-induced stress. This involves fostering a community spirit, encouraging team collaboration, and building collective efficacy to manage climate-related challenges.
7. **Invest in Health Initiatives**: Offer health-related initiatives such as providing light therapy for employees suffering from SAD, ensuring proper hydration, and maintaining clean air quality within office environments to mitigate the negative effects of poor environmental conditions.
8. **Policy Advocacy and Community Engagement**: Engage with wider community and policy initiatives to support environmental responsibility both at a corporate and community level. This could include supporting local climate resilience efforts and advocating for policies that protect and promote environmental and workplace health.

Implementing these actions requires a commitment from both management and employees to recognize the complex relationship between climate and work attitudes, and to actively engage in creating a supportive and adaptive work environment.

Recommendations for Further Research

To advance the research on the impact of climate on work-related attitudes and behaviors, several areas of investigation are recommended:

1. **Longitudinal Research**: There is a need for longitudinal studies that track changes in work attitudes over time in response to climatic changes. By tracking the same individuals or groups over extended periods, researchers can identify patterns of change, establish cause-and-effect relationships, and predict future trends. This is particularly important in the context of climate change, where both acute and gradual shifts in climatic conditions can have profound, yet markedly different, impacts on the workforce.
2. **Experimental Designs**: Employing experimental or quasi-experimental designs in research could help establish causality between specific climatic conditions and changes in work attitudes. Experimental designs offer a robust methodology for understanding the causal relationships between climatic conditions and work-related attitudes and behaviors. By manipulating environmental variables within controlled settings, researchers can directly observe the effects on worker productivity, job satisfaction, stress levels, and overall psychological well-being.
3. **Cross-Cultural Studies**: Given the global nature of climate change, cross-cultural research is essential to compare how different cultural contexts influence the perception of and adaptation to climate impacts. Cross-cultural studies are vital in the context of global climate change, given the diverse ways in which different cultures perceive, react to, and manage environmental challenges. These studies help uncover cultural variations in work-related attitudes and behaviors in response to climate factors, enhancing the development of universally effective, yet culturally nuanced, workplace policies and practices.
4. **Interdisciplinary Approaches**: Further integration of insights from environmental psychology, organizational behavior, climate science, and sociology could enrich the theoretical frameworks used to study the interplay between climate and work-related behaviors. Collaborations across these disciplines can lead to more holistic approaches and innovative solutions. Each discipline brings unique insights that can deepen the understanding of how climate affects human behavior in work environments. By integrating environmental psychology, organizational behavior, climate science, and sociology, research can more comprehensively address both the human and environmental dimensions of climate impacts.

5. **Sector-Specific Impacts**: More research is needed to delineate how various sectors uniquely experience and respond to climate-related challenges. Industries such as agriculture, construction, and others that are highly exposed to environmental conditions may require tailored strategies to mitigate the adverse effects on workers. Different industries face unique challenges related to climate, largely due to their dependence on and exposure to specific environmental conditions. Understanding how climate affects various sectors is crucial for developing effective, tailored strategies to improve worker productivity and well-being, and ensure sustainable business practices.
6. **Impact of Technological and Organizational Innovations**: Exploring how technological advancements such as artificial intelligence, remote sensing, and personalized climate control systems in workplaces can mitigate the negative impacts of climate on worker productivity and health would be beneficial. Additionally, examining the effectiveness of organizational changes like flexible working conditions and remote work arrangements in different climatic scenarios could provide valuable insights.
7. **Policy Impact Studies**: Investigating the role of policy interventions at both the organizational and governmental levels can help understand how regulatory frameworks influence organizational practices related to climate adaptation. This includes policies on workplace safety, environmental responsibility, and sustainable development goals. Policies can guide and mandate actions that significantly affect how organizations respond to climate challenges, ensuring safety, sustainability, and resilience.
8. **Qualitative Research**: Qualitative methods can offer in-depth insights into the personal experiences and narratives of employees dealing with climate impacts. This approach can uncover nuanced psychological and social dynamics that quantitative methods might overlook. By capturing detailed personal experiences and narratives, qualitative studies can uncover the subtle psychological and sociocultural dynamics that shape how individuals and organizations respond to climate impacts.
9. **Psychological Interventions**: Developing and testing psychological interventions that could help employees cope with climate-induced stress and uncertainties is crucial. These interventions can equip employees with the tools needed to manage stress effectively, enhance resilience, and maintain productivity in the face of environmental uncertainties and changes.
10. **Economic Modeling**: Employing economic models to predict the potential financial impacts of climate change on business operations and workforce productivity could aid in strategic planning and resource allocation. Economic modeling provides a critical tool for forecasting and quantifying the financial impacts of climate change on businesses. By predicting potential scenarios, organizations can make informed decisions about resource allocation, strategic planning, and risk management, ensuring sustainability and resilience in the face of climate challenges.

These recommendations aim to broaden the scope of research on climate impacts on work, ultimately contributing to more effective strategies to ensure workforce resilience and productivity in the face of changing global climate conditions.

REFERENCES

Adger, W. N. (2003). Social capital, collective action, and adaptation to climate change. *Economic Geography, 79*(4), 387-404. https://doi.org/10.1111/j.1944-8287.2003.tb00220.x

Adger, W. N., Barnett, J., Brown, K., Marshall, N., & O'Brien, K. (2013). Cultural dimensions of climate change impacts and adaptation. *Nature Climate Change, 3*(2), 112-117. https://doi.org/10.1038/nclimate1666

Allen, N. J., & Meyer, J. P. (1996). Affective, continuance, and normative commitment to the organization: An examination of construct validity. *Journal of Vocational Behavior, 49*(3), 252-276.

Amabile, T. M., & Kramer, S. J. (2011). *The progress principle: Using small wins to ignite joy, engagement, and creativity at work.* Harvard Business Review Press.

American Psychological Association. (2009). *Psychology and global climate change: Addressing a multi-faceted phenomenon and set of challenges.* https://www.apa.org/science/about/publications/climate-change

Bandura, A. (2000). Exercise of human agency through collective efficacy. *Current Directions in Psychological Science, 9*(3), 75-78. https://doi.org/10.1111/1467-8721.00064

Basner, M., Babisch, W., Davis, A., Brink, M., Clark, C., Janssen, S., & Stansfeld, S. (2014). *Auditory and non-auditory effects of noise on health.* https://www.ncbi.nlm.nih.gov/pmc/articles/PMC3988259/

Bates, G., Miller, V., Joubert, D., & Markham, C. (2020). Climate change and heat stress resilient outdoor workers: Findings from systematic literature review. *BMC Public Health, 20,* Article 1749. https://doi.org/10.1186/s12889-020-09874-0

Bloom, N., Liang, J., Roberts, J., & Ying, Z. J. (2015). Does working from home work? Evidence from a Chinese experiment. *The Quarterly Journal of Economics, 130*(1), 165-218.

BMC Public Health. (2023). *Climate change and heat stress resilient outdoor workers: Findings from systematic literature review.* https://bmcpublichealth.biomedcentral.com

Brown, M. E., Treviño, L. K., & Harrison, D. A. (2005). Ethical leadership: A social learning perspective for construct development and testing. *Organizational Behavior and Human Decision Processes, 97*(2), 117-134.

Christensen, K. E., & Schneider, B. (2010). Workplace flexibility: Realigning 20th-century jobs for a 21st-century workforce. *The Annals of the American Academy of Political and Social Science, 638*(1), 43-55.

Cialdini, R. B., & Goldstein, N. J. (2004). Social influence: Compliance and conformity. *Annual Review of Psychology, 55,* 591-621.

Clayton, S., Manning, C. M., & Hodge, C. (2014). Beyond storms and droughts: The psychological impacts of climate change. *American Psychological Association.*

Climate Data. (2020). *Dubai climate: Average Temperature by month, Dubai water temperature.* https://en.climate-data.org

Cohen, S., & Wills, T. A. (1985). Stress, social support, and the buffering hypothesis. *Psychological Bulletin, 98*(2), 310-357. https://doi.org/10.1037/0033-2909.98.2.310

Corporate Wellness Magazine. (2020). *Winter Wellness: Fighting Seasonal Affective Disorder at Work.* https://www.corporatewellnessmagazine.com

Dai, S., & Zheng, Y. (2019). Individualist–collectivist differences in climate change inaction: The role of perceived intractability. *Frontiers in Psychology*, *10*, Article 98. https://doi.org/10.3389/fpsyg.2019.00098

Deci, E. L., & Ryan, R. M. (2000). The "what" and "why" of goal pursuits: Human needs and the self-determination of behavior. *Psychological Inquiry*, *11*(4), 227-268.

Demerouti, E., Bakker, A. B., Nachreiner, F., & Schaufeli, W. B. (2020). The job demands-resources model of burnout. *Journal of Applied Psychology*, *86*(3), 499-512.

De Smet, A., Dowling, B., Mugayar-Baldocchi, M., & Schaninger, B. (2021). The future of work after COVID-19. *McKinsey Quarterly*. https://www.mckinsey.com/business-functions/organization/our-insights/the-future-of-work-after-covid-19

Eisenberger, R., Stinglhamber, F., Vandenberghe, C., Sucharski, I. L., & Rhoades, L. (2002). Perceived supervisor support: Contributions to perceived organizational support and employee retention. *Journal of Applied Psychology*, *87*(3), 565.

Ganster, D. C., & Rosen, C. C. (2013). Work stress and employee health: A multidisciplinary review. *Journal of Management*, *39*(5), 1085-1122.

Gifford, R. (2014). Environmental psychology matters. *Annual Review of Psychology, 65*, 541-579.

Gifford, R., & Chen, A. (2017). Why aren't we taking action? Psychological barriers to climate-positive food choices. *Climate and Development*, *9*(3), 215-229. https://doi.org/10.1080/17565529.2016.1149447

Golden, T. D. (2006). The role of relationships in understanding telecommuter satisfaction. *Journal of Organizational Behavior, 27*(3), 319-340.

Grant, A. M. (2008). The significance of task significance: Job performance effects, relational mechanisms, and boundary conditions. *Journal of Applied Psychology*, *93*(1), 108-124.

Gurung, R. A. R. (1989). Coping with climate change: The roles of social support and environmental factors. *Journal of Applied Social Psychology*, *19*(7), 552-568. https://doi.org/10.1111/j.1559-1816.1989.tb00035.x

Hackman, J. R., & Oldham, G. R. (1980). *Work redesign*. Addison-Wesley.

HealthLink BC. (2022, October 20). Seasonal Affective Disorder: Using Light Therapy. https://www.healthlinkbc.ca

Hill, E. J., Hawkins, A. J., Ferris, M., & Weitzman, M. (2001). Finding an extra day a week: The positive influence of perceived job flexibility on work and family life balance. *Family Relations, 50*(1), 49-58.

Hom, P. W., Lee, T. W., Shaw, J. D., & Hausknecht, J. P. (2019). One hundred years of employee turnover theory and research. *Journal of Applied Psychology*, *102*(3), 530-545.

Human Rights Watch. (2020). Gulf States: Migrant Workers at Serious Risk from Dangerous Heat. https://www.hrw.org

Hulme, M. (2011). Reducing the future to climate: A story of climate determinism and reductionism. *Osiris, 26*(1), 245-266.

Ichalak, E. E. (2016). Serotonin and seasonal affective disorder. *Journal of Psychiatry & Neuroscience*, *41*(5), 356-364

Isen, A. M., & Baron, R. A. (1991). Positive affect as a factor in organizational behavior. In L. L. Cummings & B. M. Staw (Eds.), *Research in organizational behavior* (Vol. 13, pp. 1-53). JAI Press.

Judge, T. A., & Larsen, R. J. (2001). Dispositional affect and job satisfaction: A review and theoretical extension. *Organizational Behavior and Human Decision Processes, 86*(1), 67-98.

Judge, T. A., Weiss, H. M., Kammeyer-Mueller, J. D., & Hulin, C. L. (2017). Job attitudes, job satisfaction, and job affect: A century of continuity and of change. *Journal of Applied Psychology*, *102*(3), 356-374.

Kaniasty, K., & Norris, F. H. (2000). Social support dynamics in adjustment to disasters. *Handbook of Coping: Theory, Research, Applications*, 395-409.

Kelloway, E. K., & Day, A. L. (2005). Building healthy workplaces: What we know so far. *Canadian Journal of Behavioural Science/Revue canadienne des sciences du comportement, 37*(4), 223-235.
Kossek, E. E., Roberts, K., Fisher, S., & Demarr, B. (1998). Career self-management: A quasi-experimental assessment of the effects of a training intervention. *Personnel Psychology, 51*(4), 935-960.
Kossek, E. E., Thompson, R. J., & Lautsch, B. A. (2015). Balanced workplace flexibility: Avoiding the traps. *California Management Review, 57*(4), 5-25.
Kossek, E. E., & Lautsch, B. A. (2018). Work-life flexibility for whom? Occupational status and work-life inequality in upper, middle, and lower level jobs. *Academy of Management Annals, 12*(1), 5-36.
Lan, G., McNall, L.A., Kim, S., & Ferris, D.L. (2019). The role of job satisfaction, organizational commitment, and job involvement in predicting turnover intentions. *Journal of Organizational Behavior, 40*(3), 313-329.
Lan, L., Wargocki, P., & Lian, Z. (2011). Quantitative measurement of productivity loss due to thermal discomfort. *Energy and Buildings, 43*(5), 1057-1062. https://doi.org/10.1016/j.enbuild.2010.09.001
Lan, L., Lian, Z., Pan, L., & Ye, Q. (2019). Neurobehavioral approach for evaluation of office workers' productivity: The effects of room temperature. *Building and Environment, 148*, 504-512.
Lazarus, R. S., & Folkman, S. (1984). *Stress, appraisal, and coping.* Springer Publishing Company.
Lee, T. M., Markowitz, E. M., Howe, P. D., Ko, C. Y., & Leiserowitz, A. A. (2015). Predictors of public climate change awareness and risk perception around the world. *Nature Climate Change, 5*(11), 1014-1020. https://doi.org/10.1038/nclimate2728
LePine, J. A., Podsakoff, N. P., & LePine, M. A. (2005). A meta-analytic test of the challenge stressor–hindrance stressor framework: An explanation for inconsistent relationships among stressors and performance. *Academy of Management Journal, 48*(5), 764-775.
Life in Norway. (2020). Surviving the Dark Time. https://www.lifeinnorway.net/surviving-the-dark-time
Locke, E. A. (1976). The nature and causes of job satisfaction. *Handbook of Industrial and Organizational Psychology, 1*, 1297-1343.
Magnusson, A., & Boivin, D. (2003). Seasonal affective disorder: An overview. *Chronobiology International, 20*(2), 189-207.
Mathieu, J. E., & Zajac, D. M. (1990). A review and meta-analysis of the antecedents, correlates, and consequences of organizational commitment. *Psychological Bulletin, 108*(2), 171-194.
Mehta, N., & Ticku, A. (2021, August 19). Does culture shape our environmental attitudes? *Psychology Today*. https://www.psychologytoday.com/intl/articles/does-culture-shape-our-environmental-attitudes
Melrose, S. (2015). Seasonal affective disorder: An overview of assessment and treatment approaches. *Depression Research and Treatment*, 1-6.
Meyer, J. P., & Allen, N. J. (1991). A three-component conceptualization of organizational commitment. *Human Resource Management Review, 1*(1), 61-89.
Meyer, J. P., Stanley, D. J., Herscovitch, L., & Topolnytsky, L. (2002). Affective, continuance, and normative commitment to the organization: A meta-analysis of antecedents, correlates, and consequences. *Journal of Vocational Behavior, 61*(1), 20-52.
Meyer, J. P., & Allen, N. J. (1991). A three-component conceptualization of organizational commitment. *Human Resource Management Review, 1*(1), 61-89.
Meyer, W.B., & Guss, D.M. (2017). Environmental Determinism: What Is It? In *Neo-Environmental Determinism*. Palgrave Macmillan, Cham. https://doi.org/10.1007/978-3-319-54232-4_2
Nieman Foundation. (n.d.). Culture contributes to perceptions of climate change: A comparison between the United States and Germany reveals insights about why journalists in each country report about this

issue in different ways. *Nieman Reports.* https://nieman.harvard.edu/articles/culture-contributes-to-perceptions-of-climate-change

Putnam, R. D. (2000). *Bowling alone: The collapse and revival of American community.* Simon & Schuster.

Quick, J. C., Quick, J. D., Nelson, D. L., & Hurrell Jr, J. J. (2003). *Preventive Stress Management in Organizations.* American Psychological Association.

Robertson, J. L., & Barling, J. (2015). *The psychology of green organizations. Oxford University Press.*

Rohan, K. J., & Rough, J. N. (2013). Seasonal affective disorder: An overview and update. *Psychiatric Clinics of North America, 36*(2), 205-218.

Rohan, K. J., Evans, M., Mahon, J. N., Sitnikov, L., Nillni, Y. I., Roecklein, K. A., & Halverson, J. L. (2016). Cognitive-behavioral therapy vs light therapy for preventing winter depression recurrence: A randomized controlled trial. *American Journal of Psychiatry, 172*(9), 862-869.

Rousseau, D. M. (1995). P*sychological contracts in organizations: Understanding written and unwritten agreements.* Sage Publications.

Sambrook, K., Konstantinidis, E., Russell, S., & Okan, Y. (2021). The role of personal experience and prior beliefs in shaping climate change perceptions: A narrative review. *Frontiers in Psychology, 12*, 669911. https://doi.org/10.3389/fpsyg.2021.669911

Sampson, R. J., Morenoff, J. D., & Gannon-Rowley, T. (2002). Assessing "neighborhood effects": Social processes and new directions in research. *Annual Review of Sociology, 28*, 443-478. https://doi.org/10.1146/annurev.soc.28.110601.141114

Schaufeli, W. B., Salanova, M., González-Romá, V., & Bakker, A. B. (2002). The measurement of engagement and burnout: A two-sample confirmatory factor analytic approach. *Journal of Happiness Studies, 3*(1), 71-92.

Schein, E. H. (2010). *Organizational culture and leadership* (4th ed.). Jossey-Bass.

Shi, T., Zhang, X., & Zhao, D. (2015). Public perception of climate change and support for climate policies in China: Evidence from a national survey. *Climate Policy, 15*(4), 433-452. https://doi.org/10.1080/14693062.2014.937388

Spector, P. E. (1997). *Job satisfaction: Application, assessment, causes, and consequences.* Sage Publications.

Spill. (2022). 8 ways to beat the winter blues at work. https://www.spill.chat

Sverke, M., Hellgren, J., & Näswall, K. (2002). No security: A meta-analysis and review of job insecurity and its consequences. *Journal of Occupational Health Psychology, 7*(3), 242-264.

Ulrich, R. S., Simons, R. F., Losito, B. D., Fiorito, E., Miles, M. A., & Zelson, M. (1991). Stress recovery during exposure to natural and urban environments. *Journal of Environmental Psychology, 11*(3), 201-230.

VA Research. (2015). *Cognitive behavioral therapy as effective as light therapy for seasonal affective disorder.* https://www.research.va.gov

Vroom, V. H. (1964). *Work and motivation.* Wiley.

Wiboonchutikul, S., Patumanond, J., & Boonchoo, B. (2020). The effects of cold exposure on cognitive and physical performance. *Environmental Research, 185*, 109449.

Wiener, Y. (1982). Commitment in organizations: A normative view. *Academy of Management Review, 7*(3), 418-428.

Wilson, S. H., & Walker, G. M. (2004). Unemployment and health: A review. *Public Health, 118*(3), 182-186.

Xue, W., Hine, D. W., Marks, A. D., Phillips, W. J., Zhao, S., & Nunn, P. (2016). Combining threat and efficacy messages to increase public engagement with climate change in Beijing, China. *Climatic Change, 137*(1), 43-55. https://doi.org/10.1007/s10584-016-1673-6

Zivin, J. G., & Neidell, M. (2014). Temperature and the allocation of time: Implications for climate change. *Journal of Labor Economics, 32*(1), 1-26.

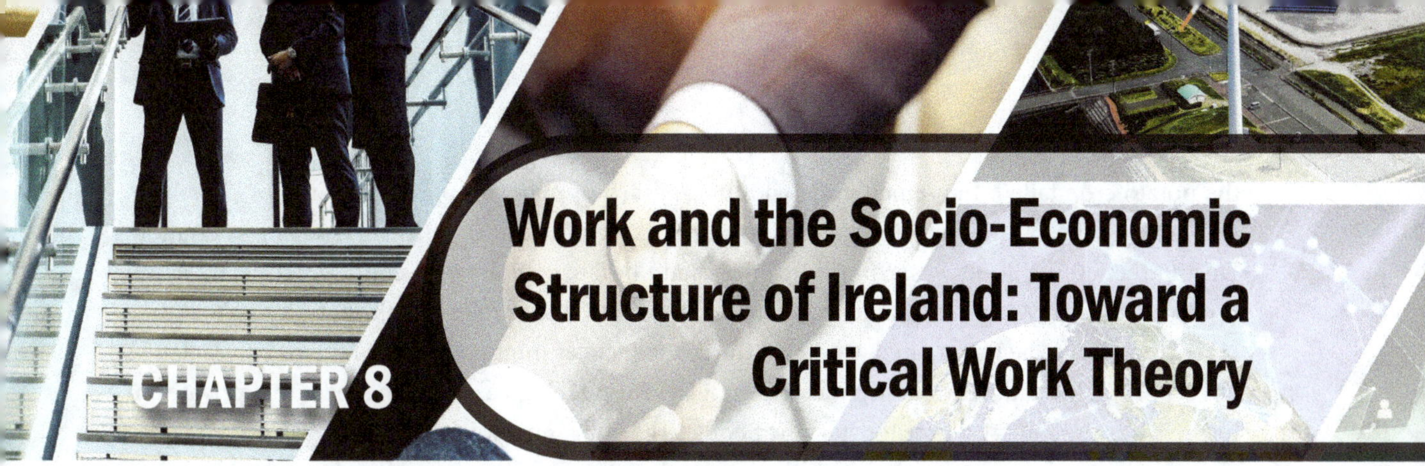

CHAPTER 8

Work and the Socio-Economic Structure of Ireland: Toward a Critical Work Theory

Ted Fleming, Maynooth University, Ireland

The well-known photograph, 'Lunch atop a skyscraper' shows construction workers sitting on a beam 800 feet high on top of Rockefeller Centre, New York. The picture is part of a publicity shot promoting the building as it was being built in 1932 (Cross, 2003). Today visitors can replicate the experience in a tourist attraction called "The Beam" (Rahmanan, 2023). It seems that at least one of the men was Irish (Ó Cualáin, 2012). This photograph of a confident America expanding upward required workers. Emigration from Ireland began in the 1720s and by 1790 almost half a million of the 3 million Americans were Irish. Millions emigrated from the early 19th century, driven by poverty; in the 1850s by famine; attracted by promises of work and a better life. The impact on the industrial, social and political life of both the United States and Ireland was significant.

In this chapter, I will map the story of work and society in Ireland and create an awareness that this story is best understood as a long historical journey through colonial (including famine) exploitation, independence, the famous Celtic Tiger, and its demise until today. Work and society in Ireland have reached a place where emigration is historically low, as is unemployment. Never before have so many immigrants re-defined work and society leading to historically high population levels. Despite the obvious success of the model of work in Ireland, there still remain serious problems of housing, homelessness, and relative poverty and inequality. This entire experience, over almost 200 years, is outlined in this chapter and leads toward a critical work theory.

Work and the Famine

One hundred years before the famous photo on the beam, during the potato famine (1845-1852), one million died and another million emigrated from Ireland. Delaney (2012) states that though the potato crop failed, the remedy was within the grasp of many, in particular Charles Travelyan, who was the most senior administrator controlling expenditure at the British Treasury in London. During the famine, food was exported from Ireland because the liberal economic imperative, administered by Travelyan, of maintaining free trade ensured that relief would not be forthcoming: "Free trade was to be maintained, whatever the consequences might be for the Irish poor" (Delaney, 2012, p. 107). Instead, self-reliance was encouraged. This ideological position meant that private enterprise was the chief resource for starving people. The poor must work; earn money; and buy relief; all in the midst of mass starvation. The ideology of the free market trumped humanitarian concerns. This chapter highlights concern for those for whom the economy and work do not deliver in Ireland.

To understand work in Ireland this colonial experience must be understood as well as the associated work schemes, workhouses, and the cruel idea that starving peasants must work to live. The history and memories of famine live long; in song, in mass burial sites, and in the subsequent political desire to reform the ownership of land. National identity became closely associated with a particular place and its history, Ireland.

The British, at that time, believed that a diet of potatoes was insufficient and led to "indolence and vice" (Kelly, 2012, p. 56). Instead, people were expected to earn money by working for wages on farms producing Indian corn. For this work, they were promised "a vast accumulation of capital" would arise (Kelly, 2012, p. 56). This required a transformation of the labor market; in the interest of colonial profits. This was the not-so-hidden message of British colonial power and its liberal political economy. The indolence of the Irish is countered by the skilled work projects undertaken in places such as New York. It brings into focus the ability of the Irish to work hard, for low wages, in vastly different social environments. This study attempts to begin a critical work theory (akin to critical race theory) and understand how history, and other disciplines, help us understand work in Ireland today. It is not a simple story, but step by step the story can be told.

The money earned by Irish immigrants in America and the UK flowed back to Ireland in huge amounts and was a significant factor in the economy of Ireland. Historian Arnold Schrier has calculated that the Irish in America sent home $260 million during the latter part of the nineteenth century (Schrier, 1958). Even as recently as 1961, £14 million ($36 million) was sent home by Irish emigrants from the UK alone and it continued "unabated until about 1970" (Schrier, 1958, p. 106)[1]. A study by Horgan-Jones (9 April, 2014) found that between 1940 and 1970 those working in the UK returned €5.7 billion ($6.4 billion) in today's equivalent. Remittances were part of the economic safety valve of Irish emigration. But such huge amounts of income hard earned abroad, masked the emotional sacrifice of emigrants who were doubly burdened with the need to send money home and find their way in a foreign country. And there were so many. Today about 31.5 million US residents

1. Euro or British sterling are expressed in US Dollars, according to exchange rates at the time

claim Irish ancestry and their earnings from work abroad kept the economy in Ireland afloat. This level of immigration in America helped preserve a threatened Irish culture and contributed in no small way to American culture and music.

The struggle for Irish independence was supported financially by contributions from abroad. Of the 46 U.S. presidents, 23 trace part of their roots to Ireland (Moore, Vasquez, & Dolan, 2021). If goodwill toward Ireland underpins American economic investment in Ireland today and support for peace in Ireland too, it is deeply grounded in history. It is a deeply felt emotional connection. The Irish in America were able to hold on to and adapt its rich culture and traditions, especially through music, dance, and literature, they have managed to carve a distinct Irish-American identity and influence American culture, e.g., the integration with Appalachian music. Organizing trade union representation was a strong influence and for instance, the famous Mary Harris, better known as Mother Jones, spent over fifty years unionizing workers across America. In the late 19th and early 20th centuries, Irish immigrants in America began to make significant progress through work. But the sheer numbers, their unity of purpose and political prowess, along with their commitment to voting in elections, meant they contributed hugely to their adopted country. In major cities like New York, Boston, and Chicago labor unions became inundated with Irish workers who ensured good-paying jobs for their colleagues. Irish organizations sprang up and gave immigrants a sense of belonging.

New York was the seaport through which 75% of the famine Irish passed, and by 1860 a quarter of New York City's population was Irish. Within a few decades, the Irish held firm control over Tammany Hall, the Democratic Party-political machine controlling New York politics. The power of their work ethic was symbolized by the first Irish descendant to rise from the tenements of the Lower East side to become governor of New York in the 1920s. A new Irish-American identity, confident, proud, and irrepressible, emerged and pointed to the results of hard work by so many who stepped off boats with nothing. I suggest that it is not possible to understand work and society in Ireland without this American perspective.

I have chosen to introduce a study of work and society in Ireland through this historic lens for other reasons too. Firstly, I want to show how work and society can be better understood through a complex matrix of factors and perspectives; history is often neglected here. Secondly, today we are aware of the resentments among the host nation toward immigrants, often resulting from competition for scares resources. This is balanced by the impact on the country losing its citizens; leading to a multi-dimensional understanding of how work, or its absence, impacts on a society. Thirdly, we can see that work has evolved over time. Fourthly, employers have always sought flexible workers but we also know that there could not have been more flexibility among immigrant workers in America. Fifthly, work is in a dialectic relationship with its broader social and cultural context; it might even seem that context is everything. A critical work theory is grounded in such multi-dimensional perspectives as culture, language, economics, religion, and history.

Work and Society in 1950s Ireland

The 1950s in Ireland were bleak. Books and movies were banned under oppressive censorship laws. Tuberculosis (TB) and polio were widespread; pandemics. Workers on farms declined from 300,000 in 1911 to 100, 000 by 1936, and declined again according to the Census of 1951 to 66,000. Lee states that it is difficult to find a government intervention to "prevent the continuing dispersal of families ravaged by the cancer of emigration" (Lee, 1989, p. 159). The *Report of the Commission on Emigration and other Population Problems* (Government of Ireland, 1955) admitted that the "ready outlet of emigration has provided the remaining population with a reasonably satisfying standard of living and this has been responsible for an acquiescence in conditions of under-development…." (p. 139). In the 1950s, from a population of about 3 million, a total of 500,000 emigrated. In 1939 unemployment was 16%; by 1945 it had dropped to 10% due to the emigration of 100,000. Just as the European Economic Community (EEC), now the European Union (EU), was formed in 1957 as a response to the widespread desire not to have another war in Europe, it could be argued that the motivation for Ireland's membership of the EEC (in 1972) included a widespread desire to avoid the national debilitating scourge of emigration. Emigration in search of work provided an outlet, at least for those who were successful abroad, that was beyond the control and influence of a dark conservative inward-looking Ireland. Working abroad was a counter weight, a protest against the dull, blind, bland, closed, conservative, sexually ignorant, and misogynistic place restricted by the Catholic Church - the strict enforcer in a cruel land. The cruel, degrading, bordering on slavery, work of the Irish picking potatoes in Scotland continued. Irish workers built the American catholic church giving one the distinct impression that the only experience Ireland had as a colonial power was as a powerful promoter of catholic church power and values throughout the English-speaking world.

In contrast, at home, the Catholic church, with close links to Rome, was a powerful player in the construction of Ireland as it existed in the 1950s and before it. Pope Leo XIII (1891) in *Rerum Novarum*, (subtitled *On the Conditions of Work*) and subsequently Pius XI (1931), in the encyclical *Quadragesimo Anno (QA)*, formed a complex web of ideas asserting the importance of private property and the critique of elements of current versions of liberalism. On the other hand, these teachings were stridently opposed to socialism and fed a constant reaction in Ireland against the illusion that communism and/or socialism were real enemies of modernizing Ireland. Above all, and of great importance for work, these teachings were a powerful affirmation of the dominance of men as the workers earning wages within the family. Pius XI reaffirmed traditional gender roles and used the idea of a family wage for fathers to achieve this:

> That the rest of the family should also contribute to the common support, according to the capacity of each, is certainly right, as can be observed especially in the families of farmers, but also in the families of many craftsmen and small shopkeepers.... Mothers, concentrating on household duties, should work primarily in the home or in its immediate vicinity. It is an intolerable abuse, and to be abolished at all cost, for mothers on account of the father's low wage to be forced to engage in gainful occupations outside the home to the neglect of their proper cares and duties, especially the training of children. Every effort must therefore be made that fathers of families receive a wage large enough to meet ordinary family needs adequately. (*QA*, 71)

This is only one example of how the church has been in so many instances on the wrong side of the imperative to modernize Ireland. Censorship laws of the state were confirmed by the practices of the church. The bar on married women working was confirmed in Leo's encyclical and helped bolster the arguments of the Irish government that kept a marriage bar and other anti-woman laws on the statute books until The Employment of Married Women Act, 1973 (Foley, 2022) ended the practice. Many other examples could be found (women could not sit on jury trials) but this one directly impacts on work.

A New Era of Work and Society: The 1960s

A new younger generation emerged in the 1960s who experienced a cultural shift exemplified by popular music and literature (O'Brien, 1960), and a sexual revolution; or at least the beginnings of one. The government prioritized work-related policies. The first economic development plan was introduced; and other initiatives including: the first OECD report on education (Government of Ireland, 1965); free secondary school education; free school transport; and new third level colleges (National Institutes of Higher Education called NIHE and Regional Technical Colleges known as RTCs).

The first joint OECD/Irish Government research, *Investment in Education* (Government of Ireland, 1965) found universities were underfunded with low levels of participation. Universities suffered from "benign neglect" (Walsh, et al., 2014, p. 8) and were attended by only 3.4% of the population aged 20-24; prioritizing the children of professionals (Government of Ireland, 1965, p. 172). The report made sweeping recommendations about the future of education. The government introduced free secondary school education and raised the school leaving age to 15 in 1972. In turn, it produced a demand for the expansion of higher education (HE); the beginning of a move toward mass HE. The first RTCs were opened in 1970 followed by 7 more before 1974. These are now either Technological Universities or being upgraded.

The *First Programme for Economic Expansion 1959-1963*, (Government of Ireland, 1958) transformed the economy. Industrial output increased by almost one-quarter, unemployment fell by one-third, and emigration declined sharply. This planned progress led to a period of prosperity and higher expectations redefining work and forming a bridge between an emigration-oriented country and a more open economy with migration eventually becoming more like an option than a compulsion. This synopsis is precisely that. The reality hides nuances, problems, disagreements, and indeed failures. But in this decade work in Ireland was redefined. This story is bound up with educational changes in which HE has contributed to the success. HE became more tightly integrated into state planning and more orientated to producing highly skilled graduates to work in a new economy.

This orientation to work is now deeply embedded in Irish society and public policy. It is also closely linked with the belief that markets will bring growth, social cohesion, and equality. This has a strong international dimension, based on considerable foreign investments that survived a civil war in Northern Ireland (1969 to 1998) and built on the rapid transformation of education and society, supported by international bodies, especially the OECD and the EU.

Similarly, Irish educational policy is tightly bound to the EU's conception of lifelong learning and the enhancement of human capital in a knowledge-based economy (European Commission, 2000). The European Union adopted lifelong learning in the early 1990s, amid the break-up of the Soviet bloc and the rise of neoliberal globalization. It is difficult to overstate the influence these international bodies have had, and in particular, the policy adopted toward lifelong learning. In this sense, Ireland is an interesting case study of a small, peripheral, open, and globalized economy that is part of a much larger project thinking about the role of education in relation to work and society envisaged by the EU and the OECD.

In these years of transition between the 1960s and the infamous Celtic Tiger the adoption of the lifelong learning agenda is a noteworthy development (Fleming, 2021). An EU wide adoption of a policy of cultural change was required and this involved citizens and workers learning not only to understand the new world emerging in the new century (as 2000 approached) but also understanding and adapting to the new social and work environments. Only a learning society, only workers who learn could be seen as having the abilities to thrive in the future.

Work in Celtic Tiger Ireland (1995-2007)

But Ireland still had a long way to go in the year 2000. Only Mexico (23%) and Turkey (21%) had more young people than Ireland (16%). Sometimes it was the countries doing better, so to speak, that provided meaningful statistics. In the working population (15-64 years) Germany, Canada, Austria, and Japan had more people of working age with upper-secondary schooling. More significantly, only Turkey, Portugal, Mexico, Greece, and Italy had fewer secondary school completions among the working population. Only Korea and New Zealand had more pupils for each teacher than Ireland. Comparative figures, or scales of where Ireland was located relative to other countries and the OECD averages were revealing in a world where competition for investments was strong. Important work remained to be done, apart from the adoption of a lifelong learning policy mantra.

The idea was widely believed that when everybody is working, and the benefits are distributed by government tax policies a fair society will be created and sustained. The idea that everybody benefitted from the Celtic Tiger is a myth. After generations of looking forward to full employment, its arrival proved disappointing. Work was not sufficient to cure all ills. Inequalities of the social class continued, and housing, education, and health compared poorly in comparison with other developed countries, e.g., in the EU and OECD. The accumulation of wealth by a few was a major scandal showing how work is not necessarily the source of more equality, or better housing, or better health care, or any other measure of equality. Ireland was the second most unequal society in the EU. With 15.3% living in poverty, only the US, among Western countries was worse with 15.8% in poverty (Paul Cullen, 2002).

The US economy grew during the 1990s particularly in computers and health-related technologies. America needed to access new markets in the EU. In Ireland, a tax system that allowed foreign companies to process unprecedented profits, avail of lower labor costs, and benefit from tax shelters lay behind Ireland's work expansion. The Irish economy grew at an average annual rate of 9.4% between 1995 and 2000. O'Hearn (2003) points out that between 1990 and 1999 the output of workers in American companies in Ireland grew by 375%; the number of workers grew by only 73%. Almost 50% of Ireland's GDP was due to chemical, computer, and electronic engineering firms. In the Celtic Tiger years, the number of people at work increased dramatically. Ireland became an off-shore account for hiding profits and paying low taxes. Allen (2003, p. 71) asserts that government policy turned "...the whole island into an Atlantic tax haven". Even Habermas who broadly supports the EU has explained that;

> The more policy matters are settled through intra-state negotiations, and the more important these matters are, the more political decisions are withdrawn from arenas of democratic formation and will formation. (Habermas, 1999, p. 49).

O'Hearn (2003, p. 41) also reminds us that in the 1990s;

> ...unemployment rates still exceeded fifteen percent and possibly approached twenty percent in 1994. Yet, by 2000, the number of jobs in the southern Irish economy had risen by nearly half compared with 1990, with the total employment rising by more than half a million during the decade. As a result, official unemployment rates fell to around four percent at the end of the decade.

Knowing that each job in a foreign direct investment (FDI) company created a number of jobs, especially in the service sector, O'Hearn goes on to explore how manufacturing industries accounted for economic growth (increased GDP) but services accounted for the numbers at work. By 1999 two out of three jobs were in services; service jobs paid lower wages. Other structural issues such as part-time work and fixed-term contracts were widespread. The policies on work in Ireland in those years involved the transferring of the burden of taxation from companies (who paid low taxes in Ireland) to workers (who paid a disproportionately high amount of government tax income). Tax on workers' pay replaced tax on company profits. From 1995 to 2000, 44% of state revenue came from taxing workers' income. O'Hearn (2003, p. 49) concludes: "It is significant that corporate taxes were not the major source of rising state revenues, despite the fact that trading profits of companies tripled between 1995 and 2000.

Economic growth was certainly achieved but inequality continued. It seems that irrespective of how the economy flourished, widespread inequality remained. Any critical exploration of work in Ireland has to explain this phenomenon. During the boom economic growth led to increases in profits, without a corresponding rise in wages for work. This increased class divisions (O'Hearn, 2003). The proportion of workers on low wages was "twice the EU average" (O'Hearn, 2003, p. 47); progressively getting worse through the Tiger years. The UN declared that at the end of the 1990s, the poverty rate according to the UN Human Development Report was the highest in the EU (O'Hearn, 2003, p. 48); the government providing tax breaks for the wealthy rather than increasing welfare and public services for the poor. The breakdown of the social housing program in those years had a knock-on effect on the current housing crisis; housing workers on low wages was not a national priority. On many indicators, Ireland was a poorly served country in terms of expenditure per capita on the number of hospital beds, affordable housing, *per capita* funding of primary education, and health. The greatest indicator that something was wrong concerned corporate taxes. Despite trading profits trebling between 1995 and 2000; huge profits were not a major source of rising state revenue.

What is the most critical comment that can be made? The capital was increasingly being removed from democratic decision-making. Those who did the work and paid the taxes received minimal and inadequate recompense from their tax contribution to the state. One can argue that work was a means for government to redistribute wealth, upward. The political mantras or memes, as they might be called now, were not true: a rising tide raises all boats; trickledown economics; and encouraging supply-side economics.

A number of factors led to this expansion and the inevitable, sudden collapse. Houses were built at a pace and in locations where they were not needed. The building industry borrowed cheaply from banks who flouted common sense (and borrowing regulations?) to attract these borrowers. Home buyers borrowed too; increasing debt and fueling salary increases to keep the vicious circle moving. Low levels of monitoring by the Central Bank, a delighted government basking in the increased revenue from taxes based on increasing prices, lax planning laws, citizens seeking to get rich by also borrowing to get on the fashionable "housing ladder" and widespread buying of second homes either at home or abroad. House prices rose, workers demanded higher salaries, and a cycle of greed fed on its own energy. Work in Ireland was the way for citizens to get rich; quickly.

Encouraged by the economic ideas of Ronald Regan (US President from 1979-1980) and Margaret Thatcher (UK Prime Minister from 1979-1990) economies around the world based their work policies on a set of ideas, widely known as neoliberalism. Only by interrogating this form of capitalism can we understand fully the nature of work in any society. Work in Ireland, economic expansion and development progressed until the Celtic Tiger economy of the mid-1990s to 2007.

Beyond the fall of the Celtic Tiger, and the rise again (2008-)

These figures highlight the successful economy and experience of work. There are glitches and problems too that will be returned to later. According to the 2022 Census (CSO, 2024) the number of people in Ireland aged 15 and over was 4.1 million. This increased from 2.5 million in 1986. The total population in 2024 is 5.2 million. In the census of 2016 (Central Statistics Office (CSO), 2017) there were 195,000 people not working (8% percent unemployment), rising to almost 400,000 in 2011. This fell to 176,000 in 2022 (4.3% unemployment). In 2016 about 43% of the workforce worked, today 56% work. The participation rates for women at work in the over-15 age cohort rose from 30% in 1981 to 56% in 2006. In 2022 there were 2.3 million people in work, up from 1.1 million people in 1986. These current levels of work and unemployment are impressive. One would think that there is the possibility that this would make a significant change to many long-term social problems.

In 1986 there were less than 200,000 retired persons and in 2022 that has increased to just over 540,000. Those on disability and unable to work increased in that period from 81,000 to just over 158,000. The increase in the number of retired workers makes demands on public expenditure (pensions and health care) but these groups also contribute significantly to child care, allowing parents to work. Unpaid work by family members in the family is a powerful economic force. The impact of rising population numbers and numbers working has complex consequences.

The kinds of work available have changed too. With the attraction of pharmaceutical and computer manufacturing, software, medical instruments, and financial services the nature of work has been transformed in Ireland. These global industries represent many of the big names in these fields. Today, more than 75,000 people are directly employed by over 200 pharmaceutical and medical device manufacturing companies across 213 sites. Many thousands more are employed indirectly and downstream in these and other foreign companies.

Agricultural work, the main sector continues to decline, from 91,000 in 2011 to 82,000 in 2022. However, food production, not surprisingly has expanded. In the same period 2011 to 2022 the number working in manufacturing increased from 183,000 to 242,000; in construction from 87,000 to 134,000; information technology and communications from 69,000 to 125,000; professional and scientific from 92,000 to 158,000; work in education grew from 167,000 to 215,000 and in industry (where the sector was not identified) increased from 101,000 to 150,000. Women now account for 47% of the workforce; mainly concentrated in health, social care, and education; and less so in agriculture, fishing, and transport. Recent (Bolton, 2024) research reveals that the current work week does not suit 70% of Irish professionals and the conventional 40-hour work week is falling out of favor. Productivity is a concern for employers and 25% of employers indicate that they would extend the work week to solve productivity. If this were to happen the same research shows that 85% of employees would leave their current job if this was to happen. There is widespread support for a four-day week with 53% of professionals saying a four-day week model could improve productivity. Workers want more flexibility.

The growth of part-time staff (job-sharing, limited duration contracts) points to vulnerabilities in these sectors, brought about by the restructuring of work. Any sudden changes in the markets for these industries have a disproportionate impact on work in Ireland. But government agencies have bet heavily on these sectors, exploiting easy access to EU and US markets. Those who do emigrate now are better qualified and prepared for work abroad. The impact of automation is similar to that of the US.

Government policies prioritize tax breaks for foreign investments, despite objections from the OECD. High levels of educational achievement form a capital investment that did not have to be made by the incoming industry. Favorable tax breaks, light touch regulation, and easy access to EU markets from an English-speaking base all played a role in the current transformation of work following the recession. When the UK left the EU in 2020 (following a referendum in 2016), the ability to compete for this foreign investment was enhanced and the economy has continued to flourish.

The COVID-19 pandemic (started in 2022) has changed work in ways we are not yet able to assess. But some trends are emerging. Responses by the government to COVID required that as many people as possible would work from home. This was a welcome and long-sought change, for some. For others, it was an imposition on the living space within the family home. Modest tax deductions were a token gesture for those who worked from home. But it was also a structural change in work. It reduced travel time and impacted the road network that seemed less crowded. Now 32% of workers work from home (CSO, 2024). About 750,000 work at least some part of the week at home. Secretarial, occupations with leisure and travel-related work as well as sales occupations all had between 36% and 39% working part-time. The opposite is true of emergency services, science, engineering, and technology all had between 92-94% working full time.

This chapter underlines the key role of education (informed by the public policy adoption of lifelong learning as its informing idea) in defining and redefining work in Ireland. According to CSO (2024), in 1986 there were 245,000 students in Ireland. Today, with huge implications for work and especially the kind of work for which young people are qualified, that number is now 460,000. In this study, education is presented as one of the key ingredients in understanding work in Ireland. The 2016 (CSO, 2017) census shows that the number who left school at or under 15 years was 388,000 and this number dropped to 269,000 in 2022 (CSO, 2023) from a much larger population. The most dramatic change occurred in the numbers who continued their education beyond the age of 25. In 2011 this was 190,000 but by 2022 this number increased to 374,000. These numbers are impressive and indicate a young workforce on the move utilizing education to access work.

The number of adults with only primary school education dropped from 414,000 to 251,000 in the period between 2016 and 2022. Those with honors degrees and professional diplomas increased among the working population from 271,000 to 450,000, in the period from 2016 to 2022. Across the HE system, there has been an increase in the numbers who have graduated and these impressive but gradual changes have allowed a managed economy to attract employers from abroad who increasingly offer work requiring higher-level skills. It is not a long time since literacy levels in the general population were stubbornly high. The OECD *Adult Skills Survey* shows that in the 1990s, 17.9% or about 1 in 6, Irish adults were at or below level 1 on a five-level literacy scale. Numeracy levels also remained low (Morgan, Hickey, Kelleghan, Cronin, & Miller, 1997; OECD, 1995).

Emigration is not now a relentless drain on young people. Though not eliminated, most of those leaving now are better qualified, and in a position to work abroad (and possibly return later?). Many leave to take advantage of better work opportunities and gain experience. In the 12 months to April 2023, 64,000 emigrated; of these, only 30,500 were Irish citizens. Remarkably, 29,000 Irish citizens returned in the same period. Immigration is indeed a significant demographic change with 141,000 arriving in 2023. That was the second successive twelve-month period in which over 100, 000 new immigrants arrived. In the 2023 figures, the numbers who were non-UK, non-EU, and non-Irish accounted for about 81,000, of which approximately 42,000 were Ukrainian.

As a general contextualizing of these figures: Ireland has a current total population of 5.2 million; there were 55,000 births and 35,000 deaths in 2023. The pressure on an economy to provide work is significant and the ability of the economy to absorb these numbers is challenging and there are resulting pressure points. The health system is strained, but let us not blame immigrants. The total population over 65 years of age has risen since 2017 by 153,000 to 806,000. But rising immigration, including refugees from a range of countries, allied with a general increase in population, have placed affordable housing, homelessness, child care, and child poverty (Cullen, 2002) among the continuing problems remaining to be solved with resources mostly provided by those who work. Public policy has been dramatically unsuccessful in all these areas. Far-right influencers are coming to the fore; there is an increase in street protests and violence. Social unrest can be an unpredictable source of instability also impacting work.

The Neoliberalism Story

The Celtic Tiger era (1995-2007) was followed by the dramatic collapse in 2008 that had catastrophic consequences for the national debt and workers' wages – both their income and tax deductions. But before we look at work or even the beginnings of a critical work theory, we examine the neoliberal model of economic activity adopted in Ireland. It is the contemporary iteration of liberalism that informed the actions of Travelyan during the famine in the 1840s. Neoliberalism, the dominant ideology in Ireland and the EU, is, according to Harvey (2005, p. 2):

> A theory of political economic practices that proposes that human wellbeing can best be advanced by liberating individual entrepreneurial freedoms and skills within an institutional framework characterized by strong private property rights, free markets and free trade.

In this system, the state is restructured to reflect the interests of businesses and drive privatization. The state is encouraged by the economy to dismantle the welfare system and support the growth and reach of the market and its priorities. Government cutting of expenditure is part of this process of undermining the welfare state, as is the perennial promise by governments to reduce taxes. Economies are driven by an unshakable and fiercely held belief in the free market. This belief, among others, is held to be common sense, self-evident, and beyond questioning, by the neoliberal economic class. The core belief is that the market and not politics solve all problems. Neoliberalism is not just an economic policy designed to cut government spending, it is also a political and philosophical ideology that affects every dimension of social life (Giroux, 2004). Citizens are defined as consumers, customers, clients, and workers. The market is sovereign. Political sovereignty is reduced. Neoliberalism does not aim to increase the well-being of everybody and increases social inequality to drive a more competitive society and economy.

The Irish government is not alone in uncritically accepting a neoliberal ideology or set of guiding ideas that were adopted without great intellectual or public debate but with the active support of most economists; and cheerleaders for these ideas and values. Linked to the idea that the market will be the organizing principle for the delivery of state services is the equally deeply held view of the neoliberal establishment that the government must be made small. Big government is bad. This oversimplifies what the markets (economy) have succeeded in doing. It has not led to a retreat by the state and a loss of importance but rather an increase in importance "of the state in a different form, operating in conformity with market rules" (O'Riain, 2014, p. 24). By reducing government regulation, the economy is allowed to get on with it. As McChesney (1999, p. 7) explains;

> neoliberalism is a political economic paradigm that refers to the policies and processes whereby a small number of private interests are permitted to control as much as possible of social life in order to maximize their personal profits.

Neoliberal initiatives encourage private enterprise; consumer choice; reward personal responsibility; encourage entrepreneurial initiatives; and hold the view that everyone has equal opportunities - if only they are willing to work hard. Central to this thesis is the belief that the market should be the guiding force for all political, social, and economic decisions of a nation-state. Profit-making (Giroux, 2004) and the exchange of capital take precedence over social justice, the development of socially-responsible citizens, and the building of democratic communities (Alfred, 2016).

But the neoliberal position is riddled with contradictions, most obviously when the economy gets into trouble, then the state must bail out the economy. In reality, the state in a capitalist system has become increasingly "both the embodiment and the representative of capital" (Coleman, 2003, p. 178). The economy is privileged over the civic purposes of the state (O'Riain, 2014). The belief that the government must be kept out of the economy because it is incompetent, is a contradiction. The belief that power resides in the markets needs careful interrogation. The market will not sort everything. As part of the process of keeping 'big' government small, the pressure from the economy demands a range of measures that include; privatization, lower taxes on wealth and salaries, and cuts in public spending (incl. health, education, and social welfare). The pressure to control workers' wages under the guise of being competitive is also part of the list of priorities that the economy tries very hard to impose on government policy.

Ireland has not adopted a textbook version of neoliberalism but one adapted to the social and political environment of Ireland. The history of unions, and the concerns of citizens for their social priorities, have led to the current iteration of neoliberalism in Ireland. Government policies on workers' wages, labor policy, industrial development, and pay-related welfare benefits, all mark Ireland's unique adaptation of liberal economics (O'Riain, 2014). Ireland's version of neoliberalism includes light touch regulation of financial and commercial institutions, for example, this model of neoliberalism is "at the root of Ireland's social failure of income equality, high poverty rates and weak structures of social protection" (O'Riain, 2014, p. 9). Neoliberalism is a capitalist class project that has increased inequalities and consolidated elite power (Sayer, 2015). O'Riain identifies the weakness in Irish neoliberalism as cronyism between business and government, and the absence of a vibrant public sphere informing democracy. It is likely, he concludes, that small open economies, with post-colonial experience, may be particularly vulnerable in this regard (O'Riain, 2014).

In this model, economic growth, based on competitiveness and flexibility, is expected to modernize society and bring about equality. The Irish state has defined the pursuit of equality in remarkably narrow terms. The structural weaknesses in the world of work and the economy in general are rooted in neoliberalism. Social failures in housing, education, and public health cast a shadow on the social agenda of the nation. Governments have attempted to privatize widely, and have had some successes but the inequalities, inefficiencies and structural flaws have not brought the benefits of almost full employment to enough people, i.e., housing. We will see how this works in the coming years as tensions play out and are exploited by far-right elements in the community. In this configuration, the state may appear to remain aloof from intervening in the markets. Yet, when the economy and work collapsed in 2008, there was widespread expectation that the state would intervene; which it did. But the state continues even in those moments to act to the advantage of enterprise, rather than workers, the citizen, and other civic purposes.

The economic collapse led to the imposition of a decade of austerity as the state attempted to rescue the banks, and insist that workers pay for the mishandling of the economy. The rules of the neoliberal game ensure that if conflicts arise between collective well-being and saving feral banks, the banks are saved (McCabe 2011; Sayer, 2015). The social good is secondary to the economic good; vociferously asserted by banks (McCabe, 2011). Austerity requires that we do more with less and manage scarce resources as a result of deep cuts in public expenditure. It seems that irrespective of how workers re-negotiate wages they are, through the tax system, involved in a transfer of wealth from the lower and middle classes to the classes above them.

The Irish government's bailout program for the banks required €67.56 billion funded from abroad. Increased flows of foreign direct investment in the following decade rewarded the state for conforming to the austerity imposed by the IMF. The economy and work had already been transformed and bore a heavy burden. Foreign direct investment in Ireland increased by €109bn to €1,208bn in 2021. But for a wide range of reasons the job market, and the economy recovered, but huge debts are carried into the long-term future as a lean on the earnings of workers. Austerity, the consequence of economic crises, is an opportunity to further the neoliberal project of increasing inequality under the guise of freeing lower socio-economic groups from their social welfare supported unwillingness to work. Their unemployment is seen as both their own fault and an inevitable of a soft social welfare supported life.

Allen states clearly that the EU in its transition to a single market and currency, also adopted neoliberal policies (Allen, 2003). Complicated bureaucratic directives, Allen states, hide the extent to which the EU has been "increasingly removing decision making from democratic pressures" (p. 65). In addition, the elaborate deregulation of most of the economy, with the exception of work shows that only workers "wages are controlled" (Allen, 2003, p. 67). He concludes that this contributes to a "transfer of wealth upward" (p. 67). Allen provides the example of how tax cuts benefit the wealthy and how the banks, who pay corporation tax, have seen their tax contribution fall as a percentage of their increasing profits. They pay less tax, as a proportion of their profits, than workers! (Allen, 2003, p. 69). In addition, following the collapse of the Celtic Tiger (the collapse more correctly of the poorly regulated banks) the taxpayers of Ireland – a euphemism for workers – were burdened through their payment of taxes to service the €67 billion extra borrowings by the government to pay off IMF, EU Central Bank rescue package, known locally as a 2010 bailout. There was also the burden of cutbacks, known as austerity as the government was required, by these external forces, to reduce its expenditure (while increasing income!) and reduce the wages of workers. The rise and fall of the Celtic Tiger highlight the fragile nature of neoliberal capitalism as well as the cyclical nature of the cycles of periods of boom and bust, mostly paid for by workers. In a world where globalization complicates these relationships the looser is likely to be democracy. The forces of capital are irresistible, it seems.

According to Stanley Aronowitz (2003, p. 21) neo-liberalism has also become the prevailing logic in the United States;

> The neo-liberal economic doctrine proclaiming the superiority of free markets over public ownership, or even public regulation of private economic activities, has become the conventional wisdom, not only among conservatives but among the progressives.

As a result, inequalities have increased and the real income of those in the top 1% in Ireland rose from €90,000 in 1975, to €450,000 in 2007 (Mercille & Murphy, 2015, p. 3), rising to €190,000 in 2023. According to Cullen (2002) Ireland has the highest level of poverty among developed countries apart from the US. Gilmore (2024) continues this point; "while the number at-risk-of-poverty has decreased, a significant portion of the population continues to experience low living standards and high levels of social insecurity" (p. 4).

The most recent figures show that nearly half (45.6%) of the individuals in lone-parent families experience enforced deprivation. Among those out of work due to longstanding health problems, 44.7% experienced enforced deprivation, as do 37.8% of unemployed workers. The ongoing housing crisis is a major problem, even for those who work, and 36.5% of those in rented or rent-free accommodation experience enforced deprivation. The housing crisis has led to an alarming increase in the number of homeless children accessing state-run emergency accommodation. This has increased nearly 6-fold in ten years—from 749 in July 2014, to 4,206 in April 2024. Gilmore (2024, p. 4) concludes that;

> the extremely high market inequality; the fluctuations and recent increase in deprivation rates; the high levels of deprivation experienced by lone-parents, those out of work, and renters; the high level of child homelessness; and the dependence of large numbers on stop-start emergency interventions to support incomes – demonstrate the profound income insecurity faced by many in Irish society.

It seems that work and the promise of work have not delivered for everybody.

The OECD's Programme for International Student Assessment (known as the PISA project) assesses the knowledge and skills of 15-year-old students in mathematics, reading, and science. Irish students are significantly above the OECD average in all three domains. Ireland has moved from eighth place to second place among OECD (2022) countries. Irish students remain in secondary education longer than their counterparts in other developed countries, with 92% of students in Ireland completing secondary school, surpassing the average completion rate of 88.9% for all OECD countries. School completion rates among the 20–24-year-old cohort in the population, are relatively high by EU standards; at 95% compared to the EU average of 85%. Of all 20-year-olds in Ireland, 59% are enrolled in some form of tertiary education. This is the third highest level of tertiary enrolment in the EU; significantly surpassing the EU average of 44%. However, with an enrolment of only 12.3% in adult education among the 25-to-64-year age group, Ireland falls just below the EU average of 12.7%. The record of Ireland addressing inequalities is limited and at best patchy. The advantage that 'advantaged' school students have over disadvantaged schools through Delivering Equality of Opportunity In Schools program (DEIS) remains stubbornly constant; despite some modest successes.

Neoliberalism, however, supports less government involvement in the lives of individuals. Now the knowledge economy requires significant investment in human resource development to meet labor needs. Workers need to be educated, especially as the economy is not going to invest in education and training. One solution, of course, was for the economic sector to influence governments to tailor existing educational systems to fit with the imperatives of the market. Instead of supporting a broad-based educational system, the OECD for instance, and other neoliberal policy development agencies promoted the development of leaner, more focused, and more accountable educational systems that met the specific, and oftentimes, shifting needs of work. As Joel Spring (1998) observes;

> OECD experts want knowledge to be measured according to its contribution to economic growth. In contrast, Confucius and Plato were interested in determining the ability of individuals to create moral and just societies. (p.168).

This is the core of the tension for society in Ireland - whether it wants to allow the economy or society to dictate national, including education and learning agendas. To frame this with different concepts we could ask: Whether the concept of nation-building only involves building an economy, or is there also a project that involves building a society? An economy has a sharp focus on profits. A society, at least according to the foundational documents of the State, involves, fairness, equality, and cherishing all the children of the nation equally:

> The Republic guarantees religious and civil liberty, equal rights, and equal opportunities of all its citizens, and declares its resolve to pursue the happiness and prosperity of the whole nation and of all its parts, cherishing all the children of the nation equally,... (Easter Proclamation, 1916)

Instead, today the economy has the last word. This is hugely problematic. In every age education finds itself navigating different social and political landscapes and today in Europe the neoliberal iteration of capitalism, and its close relative austerity, provide the dominant context. Education is caught between long-standing visions of learning as emancipatory and a determined drive by governments to prioritize learning and education for economic development.

Lifelong Learning: Toward a Critical Work Theory

Increased pressure is placed on the educational system to be more work-friendly and produce graduates who are better prepared for work (Finnegan & O'Neill, 2016). In addition, the knowledge economy demands higher learning. The preoccupations with the economy and with work and with defining citizens as workers, lead to misreading the importance of education, and the ways in which students perceive the benefits of education. Considerable effort has gone into building an economy, huge resources, imagination, and work have been brought to bear on this issue, and rightly so. But one is entitled to wonder what may have been the outcome if similar energy resources and imagination had been expended on nation-building, including support for learning for citizenship and community engagements (Finnegan & Fleming, 2023). We are not only an economy, but also a society and a nation.

One of the most intriguing questions in this study is how Irish education policy can be specifically aligned with lifelong learning policy, which is too often seen as narrow and economistic but has the potential to respond to the learning needs of active citizens. This latter dimension has been neglected (Fleming, 2021). In addition to supporting the development of a formal educational system more focused on the economy (and far less focused on personal, social, cultural, or aesthetic development), the OECD has also begun to advocate expanding non-formal structures for recurring and continuing education. As part of this effort, the learning society has been promoted, as has lifelong learning, in order to find ways of addressing the changing labor market needs beyond what could be provided by traditional educational structures.

In Ireland the economic sector relies heavily on government to educate and train the workforce at all levels including HE and SOLAS. SOLAS is the agency responsible for further education and training in Ireland. Its mandate is to support labor markets and society with better educated adults. As long as the workers are educated for work the demand for cut backs in education/training budget is muted. With one of the lowest levels of financial investment by the economic sector in training of any of the OECD countries, the Irish economy has been particularly successful in maximizing government expenditure (grant aid for business) and minimizing the take from corporations (low tax on corporations).

In the process of colonizing the social system for its own economic agenda neoliberalism attempts, and partly succeeds, in destroying all the "public spheres necessary for the defense of a genuine democracy" (Giroux, 2004). In this situation, public concerns collapse into private considerations. The government becomes the enemy of freedom and does not see itself as the guardian of the public interest. This is the context for lifelong learning. But as the neoliberal government accepts less and less responsibility or obligation concerning the poor;

> As the laws of the market take precedence over the laws of the state as guardians of the public good, the government increasingly offers little help in mediating the interface between the advance of capital and its rapacious commercial interests. (Giroux, 2004)

In addition, the government does not support the discursive conditions vital for critical citizenship and a democratic public life. Instead, it governs by sound bite, photo- opportunity, public relations, and restricts the activities of trades unions.

In this environment education is tasked with producing resources for the workplace and through a leaner system of education it is required to meet the needs of the economy for skilled workers. It also attempts to re-focus the educational curriculum to be more business friendly and produce graduates who are more work-ready. In a system of education driven by economic and political agendas that are removed from the interest in creating a society (as distinct from an economy), there is a rejection of critical thought and social responsibility that is supported by what Bauman (2006) calls "ethical tranquillization" (p. 86). Under such situations, to cite C Wright Mills (2008), we are witnessing the breakdown of democracy, the disappearance of critical intellectuals, and "the collapse of those public spheres which offer a sense of critical agency and social imagination" (p. 200). Missing from neoliberal market societies are those public spheres (in some education situations and classrooms) where people can develop civic imagination. Many institutions of higher education are now committed to economic goals, such as preparing students for work. The idea that going to college is not just about a job, a career, or maximizing one's salary is not new, but appears to be under threat in new ways in this era of neoliberalism. Today neoliberalism attempts to subordinate education to the economy. Having its roots in addressing social inequality HE is now clearly asked to be subordinate to the markets and the emerged "neoliberal knowledge regime" (Holmwood, 2014, p. 62). In the EU, by creating a Bologna Process, now rebranded as the European Higher Education Area (EHEA), a European-wide university system is brought into being so that degrees and qualifications are made, along with European culture, more appealing for other (non-EU) countries (Holford, 2014).

These changes are not simply to achieve integration across Europe but so that global HE would be transformed in the image of the European model. The global market in higher education has arrived. The EHEA is "aimed mainly at promoting higher education as an export business" (Holford & Milana, 2014, p. 7). The often quoted but much-ignored social dimension of both HE and lifelong learning (EC, 2000) falls short of the declared policy ambition and the EU practice never matched the rhetoric (Holford & Milana, 2014).

The state prefers to uncouple the political decision–making processes from the political public arenas, that have been hollowed out and whose infrastructure is crumbling. This colonialization of societies, which disintegrates from within and takes up right–wing populist positions against each other, will not change as long as no political power can be found with the courage to take up the cause of achieving the political aim of creating a democracy. Instead, neoliberalism insists on the rationality of leaving market mechanisms to their own devices (Fœssel & Habermas, 2015).

This chapter began by reflecting on the workers who built the Rockefeller Centre in New York. To move forward toward a critical work theory, it is important to study how workers experience their work. Studies such as Lilian Rubin's (1976) *Worlds of Pain* and Richard Sennett and Jonathan Cobb's (1972) *The Hidden Injuries of Class* bring the experiences of working-class workers and their families to the attention of social theory and the general population as they redefined the class divisions and conflicts in society. Sennett in particular outlines the corrosion of character (Sennett, 1998) resulting from work in what he terms the new capitalism. These authors study the corrosive impact on the self-worth of workers in the working- class (blue collar) as workers compare and measure their self-worth against the work and lives of other more privileged people and classes in society: "They are afraid that what they have to give for love, however, depends on their standing in the larger world" (Sennett, & Cobb, 1973, p. 249). They conclude, that to see them as having been "bought off" by the system misses the point and will fail to understand "the intensity of pent-up feelings that pour out when working people do challenge higher authority" (p. 251). They warn against "inferring a man's dignity from his social standing" (p. 251). In the end, because the system seems impervious to change and the value of workers' contributions is diminished in society, the injuries are hidden but no less real. This inflexibility of capitalism to deliver equality of respect across the social classes is a new form of oppression (Sennett, 2000).

Conclusion

When one recalls the 1932 photograph of the workers eating lunch atop Rockefeller Centre in New York, various memories come to mind. The awful and constant drain on the population in search of work abroad. We capture the story of these 150 years from famine to independence; to EU membership; and survival through economic catastrophe; and COVID; one is left to look in awe at the achievements, the successes, including the internationally brokered Northern Ireland peace process concluding nearly 30 years of civil conflict (1969-1998). So much has been achieved, at a cost. So much has to be achieved, but one must only hope that the learning gleaned will motivate the future without workers disproportionally paying the price. Social progress includes economic progress. Work is a means to an end, surely, and the benefits of this progress are worth sharing widely.

REFERENCES

Alfred, M. (2016) Creating space for social justice education in an era of global and neoliberal capitalism: An imperative for adult education, *Dialogues in Social Justice: An Adult Education Journal, 1*(1), 31-34.

Allen, K. (2003). The Celtic Tiger, inequality and social partnership, *Administration, 51*(1), 119-142.

Aronowitz, S. (2003). *How class works.* Yale University Press.

Bauman, Z. (2006). *Liquid fear.* Polity.

Bolton, M. (2024, August 27) Research reveals the current work week does not suit 70% of Irish workers. *BreakingNews.ie.* https://www.breakingnews.ie/ireland/research-reveals-the-current-work-week-does-not-suit-70-of-irish-workers-1666051.html

Cross, A. (2003, October 26). Up in the air: Mystery deepens in old pic. *The New York Post.* https://nypost.com/2003/10/26/up-in-the-air-mystery-deepens-in-old-pic/

Central Statistics Office (CSO) (2017). *Census of population 2016.* Central Statistics Office. https://www.cso.ie/en/census/census2016reports/

Central Statistics Office, (2023). *Census of population 2022.* Central Statistics Office.

Central Statistics Office (CSO). (2024). *Census of population 2022*. Central Statistics Office. https://www.cso.ie/en/census/census2022/

European Commission. (2000). *A memorandum on lifelong learning*. Commission of the European Communities.

Coleman, S. (2003). The centralized government of liquidity: Community language and culture under the Celtic Tiger. In C. Coulter, & S. Coleman, (Eds.), *The end of Irish history: Critical reflections on the Celtic Tiger* (pp. 175-191). Manchester University Press.

Coulter, C., & Coleman, S. (Eds.), (2003). *The end of Irish history: Critical reflections on the Celtic Tiger*. Manchester University Press.

Cullen, P. (2002, July 24). Ireland a society of poverty, inequality, UN study finds. *The Irish Times* https://www.irishtimes.com/news/ireland-a-society-of-poverty-inequality-un-study-finds-1.1089540

Delaney, E, (2012). *The curse of reason: The great Irish famine*. Gill & Macmillan.

Department of Education and Skills. (2011). *National strategy for higher education to 2030: Report of the strategy group*. Department of Education and Skills.

Easter proclamation (1916). The Provisional Government of the Irish Republic to the people of Ireland. http://www.easter1916.net/proclamation.htm

Fleming, T. (2021). Models of lifelong learning: An overview. In M. London (Ed.), *Oxford handbook of lifelong learning* (2nd ed., pp. 1-26). Oxford University Press. DOI: 10.1093/oxfordhb/9780197506707.013.3

Finnegan, F., & O'Neill. J. (2016). Building critical visions on employability in European higher education: Listening to students' voices. ESREA 8th Triennial European Research Conference: Maynooth University, Maynooth

Finnegan, F. & Fleming, T. (2023). Adult education and critical democratic citizenship: Revisiting key concepts in a time of crisis. In T. Mabrey, T. Hoggan-Kloubert, & C. Hoggan, (Eds.), *Civic education across ever-changing societies: Transforming lives, cultures, and nation-states* (pp. 19-44). Michigan State University Press.

Foley, D. (2022). 'Their proper place': Women, work and the marriage bar in independent Ireland, c. 1924–1973. *Social History*, *47*(1), 60–84. https://doi.org/10.1080/03071022.2022.2009692

Fœssel, M. & Habermas, J. (16 October, 2015). Critique and communication: Philosophy's missions - A conversation with Jürgen Habermas. *Esprit.* http://www.eurozine.com/pdf/2015-10-16-habermas-en.pdf

Gilmore, O. (2024). *The state we are in: Inequality in Ireland 2024.* Think-Tank for Action on Social Change (TASC).

Giroux H. (August 7, 2004). Neoliberalism and the demise of democracy: Resurrecting hope in dark times. *Dissident Voice.* https://dissidentvoice.org/Aug04/Giroux0807.htm

Government of Ireland (1955). *Report of the Commission on Emigration and other Population Problems, 1948-1954.* The Stationery Office.

Government of Ireland (1958). *First programme for economic expansion: Laid by the government before each house of the Oireachtais, November 1958.* The Stationary Office.

Government of Ireland (1965). *Investment in education: Report of the survey team appointed by the Minister of Education in October 1962.* The Stationery Office.

Habermas, J. (May-June 1999). The European State and the pressures of globalization, *New Left Review, 235*, 49.

Harvey, D. (2005). *A brief history of neoliberalism.* Oxford University Press.

Holford, J., & Milana, M. (2023). The European Union and lifelong learning policy. In K. Evans, W.O. Lee, J. Markowitsch, & M. Zukas (Eds.), *Third international handbook of lifelong learning.* Springer.

Holmwood, J. (2014). From social rights to the market: Neoliberalism and the knowledge economy, *International Journal of Lifelong Education, 33*(1), 62-76.

Horgan-Jones, J. (9 April 2014). Irish emigrants sent €5.7 billion back from the UK over 30 years: Central Statistics Office data. *The Journal*. https://www.thejournal.ie/irish-emigrant-remittances-uk-1405087-Apr2014/

Kelly, J. (2012). The graves are walking: The history of the great Irish famine. Faber & Faber.

Lee, J.J. (1989). *Ireland 1912-1985*, Cambridge University Press.

Leo XIII, (1891). *Rerum novarum*: Encyclical of Pope Leo XIII. https://www.vatican.va/content/leo-xiii/en/encyclicals/documents/hf_l-xiii_enc_15051891_rerum-novarum.html

McCabe, C. (2011). *Sins of the fathers: Tracing the decisions that shaped the Irish economy*. History Press.

McChesney, R. W. (1998). Introduction. In N. Chomsky (Ed.), *Profit over people: Neoliberalism and global order* (pp. 7-16). Seven Stories Press.

Mercille, J. & Murphy, E. (2015). *Deepening neoliberalism, crisis and austerity: Europe's treasure Ireland*. Palgrave Macmillan.

Moore, D., Vasquez, D., & Dolan, R. (21 March, 2021). *Residents with Irish ancestry are in all 3,142 US counties and make up 20% of the population in some.* United States Census Bureau. https://www.census.gov/library/stories/2021/03/happy-saint-patricks-day-to-one-of-ten-americans-who-claim-irish-ancestry.html

Morgan, M., Hickey, B., Kelleghan, T., Cronin, A., & Miller, D. (1997). *Report to the Minister for Education on the International Adult Literacy Survey: Results for Ireland.* St. Patrick's College Drumcondra.

O'Brien, E. (1960). *The country girls*. Hutchinson.

Ó Cualáin, S. (2012). *Men at lunch: A documentary*. RTE. http://www.rtve.es/television/20130925/documentos-tv-hombres-viga/750861.shtml

OECD (1995). *Literacy, economy and society: Results of the first international literacy survey*. OECD.

OECD. (2022). *Education at a glance 2022: OECD Indicators*. OECD. https://www.oecd.org/education/education-at-a-glance/

O'Hearn, D. (2003). Macroeconomic policy in the Celtic tiger: A critical assessment. In C. Coulter, & S. Coleman (Eds.), *The end of Irish history: Critical reflections on the Celtic Tiger*. Manchester University Press.

O'Riain, S. (2014). *The rise and fall of Ireland's Celtic Tiger.* Cambridge University Press.

Pius XI, (1931). *Quadragesimo anno* [Forty years]. Encyclical of Pope Pius XI. Retrieved fromhttps://www.vatican.va/content/pius-xi/en/encyclicals/documents/hf_p-xi_enc_19310515_quadragesimo-anno.html

Rahmanan, A. (December 1, 2023). Recreate this historical photo on top of Rockefeller Center right now. *Time Out New York*. https://www.timeout.com/newyork/news/recreate-this-historical-photo-on-top-of-rockefeller-center-right-now-120123

Rubin, L. (1976). *Worlds of pain: Life in the working-class family.* Basic Books.

Sayer, A. (2015). *Why we can't afford the rich.* Bristol: Policy Press. https://doi.org/10.2307/j.ctt1t89fd6.

Schrier, A. (1958). *Ireland and the American emigration, 1850-1900*, (University of Minnesota Press.

Sennett, R. (1998). *The corrosion of character, The personal consequences of work in the new capitalism*, W.W. Norton.

Sennett, R. & Cobb, J. (1973). *The hidden injuries of class*. Vintage Books.

Spring, J. (1998). *Education and the rise of the global economy*. Lawrence Erlbaum Associates.

Walsh, J. (2014). The transformation of Irish higher education 1945-1980. In A. Loxley, A. Seery, & J. Walsh (Ed.), *Higher education in Ireland: Practices, policies and possibilities*. Palgrave.

Wright Mills, C. (2008). *The politics of truth: Selected writings of C. Wright Mills*. Oxford University Press.

CHAPTER 9

The Evolution of Gender-Specific Occupations in Various Cultures

Praveen K. Dubey and Mattius Rischard, Montana State University, Northern, USA

Abstract

The cultural norms, societal expectations, economics, and social movements influence the evolution of gender-specific occupations. This chapter examines the change in gender-specific roles within the workforce across different cultures: the United States, India, and the United Arab Emirates. For each of these countries, we explore historical contexts and contemporary shifts in gender-specific roles toward gender equity and the persistent challenges. The authors highlight how educational attainment, legislation, cultural attitudes, and economic transitions have shaped gender roles in these societies. The analysis explored the importance of continued efforts in addressing work-life balance, the gender pay gap, and how leadership plays a role in achieving true gender equality in the global workforce.

Introduction

Gender-specific occupations have evolved significantly over time, influenced by cultural norms, economic needs, and social movements. In this chapter, we examine the evolution of gender-specific occupations in some of the most historically stratified fields, such as education, in three distinct cultures: the United States, India, and the United Arab Emirates (UAE). By exploring historical contexts and contemporary shifts, we can gain insights into the progress made and the challenges that remain in achieving gender equity in the educational workforce.

Historical Context of Gender-Specific Educational Occupations

UNITED STATES

Gendered trends in educational professions in the United States emerged through a complex interplay of social, economic, and cultural factors. These trends were influenced by the evolving roles of men and women in society, the professionalization of teaching, and broader historical changes.

In the colonial period and early 19th century, teaching, particularly at the higher levels of education, was predominantly a male profession. This was largely because education was closely tied to religious instruction, and men held most religious leadership roles. Teaching was also seen as a stepping stone to other professions, such as ministry or law, which were exclusively male domains. Women's participation in education was largely confined to informal settings, such as teaching within the home or running small private schools for young children, often referred to as "dame schools." These roles were extensions of women's perceived natural duties as nurturers and caregivers (Cortes & Pan, 2018).

The common school movement, which sought to provide universal, publicly funded education, created a significant demand for teachers. The expansion of elementary education coincided with the growing belief that women were naturally suited to teach young children due to their supposed inherent nurturing qualities. This led to the feminization of the teaching profession, particularly at the elementary level. Women were hired as teachers because they could be paid less than men (Cortes & Pan, 2018). This was justified by the prevailing societal belief that women's primary role was in the home, and thus, any income they earned was supplementary. Teaching was one of the few respectable occupations available to middle-class women, further entrenching their dominance in the profession.

INDIA

Gendered trends in educational professions in India emerged through a combination of traditional cultural norms, colonial influences, and socio-economic developments. These trends have been shaped by the intersection of gender roles, education policies, and broader social changes over time.

In pre-colonial India, education was largely the domain of men, particularly among the upper castes, where teaching and scholarship were largely the domain of groups such as the Brahmin.

Women's education was minimal and often limited to domestic skills, religious instruction, and the arts, reflecting the broader societal view of women's roles as primarily within the home. Education for women was generally not formalized and was typically provided within the family or local community.

With the advent of British colonial rule in the 18th and 19th centuries, there was a gradual shift in the educational landscape. The British introduced Western-style education, but initially, it was largely male-dominated, with few opportunities for women (Cortes & Pan, 2018). Missionary efforts, however, began to focus on educating girls, often as a means of moral and religious instruction. This laid the groundwork for the gradual inclusion of women in formal education.

UNITED ARAB EMIRATES

Gendered trends in educational professions in the United Arab Emirates (UAE) have emerged from a unique blend of cultural, religious, and socio-economic factors, influenced by rapid modernization and state-driven efforts to expand education.

Before the discovery of oil in the 1950s, the UAE, like much of the Arabian Peninsula, was a tribal society where formal education was limited. Education, especially for women, was not widespread. Traditional gender roles were deeply ingrained, with men primarily responsible for external affairs and women focusing on domestic responsibilities. Education that did exist was largely informal and religious, focusing on the Quran and other religious texts. Boys were often taught by local scholars (sheikhs) in small, informal settings, while girls' education if it occurred, was usually conducted at home by family members (Cortes & Pan, 2018).

The discovery of oil in the 1950s and 1960s led to rapid economic transformation, resulting in significant investment in infrastructure, including education. The UAE government, established in 1971, prioritized the development of a national education system as part of its modernization agenda. The government's focus on education led to the establishment of public schools for both boys and girls. Education became a key pillar of national development, with the state providing free education to all citizens. This period marked the beginning of formal educational opportunities for women, although initial enrollment was lower for girls compared to boys. Reflecting cultural and religious norms, the UAE's education system developed with gender-segregated schools. While both boys and girls had access to education, they were often educated in separate institutions with different curricula, reinforcing traditional gender roles.

The Impact of Social Movements and Economic Changes

UNITED STATES

As teaching became more professionalized in the 19th Century, a clear gendered hierarchy emerged. Women dominated elementary education, while men continued to control secondary education, administration, and higher education roles. These higher-status and higher-paying positions were often closed to women. Furthermore, during the Progressive Era, the establishment of normal schools (teacher training institutions) further solidified women's role in education. These schools were initially designed to train women for elementary teaching, reinforcing the idea that teaching young children was women's work.

The feminist movements of the 1960s and 1970s in the United States significantly challenged traditional gender roles. Women increasingly pursued higher education and entered professions such as law, medicine, and business. Legislative changes, such as the Equal Pay Act of 1963 and the Civil Rights Act of 1964, also helped to dismantle institutional barriers, promoting gender equality in the workplace. In recent decades, there has been a slow but noticeable increase in men entering elementary education and women rising to higher educational administration roles. However, the legacy of gendered expectations in education remains influential.

It should also be noted that different states have varying degrees of gender conformity because of modern social movements. Qin et al. (2023) examine the cultural constraints that women face compared to men across the United States. It applies the concept of cultural tightness—where societal norms are rigid and sanctions for deviation are strong—to understand how these cultural norms impact gender dynamics. The research, based on data from over 15,000 respondents, maps state-level gender bias in cultural tightness and reveals that states with higher cultural tightness tend to have greater gender inequality in leadership positions and innovation sectors. Key factors associated with this bias include religious and political ideologies, as well as gender-related threats. The study highlights that women in culturally tighter states experience more significant barriers, perpetuating gender disparities in professional and innovative fields.

Overall, the situation has improved over the last 40 years. Blau et al (2013) analyze the evolution of gender occupational segregation in the U.S. labor market over nearly four decades, finding a significant decline in gender occupational segregation from 1970 to 2009. However, the pace of this decline has varied over the years, with more substantial changes occurring in the earlier decades.

INDIA

The 19th century saw the rise of social reform movements that advocated for women's education as part of a broader push for social progress. Reformers like Raja Ram Mohan Roy, Ishwar Chandra Vidyasagar, and Jyotirao Phule emphasized the importance of educating women, arguing that it was essential for the upliftment of society. This period saw the establishment of the first schools for girls, often run by reformist organizations or Christian missionaries.

The emergence of women like Savitribai Phule, who became one of India's first female teachers and a pioneer of women's education, marked a significant milestone. These early female educators played a crucial role in challenging traditional gender norms and opening up educational opportunities for women.

As education expanded in the late 19th and early 20th centuries, there was a growing demand for teachers, particularly at the primary level. Teaching, especially at the elementary level, became increasingly associated with women, paralleling trends seen in other parts of the world. This was partly due to societal beliefs that women were naturally suited to teaching young children, and partly because women could be employed at lower salaries than men. Furthermore, the colonial education system often reinforced gendered divisions by establishing separate schools and curricula for boys and girls. While boys were educated for public and professional roles, girls' education was often focused on domestic skills, religious instruction, and moral education, reinforcing traditional gender roles.

After India gained independence in 1947, the government prioritized expanding education as a means of national development. Efforts were made to increase access to education for all, including women. The focus was on achieving universal primary education, and women became the primary educators in many rural and urban schools. Despite these advances, education in India continued to reflect traditional gender norms. Women were still largely confined to teaching roles in primary and secondary education, while men dominated higher education and administrative positions. The higher the level of education, the fewer women were found, a trend that persists to some extent even today.

Economic liberalization in the 1990s opened new opportunities for women in India. As the country transitioned from an agrarian economy to a more diversified one, women began to enter fields like information technology, finance, and education. Social movements advocating for women's rights and education have also contributed to shifting perceptions of gender-specific roles. Government initiatives, such as the National Education Policy and various scholarship programs, have aimed to promote women's education and professional development in the field of education.

It should also be noted that India, given its size and regional diversity, is not a monolithic ethno-state when it comes to gender roles in the workplace. Mitra et al. (2018) examined labor market dynamics in India, focusing on the influences of region and gender on employment participation rates. The study reveals significant regional variations in labor market participation across India, where more rural or Islamic states such as in Eastern India or Kashmir exhibit stronger cultural tightness around traditional roles, while states on the coast, on commercial routes, and centered around large cities tend to feature more diverse economic conditions, cultural practices, and social norms, leading to varying levels of employment opportunities.

UNITED ARAB EMIRATES

By the 1990s, the UAE government recognized the importance of women's education for national development and began promoting female participation in education more actively. Initiatives were launched to increase female enrollment in schools and universities. The government also began to advocate for women's rights in various sectors, including education. During this period, teaching, especially in primary and secondary education, became a predominantly female profession in the UAE. Cultural norms that viewed teaching as an extension of women's nurturing roles contributed to this trend. Additionally, teaching was seen as a respectable and socially acceptable profession for women, providing them with a stable career while allowing them to fulfill traditional family roles.

The 1990s and 2000s also saw a significant increase in the number of women pursuing higher education. Women began to outnumber men in university enrollments, particularly in fields like education, humanities, and social sciences. This shift further cemented the feminization of the teaching profession, as many of these graduates entered the education sector as teachers or administrators.

Contemporary Gender-Specific Disparities and Shifts

UNITED STATES

Schools are agents of socialization and play a vital role in how the world around us perceive them. Because of the differences across race, language, disabilities, and culture; schools have a responsibility to model, teach, and create learning conditions for equal opportunities. The declining gender segregation in the occupational landscape has changed the US economy in the last few decades. In the United States, the recent national study of gender disparity in educational achievement showed that, on average, both genders have scored similar on standardized math tests; however, female students outperformed male students on reading or English language arts (ELA). More precisely, such achievement gaps vary among students.

The variation is more interesting when measured among the geographic regions as smaller local areas portrayed interestingly a different picture. Considering the relationship between gender achievement and socioeconomic status (SES) suggests that achievement gaps differ substantively in local communities. Further investigations suggest that social, community, and family socioeconomic contexts affect differently for both male and female students in educational attainment which produces large variation in gender achievement gaps when measured locally from Grades 3 through 8. Notably, female students outperformed male students in ELA and math in Grades 3 through 8 favoring female students. The achievement gaps did not stay the same in high school. In high school, male students outperformed female students in math and the ELA gap is reduced substantially between genders. Such findings suggest that societal and cultural forces that shape achievement gap patterns vary substantially during child and adolescent development years in communities.

Researchers and policymakers have tried to explain the reasons behind these changes, but no clear explanation exists behind the forces driving these achievement gap patterns. One possibly explainable reason is that gender norms have changed in recent years and puts pressure on working conditions due to the economic recession. For example, during the recession, lower family incomes affected male workers more than female and reduced the male-female income, educational and occupational disparity, and lowered socioeconomic status which are associated with less male-favoring math achievement gaps. These assumptive hypotheses need to be verified with a proper examination of how community norms, wages, and societal conditions played a role in math and reading achievement gaps in local communities.

INDIA

Gender equality is a culturally constructed phenomenon that is relative to other contexts within society. In some societies, men have been given their socially sanctioned gender privileges but in certain parts of the world, it still exists. India is an example of the mixture. In contemporary India, some women have powerful voices in their respective fields and are global leaders representing their societies. However, in India, gender inequality results in unequal opportunities while impacting both genders but girls are affected most. The gender inequality has been seen in communities, homes, textbooks, movies, and among the care provider men and women. While growing up, boys and girls have different experiences where boys have more freedom compared to girls in making decisions which affects their work, education, marriage, and social relationships. With the existence of gender discrimination, and social norms and practices, girls are exposed to child marriage, teen pregnancy, child domestic work, sexual abuse, and poor education (Gupta, & Kothe, 2024).

As a collectivistic culture with a strong patriarchal society, India is at the intersection of traditional gender roles with egalitarian commitment. Currently available data-position India at a crossroads where women's participation at work is still far from equal. Gender equality has improved in the last several decades but does not necessarily reflect gender parity (Sahoo & Klasen, 2018; Gupta, & Kothe, 2024). A substantial portion of female students drop out of school before they hit puberty. Somehow if they end up completing the school, they often compromise on their career choices due to factors associated with safety, proximity to work, or some household responsibility. Even if they manage to work, they are most likely to be overburdened with their responsibilities at work as well as at home. These situations hinder the nation socially and economically and prevent it from moving up the ladder to become a first-world nation.

To fully develop India's social construct for gender-specific occupations, it is necessary to support both genders to reach their full potential through educational opportunities, freedoms for career choices, flexibility in working conditions, and job specific training without biases. Additionally, if the girls are not valued the same or equally as the boys, the economic and social growth hinders which creates the situations of social justice, equity, and vulnerabilities. Thus, changing the value system that involves men and women, is necessary to mobilize the society that advocates the rights of all equally and promotes development and growth.

UNITED ARAB EMIRATES

The recent demographic, economical, and political developments created a new value system for the citizens of UAE that changed already existing guiding principles revolving around gender, equity, roles, cross-sex relationships, marriage, professional life, and family for Emirati women. Traditional cultural values encouraged self-submissiveness, strong family values, and preservation of traditional cultures; however, contemporary modern cultural values influenced by urbanization, education and technology, and increased autonomy promoted a higher role of females in family, society, and professionally.

The establishment of the federation in 1971 directed the deployment of oil wealth to boost the economic and social infrastructure of the UAE. Additionally, the UAE Constitution guarantees equal rights and protection for all citizens and gives rights of their entitlements of legal status and access to health, education, and employment. These efforts helped to boost the economic development and advanced education for Emirati girls. The initiatives for social and economic developments have changed the role of Emirati women in the last few decades. The women are empowered with better educational opportunities including access to higher education and greater penetration to the job market.

Gender equality is part of the UAE's Vision 2021 National Agenda to provide protection to women from all forms of discrimination at work, in society, and empowers Emirati women. Such government initiatives have improved the social, cultural, and economic status of Emirati women. The recent data looks very promising for females. As of October 2019, 60% of Emirates Diplomatic Academy graduates are women and roughly 50% of the Ministry of Foreign Affairs employees are women which include high-profile female ambassadors in major embassies such as the UN Mission in New York and postings in the Netherlands, Germany, Finland, and Denmark.

The UAE government promotes the equal rights of education for every girl as it is key to economic empowerment for women. The student enrollment in higher education represents 77% women students and out of which 70% graduate from the university. In the last few decades, the UAE government has taken several measures to reduce gender-specific gaps; however, a report

from the World Economic Forum ranks UAE at 115 and stated that as a country the performance was below average on Economic Participation and Opportunity and Political Empowerment sub-indexes. On another note, the UAE performed above average on the Educational Attainment and Health and Survival sub-indexes. Such reports suggest mixed results for gender-specific attainments. Additionally, due to the government initiatives the UAE showed the highest percentage change on the Political Empowerment sub-index. Considering these findings, the future looks promising in reducing gender-specific gaps in the UAE.

Educational Attainment

Educational attainment has been a predicator in reducing gender-specific occupational gaps in all three cultures. Higher education provides opportunities for both genders to explore the work and improve their economic prospects. College education is extremely helpful to young adults to grow personally and intellectually. Additionally, college experience helps in developing skills and knowledge which are useful at work and wider penetration to the job market. The strong correlation between college completion and lifetime earnings and wealth accumulation promotes the young generation for educational attainment. In all three countries, policies have been initiatives to provide opportunities for women to earn college degrees and raise the ladders of professional careers which suit their future social and economic goals.

As of 2014, in the USA, the educational attainment gap has been closed by 94% where USA ranked 20. The recently released US Census Bureau Data Educational Attainment suggests that as of 2022, 39.0% of women aged 25 and older had completed a bachelor's degree or more as their highest level in comparison to men 36.2% of men in the same age range. This data suggests that the women are earning higher education at a higher rate than men. Additionally, between 2020 and 2021, the mean nominal earnings rose to workers at all levels of educational attainment.

Based on the World Economic Forum report 2024, India ranks 129th out of 148 countries; however, on educational attainment India ranks 124th. The women share in primary, secondary and tertiary education enrolments have been modestly increasing and the gap between men and women's literacy rate is still 17.2 percentage points. The average women literacy rate is roughly 65% as compared to 82% for men. At federal (ministerial level) and in parliament the Indian women's representation is 6.9% and 17.2% respectively which is relatively lower than other developed countries. These statistics depict India's commitment to gender parity.

The UAE Vision 2021 is a National Agenda to protect women and provides them gender equality and opportunity to earn higher education. Such actions resulted in a higher literacy rate in the UAE. The literacy rate in the UAE is above 95% for both men and women. The women are completing higher education and being an integral part of the society. The participation of women in higher education at 70% represents increased opportunities for women to graduate from Emirati University and enter the professional workforce. As of 2019, women hold 66% of public jobs, 75% occupy health and education sectors, and 23,000 Emirati women's running businesses. All these results in women empowerment and increased opportunities for Emirati women to contribute to family, culture, and society.

Legislation and Policy

Legislation and policy play a critical role in removing gender gaps and promoting gender equality. To prohibit discrimination based on sex, gender, disparities in education, employment and earnings, retirement, and health care, several legislations have been passed in the USA, India, and UAE. The purpose of these policies is to create equality, equal pay, and equitable opportunities at work.

In the USA, Title VII of the Civil Rights Act of 1964 prohibits discrimination based on race, color, religion, sex and national origins. This law protects against sex discrimination in the workplace and stops employers from treating employees differently based on their sex, pregnancy, sexual orientation or gender identity. Additionally, in 1972, President Nixon signed Title IX of the Education Amendments into law. Title IX is a comprehensive federal law to remove barriers that prevent people based on sex from participating in educational opportunities and careers of their choice. The Congress enacted Title IX with two principal objectives: 1) to avoid the use of federal funding to support discriminatory practices in education programs, and 2) to provide individual citizens effective protection from discrimination.

In India, on 10th December 1948, General Assembly affirmed that all human beings are born free and have equal rights and their rights and freedom are protected without distinction on race, color, sex, language, religion, birth, or other status. Similar provisions have been included in the Indian Constitution. In fact, the Indian constitution grants gender equality as a Fundamental Rights. It empowers women's equality before law (Article 14), protection against discrimination (Article 15), special provision in favor of women and children (Article 15(3)), Equality of opportunity related to employment (Article 16), equal rights for livelihood (Article 39(a)), equal pay (Article 36 (d)), maternity relief (Article 42), and several other provisions. Additionally, in 1979, the General Assembly eliminated all forms of discrimination against women under the International Bill of Rights for Women.

The UAE constitution guarantees equal rights to all its citizens. It empowers women's equality, social justice, equal opportunity, and security (Article 14), right to free primary education (Article 17), special school (Article 18), health and medical protection (Article 19), and no discrimination based on race, nationality, religious belief or social position (Article 25). Under the constitution of UAE, women enjoy gender equality, protection of legal status, claim to titles, access to education, the right to practice professions, and the right to inherit property same as men. Due to these protective laws, Emirati women are accessing higher education and are more university graduates. They have higher literacy rates (95.8%) and are more business owners.

Cultural Attitudes

Cultural attitudes influence gender equality in occupations. In different cultures, traditional views impose limitations on both genders for their career choices and advancements. The societal norms prevent both genders in exploring different career choices as they are not approved based on preconceived notions and limiting freedom of career choices. To truly change these practices, change in attitude is required through education, public discourse, resetting societal norms, acceptable policy formation, and creating positive representations of different profession roles. These steps would create a new societal environment for acceptance and creating new opportunities based on economic reality, not on preferences.

In the United States, social norms provide direction for individual and group behavior and influence people's opinion regarding education, jobs, and social cultures. Women are more constrained by cultural norms compared to men and these variations influence gender biases in cultural tightness. These variabilities are associated socio-political factors such as religion and political ideology and connected with gender-related threats. Due to these gender biases, cultural tightness is associated with gender inequality and favoring men in business, innovation, and political leadership. Thus, to improve gender equality, it is paramount to understand social norms and create policies and procedures that do not favor based on gender, location, religion, and political ideologies.

Indian culture is deeply rooted in social norms, traditions, and structures which drives everyday life of the citizens. The societal norms, family, and household influence girls at a very young age and form gender-based discrimination and inequitable perceptions. While adolescents begin forming gender equity attitudes and perceptions at a young age where boys have lower gender-equitable attitudes compared to girls. When children mature, gender equitable attitudes are strongly influenced by gender norms practiced in households by their parents and understanding of what the acceptable gender roles in the community are. Such structures construct children's gender-based understanding of what it means to be a male or female and continue to harm the lives of girls. The existing attitudes and mindsets within the communities and schools create obstacles in girls' lives where they experience higher rates of gender discrimination. Thus, to resolve such situations, more attention must be paid to the adolescent boys to increase their awareness and sensitivity toward the pre-existing discrimination against girls and use it as a unique opportunity to address gender attitudes before it solidifies into their brains. Considering such measures will yield better outcomes for families, greater-economic prospects for families and communities, and stability and peace with higher country GDP.

The UAE society is considered as culturally conservative with tribal affiliations and a patriarchal family structure. The Emirati women are discouraged to work outside home due to cultural barriers and viewed their roles as housewives and caregivers (Hussain 2015). However, there is significant change in societal attitudes toward the everyday life of people. In fact, the UAE government has initiated female supportive policies to increase their access to education and employment opportunities for women. All these changes had been created with the rapid expansion of information technology which influenced attitudes toward women, gender roles, and the relationships between men and women. Such social and cultural changes will provide Emirati women an opportunity to explore new avenues and remove the gender-based gaps in UAE society.

Challenges and Future Directions

It has been theorized that persistence in gender-specific occupations is a result of either the devaluation of jobs considered suitable for women, or the hyper valuation of jobs requiring specialized training that is accessed through male-dominated educational tracks, or some combination of both. Cohen and Huffman (2003) argued that occupations dominated by women are often undervalued, leading to lower wages. This devaluation is not merely a reflection of skill level but is influenced by societal perceptions of gender roles and the importance of various jobs. The study also considers how specialized training impacts occupational choices and earnings. Tam (1997) suggests that the differences in training and education contribute to the gender wage gap, as men and women may have unequal access to high-paying fields requiring specialized skills, and may be expected to maintain a stricter work-life balance due to family responsibilities that are more often placed on women, while men spend more of their time in leadership positions and technically specialized work that places more demands on one's time away from familial obligations.

WORK-LIFE BALANCE

Work-life balance is challenging for all working professionals but especially for working women. Balancing work and personal life can create challenges as many responsibilities and societal expectations differ between men and women. In the 21st-century working environment, all the working women are struggling to maintain their professional identity. To maintain the work-life balance, setting boundaries is the first important step to manage and separate personal and professional life. This is easier said than done, especially if countries lack the infrastructure and legal protections to enable women to make choices between paid work and domestic spheres.

Balancing work and family responsibilities remains a challenge, particularly for women. In cultures where long working hours are the norm, such as China or India, achieving work-life balance is crucial for increasing female workforce participation. Flexible work arrangements and parental leave policies are essential. As Jong-Wha and Wie (2017) have shown, state-owned enterprises, civil service, education, and the informal/domestic industries of such large-scale, emergent economies such as India's can create enormous demands on an individual's time with relatively few benefits for the individual or their family to create a desirable work-life balance. Indeed, Sinha (2022) demonstrates that in the development of the modern Indian economy, women's participation in agriculture remains high, though there are notable declines in manufacturing jobs, which historically employed many women. Economic transitions in India, particularly the move towards a service-oriented economy, affect female employment opportunities. While the service sector offers new job avenues, barriers such as gender discrimination and lack of supportive infrastructure continue to hinder women's full participation. More funding for benefits in public service, childcare services, universal healthcare, and other solutions are possible remedies to the current political economy found in such nations.

However, there is still a generational gap in the way that family and work life balance is valued in relation to gendered responsibilities and expectations. In the UAE, Alteneiji (2023) explores how gender roles and perceptions have evolved across three generations of women. Alteneiji investigates how traditional roles are being redefined as women gain increased access to education and professional opportunities, alongside broader societal changes. The study highlights the shift from more rigid, traditional gender expectations to more fluid and egalitarian roles, although older generations tend to maintain more conservative views.

Yet scholars have offered creative solutions to resolving the work-life balance issue in formerly colonized societies such as the UAE. Fiteni (2022) critiques existing home economics curricula, highlighting their colonial roots and the lack of relevance to the local cultural context. It emphasizes that traditional pedagogies often reinforce gender stereotypes and limit the potential of women in the UAE. Fiteni argues for the need to decolonize the home economics curriculum by incorporating indigenous knowledge and practices. This involves recognizing local traditions, values, and gender roles that can empower Emirati women and provide them with practical skills relevant to their cultural context, and also shifting some of the domestic labor responsibilities onto men.

GENDER PAY GAP

The gender pay gap persists across all cultures, with women generally earning less than men for similar work. Damelang and Ebensperger (2020) have highlighted in a longitudinal analysis that higher female representation in an industry often correlates with lower wages and less job security across multiple countries over time. Addressing this issue requires transparency in pay practices, as well as policies that promote equal pay for equal work.

The Equal Remuneration Act of 1976 is a law that protects women from discrimination in the workplace in India, formally ending gender discrimination in pay. However, Duraisamy and Duraisamy (2014) analyze the trends and patterns of occupational segregation and discrimination faced by women in India over a 27-year period, finding that prejudicial hiring and promotion as well as pay rates continue to exist in India, despite gains in educational access for women. However, Landry et al. (2019) shows how adolescents in India are developing gender equity attitudes, highlighting the impact of social, cultural, and educational influences during this critical stage of their development. Key findings emphasize that exposure to gender-sensitization and empowerment programs during adolescence is crucial for promoting equitable attitudes and reducing gender-based discrimination in pay and on-the-job treatment. The study acknowledges that adolescence is a pivotal time when gender attitudes can be shaped, potentially diminishing gender inequity in the long term. Despite the study's focus on specific communities, its broader implications suggest that gender equity programs could play a significant role in transforming societal views on gender and improving the well-being of both men and women across various aspects of life, including education and health.

Furthermore, Chowdhury et al. (2018) demonstrates how gender roles in India are still perpetuated by the employers themselves in the way that they structure advertising for job openings. The study highlights variations across different sectors, where some industries show a higher inclination towards hiring one gender over the other. For instance, jobs in caregiving and education are often skewed towards females, while technical and managerial positions lean towards males in language, framing, and imagery. Thus, the gendering of specific occupations is still associated with different industries that openly seek one gender or the other for differential pay rates and job responsibilities on the labor market.

In the USA, women, on average, still earn less than their male counterparts, even when controlling for factors such as education, experience, and hours worked, even in highly specialized professions such as engineering or biomedical science (Graham & Smith, 2005). While institutions such as the EEO Commission, OSHA, the Office of Civil Rights (in educational professions), and others have stepped up efforts to curb open discrimination based on gender and sexuality in the workplace, women suffer from lower pay, less promotional opportunities, and lack of psycho-emotional wellbeing, especially in male-dominated industries (Damelang, & Ebensperger, 2020; Qian, & Fan, 2019).

Phenomenological studies of the UAE have demonstrated that many women express a desire for financial independence and skill development, which are seen as empowering and essential for personal growth (Amro, 2022). Yet, Adamson (2015) identifies several barriers women encounter, such as limited access to leadership positions, gender bias in hiring and promotions, and the perception that women prioritize family over career. These factors contribute to the persistence of the "glass ceiling" in organizational contexts. In response, many women have turned to their own forms of entrepreneurship in the UAE. In their interviews with female business leaders, Hermayen et al. (2022) emphasize that family support, including emotional, financial, and social backing, plays a crucial role in enhancing women entrepreneurs' confidence and resilience. This support helps them navigate challenges and encourages them to pursue their entrepreneurial goals.

REPRESENTATION IN LEADERSHIP/ADMINISTRATION

Despite progress, women remain underrepresented in leadership positions. Mentorship programs, leadership training, and corporate policies that support career advancement for women are necessary to bridge this gap. In the context of education, although there have been societal changes and increasing gender equality, teaching, especially at the elementary level, remains a feminized profession. The gender pay gap, along with the lower status accorded to teaching compared to other professions, continues to reflect this historical trend.

In the USA, for instance, Gjerde (2002) investigates the disparity in promotion standards applied to male and female employees within organizations in the United States. The study examines whether different criteria are used for assessing the qualifications and performance of employees based on their gender. Key findings indicate that women often face higher standards for promotion compared to their male counterparts, which can hinder their career advancement. The analysis suggests that these gender-specific standards are influenced by organizational culture and systemic biases that favor male employees, contributing to the underrepresentation of women in leadership positions.

In the UAE, there are conflicting religious and social interpretations of a woman's place in the job market, such that it often comes down to individual family support for women finding suitable work and career success. Hussain (2015) explores how religious beliefs and family dynamics influence the career choices and professional engagement of Emirati women, highlighting how religious teachings can either encourage or discourage women from pursuing high-level careers, depending on individual interpretations and family beliefs. Al-Othman (2011) explores the mixed attitudes towards women's public participation outside of the family, highlighting both supportive and resistant views. While some citizens advocate for increased involvement of women in public life, others maintain conservative perspectives that prioritize traditional gender roles. The study identifies several factors influencing these attitudes, including education, socioeconomic status, and exposure to modern ideas. Higher educational attainment often correlates with more progressive views on women's roles as leaders in politics, enterprise, and education.

There is also the fact of male-dominated workplaces becoming hostile and competitive in and of themselves, which can create barriers to the success of women in such environments. Qian and Fan (2019) find that the proportion of men and women in an occupation significantly influences the affective well-being of employees. Higher representation of women in a workplace is associated with lower levels of job satisfaction among men, while the opposite is true for women, who tend to report higher satisfaction in gender-balanced or predominantly female environments. Busch and Holst (2011) also find that women face barriers to reaching higher-level positions within organizations despite having similar qualifications and experience as their male counterparts. The authors employ a fixed effects model to control for various variables, reinforcing the idea that gender remains a crucial determinant of income.

Conclusion

The evolution of gender-specific occupations across the United States, India, and the UAE highlights the challenges as well as progress over time. In the last few decades, changes in economic landscapes, societal expectations, and attitudes toward gender roles have driven several movements to increase the expectations of equal participation between genders. To achieve such goals, the governments in these countries have introduced several laws and policy measures to promote inclusive societal norms for both genders. The government initiatives are successful up to a certain extent in promoting equal opportunities for primary education, and higher education, equal opportunities in jobs, and uplifting the overall social status of women.

The legislation and policy initiatives have improved educational attainment and cultural attitudes with respect to defying traditional gender roles in all three countries, yet challenges still remain. For instance, trade liberalization has had mixed effects on gender inequality in India. While some sectors saw increased opportunities for women, many women faced wage disparities and limited access to high-skilled jobs compared to men (Gupta 2021). The USA has made great strides in female representation at the top of educational administrations, politics, and industry since the Civil Rights-era legislation, but with diminishing improvements over the years since at least the 1980s (Blau et al., 2013), and still demonstrates a pay gap in most professions, even highly skilled STEM disciplines (Graham & Smith, 2005; Pal et al., 2024). In the UAE, the importation of Western educators and models of schooling, along with strategic government initiatives, have the effect of providing opportunities for work and entrepreneurship to women that weren't available even a decade ago (Hermayen 2022); however, the experiences of women who try to work or are even supported in finding work can be dependent upon whether or not an individual's family consents to or encourages their ability to do so (Amro, 2022; Biju et al., 2021). The certainty of these initiatives and their efficacy in moving the public towards greater gender equity in the workforce in different cultures relies on how quickly and effectively women's social status improves. This improvement can measured in concrete steps to address the issues of work-life balance, gender pay gap, and resources available to meet the new roles that all genders must inevitably assume.

REFERENCES

Adamson, I. (2015). Breaking through the glass ceiling? The United Arab Emirates case. In *Women's voices in management: Identifying innovative and responsible solutions* (pp. 162-176). Palgrave Macmillan UK.

Al-Othman, H. M. (2011). Attitudes toward women's participation in public life in the United Arab Emirates. *Journal of International Women's Studies, 12*(3), 234-246.

Amro, S. M. (2022). The impact of internal and external factors on female enrollment in vocational training institutes in the United Arab Emirates: A phenomenological qualitative study. https://scholarworks.uaeu.ac.ae/all_dissertations/257/

Biju, S., Shetty, K., & Fitzsimmons, J. R. (2021). Perceived barriers to career progression amongst female students: evidence from India and the United Arab Emirates. *Gender in Management: An International Journal, 36*(6), 697-713.

Blau, F. D., Brummund, P., & Liu, A. Y. H. (2013). Trends in occupational segregation by gender 1970–2009: Adjusting for the impact of changes in the occupational coding system. *Demography, 50*, 471-492.

Busch, A., & Holst, E. (2011). Gender-specific occupational segregation, glass ceiling effects, and earnings in managerial positions: Results of a fixed effects model. https://www.diw.de/documents/publikationen/73/diw_01.c.367559.de/dp1101.pdf

Chowdhury, A. R., Areias, A. C., Imaizumi, S., Nomura, S., & Yamauchi, F. (2018). Reflections of employers' gender preferences in job ads in India: an analysis of online job portal data. *World Bank Policy Research Working Paper*, (8379).

Cohen, P. N., & Huffman, M. L. (2003). Occupational segregation and the devaluation of women's work across US labor markets. *Social Forces, 81*(3), 881-908.

Constitution of India. (2023, November 1). Legislative Department. https://legislative.gov.in/constitution-of-india/

Cortes, P., & Pan, J. (2018). Occupation and gender. *The Oxford handbook of women and the economy*, 425-452.

Damelang, A., & Ebensperger, S. (2020). Gender composition of occupations and occupational characteristics: Explaining their true relationship by using longitudinal data. *Social Science Research, 86*, 102394.

Duraisamy, M., & Duraisamy, P. (2014). Occupational segregation, wage and job discrimination against women across social groups in the Indian labor market: 1983–2010. *Preliminary Draft, 11*(08), 2017.

Ebtesam Alteneiji. (2023). Value changes in gender roles: Perspectives from three generations of Emirati women. *Cogent Social Sciences, 9*(1), 2184899.DOI: 10.1080/23311886.2023.2184899

Fiteni, D. B. (2022). Decolonising and Indigenising home economics pedagogies to advance gender roles in UAE. *International Journal of Home Economics, 15*(1), 55-69.

Gender equality. (n.d.). Unicef for every child, India. https://www.unicef.org/india/what-we-do/gender-equality

GENDER EQUALITY. (2020, January). Gender Equality. https://loksabhadocs.nic.in/Refinput/New_Reference_Notes/English/26022020_120723_102120474.pdf

Gjerde, K. A. P. (2002). The existence of gender-specific promotion standards in the US. *Managerial and Decision Economics, 23*(8), 447-459.

Global gender gap index 2014. (2014). The Gender Gap Report 2014. https://widgets.weforum.org/gender-gap-report-2014/index.html

Graham, J. W., & Smith, S. A. (2005). Gender differences in employment and earnings in science and engineering in the US. *Economics of education review*, *24*(3), 341-354.

Gupta, P., & Kothe, S. (2024). Gender discrimination and the biased Indian labour market: evidence from the national sample survey. *World Development Perspectives*, *35*, 100613

Gupta, A. (2021). Effect of trade liberalization on gender inequality: The case of India. *IMF Economic Review*, 69(4), 682-720.

Hermayen, A., Tarique, A., Bhardwaj, A. B., Bishnoi, M. M., & Gupta, R. (2022). Family support and psychological empowerment: women entrepreneurs in the UAE. *Journal of Positive School Psychology*, *6*(9), 4244-4253.

Hussain, N. (2015). Assessing the impact of religion and family in shaping UAE national women's choice of, and engagement with their careers. https://dspace.lib.cranfield.ac.uk/items/5a3482f9-61ca-457a-b907-a19b2791fd12

Jong-Wha, L. E. E., & Wie, D. (2017). Wage structure and gender earnings differentials in China and India. *World Development*, *97*, 313-329.

Landry, M., Vyas, A., Malhotra, G., & Nagaraj, N. (2019). Adolescents' development of gender equity attitudes in India. *International Journal of Adolescence and Youth*, *25*(1), 94-103. https://doi.org/10.1080/02673843.2019.1590852

Mitra, A., Okada, A., Mitra, A., & Okada, A. (2018). *Labour market participation in India: A region-and gender-specific study* (pp. 1-51). Springer Singapore.

Pal, K. K., Piaget, K., & Zahidi, S. (2024). *Global Gender Gap Insight Report June 2024*. World Economic Forum. https://www.weforum.org/publications/global-gender-gap-report-2024/

Qian, Y., & Fan, W. (2019). Men and women at work: Occupational gender composition and affective well-being in the United States. *Journal of Happiness Studies*, *20*(7), 2077-2099.

Qin, X., Chua, R. Y., Tan, L., Li, W., & Chen, C. (2023). Gender bias in cultural tightness across the 50 US states, its correlates, and links to gender inequality in leadership and innovation. *PNAS Nexus*, *2*(8). https://doi.org/10.1093/pnasnexus/pgad238

Reardon, S. F., Fahle, E. M., Kalogrides, D., Podolsky, A., & Zárate, R. C. (2019). Gender Achievement Gaps in U.S. School Districts. *American Educational Research Journal*, *56*(6), 2474-2508. https://doi.org/10.3102/0002831219843824

Sahoo, S., & Klasen, S. (2018). Gender segregation in education and its implications for labour market outcomes: Evidence from India. https://docs.iza.org/dp11660.pdf

Siddiqi, N. (2021). Gender inequality as a social construction in India: A phenomenological enquiry. *Women's Studies International Forum*, *86*, 102472. https://doi.org/10.1016/j.wsif.2021.102472

Sinha, D. (2022). Unpacking sectoral trends in female employment in India. In *Gender, unpaid work and care in India* (pp. 67-85). Routledge India.

Tam, T. (1997). Sex segregation and occupational gender inequality in the United States: Devaluation or specialized training? *American Journal of Sociology*, *102*(6), 1652-1692.

Title IX. (2021, August 12). Civil Rights Division. https://www.justice.gov/crt/title-ix#Introduction

Tlaiss, H. (2015). Neither-nor: career success of women in an Arab Middle Eastern context. *Employee Relations*, *37*(5), 525-546.

UAE women's rights. (n.d.). Promoting women's rights. https://www.mofa.gov.ae/en/The-Ministry/The-Foreign-Policy/Women-rights

United Arab Emirates Ministry of Foreign Affairs & International Cooperation. (2019).

Women's rights. https://www.mofaic.gov.ae/en/The-Ministry/The-Foreign-Policy/Women-rights
United Arab Emirates 1971 (rev. 2004) constitution. (n.d.). Preamble. https://www.constituteproject.org/constitution/United_Arab_Emirates_2004
US Census Bureau. (2023, February 16). *Census Bureau releases new educational attainment Data.* https://www.census.gov/newsroom/press-releases/2023/educational-attainment-data.html#:~:text=In%202022%2C%2039.0%25%20of%20women,highest%20level%20of%20educational%20attainment
What's behind the growing gap between men and women in college completion? (2021, November 8). https://www.pewresearch.org/short-reads/2021/11/08/whats-behind-the-growing-gap-between-men-and-women-in-college-completion/

CHAPTER 10

The Effects of the Practice of Art, Music, and Religion on the Practices of Work

Linda Ellington and Mona Stephens, Southern New Hampshire University, USA

Abstract

This chapter delves into the transformative potential of integrating art, music, and religion in work practices. It underscores how these elements shape work attitudes, behaviors, and organizational culture by examining their impact on workplace dynamics. Artistic practices foster creativity and well-being, music enhances productivity and therapeutic outcomes, and religious frameworks guide work ethics and cultural understandings. This integration enriches and transforms the work environment, making it more engaging, creating a higher awareness and appreciation of others, and impacting organizational productivity and results.

Introduction

The practice of art in the workplace has evolved significantly over time. It serves various purposes and impacts employees in multiple ways. Research indicates that workplace art promotes social interactions, elicits emotional responses, facilitates personal connections, enhances the environment, and fosters learning (Smiraglia, 2014). Historically, the relationship between art and labor has transformed from the traditional guild systems to modern galleries, reflecting changes in production modes and artistic identity (Beech, 2020). In the post-industrial era, artistic models of collaboration and creativity influence corporate practices, inadvertently contributing to labor restructuring (Bernes, 2017). In business settings, contemporary applications of artistic techniques aim to encourage creative problem-solving and embed arts into the organizational culture. Antal and Bitran (2018) stated that the complex interplay between art and workplace dynamics highlights the multifaceted role of art in the professional environment throughout history.

Music in the workplace has evolved with technology, becoming more prevalent and personalized (Haake, 2011). It serves multiple functions beyond mood enhancement, including inspiration, concentration, and stress relief (Haake, 2011; Landay & Harms, 2019). The impact of music on work performance is mediated by mood and emotion, with factors like extraversion, task complexity, and listening autonomy influencing individual reactions (Landay & Harms, 2019). It is crucial to manage the use of music effectively, as different uses of music have varying effects: emotional use positively relates to performance job satisfaction. In contrast, background use negatively affects satisfaction (Sanseverino et al., 2023). Therefore, management and employees need to be mindful of the type and volume of music played in the workplace. Appropriate music can increase motivation, creativity, and attention, potentially leading to better outcomes and job satisfaction. However, overly loud or lyrically distracting music may hinder productivity (Singh, 2023). Overall, music in the workplace can be a positive organizational practice when managed effectively, putting the responsibility in the hands of management and employees.

The history of religion in the workplace is rooted in the Protestant Work Ethic and emerged through the Faith at Work movement (Benefiel et al., 2014; Geigle et al., 2013). Over the past two decades, expressing religious views and seeking accommodation at work has become more common (Borstorff & Arlington, 2011). The regulation of religion in secular work environments often embraces certain cultural and religious practices (Van Laer & Essers, 2023). Demographic shifts, including increased immigration from non-Christian countries, have led to greater religious diversity in the workplace, necessitating more accommodations (Borstorff & Arlington, 2011). This diversity has also resulted in a rise in religious discrimination complaints. The interplay between work practices and religious expression continues to shape the landscape of religion in the workplace.

Research indicates that incorporating art into the workplace significantly impacts employees. Artworks promote social interactions, elicit emotional responses, facilitate personal connections, enhance the work environment, and foster learning (Smiraglia, 2014). The presence of art interrupts routine perceptions of space, stimulates conversations, and enriches relationships among colleagues (Antal & Bitran, 2018). Art triggers questions and conversations, which stimulate sensemaking processes. It also allows managers and employees to holistically see everyday life and customer relationships.

The Role of Art on Work Practices

Artistic practices influence work by fostering creativity and innovation. Organizations encouraging artistic expression through design, visual arts, or creative problem-solving often benefit from a more dynamic and adaptive workforce. Art provides a means for workers to think outside the box, leading to unique solutions and the ability to approach tasks from multiple perspectives.

EXPLAINING THE ARTS

While the arts have always been conceptually tricky to define, many cross-cultural characteristics are recognized as fundamental to art. These include the art object (whether physical or experiential) being valued in its own right rather than merely as a utility, providing imaginative experiences for both the producer and the audience, and comprising or provoking an emotional response. In addition, the product of art is characterized by requiring novelty, creativity, or originality, requiring specialized skills, and relating to the rules of form, composition, or expression (Adajian, 2024). Adajian goes further and states that art has been proposed to consist of five categories (1.1.1):

- Performing arts (music, dance, theatre, singing, and film).
- Visual arts, design, and craft (painting, photography, sculpture, and textiles.
- Literature (writing, reading, and attending literary festivals.
- Culture (going to museums, galleries, art exhibitions, concerts, community events.
- Online, digital and electric arts (animations, filmmaking and computer graphics.

In recent years, much attention has been paid to how art might benefit business organizations, marketing, and strategic planning. For instance, exposure to art positively influences profitability and marketing persuasiveness, external and internal company relationships, the development of leadership and organizational culture, self-discovery and personal growth, collaboration, activation of emotions and energy, and creativity through openness to new experiences and widened perspectives (Donghwy & Nara, 2018). Among these effects, the last has generated some of the most interest, as creativity is essential for generating unusual and novel ideas, which can drive organizational success—especially in a rapidly changing and competitive economic climate.

Organizations must create an environment where technology and creativity are fully integrated and intertwined in the digital era. The instrumental use of the arts as a management tool nurtures human potential and creative thinking by bringing artistic projects and attitudes to trigger critical and creative thinking (Schiuma, 2017). On a societal level, art challenges norms and stimulates cultural progress, driving social change and innovation. By integrating art into daily practices, organizations and communities can cultivate environments where creativity thrives, leading to meaningful advancements and a more vibrant, forward-thinking society.

Creativity and Innovation

EXPLAINING CREATIVITY

Creativity is the catalyst that propels both work and society toward growth and transformation. It involves thinking beyond conventional boundaries and generating novel ideas and solutions that transform challenges into opportunities. In the workplace, creativity fuels innovation, enabling organizations to adapt to changing environments, stay competitive, and meet evolving needs. Beyond the workplace, creativity plays a crucial role in societal practices by influencing cultural shifts, driving social change, and inspiring individuals and communities to envision and create better futures.

As the source of anything new and compelling that comes about through human efforts, creativity is also the driver for most societal growth, change, and discovery. It allows us to adapt, to solve problems, and to learn new things. Sawyer and Henricksen (2024) tell us that creativity has increased in importance due to several broad societal and economic trends:

- Globalized markets have resulted in greater competitiveness, even for industries that historically had been protected from significant change.
- Sophisticated information and communication technologies result in shorter product-development cycles.
- Jobs that do not require creativity have increasingly been automated or have moved to lower-wage countries.

Creativity in the workplace has significant organizational and individual implications, influencing employee performance and maintaining competitiveness in the modern business landscape (Appu et al., 2015). Research indicates that various factors contribute to workplace creativity, including personal control over the physical work environment, motivation, self-efficacy, social support, job autonomy, and cognitive styles (Samani et al., 2015; Appu et al., 2015).

As companies recognize that the benefits of creativity have increased, many art programs have been employed in workplaces as a fresh approach to bring about innovation (Berthoin & Straub, 2013). Managers have discovered that using an innovation to generate innovation makes much sense. So, they are experimenting with the potential of artistic interventions: bringing in people, practices, and products from the arts to help address issues their organizations face. This can inspire organizational members to think about interrupting routines and possibly encourage them to try new approaches.

Berthoin and Straub's (2013) study found that establishing artful ways of working to tap the rich creative potential of all organizational members entails profound counterintuitive changes in processes and culture. It implies a shift in emphasis from efficiency and control to embracing possibility and unexpectedness, increasing the chances that newness will emerge.

Being incapable of creativity in the workplace is a problematic failure that can be overcome by involving artistic expression. Organizational leaders who consciously leave creative potential unused and avoid creatively bringing about new things would seem absurd (Reckwitz, 2017). Taking aesthetic practices in contemporary workplaces is essential, as Reckwitz calls *aesthetic sociality* (2017, p. viii). In the sphere of work and organizations, the coupling of the wish to be creative with the imperative to be creative encompasses the whole structure of contemporary society. From a sociological viewpoint, creativity is not simply a superficial semantic phenomenon but a crucial organizing principle of Western societies (Reckwitz, 2017). This development was initially most noticeable in capitalist societies' economic and technical professions. The older forms of artistic endeavors are now social media texts, communication, aesthetic objects, and body modifications for the consumer public. The potential of art in the workplace stimulates tacit knowledge, provides new perspectives, and facilitates intrinsic motivation among participants in innovation activities, which are essential for maintaining competitiveness in a market (Kamiya, 2024).

EXPLAINING INNOVATION

Innovation is pivotal in transforming work practices, driving organizations to adapt and thrive in an ever-changing landscape. By integrating innovative approaches, companies can streamline processes, enhance productivity, and foster a culture of continuous improvement. Innovation encourages the exploration of new technologies, methodologies, and business models that can lead to more efficient operations and better customer experiences. It also empowers employees to think creatively, collaborate more effectively, and take calculated risks, contributing to long-term success. Ultimately, work practice innovation strengthens a company's competitive edge and ensures it remains resilient and responsive to future challenges.

There is empirical evidence of artistic practice—art thinking—that an artistic reframing of research and development (R&D) equates to a cultural shift in organizational thinking about the value of art in the workplace. Robbins and Sandberg (2023) introduce art thinking as a novel innovation paradigm. The shift requires art-based double-loop learning, which innovation management needs to champion. Art thinking means challenging the status quo. It entails an interplay between building on precedents on the one hand and questioning them on the other (Alexandre, 2017). Art thinking is a framework and a set of tools or practices that encourages organizations to embrace the attitude that requires a shift into R&D practices (Robbins & Fu, 2022).

Art thinking is an organizational competence that promises sustained competitive advantage, not simply one-off innovation outputs (Beuhring & Liedtka, 2018). This fundamental shift in culture and mindset does not fundamentally change the organization or question its structure or business model. However, it does extend beyond adopting new templates or practices (Seifried & Wasserbaech, 2019). For organizations who want to advance in the direction of more transformational innovation, Siefried and Wasserbaech (2019, p. xv) propose that organizational leaders integrate art thinking in their innovation process by:

- Change your point of view. Look at an issue from different analysis levels or through another discipline's eyes.
- Engage multiple stakeholders to encourage multivalency.
- Acknowledge the need to balance the precision of operational excellence when you execute and the chaos of art thinking as you innovate.

Art and the Competitive Environment

Interactions with art and the work environment promote social interactions, generally enhancing the workplace environment, eliciting emotional responses, facilitating personal connection-making, and fostering learning (Smiraglia, 2014). There is a belief that the salient features of the art collection connect employees to the organization's missions and its diversity, quality, creativity, and changing nature (Smiraglia, 2014, p. 3). The findings from a 2014 study conducted by Smiraglia found that art fosters discussions and socialization between colleagues, fosters learning opportunities, and promotes cognitive engagement. Their results also showed the art's diversity, quality, creativity, and connection to the organization's mission. The research question Smiraglia asked was: "What impact do organization affiliates believe the art in their workplace has on their experience at work?" (2014, pp. 287-292). Smiraglia posited that the study found social interactions, environment enhancement, and mission connection were present when art is in a work environment.

Social Interactions:

The social interactions around the artwork are conversation starters that offer everyone something to contribute. The discussions were usually spontaneous and spur-of-the-moment, thus facilitating discussions between new employees and providing new insights into coworkers.

Enhancement of Workplace Environment:

The presence of art in the environment affected employees' feelings about the organization and their work. They felt it aesthetically enhanced the environment by giving it color rather than having drab, boring walls.

Mission Connection:

In addition to reflecting the organization's values, the art identifies a connection to the mission. It reflects learning, which adds to the atmosphere of the organization and the feeling of belonging.

Art is a powerful catalyst in the competitive environment, offering businesses a unique edge through enhanced creativity, innovation, and emotional engagement. By integrating art into their strategies, companies can differentiate themselves, foster a culture of creativity, and build stronger connections with their stakeholders. In a rapidly changing market, those who embrace the transformative power of art are better positioned to navigate challenges, inspire their teams, and achieve sustained success.

TEAM BUILDING AND COLLABORATION

Art projects and activities can serve as practical team-building exercises. Collaborative art projects encourage communication, cooperation, and mutual respect among employees. These activities can break down barriers, foster community, and enhance teamwork, ultimately contributing to a more cohesive and productive work environment. In healthcare settings, visual and performing arts have been used to develop teamwork and create a greater awareness of the importance of teamwork and communication skills in their professional practice (Acai et al., 2017).

An approach to developing teamwork is through visual and performing arts. Understanding performance theory and the role of art practice is essential because it provides insights into how performing elements in building teams and collaborations influence human expression, interaction, and communication. Performance theory offers a lens to analyze how we present ourselves, engage with others, and create meaning in various contexts, whether in everyday life or professional settings. For instance, how one presents ideas in a meeting, navigates office dynamics, or leads a team can be understood as performative acts requiring creativity, adaptability, and awareness – qualities central to artistic practice. This perspective encourages a more dynamic, engaged approach to work, where employees can draw from artistic techniques to foster innovation, build strong relationships, and create a vibrant workplace culture.

The performance theory could be applied to a team-building activity during a 'brown-bag' lunch. By listening to a poetry reading, participants can learn that listening to others may expose them to ideas that they would not have thought of on their own—innovative thinking. Watching a theatrical performance may lead to a heightened experience by observing actors' verbal and nonverbal cues (Acai et al., 2017). Recognizing that performance occurs in everyday situations allows people to consider the role of the arts in team interactions with others.

Collaborative performance theory in workplaces is a complex, multifaced concept that can be analyzed through various theoretical lenses, including performance theory and its link to intersubjectivity theory. This theory highlights the importance of perspective as a critical factor in collaborative performance (Fauquet-Alekhine & Lahlou, 2022). By integrating art into team-building efforts, organizations can create a culture that values diverse perspectives and promotes a sense of connection and cooperation within the team.

Art Therapy and Employee Well-being

Engagement with art in the workplace also contributes to employee well-being. Access to visual arts, whether through workplace art installations or creative workshops, can reduce stress and enhance job satisfaction. The presence of art can make work environments more aesthetically pleasing and mentally stimulating, which, in turn, can improve productivity and employee morale. According to Fujiwara et al. (2015), there are three types of well-being: evaluative subjective well-being (such as people's overall assessments of their lives or domains of their lives), affective subjective well-being (such as positive and negative feelings), and eudaimonic subjective well-being (such as meaning, autonomy, control, and connectedness).

Art therapy provides a creative outlet for expression and stress relief, helping employees manage anxiety, improve mental health, and boost overall job satisfaction. As companies increasingly prioritize employee well-being, integrating art therapy into wellness programs offers a powerful way to support mental health, create a more positive and productive work environment, and help reduce stress and lower turnover rates. Moreover, it improves emotional resilience (Mastandrea et al., 2019).

In a report published by the World Health Organization in 2020, Fancourt and Finn provide evidence that art in the workplace is possible if the leaders recognize the added health value of engagement with the arts:

- Ensuring that culturally diverse art forms are available and accessible to various groups across the life course, especially those from disadvantaged minorities.

- Encouraging arts and cultural organizations to make health and well-being an integral and strategic part of their work.
- Actively promoting public awareness of the potential benefits of arts engagement for health.
- Developing interventions that encourage arts engagement to support healthy lifestyles.

Integrating music-based programs into broader wellness initiatives offers a comprehensive approach to improving mental and emotional health across diverse groups. This sets the stage for understanding how music contributes to employees' well-being, increasing productivity, creativity, and job satisfaction as part of these wellness initiatives. By leveraging the therapeutic potential of music, organizations can create a more supportive and enriching work culture where mental and emotional health is prioritized.

The Role of Music in Work Practices

MOTIVATIONAL TOOL AND PRODUCTIVITY

Music has long been used to enhance productivity and improve the work environment. Background music in workplaces, such as retail stores, offices, or manufacturing plants, can create a pleasant and motivating atmosphere, helping employees focus and perform tasks more efficiently. According to Singh (2023), employees who listen to energizing and rhythmic music may have increased productivity and lower stress levels than their non-listening colleagues. However, Sanseverino et al. (2023) found that cognitive music has no significant effect, and background music negatively affects motivation.

Research shows that productivity for specific types of tasks is influenced by four music characteristics: tempo, complexity, key, and volume- for people who listen to music at work (Keeler & Cortina, 2020). Tempo relates to the beat of the music. Complexity relates to how complex the music sounds to the listener. Key is categorized by major and minor. Major keys generally positively affect the listener, whereas minor keys create adverse effects. Volume is the decibel level of the music as it is played (Keeler & Cortina, 2020). Keeler and Cortina posit that different combinations of those characteristics contribute to different performance outcomes (2020). For example, a major key, with low complexity, fast tempo, and high volume, is best for complex tasks, while a minor key, with low complexity, slow tempo, and low volume, is best for routine tasks. This information may help employers consider what type of music to play in common areas where many employees work together.

Given the increase in remote work, now followed by a gradual return to in-person work, allowing employees to select their own music appears to impact productivity. Music tastes are personal and influenced by, among other things, age, culture, and individual life experiences. Studies suggest that music that aligns with an employee's preferences can create a more engaging and stimulating experience for that employee (Landay & Harms, 2019). In many work situations, allowing employees to listen to music via headphones or in separate working spaces can improve employee mood and motivation, leading to increased productivity (Landay & Harms, 2019).

Incorporating music into the workplace by allowing employees to use headphones or providing designated areas for listening can be a powerful tool for enhancing overall job satisfaction and performance. Music can elevate mood, reduce stress, and create a more focused and enjoyable work environment, directly translating into increased motivation and productivity. This practice acknowledges the diverse needs of employees, recognizing that a one-size-fits-all approach to work environments may not be ideal. Companies can foster a culture that values well-being and encourages creativity and efficiency by allowing employees to personalize their auditory environment. This can lead to higher employee engagement, lower turnover rates, and more substantial organizational commitment. Integrating music into the workplace is a cost-effective strategy to improve individual and collective performance, contributing to the organization's long-term success (Serpian et al., 2023).

MUSIC IN STRESS REDUCTION

Music plays an influential role in stress reduction, offering a therapeutic escape from the pressures of daily life, including the workplace. Music is a valuable tool to alleviate tension and promote mental well-being in a fast-paced work environment, where deadlines, multitasking, and constant communication can heighten stress levels. Music can resonate with emotions as a universal language, providing solace and calm.

From a physiological perspective, music has been shown to reduce cortisol levels, the hormone associated with stress, and promote relaxation (Finnerty et al., 2022). This effect is especially beneficial in high-stress professions, such as healthcare, where job demands can lead to chronic stress and burnout. For example, a review by Finnerty et al. (2022) found that music therapy significantly reduced stress levels among nurses, improving their mental health and job satisfaction.

A 2021 report by the State of Global Workplace concluded that almost 50% of employees felt stress in their workplace (GALLUP, 2021). Constant stress influences well-being indicators, including mental stability, mental health, and physical health (Casey, 2017). Mental states such as anxiety, depression, burnout, and addictions or physical conditions are associated with high stress levels (APA, 2023). Managing stress within an organization is a crucial factor in a company's success, so focusing on stress management practices is essential and beneficial for enhancing employees' work motivation and ability to handle stress (Panigrahi, 2016). Managers can consider several stress practices, such as meditation, art, or music (Glazer & Liu, 2017; Holman et al., 2018).

MUSIC THERAPY

For the past decades, there has been a strong need for new and innovative interventions to match the fast-developing life and growing demand in today's society (Kovaleva, 2023). One of the latest modern interventions to combat stress worldwide has caught managers' attention: Creative Arts Intervention (CAT) (Martin et al., 2018). CAT is the creative use of media (art, music, dance, and dance/movement) for non-verbal and symbolic communication (Kovaleva, 2023). CATs enable people to express, explore, and perceive on different levels by encouraging attention and concentration, which has been proven by the research of Martin et al., (2018), stating that after interventions, anxiety levels were reduced, and the individual's mood was improved. Thus, CATs could be potentially effective in stress management practices.

Music intervention (or music therapy) is one of the CAT techniques that can be implemented in an organization to fight a stressful environment. Implementing music into the work environment is cost-effective and engaging since it induces employees' concentration (Nao, 2022). Gang (2022) depicts such benefits as improved work efficiency, alleviated work pressure, enhanced feelings between employees, and energized employees due to music interventions employed in the organizational environment. Depending on the type of organization and needs of workers, such kinds of music interventions as background music, music while on breaks, or the use of noise-canceling headphones could be one of the options to employ in the working environment (Nao, 2022; Schwartz et al., 2017). However, while some music methods could work for one organization, it does not necessarily mean they would benefit another.

The effectiveness of music strategies can vary greatly depending on each organization's unique culture, goals, and challenges. Despite this, music has a universal aspect that transcends individual differences by fostering a shared emotional experience, bridging gaps, improving understanding, and strengthening connections within a team, ultimately leading to more effective communication.

IMPROVING COMMUNICATION AND TEAM DYNAMICS

In addition to lowering stress, which can help employees be more open to honest communication in their teams, music can improve communication and team dynamics in other ways. According to Meyer (2019), music can stir emotional responses in employees, which can help to create a positive environment. Employees need to feel a sense of psychological safety to communicate effectively and work together. Meng and Yang (2022) note that psychological safety can be enhanced by the presence of music in the workplace. Their study found that music helps employees feel comfortable enough to engage in voice behavior—expressing constructive opinions and ideas to improve organizational performance. Music activities can create an environment where employees connect personally, meet people of different backgrounds, and build a sense of community, strengthening employee communication and teamwork.

For example, musical workshops are group sessions where employees participate in various musical activities such as songwriting, singing, playing instruments, or making music together. These workshops have been found to generate innovative ideas while working as a team and improve employees' performance, productivity, and communication. Rabinovitch (2020) indicated that creating music together enhanced social connection, increasing team understanding. Music helps switch roles within an established team to give freedom and more responsibility to employees in lower positions. Another point is that while completing tedious, less likable tasks, playing music helps make routine team assignments more bearable and fun (Kovaleva, 2023).

Keeler and Cortina (2020) suggest that organizations create listening activities, such as choosing a song of the week for different team members. Moss and O'Donoghue (2020) posited that workplace choirs enhance social connectedness and improve relationships among staff members across different professional levels. These activities can facilitate social bonds and teamwork, promote collaboration, and help build a robust and supportive workplace culture.

In addition to fostering social bonds and promoting collaboration, creating a supportive workplace culture can be further enhanced by customizing the environment to fit employees' preferences. One effective way to do this is through the use of music. Incorporating music into the workplace not only boosts morale and productivity but can also be tailored to reflect the unique dynamics and needs of the team. Whether through shared playlists or background tunes in common areas, music helps to personalize the workspace, making it more engaging and conducive to creativity.

CUSTOMIZING WORKSPACES WITH MUSIC

A key benefit of personalizing music in the workplace is the sense of autonomy it provides employees. Landay and Harms (2019) state that autonomy is essential to employee motivation and well-being. When employees have control over their work environment, including their choice of music, they are more likely to feel valued and engaged in the work. This leads to higher levels of job satisfaction, reduces turnover intentions, and overall improves organizational outcomes. Allowing employees to customize their music makes sense because each person can react differently to music and create a sense of autonomy. Personality traits, particularly extraversion, can influence how individuals respond to music in the workplace. Extraverts may benefit more from music in tasks requiring higher stimulation, while introverts might find it distracting (Landay & Harms, 2019).

Given the ease of access to multimedia content, the ability to isolate from outside noise and chatter, and the opportunity to enjoy music, especially in environments with high work autonomy, understanding the benefits of listening to music in the workplace could improve the work experience of workers, especially those who use music for emotional regulation. This understanding of the role of customizing the work environment with music could also contribute to a shift in thinking such that music is not only used as a one-time intervention to calm anxiety but could be a work practice that is more widely accepted and shared by management (Ploukous & Panagopoulou, 2018).

From a management perspective, it would be interesting to examine employee preferences for listening to music in the workplace, both in terms of listening modality and genre, and their impact on organizational outcomes. Indeed, meeting music-listening preferences could be another environmental characteristic of some workplaces that enhances employee autonomy, according to self-determination theory, could be a motivational boost and thus improve job performance (Deci et al., 2017). Considering situations where listening to music at work is impossible, deepening the reasons for this would be noteworthy. Sometimes, it is related to the nature of the job itself, which may not allow one to isolate oneself and listen to music (e.g., in customer service). However, in many occupations and workplaces where the work characteristics would allow this practice, it is nevertheless not always performed. Thus, some obstacles or resistance from supervisors may cement the view that listening to music at work is counterproductive. This role of music could be more nuanced when considering the relationships in different work contexts (e.g., service sector or factory) and with different levels of autonomy.

Music in the workspace has been shown to influence productivity and employee morale, but it is not the only factor shaping workplace dynamics. Another significant element that plays a vital role in how people approach their work is religion. Just as music can affect an individual's focus and creativity, religious beliefs and practices can shape attitudes toward work, ethics, and collaboration. To explore this further, it is essential to examine the impact of religion on work practices and how faith-based values can influence individual behavior and organizational culture.

The Impact of Religion on Work Practices

Religion profoundly influences work ethics and practices across cultures. Many religious traditions provide a moral and ethical framework that guides behavior in the workplace. For example, the Protestant work ethic, which emphasizes hard work, discipline, and frugality, has significantly influenced Western work practices, particularly in the context of capitalism.

Research suggests that religion significantly impacts work practices, though its influence varies across contexts. Religious beliefs and commitments can affect employee behavior in organizations, ranging from firm to negligible effects (Weaver & Stansburgy, 2014). Work practices often may conflict with religious practices, particularly for Muslim employees who must negotiate rhythms, space, and bodies of work (Van Laer & Essers, 2023). For religious entrepreneurs, faith shapes their work activities, often requiring a reinterpretation of work in religious terms to reconcile potential tensions between faith and business (Griebel et al., 2014). The impact of religion on work practices is complex and individualized, influenced by factors such as organizational context, cultural norms, and personal interpretations of religious commitments, as well as the impact on business operating decisions and procedures in the workplace.

BUSINESS OPERATING PROCEDURES PRACTICES

Employees' and customers' religious beliefs influence business decisions, such as location, layout, shift scheduling, and compliance. These issues are especially salient for global corporations extending operations overseas and utilizing expatriate management (Metters, 2019).

Table 1 is an example of the effects on business operations by religion:

Religious Tradition	Countries	Issue/Operational Concern
Animism	S. America: Bolivia, Peru Asia: Cambodia, Malaysia, Nepal, Singapore	Operational shutdown
Islam	Bangladesh, India, Pakistan	Factory location; Shift scheduling; Office layout
Judaism	Israel	Technology use; Gender segregation
Confucianism	South Korea, China	Contract adherence
Christianity	USA: Jehovah's Witness, Christian Science	Medical operations

Source: Metters, 2019, p.4.

The religious beliefs of either employees or customers can disrupt operational choices, such as seats sold on an airplane, where to locate a facility, and conflicts between the expression of occupational and religious identities.

WORKPLACE IDENTITY

Identity is core to diversity in the workplace, reflecting fundamental social differences among people. Workplace diversity entails more than visible or surface-level diversity (e.g., age or ethnicity) but also includes the deep-level diversity associated with sexual orientation, class, or religion (Ghumman et al., 2016; Harris & Yancey, 2017). Although some religious identities can be invisible to coworkers, others have visible signifiers, such as the wearing of a hijab, kippah, or turban by some Muslim women, Jewish men, and Sikh men, respectively. Visible signifiers became a concern in diversity policy during the mid-1980s with the changing composition of the workforce (Sauer, 2009) and continue to be necessary to diversity policies (Bond & Haynes, 2014).

In the context of the religious self in the workplace, to be authentic, employees must experience congruence between their internal values and external expressions (Roberts, 2013). Workplace behavior and practice can create challenges for expressing an authentic self. For example, some religious police officers may see their work furthering a religiously understood common good. Within Christianity, forgiveness is a prominent theme in scripture and theology, alongside concepts of sin and mercy. Nevertheless, Christian officers typically act on behalf of the legal system and do not have the right to offer forgiveness on its behalf. However, occasionally, they may exercise mercy through discretion. That means that divergent identity demands may create internal conflict and tension that individuals need to manage (Heliot et al., 2020).

Key variables affecting how religious employees negotiate role demands include the value-fit between religious identity and job-related concerns (e.g., empathy with clients, clinical decision-making (Morrison & Borgen, 2010), the organization's culture, policies, and practices, as well as role expectations (Kutcher et al., 2010) along with an employee's formal status and the nature of the employment relationship (Haines & Saba, 2012). Kutcher et al. (2010)) found that religious practice at work—notably, the freedom to express religious identity—was negatively related to work-related stress and burnout and positively related to job satisfaction, organizational citizenship behavior, and commitment. They conclude that where religious identity is given room for expression and thus can be either highly congruent or coexistent with an occupational identity, positive behaviors, and job attitudes are likely; where expression is not permitted, outcomes are more harmful.

The nature of the organization's workforce is likely to contribute to the importance of support for religious expression in terms of engendering well-being and other positive consequences. Organizations encouraging such expression will likely positively affect employees' job attitudes, performance, and retention (Cabel et al., 2013). Henderson noted that religious involvement has been found to positively affect the well-being of African American employees, helping them cope with stressful job situations (2016). This finding is echoed in Abu-Ras and Hosein's (2015) study of Muslim military personnel in the United States, demonstrating the central role of religion and practice in their lives. Religious identity can function as a coping mechanism and may be both a protective and risk factor in well-being, depending on workplace support for religious expression. Further, religious expression is significant in workplace relationships, perceptions, and organizational attractiveness and fit (King & Franke, 2017).

Moral and Ethical Frameworks

Focusing on the effects of religious or spiritual orientation, as well as on the values, norms, and goals present in a business, can gain a nuanced understanding of the relationship between religious and spiritual beliefs and sustainable, ethical behavior in an organization. In its most basic form, ethical behavior in business alludes to adherence to honesty, transparency, and fairness in one's interactions with stakeholders (Crossan et al., 2013). While we want to believe that others share our perceptions of honest and fair behavior and, thus, our understanding of ethicality, these largely depend on an individual's underlying principles and values (Driscoll et al., 2019; Pirson et al., 2017).

Moral failures have become common in society and for multinational corporations. FTX, Volkswagen, Enron, and others have demonstrated poor institutional governance, a lack of accountability, or a lack of strategic clarity (Yaffe-Bellany, 2022). This raises the question: Do we genuinely comprehend the ethical decision-making process? For instance, a corporation operating simultaneously in multiple countries introduces complexity to decision-making, such as national culture and moral virtues (Ellestad et al., 2024).

Ellestad and Winton (2022) sought to bridge a significant gap in existing ethical frameworks by advocating for the inclusion of moral virtues. For individuals of faith, religious nonprofits, or those with strong personal convictions, moral virtues can be a potent and crucial force in organizational decisions. Virtues are hallmarked by honesty, integrity, and cultural values, all with high ethical standards.

ROLE OF HONESTY

A definition of honesty implies a refusal to be deceptive, lie, cheat, or steal even when allowed to (Ashton et al., 2014). Honesty focuses on sincerity, fairness, greed avoidance, and modesty. Openness and transparency are forms of honesty that allow informed choice (Schroeder et al., 2019).

ROLE OF INTEGRITY

The principles of integrity include trustworthiness, loyalty, dependability, accountability, commitment, cooperation, congeniality, obedience, and courage (Ellestad & Winton, 2022). A simple definition is having strong and consistent moral values that a person refuses to waiver on.

ROLE OF CULTURAL VALUES

While national and organizational cultures are similar, they should not be used interchangeably. Both refer to rituals, values, beliefs, and ceremonies that hold individuals together but function on different levels. Organizational culture is specific to the individuals within the organization regardless of the country the employee resides in. National culture reflects the broader traditions and values that unite all people within a country, not just via one employer.

Social norms influence honesty, especially how individuals interact with situations involving honesty and dishonesty (Heintz et al., 2016). Corruption and scandal provide evidence of the underlying disingenuous nature of the national culture, where lying, cheating, and stealing do not strongly offend the sensibilities of leaders and employees alike

Honesty, integrity, and cultural values play a vital role in shaping ethical behavior and social cohesion, and these principles also influence how societies approach religious holidays and work-life balance. Religious holidays, rooted in cultural and spiritual traditions, are significant for many individuals, providing time for reflection, family, and community engagement. Balancing work commitments with these observances requires respect for cultural diversity and an understanding of the importance of these days in maintaining a healthy work-life balance. Employers who acknowledge and accommodate religious holidays demonstrate a commitment to inclusivity and the well-being of their employees, fostering an environment where both personal values and professional responsibilities are respected.

Religious Holidays and Work-Life Balance

> Work-life balance affects attitudes, behavior, welfare, and organizational effectiveness. Therefore, it is necessary to have an attitude of appreciation from a sense of diversity towards a religion. Dewi et al., 2020

Religiosity can positively influence work-life balance by reducing conflict experiences and providing coping mechanisms (Khan & Kirmani, 2018). Studies have found that religiosity can be beneficial for achieving a work-life balance rather than competing with work and other non-work roles for time and energy (Sav, 2019). Religiosity has been shown to moderate the relationship between satisfaction with work-life balance and job satisfaction, acting as a personal resource that helps individuals cope with work-life imbalance challenges (Karim et al., 2016). Life quality depends on the balance of work and life. Among the determinants of life quality is religious freedom in the workplace, which contributes to physical and mental health and leads to employee stability. Religious activities are closely linked to religiosity and can predict a person's behavior at work, emphasizing the importance of considering religious commitments alongside work and family roles in work-life balance helps to foster resilience (Dewi et al., 2020).

The employee work-life balance depends on the strategy used to improve life quality, such as the role of religious freedom in the workplace (Kasmuri et al., 2021). "By considering religious aspects in the organization's policies, an improvement in workplace harmonization can occur and at the same time work-life quality" (Kasmuri et al., 2021, p. 326). It has been suggested that religious matters should be supported with an equality of resources policy (Alon & Wu, 2017).

Religion issues at workplaces are seen in the demand for religious freedom, the colleague acceptance of religious beliefs, and the effect on freedom of religion at the workplace. It can be summarized that an organization's role in entertaining employees' religious beliefs and commitments could be managed wisely by reviewing management policy (Heliot et al., 2020; Hashim et al., 2019). Additionally, organizational management policy could reduce the possibility of employment discrimination in the workplace. Kasmuri et al. (2021) identified themes that involve religious issues in the workplace, such as freedom of religion, colleagues' acceptance, and the effect of religious issues.

DEMAND FOR FREEDOM OF RELIGIOUS COMMITMENTS

Reasonable religious decision-making should be considered when managing an organization with various religions. Organizations should support employees' religious beliefs through freedom of religious practice work (Gonzalez-Gonzalez, 2018). Two religious-based approaches can be executed: the individual and the organization (Fanggidae, 2018). Religious accommodation could be the basis for the management to explore the various religious beliefs in the workplace as part of the organization's values, thus promoting workplace harmonization.

The demand for freedom of religious commitments in the workplace reflects the growing recognition of employees' rights to observe and practice their faiths. As workplaces become more diverse, employees increasingly expect their employers to accommodate religious practices, such as observing prayer times, dietary restrictions, or religious holidays. This demand challenges employers to balance operational needs with respect for individual religious commitments, ensuring that policies are flexible enough to allow religious expression without compromising productivity. When employers respond positively to these demands, it not only upholds legal and ethical standards but also enhances employee morale and loyalty by showing that the organization values diversity and inclusivity.

COLLEAGUE ACCEPTANCE

Colleague acceptance of religious beliefs is crucial for fostering a harmonious and respectful workplace. When employees are open to understanding and accepting their coworkers' diverse religious practices and beliefs, it creates an environment of mutual respect and inclusivity. This acceptance involves refraining from discrimination or ridicule and showing support by respecting religious customs. Such an environment encourages collaboration and reduces workplace tension, increasing job satisfaction and productivity. When colleagues accept and value each other's religious beliefs, it ultimately contributes to a more cohesive and positive work culture.

EFFECT ON FREEDOM OF RELIGION AT WORKPLACE

Religious commitment is seen in positive work outcomes through assistance in work-life balance (Hassan et al., 2021), task flexibility (Ang et al., 2019), work pressure (Batalla et al., 2019), job performance (Li et al., 2019), and job satisfaction (Ntantana et al., 2017). Work pressure affects the employee's occupational health, which can be countered with the role of religion.

The freedom of religion in the workplace is a fundamental right that allows employees to express and practice their religious beliefs without discrimination or retaliation. However, balancing this freedom with the operational needs of a business can be challenging. Employers must create an inclusive environment that respects diverse religious practices, such as allowing time for prayer, accommodating religious attire, and avoiding scheduling conflicts with religious observances. Failing to provide these accommodations can lead to legal consequences and diminish workplace morale. Conversely, when correctly managed, respecting religious freedom enhances workplace diversity, fosters mutual respect, and contributes to a positive organizational culture.

Intersections of Art, Music, and Religion

The intersections of art, music, and religion within work practices reflect a profound and often historical connection between creative expression and spiritual life. In many cultures, religious rituals have long been accompanied by music and art, serving as a means of worship and communicating sacred narratives. These elements combine to create an immersive experience that transcends the mundane aspects of work, transforming labor into an act of devotion. Artistic expressions in religious contexts, such as illuminated manuscripts or sacred architecture, are often designed to inspire reverence and contemplation. Music, whether through chants, hymns, or instrumental compositions, enhances the spiritual atmosphere, reinforcing the sense of community and shared purpose in religious work practices. This synergy fosters a deeper connection to the divine and integrates spiritual values into the very fabric of daily life, influencing how work is perceived and performed. For example, art practices intersect with all elements in the workplace, such as human interactions, whether music or religion, as identified in Figure 1.

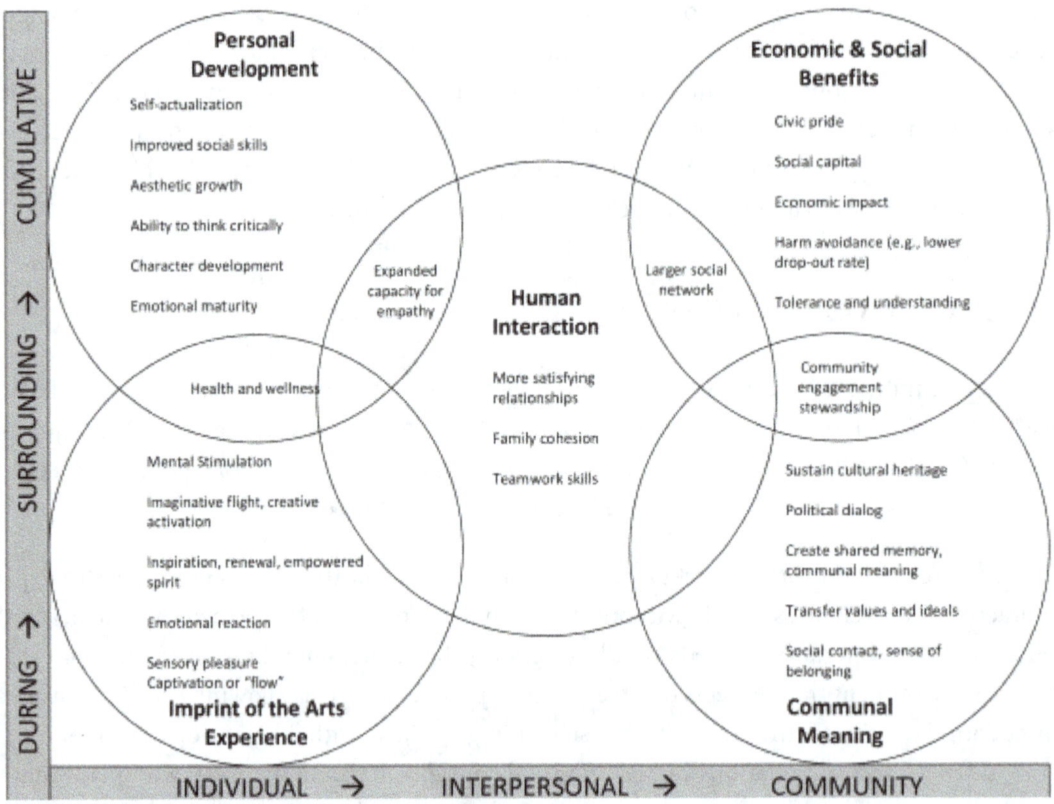

FIGURE 1: **Brown, 2006, p.21 in Byrnes, 2022, p. 7.**

Alan Brown's map, included in Byrnes's 2022 book, identifies the value of the arts using a scale that starts with the arts experience and extends left to right from the individual to the community and vertically during the event to the cumulative value that results.

The five overlapping dimensions of value include the imprint of the art experience, personal development, human interaction, economic and social benefits, and communal meaning. Within each dimension, Brown plugs in various outcomes significant to that dimension and notes overlapping areas. For example, personal development and human interaction share an expanded capacity for empathy (Byrnes, 2022).

An organization's ability to interact with its external environment is essential for transforming resources into products and services. These environments' demographic, economic, political, social, and technological factors significantly influence the organization's strategies, operations, and success. By recognizing and adapting to these external forces, organizations can remain competitive and responsive to the evolving needs of their customers and markets.

The interaction of art, music, and religion in work practices is increasingly important in today's dynamic environments. They foster creativity, innovation, and fresh perspectives critical in problem-solving and adapting to external challenges. They incorporate approaches to enhance team collaboration, drive meaningful engagement, and inspire the development of unique products and services. This emphasis on such approaches empowers organizations to tackle challenges with resourcefulness and creativity, using tools for creative expression, a component for cultivating innovation, resilience, and a deeper connection to the values that shape both the organization and its relationship with the world.

Case Studies and Practical Applications

Examining case studies of organizations that successfully integrate art, music, and religion into their work practices provides valuable insights. For instance, companies that have implemented art programs, music initiatives, or religious accommodations can serve as models for how these elements can effectively enhance the workplace.

CASE STUDY: IMPLEMENTING ART PROGRAMS IN CORPORATIONS

Company Overview: XYZ Tech Solutions is a global leader in cloud computing services. With 10,000 employees across multiple countries, XYZ has long been committed to fostering innovation and creativity. The company has consistently ranked as a top workplace due to its employee-centric culture and forward-thinking leadership.

The Challenge: As the company expanded rapidly, XYZ Tech Solutions began facing issues related to employee burnout, decreased creativity, and team collaboration. The high-stress environment, especially in the software development and project management departments, affected employee morale, resulting in higher turnover and lower job satisfaction rates.

Proposed Solution: Corporate Art Program The HR and leadership teams, in consultation with a local arts organization, proposed implementing a corporate art program aimed at reducing stress, increasing creativity, and improving overall employee engagement. The art program would consist of:

- **Workshops:** Regular, company-sponsored painting, sculpture, and digital art workshops for employees.
- **Art Installations:** An artist-in-residence program that allows artists to display their work in office spaces.
- **Creative Spaces:** Designating areas within the office as "creative zones," with open access to materials such as canvases, paints, and art supplies.
- **Art Exhibitions:** Biannual employee art showcases where employees could display their work.

Implementation: The art program was launched in phases over six months:

1. **Pilot Workshops:** The first phase involved small, voluntary workshops in three locations. These sessions focused on beginner-level painting and pottery, with classes held twice a month.
2. **Dedicated Creative Zones:** The second phase established "creative corners" in headquarters, with art supplies available during work hours. Employees could drop in anytime to express themselves creatively.
3. **Artist-in-Residence:** A well-known local artist was invited to work in XYZ's lobby for a month, interacting with employees and creating art inspired by the company's culture and mission.
4. **Annual Art Exhibition:** A company-wide art competition was introduced, encouraging office employees to submit their artwork. The winners were showcased in a virtual gallery.

Results: After 12 months, XYZ Tech Solutions observed the following outcomes:

- **Improved Employee Well-being:** A post-program survey indicated a 30% improvement in employee well-being and job satisfaction. Many employees cited the art program as a stress reliever and a source of fulfillment.

- **Boost in Creativity and Collaboration:** Teams participating in workshops showed a 15% increase in cross-department collaboration, as noted through increased participation in company-wide creative projects.
- **Reduced Burnout:** Absenteeism due to burnout decreased by 18% in departments where art activities were most active.
- **Cultural Impact:** The artist-in-residence program fostered a sense of connection between employees and the company's creative vision, leading to more discussions about the role of creativity in problem-solving.
- **Talent Retention:** The turnover rate dropped by 12%, particularly in high-pressure roles such as software development, where employees reported feeling more balanced and engaged due to the creative outlet provided by the program.

Conclusion: XYZ Tech Solutions successfully implemented a corporate art program that improved employee well-being and enhanced creativity and collaboration across departments. The initiative highlighted the value of integrating artistic activities into corporate culture to boost productivity, engagement, and employee satisfaction.

CASE STUDY #2: THE ROLE OF MUSIC IN ENHANCING WORKPLACE PRACTICES

Company: TechInnovators Inc.
Industry: Software Development
Size: 500 employees
Headquarters: San Francisco, CA

TechInnovators Inc. is a rapidly growing software development company known for its innovative approach to product design and employee well-being. Like many modern tech companies, it strives to foster a work environment that encourages creativity, focus, and collaboration. In 2022, the company began exploring new ways to enhance productivity and employee satisfaction, and one key initiative was introducing music in the workplace.

Problem

In 2021, TechInnovators experienced a decline in employee engagement and productivity. After an internal survey, the company found that many employees struggled to focus in their open-office environment, which had become more common in the post-pandemic hybrid work setup. Background noise, interruptions, and a lack of privacy were common issues reported by employees.

Maintaining a cohesive culture was also challenging as some workers returned to the office while others continued working remotely.

Hypothesis

TechInnovators hypothesized that carefully curated music could serve multiple purposes in the workplace, including:

- Improving focus and concentration.
- Enhancing creativity and problem-solving abilities.
- Reducing stress and promoting relaxation during high-pressure tasks.
- Strengthening team cohesion through shared music experiences.

Implementation

TechInnovators took a strategic approach to implementing music in the workplace, creating different playlists tailored to specific work tasks and environments. They partnered with a professional music consultancy to develop a multi-phase music integration plan.

1. **Focus Zones:** The company designated specific areas within the office as "focus zones," where employees could work on deep, uninterrupted tasks. Calming instrumental music, such as classical or ambient sounds, was played at a low volume in these areas.
2. **Collaborative Spaces:** For collaborative spaces where teams brainstormed and discussed projects, TechInnovators introduced more upbeat and rhythmic music to inspire creativity and energy. Playlists included genres like indie, jazz, and soft electronic music.
3. **Personalized Playlists:** For remote workers and employees in private office spaces, the company provided access to a corporate Spotify account with pre-made playlists for different moods and tasks (e.g., "Coding Flow," "Creative Spark," "Relax & Recharge"). Employees could also customize these playlists based on their preferences.
4. **Break and Relaxation Areas:** Music was also introduced in break rooms and relaxation zones. Upbeat yet relaxing music was played to promote a sense of calm during downtime.
5. **Music-Free Zones:** Recognizing that not everyone thrives in a musical environment, TechInnovators designated certain parts of the office as "music-free zones" for those who preferred silence or wanted to use their noise-cancelling headphones.
6. **Team Building with Music:** As a cultural initiative, TechInnovators encouraged teams to create collaborative playlists during virtual and in-person meetings. Music became an icebreaker during virtual team-building exercises, helping strengthen connections between remote and on-site employees.

Results

TechInnovators conducted a follow-up survey and analyzed productivity metrics six months after implementing the music initiative. The results were overwhelmingly positive:

- **Increased Focus and Productivity:** 72% of employees reported that music helped them concentrate better during tasks requiring deep focus. Productivity tracking software showed a 15% improvement in project completion times in the "focus zones."
- **Enhanced Creativity:** Teams using collaborative spaces with upbeat music reported a 22% increase in creative ideas generated during brainstorming sessions.
- **Reduced Stress:** 68% of employees indicated that background music in relaxation areas helped them manage stress, particularly during high-pressure project deadlines. HR noted a 10% reduction in stress-related absenteeism.
- **Improved Employee Engagement:** Music played a significant role in uniting teams, especially in hybrid environments. Using team playlists during virtual meetings fostered a sense of camaraderie, with employee satisfaction surveys showing a 12% increase in engagement scores.
- **Balanced Work Environment:** The music-free zones and personalized playlists ensured that all employees felt accommodated regardless of their work preferences. The mix of options led to higher satisfaction levels among those who needed quieter environments.

Conclusion

Integrating music into TechInnovators Inc.'s workplace practices resulted in several benefits, including enhanced focus, creativity, stress relief, and team cohesion. By strategically implementing music in different workplace areas and respecting individual preferences, the company created a more dynamic and flexible work environment that catered to remote and on-site employees.

CASE STUDY #3: THE ROLE OF RELIGION IN WORKPLACE PRACTICES

Background

Companies increasingly employ individuals from various religious backgrounds in today's globalized and diverse work environment. As workplaces become more multicultural, balancing religious practices with workplace operations has become crucial for fostering inclusion and employee satisfaction. This case study explores how a generic mid-sized company, Innovatech Solutions, addressed religious diversity to create an inclusive workplace that respects religious practices while maintaining productivity.

Problem

Innovatech Solutions employs 800 staff members with significant religious diversity, including Christians, Muslims, Jews, Hindus, Buddhists, and non-religious employees. The lack of formal policies regarding religious accommodation led to several issues:

1. **Prayer Accommodations**: Muslim employees who needed to pray at specific times found it challenging to adhere to their religious practices due to busy work schedules and a lack of private prayer spaces.
2. **Holiday Scheduling**: The company's holiday calendar mainly reflected Christian holidays, leaving employees of other faiths struggling to balance work and religious observances.
3. **Religious Attire**: Some employees faced subtle discrimination or discomfort for wearing religious attire such as hijabs, turbans, or kippahs.
4. **Dietary Needs**: Company events and cafeteria offerings lacked consideration for dietary restrictions required by some religious groups, such as halal, kosher, or vegetarian meals.

These challenges resulted in lower morale among religious employees, increased tension among colleagues, and inconsistent approaches by managers when handling religious accommodations.

Hypothesis

The management team at Innovatech Solutions hypothesized that by formally addressing religious practices in the workplace, they could:

- **Improve employee morale and engagement** among religious employees by fostering an inclusive environment.
- **Reduce turnover rates** by creating a workplace that respects diverse religious needs.
- **Increase productivity** by allowing employees to practice their faith without stress or conflict.
- **Enhance workplace culture** through greater understanding and respect among employees of different backgrounds.

Implementation

To address these issues, Innovatech Solutions introduced several key initiatives aimed at accommodating religious practices in the workplace:

1. **Multi-Faith Prayer Rooms**: The company converted unused office space into designated multi-faith prayer rooms for employees to use for religious practices. These rooms provided a quiet, private area with amenities like prayer mats and religious texts.

2. **Floating Holidays**: Innovatech revised its holiday policy to include floating holidays. Employees were allowed to take time off for religious observances outside of standard holidays, such as Ramadan, Yom Kippur, or Diwali. This ensured that all employees could celebrate religious events important to them without losing paid time off.
3. **Religious Inclusion Training**: Innovatech implemented mandatory religious inclusion training for all staff to foster a culture of understanding and respect. This training covered topics such as the importance of religious accommodation, understanding religious attire, and ways to respect religious practices in day-to-day interactions.
4. **Dietary Accommodations**: The company updated its cafeteria offerings and event catering to include options for employees who adhered to religious dietary laws. Halal, kosher, and vegetarian meals were clearly labeled and available at all company functions.
5. **Religious Attire and Symbols**: A formal policy was introduced to support employees' wearing religious attire or symbols. This policy ensured that employees could express their religious identity without fear of discrimination. Managers were trained to promote a respectful atmosphere and address any issues sensitively.
6. **Interfaith Employee Resource Group (ERG)**: The company established an Interfaith ERG as a forum for employees from different religious backgrounds to discuss their experiences, provide feedback on workplace policies, and organize interfaith events. This group worked closely with HR to continuously improve the company's approach to religious inclusion.

Results

After a year of implementing these changes, Innovatech Solutions experienced several positive outcomes:

1. **Increased Employee Satisfaction**: Employee engagement surveys revealed a 15% increase in satisfaction among religious employees, who cited the availability of prayer rooms, floating holidays, and dietary accommodations as critical factors in their improved morale.
2. **Reduced Turnover Rates**: The turnover rate for employees from minority religious backgrounds decreased by 10%, as employees felt more valued and respected in the workplace. Several employees who had previously considered leaving the company due to religious conflicts decided to stay, citing the new policies.
3. **Enhanced Workplace Culture**: The diversity and inclusion training and the Interfaith ERG's initiatives led to a more inclusive and respectful workplace culture. Employees reported feeling more comfortable discussing their religious practices and felt that colleagues had become more open and understanding. There was also a noticeable reduction in religious discrimination or discomfort regarding religious attire.

4. **Improved Productivity**: Employees who practiced their religion without work-related stress reported better focus and engagement. By allowing employees to take time for religious observances without feeling guilty or conflicted, the company saw a 12% increase in productivity, especially during critical religious periods like Ramadan or the Jewish High Holidays.
5. **Positive Impact on Recruitment**: Innovatech's religious accommodation policies were highlighted in recruitment materials, which helped attract a more diverse pool of candidates. New hires appreciated the company's commitment to diversity and religious inclusion, which became a selling point for top talent.

Conclusion

Innovatech Solutions' efforts to accommodate religious practices improved employee satisfaction, retention, and overall workplace harmony. By addressing the spiritual needs of its workforce through designated prayer spaces, flexible holiday policies, dietary accommodations, and education on religious inclusion, the company created a more inclusive and respectful environment for all employees.

This case study demonstrates that integrating religious practices into workplace policies enhances employee well-being, strengthens company culture, improves productivity, and attracts diverse talent. Companies prioritizing religious inclusion can create a more harmonious and productive workplace for everyone.

Chapter Conclusion

The practices of art, music, and religion have profound effects on the world of work, influencing everything from individual creativity and motivation to organizational culture and ethics. By understanding these influences, businesses and workers can create more productive, enriching, and meaningful environments. This chapter has explored the multifaceted ways art, music, and religion intersect with work, highlighting their importance in shaping the nature and experience of work across different contexts. As the global workplace evolves, these cultural elements will remain essential in guiding how work is perceived and performed.

REFERENCES

Abu-Ras, W., & Hosein, S. (2015). Understanding resiliency through vulnerability: Cultural meaning and religious practice among Muslim military personnel. *Psychology of Religion and Spirituality, 7*, 179–191.

Acai, A., McQueen, S.A., McKinnon, V.E., & Sonnadara, R.R. (2017). Using art to develop teamwork and communication skills among health professionals: A literature review. *Arts & Health, 9*, 60–72.

Adajian, T. (2024). The definition of art. In E.N. Zalta & U. Nodelman (Eds.), *The Stanford encyclopedia of philosophy*. https://plato.stanford.edu/entries/art-definition/

Alexandre, J. M. (2017). *Dance leadership: Theory into practice.* Palgrave Macmillan.

Alon, I., Li, S., Wu, J. (2017). An institutional perspective on religious freedom and economic growth. *Politics and Religion,* 689-716.

Antal, A.B., & Bitran, I.N. (2018). Discovering the meaningfulness of art in organizations. *Journal of Cultural Management and Cultural Policy / Zeitschrift für Kulturmanagement und Kulturpolitik, 4*, 55-76.

American Psychological Association (2017). Stress in America: Coping with change. https://www.apa.org/news/press/releases/stress/2016/coping-with-change.pdf

Appu, A.V., Sia, S.K., & Sahoo, B.C. (2015). Creativity at the workplace: Proposing some contributors. *International journal of innovative research and development, 4.*

Ashton, M. C., Lee, K., & de Vries, R. E. (2014). The HEXACO honesty-humility, agreeableness, and emotionality factors: A review of research and theory. *Personality and Social Psychology Review, 18*(2), 139–152.

Batalla, V.R.D., Barrameda, A.L.N., Basal, J.M.S., Bathan,A.S.J., Bautista, J.E.G., Rebueno, M.C.D.R., & Macindo, J.R.B. (2019). Moderating effect of occupational stress on spirituality and depression of registered nurses in tertiary hospital: A structure equation model. *Journal of Advanced Nursing, 75*(4), 772-782.

Beech, D. (2020). *Art and Labour.* Bill Publishing.

Benefiel, M.J., Fry, L.W., & Geigle, D. (2014). Spirituality and religion in the workplace: History, theory, and research. *Psychology of Religion and Spirituality, 6*, 175-187.

Bernes, J. (2017). *The work of art in the age of Ddeindustrialization.* Stanford University Press.

Berthoin, A., & Strauß, A. (2013). *Artistic interventions in organizations: Finding evidence of values-added.* Creative Commons Publishing.

Beuhring, J.H., & Liedtka, J. (2018). Embracing systematic futures thinking at the intersection of strategic planning, foresight, and design. *Journal of Innovation Management, 6*(3), 134-152.

Bond, M. A., & Haynes, M. C. (2014). Workplace diversity: A social-ecological framework and policy implications. *Social Issues and Policy Review, 8,* 167–201.

Borstorff, P.C., & Arlington, K. (2011). Protecting Religion in the Workplace? What Employees Think. *Journal of Legal, Ethical and Regulatory Issues, 14.*

Brown, A., (2006). An architecture of value. *Grantmakers in the Arts, 17*(1), 18–23.

Byrnes, W.J. (2022). *Management and the arts* (6th ed.). Routledge.

Cabel, D. M., Gino, F., & Staats, B. R. (2013). Breaking them in or eliciting their best? Reframing socialization around newcomers' authentic self-expression. *Administrative Science Quarterly, 58,* 1–36.

Casey, G. (2017). Stress and disease. *Nursing New Zealand, 23*(6), 20-24.

Crossan, M., Mazutis, D., & Seijts, G. (2013). In search of virtue: The role of virtues, values and character strengths in ethical decision making. *Journal of Business Ethics, 113*(4), 567–581.

Deci, E. L., Olafsen, A. H., & Ryan, R. M. (2017). Self-determination theory in work organizations: The state of a science. *Annual Review of Organizational Psychology and Organizational Behavior, 4,* 19–43.

Dewi, S.S., Madjid, A., & Fauzan, A. (2020). The role of religiosity in work-life balance. *Budapest International Research and Critics Institute-Journal, 3*(3).

Donghwy An.,& Nara, Y. (2018). The inspirational power of arts on creativity. *Journal of Business Research, 85*, 467-475.

Driscoll, C., McIsaac, E. M., & Wiebe, E. (2019). The material nature of spirituality in the small business workplace: From transcendent ethical values to immanent ethical actions. *Journal of Management, Spirituality & Religion, 16*(2), 155–177.

Ellestad, A.I., & Winton, B.G. (2024). The push and pull between culture and integrity in the workplace: An ethical decision-making context. *International Journal of Ethics and Systems, 42.*

Ellestad, A.I. and Winton, B.G. (2022). Ethical decision-making: a culture influenced virtue specific model for multinational corporations. *Ethics and Behavior, 33*(8), 656-671.

Fauquet-Alekhine, P., & Lahlou, S. (2022). Performance in collaborative activity: Contribution of intersubjectivity theory. *Journal of Psychology & Behavior Research* 4(1),11-41.

Fancourt, D. & Finn, S. (2020). What is the evidence on the role of the arts in improving health and well-being? A scoping review. *Nordic Journal of Arts Culture and Health, 2*(1), 77–83.

Fanggidae, R. E. (2018).Organizational culture and spirituality workplace: Empirical study of influence of organizational culture and spirituality workplace. *E3S Web of Conferences, 73*, 1–4.

Finnerty R, Zhang K, Tabuchi RA, Zhang K. (2022). The use of music to manage burnout in nurses: A systematic review. *American Journal of Health Promotion,36*(8), 1386-1398.

Fujiwara, D., Dolan, O., & Lawton, R. (2015). Creative occupations and subjective well-being. *Nesta Working Paper.*

GALLUP (2021). Discover how employees around the world experience life and work in 2020. State of the Global Workplace Report. https://www.gallup.com/workplace/349484/state-of-the-global-workplace.aspx

Gang Li. (2022). Probe into the role of music therapy in workplace health management. *Journal of Healthcare Engineering*, 1–6.

Geigle, D., Fry, L.W., & Benefiel, M.J. (2013). Spirituality and religion in the workplace: History, theory, and research. *Academy of Management Proceedings, 1.*

Ghumman, S., Ryan, A. M., & Park, J. S. (2016). Religious harassment in the workplace: An examination of observer intervention. *Journal of Organizational Behavior, 37*, 279–306.

Glazer S., & Liu C. (2017, April 26). Work, stress, coping, and stress management. *Oxford Research Encyclopedia of Psychology.* https://doi.org/10.1093/acrefore/9780190236557.013.30

González-González, M. (2018). Reconciling spirituality and workplace: Towards a balanced proposal for occupational health. *Journal of Religion and Health, 57*(1), 349–359.

Griebel, J., Park, J.Z., & Neubert, M.J. (2014). Faith and work: An exploratory study of religious entrepreneurs. *Religion, 5*, 780-800.

Haake, A.B. (2011). Individual music listening in workplace settings. *Musicae Scientiae, 15*, 107 - 129.

Haines, V. Y., & Saba, T. (2012). Challenges to professional identities and emotional exhaustion. *Career Development International, 17*, 120–136.

Harris, H. W., & Yancey, G. I. (2017). Values, dissonance, and rainbows: Practice tips for Christian social workers in a polarized world. *Social Work & Christianity, 44*, 123–142.

Hashim, R., Mohd Aminuddin, Z., Ghazali, A. R., & Abd Razak, N. (2019). Elderly Welfare and Quality of Life: A Qualitative Inquiry. *Environment-Behaviour Proceedings Journal, 4*(12), 109.

Hassan, Z., Tnay, J. S., Sukardi Yososudarmo, S. M., & Sabil, S. (2021). The relationship between workplace spirituality and work-to-family enrichment in selected public sector organizations in Malaysia. *Journal of Religion and Health, 60*(6), 4132-4150.

Heliot, Y., Gleibs, I.H., Coyle, A., Rousseau, D.M., & Rojon, C. (2020). Religious identity in the workplace: A systematic review, research agenda, and practical implications. *Human Resource Management, 59*(2), 153-173.

Heintz, C., Karabegovic, M., & Molnar, A. (2016). The co-evolution of honesty and strategic vigilance. *Frontiers in Psychology, 7*, 1503.

Henderson, A. K. (2016). Jesus didn't teach us to juggle: Religious involvement, work-family conflict, and life satisfaction among African Americans. *Journal of Family Issues, 37*, 1558–1584.

Holman, D., Johnson, S., & O'Connor, E.(2018).Stress management interventions: Improving subjective psychological well-being in the workplace. *Handbook of well-being.* DEF Publishers.

Kamiya, T. (2024). Fostering corporate innovation activities through artist-created boundary media. Creativity, Innovation, and Entrepreneurship. *AHFE (2024) International Conference.*

Karim, J., Bobi, Z., Aftab, F., & Karim, J. (2016). The moderating role of religiosity on the relationship between satisfaction with work-life balance and job satisfaction. *Journal of Business Studies, 12*(1).

Kasmuri, S.H., Ng, N.K., Ghani, N.A., & Shahrin, F. (2021). Towards quality of life: Analysis of patterns on religious practice at workplace. *Environment-Behaviour Proceedings Journal, 6*(16), 325-334.

Keeler, K. R., & Cortina, J. M. (2020). Working to the beat: A self-regulatory framework linking music characteristics to job performance. *Academy of Management Review, 45*(2), 447-471.

Khan, O.F., & Kirmani, M.S. (2018). A study of relationship between religiosity and work-life balance. *Advance Research Journal of Social Science, 9*(1).

King, J. E., & Franke, G. R. (2017). Faith bias or religious expression: The real religious diversity challenge? *Journal of Management, Spirituality & Religion, 14*, 81–99.

Kovaleva, A. (2023). *Benefits and drawbacks of music in stress management in a workplace.* University of Tartu.

Kutcher, E. J., Bragger, J. D., Rodriguez-Srednicki, O., & Masco, J. L. (2010). The role of religiosity in stress, job attitudes, and organizational citizenship behavior. *Journal of Business Ethics, 95*, 319–337.

Landay, K., & Harms, P. D. (2019). Whistle while you work? A review of the effects of music in the workplace. *Human Resource Management Review, 29*(3), 371–385.

Li, C., Xu, Y., Gill, A., Haider, Z. A., & Wang, Y. (2019). Religious beliefs, socially responsible investment, and cost of debt: Evidence from entrepreneurial firms in India. *Emerging Markets Review, 38*, 102–114.

Martin L., Oepen, R., Bauer K., Nottensteiner A., Mergheim K., Gruber H., & Koch S.C. (2018). Creative Arts Interventions for Stress Management and Prevention—A Systematic Review. *Behavioral Sciences, 8*(2), 28.

Meng, D., & Yang, J. (2022). Pleasant music and voice behavior in the workplace: The mediating role of psychological safety. *Social Behavior and Personality: An international journal, 50*(2).

Metters, R.D. (2019). The effect of employee and customer religious beliefs on business operating decisions. *Religions, 10*(8).

Meyer, M. (2019). The power of music: Can music at work help to create more ethical organizations? *Humanistic Management Journal, 4*(1), 95–99.

Morrison, M., & Borgen, W. A. (2010). How Christian spiritual and religious beliefs help and hinder counselors' empathy toward clients. *Counseling and Values, 55*, 25–45.

Moss, H., & O'Donoghue, J. (2020). An evaluation of workplace choir singing amongst Health Service staff in Ireland. *Health Promotion International, 35*(3), 527–534.

Nao Mao. (2022). The role of music therapy in the emotional regulation and psychological stress relief of employees in the workplace. *Journal of Healthcare Engineering, 1*, 1–7.

Ntantana, A., Matamis, D., Savvidou, S., Giannakou, M., Gouva, M., Nakos, G., & Koulouras, V. (2017). Burnout and job satisfaction of intensive care personnel and the relationship with personality and religious traits: An observational, multicenter, cross-sectional study. *Intensive and Critical Care Nursing, 41*, 11–17.

Panigrahi A. (2016). Managing stress at workplace. *Journal of Management Research and Analysis, 3(4)*,154–160.

Pirson, M., Martin, K., & Parmar, B. (2017). Formation of stakeholder trust in business and the role of personal values. *Journal of Business Ethics, 145*(1), 1–20.

Ploukou, S. & Panagopoulou, E. (2018). Playing music improves well-being of oncology nurses. *Applied Nursing Research, 39*, 77–80

Rabinovitch, T. C. (2020). The potential of music to effect social change. *Music & Science, 3.*

Reckwitz, A. (2017). *The invention of creativity: Modern society and the culture of new.* Polity Press.

Robbins, P., & Sandberg, B. (2023). Art thinking: Amplifying the 'R' in R&D. *Journal of Innovation Management, 11*(1), IX-XXI.

Robbins, P., & Fu, N. (2022). Blind faith or hard evidence? Exploring the indirect performance impact of design thinking practices in R&D. *R&D Management, 52*(4), 704–719.

Roberts, L. M. (2013). Reflected best self-engagement at work: Positive identity, alignment, and the pursuit of vitality and value creation. In I. Boniwell & S. David (Eds.), *Oxford university press handbook of happiness.* Oxford University Press.

Samani, S.A., Rasid, S.Z., & Sofian, S. (2015). Individual control over the physical work environment to affect creativity. *Industrial Engineering and Management Systems, 14*(1), 94-103.

Sanseverino, D., Caputo, A., Cortese, C.G., & Ghislieri, C. (2023). "Don't stop the music," please: The relationship between music use at work, satisfaction, and performance. *Behavioral Sciences, 13.*

Sauer, B. (2009). Headscarf regimes in Europe: Diversity policies at the intersection of gender, culture and religion. *Comparative European Politics, 7*, 75–94.

Sav, A. (2019). The role of religion in work-life interface. *The International Journal of Human Resource Management, 30*, 3223 – 3244.

Sawyer, R.K., & Henriksen, D. (2024). *Explaining creativity: The science of human innovation.* Oxford University Press.

Schiuma, G. (2017). Arts catalyst of creative organizations for the fourth industrial revolution. *Journal of Open Innovation: Technology, Market, and Complexity, 3*(4).

Schroeder, D., Chatfield, K., Singh, M., Chennells, R., & Herissone-Kelly, P. (2019). *The four values framework: Fairness, respect, care and honesty, equitable research partnerships: A global code of conduct to counter ethics dumping.* Springer International Publishing.

Schwartz R. W., Ayres K. M., & Douglas K. H. (2017). Effects of music on task performance, engagement, and behavior: A literature review. *Psychology of Music,45*(5), 611–627.

Seifried, J., & Wasserbaech, J.S. (2019). Design thinking in leading European companies: Organizational and spatial issues. *Journal of Innovation Management, 7*(1).

Serpian, S., Alzah, S.F., Jusnawati, J., & Handayani, K. (2023). Music at workplace: Is it truly improving employees' performance? *Journal Office, 8*(2).

Singh, G. (2023). Influence of music on business and performance. *International Journal of Social Science and Economic Research, 8*(6), 1520–1525.

Smiraglia, C. (2014). Artworks at work: The impacts of workplace art. *Journal of Workplace Learning, 26*, 284-295.

Van Laer, K., & Essers, C. (2023). The regulation of religion by secular work practice: Exploring Muslim employees' performance of religious practice. *Journal of Management, 50*, 1002 - 1028.

Weaver, G.R., & Stansbury, J. (2014). Religion in organizations: Cognition and behavior. *Religion and Organization Theory, 41.*

Yaffe-Bellany, D. (2022). FTX files for bankruptcy as CEO Sam Bankman-Fried resigns. The New York Times. www.nytimes.com/2022/11/11/business/ftx-bankruptcy.html

CHAPTER 11

The Nature of Work in Australia and Its Implications

Geraldine Torrisi-Steele, Griffith University, Australia

Abstract

This chapter examines the evolution and current state of work in Australia, exploring its historical context, key characteristics, and future trends. It traces the country's economic development from early reliance on agriculture and mining to its current service-based economy, highlighting the impact of significant events such as world wars, immigration policies, and economic reforms. The chapter discusses distinctive features of Australian work culture, including its strong labor laws, union presence, and emphasis on work-life balance.

Two major trends shaping the future of work in Australia are analyzed in depth: digitalization and the gig economy. The chapter explores the implications of artificial intelligence and automation on job roles, emphasizing the need for reskilling and adaptation in the workforce. It also examines the rise of the gig economy, discussing its opportunities for flexible work and its challenges for worker protection and regulation.

The chapter concludes by considering the future of work in Australia, highlighting the importance of agility in government policy, education, and individual skills development. It underscores the need for conscious technology design that enhances rather than replaces human work and emphasizes the importance of inclusion and diversity in shaping equitable work opportunities. Overall, the chapter provides a comprehensive overview of the dynamic nature of work in Australia and its broader implications for society and the economy.

Introduction

Seemingly, work is connatural to humans. The phenomenon of work is perhaps one of the greatest influences on the human condition. There are multiple perspectives on the nature and purpose of work, leading to many philosophical discussions but is loosely defined here as a culturally embedded activity in which humans engage for some kind of gain for individuals or society, whether the gain is economic, physical, social, psychological or even cognitive. In the present chapter, work is understood economically as something done for a job or employment.

Work is a reflexive phenomenon. The nature of work in a society reflects the beliefs and values of a society but at the same time the nature of work in a society shapes the form and function of societies and has an enormous impact on the lives and even well-being of the individuals (Cholbi, 2023). Because work is contextual and culturally embedded, examining the nature of work in various countries, precipitates insight into how different societies organize labor, address inequality, adapt to technological change, and manage the rights and well-being of workers. This in turn allows for better global cooperation, more equitable labor practices, and the formulation of policies and educational approaches that can bring positive change to the human condition in a rapidly changing world.

In the present article, the nature of work in Australia is considered firstly against the background of the historical evolution of the Australian economy. The nature of work in Australia and some of its prominent characteristics are briefly discussed. Digitalization, AI, and the gig economy are then discussed as dominant and highly influential features of the landscape of work in Australia. It is hoped that the article provides a platform for reflection on the dynamic nature of work and how the changes shape social structures. Most importantly, it is hoped that the article causes reflection on the central role of technologies and how these influence the nature of work and ultimately the human condition, and subsequently highlights some important considerations that are necessary for the continued evolution of work in a positive way for individuals and societies.

Evolution of the economy and work in Australia.

The evolution of work in any country reflects the country's unique history, economic transitions, and societal changes. the nature of contemporary work. Key points in Australia's economic development provide a useful backdrop against which the nature of work in Australia can be better understood. Australia's work environment has undergone significant transformation over the past century. From its early reliance on agriculture and mining, the country has diversified its economy to include a robust services sector, advanced manufacturing, and a growing digital economy. These changes reflect broader global trends, but they are also shaped by Australia's unique geographic and demographic characteristics.

The beginnings of the contemporary economy in Australia occurred in the late 18th century during which Australia established penal colonies in Australia. At this time much of the workforce consisted of convicts who were tasked with infrastructure projects, farming, and other manual labor. Over time, free settlers began arriving and establishing farms and businesses. The wool industry became especially important, with large sheep stations dominating rural work.

In the 1850s, gold was discovered in Victoria and New South Wales, which dramatically shifted the workforce. The gold rush attracted not only local workers but also migrants from around the world, particularly from China and Europe. It also gave rise to Australia's first labor and union movements as workers sought better conditions in the mining sector. The union movement has a long history in the Australian context and while its power has varied under different political climates it continues to have a strong presence in the Australian work environment.

Economic function aside, the Gold Rushes greatly influenced the establishment and layout of new settlements across Australia, especially in the area of the state of Victoria (Department of Infrastructure and Regional Development, Australian Government, 2014). The location and pattern of towns, cities, and other regional settlements are partly influenced by economic conditions and also play an important role in work within a country (given that some areas tend towards particular economic activities such as mining, farming, services, etc). The Gold rushes greatly stimulated the Australian economy (Attard, n.d.) and were pivotal in establishing the mining industry in Australia.

By the late 19th century, Australia was moving toward industrialization. The economy diversified with the growth of industries like manufacturing, transportation, and construction. Railroads and ports were built, and cities began expanding rapidly. The introduction of the White Australia Policy in the early 20th century shaped immigration and the workforce by limiting non-European labor, which impacted industries such as sugar and agriculture, previously reliant on Asian and Pacific Islander labor.

Like other economies, the Australian economy has experienced boom and downtime cycles because of surrounding social, global and environmental conditions. The two world wars inevitably made significant impact on the economy and subsequently on the evolution of work. As an island, one of the biggest disruptions due to war was the interruption of shipping and the cessation of vital imports. On the flip side, the world wars, particularly the second world war also resulted in a growing sense of self-sufficiency and resilience. Industrialization was also greatly spurred on by the war efforts. From about midway through the second world war the Australian government focused on recovering from the war and how the economic and industrial resources of the country could be used to grow the Australian economy (National Archives of Australia, n.d.). After World War II, Australia thus experienced significant industrial growth, leading to a higher demand for labor. Key industries included manufacturing, construction, and public infrastructure. There was a major shift toward urbanization, with much of the population moving from rural areas to cities.

To meet labor demands, Australia embarked on an ambitious immigration program, bringing in workers from Southern and Eastern Europe (e.g., Italy, Greece, and Yugoslavia). These migrants became a crucial part of the workforce, helping to build infrastructure and driving economic growth. The Australian government expanded welfare programs, providing unemployment benefits, healthcare, and housing, while the influence of labor unions continued to shape better working conditions and protections.

Of course, one of the most significant economic events was the great depression which peaked at around 1932 with an unemployment rate of 32 percent. (National museum of Australia, n.d.). Before the Wall Street crash in 1929 which led to a worldwide depression, the Australian economy was already suffering from falling wool and wheat prices along with the massive quantities of money borrowed from other countries and increasing competition (National museum of Australia, n.d.) . It took more than 10 years for Australia to surface from the Great Depression.

Major economic reform occurred in the 1980s and the 1990s. The government pursued economic restructuring through the liberalization of markets, the deregulation of industries, and the floating of the Australian dollar in 1983. This opened Australia to global competition. There was a marked decline in manufacturing jobs, as industries such as textiles and car manufacturing were outsourced to cheaper labor markets abroad. In response, the economy shifted toward services, particularly finance, healthcare, and education.

Workplace reforms, including the WorkChoices policy introduced in the 2000s, aimed to deregulate the labor market, giving employers more flexibility but also weakening union power and workers' rights. These changes sparked significant political debate and were eventually rolled back in 2007 after public opposition.

From the 2000s through to the 2010s, Australia experienced a mining boom and the consolidation of a resource economy. Australia's vast mineral resources, particularly coal, iron ore, and natural gas, have played a major role in the country's economy. The mining boom of the 2000s and 2010s created high-paying jobs in remote regions and contributed to a long period of economic growth. However, the reliance on the resource sector has also led to environmental concerns, such as land degradation and carbon emissions, and social challenges, including the impact on Indigenous communities and local economies dependent on mining.

From the time of penal colonies, when agriculturalism and pastoralism dominated the economy, Australia has seen a steady shift from agriculturalism, to industrialization and more recently to a service-based economy (Department of Infrastructure and Regional Development, Australian Government, 2014). Although agriculture continues to be an important component of Australia's economy, the contribution of agriculture to Australia's GDP is relatively small around 2.68% in 2022 compared to 27.48% from industry and 63.3% from services (Australia: Distribution of gross domestic product (GDP) across economic sectors from 2012 to 2022, n.d.). The shift to a services-orientated economy was greatly assisted by the advent of the internet and associated IT and communications technologies, and the consequential emphasis on knowledge work. Hence, by the 21st century, Australia became a predominantly service-based economy. Key industries include healthcare, education, financial services, retail, and tourism. This reflects a global trend of moving away from industrial work toward knowledge-based, technology-driven work.

Technological advancements have had a profound impact on the economy and subsequently work in Australia, reshaping industries and creating new opportunities while also presenting challenges. The rise of automation, artificial intelligence, and digital platforms has increased productivity across various sectors, but it has also disrupted traditional employment patterns. In manufacturing, for example, automation has led to a decline in traditional factory jobs while increasing demand for skilled workers who can operate and maintain advanced machinery. Similarly, the retail sector has seen a shift towards e-commerce, reducing the need for physical stores and changing the nature of retail work.

The gig economy has gained traction in Australia, with platforms like Uber, Deliveroo, and Airtasker offering flexible work opportunities. While this has provided income for many, particularly during economic downturns, it has also raised concerns about job security, working conditions, and the lack of traditional employee benefits.

Overview of the nature of work in Australia

In keeping with diminishing emphasis on agriculture and the shift to a services economy, alongside the prevalence of the Gig economy, many Australians now work as freelancers or contractors in industries like ridesharing, food delivery, and online services. This trend has sparked concerns over job security, fair wages, and workers' rights in this new sector. One key contributor to the expansion of the Gig economy was the COVID-19 pandemic and the rising work-from-home culture. The COVID-19 pandemic in 2020 reshaped the Australian workforce, with many businesses shifting to remote work and certain industries like hospitality and tourism taking significant hits. The gig economy expanded, but so did unemployment, leading to government interventions like the Job Keeper program to support workers and businesses.

Remote work, accelerated by the COVID-19 pandemic, has become a permanent fixture in many Australian industries. This shift has brought both benefits and challenges, including greater work-life balance for some and the blurring of boundaries between work and personal life for others. It has also highlighted the need for robust digital infrastructure and cybersecurity measures to support a distributed workforce. The pandemic accelerated the adoption of flexible work arrangements and remote work, particularly for knowledge workers in industries such as finance, IT, and education. Post-pandemic knowledge workers are commonly exposed to hybrid work arrangements in which part of the work week is spent working in locations other than 'the office'. For most this means working from home (WFH) or remotely working (Hopkins & Bardoel, 2023). An April 2022 study found that of 1421 Australian knowledge workers, 54% were in some kind of hybrid working arrangement (Hopkins & Bardoel, 2023). Interestingly, some major companies are beginning to discard hybrid and flexible working arrangements with some now mandating a full-time return to pre-pandemic 'in the office' every working day. Some of these companies include Apple, Amazon (Lebowitz, et al., 2024).

The hybrid and flexible work models post-pandemic are stimulating discussions on work-life balance and the future of office-based work. Work-life balance is emerging as a prominent feature of the nature of work in Australia. This emphasis is in the aftermath of the pandemic and in the face of the affordances of digital tools to maintain communication and work outside the confines of time and location. Most recently, a new legislation has passed in Australian Government which affords employees with a new right – the 'right to disconnect'. The legislation came into force on the 26 August 2024 for non-small business employers and comes into force one year later on the 26 August 2025 for small business employers. In summary

> *"Eligible employees will have a new 'right to disconnect' outside of work hours.*
>
> *Employees will have the right to refuse contact outside their working hours unless that refusal is unreasonable. This means an employee can refuse to monitor, read or respond to contact from an employer or a third party.*
>
> *The right also covers attempted contact outside of an employee's working hours.*
>
> *When working out whether an employee's refusal is unreasonable, the following factors must be considered:*

- *the reason for the contact*
- *how the contact is made and how disruptive it is to the employee*

- *how much the employee is compensated or paid extra for:*
  - *being available to perform work during the period they're contacted, or*
  - *working additional hours outside their ordinary hours of work*
- *the employee's role in the business and level of responsibility*
- *the employee's personal circumstances, including family or caring responsibilities.*

Other matters may also be considered.

It will be unreasonable for an employee to refuse to read, monitor or respond if the contact or attempted contact is required by law" (Australian Government, 2024)

Characteristically, work in Australia is greatly influenced by the surrounding context of laws and unions. There are numerous labor laws in Australia designed to protect employees. The Fair Work Act, provides comprehensive protections, including minimum wage, unfair dismissal laws, and rights to request flexible work. Australia's minimum wage is one of the highest in the world, and the country also has strong workplace safety regulations under the Work Health and Safety Act.

Australia has a historically strong labor union presence, with unions actively involved in wage negotiations and workplace safety. Although union membership has declined in recent years, unions still play a significant role in key sectors like healthcare and construction through collective bargaining agreements.

Australia's minimum wage is one of the highest in the world, at AUD 23.23 per hour (as of 2024). The wage-setting system is highly regulated, and the Fair Work Commission regularly adjusts the minimum wage to keep pace with inflation and living standards.

Casual work is a distinctive feature of Australia's labor market, with casual workers receiving a higher hourly wage but lacking benefits like paid sick leave or annual leave. This form of employment is common in retail, hospitality, and tourism. Australia's casual loading compensates for the lack of entitlements.

Australia has a legal framework focused on improving gender equality and diversity in the workplace. The Workplace Gender Equality Act mandates annual reporting by companies on gender equality indicators. Many workplaces also participate in diversity benchmarks like the Australian Workplace Equality Index (AWEI), which measures LGBTQ+ inclusion

Amid the legal frameworks, policies, and legislation, Australian work culture is known for its characteristic informality and emphasis on egalitarianism. This is reflected in flat organizational hierarchies, where it's common for employees to address managers by their first names and enjoy more relaxed workplace interactions

Digitalization and the gig economy – where to from here?

There are two main trends apparent in the nature of work in Australia all of which will undoubtedly shape work in the future.

One of the most apparent trends is digitalization – sometimes referred to as the fourth industrial revolution. The ubiquitousness of digital technologies has, in the past few decades, catalyzed significant changes in the type of work that is done and how that work is done. Communications technologies afford flexible work arrangements and, as seen post-covid this enabled remote or hybrid working. However, despite the 'proof' that it was possible to undertake work outside the confines of the office, there are still some doubts over the effectiveness of the models of hybrid work which linger post-COVID. One of the main concerns is the decreased opportunities for connection and 'supportive' work relationships (Mobbs, et al., 2021). Several years on from the pandemic that seemed to catalyze new hybrid work models, some employers are already re-evaluating hybrid work models, and some planning to return to old models of 'work in the office five days/week' in the next year, usually out of concern for the perceived damage of remote work to work relationships and necessary collaboration for productivity. But perhaps the scenario isn't as simple as it seems. Are we truly understanding new work models such as hybrid models? How well can remote communication tools support relationships and collaboration? Is it the tools that are insufficient or unsuitable? Do we really understand remote working and how to maximize productivity and relationship building? Many unanswered but important questions remain unanswered and therefore must be considered as models of work evolve.

Beyond digitalization is artificial intelligence. The rise of artificial intelligence (AI) is viewed with excitement about potential but also with fear about the possibility that AI will take over jobs, leaving scores of people with no work.

> *"Successful integration of automation and gen AI could boost the Australian economy and benefit businesses. Assuming all factors are in place, gen AI has the potential to increase Australian labor productivity by 0.1 to 1.1 percentage points a year through 2030…Between 79 and 98% of Australia is predicted to be automated by 2030"* (Ungur & Johnson, 2024)

> *"Recent research by LinkedIn and Mandala, using LinkedIn data covering more than 41,000 skills and 15 million Australian members, indicates that GenAI will affect the skills composition for approximately 7.2 million Australian workers."* (Lobo-Pulo, 2024, p. para 4)

Where does this leave individuals? What are the implications of this for the nature of work in Australia? These are complex considerations but surely all this points to the need for reskilling. The real question is then, what skills and capabilities are necessary to ensure a realization of the potential of AI for the economy and working individuals? At present, there is a perceived 'skills gap' that is a barrier to the realization of the potential of AI (Lobo-Pulo, 2024).

To help identify skills, it is useful to consider that job roles and the effect of AI on them fall loosely into three categories:

- *Augmented Jobs*, where the core skills required include large shares of both GenAI-replicable and GenAI-complementary skills.
- *Disrupted Jobs,* which include a large share of GenAI-replicable skills and a relatively low share of GenAI-complementary skills; and
- *Insulated Jobs*, which are relatively insulated from GenAI, having a small proportion of GenAI-replicable core skills.
  (Lobo-Pulo, 2024, p. para 7)

There is some commentary that there is 'some inertia' on the part of the government and in some industries concerning AI and that this inertia cannot be afforded (Kontic, 2024). AI is an imperative for Australia:

> *"Greater utilization of artificial intelligence (AI) in key Australian industries will lead to a short-term boost in GDP of more than $200 billion per year and the creation of an additional 150,000 jobs from 2023-2030. …Greater utilization of artificial intelligence (AI) in key Australian industries will lead to a short-term boost in GDP of more than $200 billion per year and the creation of an additional 150,000 jobs from 2023-2030"* (Kontic, 2024)

An extensive report titled "Australia's AI imperative" and published by Kingston AI group (Australian Professors of Artificial Intelligence) brings urgency to ensuring that Australia and its workforce are ready to harness AI. In the report, it is argued that it is critical to Australia's economy that the country is a leader and early adopter of AI if the potential benefits of AI are to be reaped (Mangan, 2024). A central element of AI diffusion in Australian industry is the skilling of the workforce. With the emphasis that in an AI-rich future of work there will be an increasing demand for basic literacy skills and importantly socio-emotional competencies, critical thinking, and complex problem-solving skills (Ungur & Johnson, 2024).

> *"By nature, education systems operate reactively rather than proactively in response to significant technical change. In the case of AI, skills and training issues are further complicated by its ubiquitous nature in contrast to earlier periods of technical change that tended to be confined (initially) to specific industries and particular sections of the economy.*

As a consequence, the educational and training needs for AI are diverse and require a mix of skills, including:

- *technical skills for those developing AI systems and high-end users*
- *interpretation, business, and diagnostic skills for those managing front-end usage of AI systems*
- *re-orientation and adaptive skills, particularly for those whose occupations will disappear or be transformed*
- *management for those charged with managing social dislocation and re-alignment.*

These skills mix will provide the structural and organizational changes required to make education and training more agile and responsive to rapidly changing AI needs." (Mangan, 2024, p. 55)

"We are now experiencing…a techno-axial age reliant on novel cognitive technologies that enhance human analytic and processing capabilities" (Bessant & Watts, 2021, p. 2).

For some this significant change in workplace structures and tools represents a fifth industrial revolution or Industry 5.0 (Adel, 2022). Industry 1.0 refers to the 18th century with the advent of machines in the manufacturing industry. Industry 2.0 refers to the period between 1871 and 1914 that allowed for a 'faster transfer of ideas and movement of persons' and was characterized by increased productivity but a loss of jobs as people's jobs were replaced by machines (Adel, 2022). The third industrial revolution Industry 3.0 began in the 1970s and may be considered the digital revolution which culminated in the ubiquitousness of computers, integrated circuit chips, cellular phones, and, of course, the internet in the later part of the 1990's (Adel, 2022). Industry 4.0 has been present for around the past 10 years and is characterized by the "union of physical assets and advanced technologies" such as AI, 3D printing, IOT, etc (Adel, 2022, p. 1). The adoption of Industry 4.0 characterizes industries through flexibility and data-driven decision-making (Adel, 2022).

"The revolution of industry 5.0 means that humans and machines are working together, improving the efficiency of industrial production " (Adel, 2022, p. 4).

The collaborative work of people involves working with robots and smart/advanced technologies such as AI. Within Industry 5.0 social networks exist among humans and 'electronic components' (Adel, 2022). Subsequently, industry 5.0 is characterized by focus on human factors, human-centered communications with machines (Adel, 2022). Technologies in Industry 5.0 include AI, blockchain technologies, cognitive computing, and quantum computing.

Despite the potential and promise of greater efficiencies and effectiveness in work, this close relationship and communication between humans and machines has some specific challenges that need to be addressed if the potential of Industry 5.0 is to be positively realized. The challenge includes:

- The development of human skills to work effectively with machines
- Adoption of these sophisticated and very different technologies will likely require more effort and learning from humans than what we've seen in the past
- There are additional costs for Industry 5.0 since the production of technologies is not cheap and neither is the cost of training humans

Finally, security and trust are major challenges that inevitably are much more prominent challenges in networked environments especially networked environments that involve both machine and human components (Adel, 2022). Importantly, acceptance of the technologies and trust on the part of humans will be a critical element of Industry 5.0 success.

Surrounding the discourse on digitalization, industry 5.0 and AI in industry in Australia is a consideration of the Gig economy and its implications for the future of work in Australia.

In the past 20 or so years, Australia has seen a shift from a workforce interested in predominantly secure work and relatively consistent wages to the gig economy. The characteristics of the gig economy are workers who take on short-term and varied work tasks via digital platforms (e.g. UBER) – hence the use of the term 'gig'. The gig economy is growing rapidly in Australia and presents various challenges to the Australian government in terms of how this kind of work is thought of and has brought into question how the traditional terms of the employee, contractors, and employers are thought of from a policy, law, and regulation point of view (Murphey, n.d.) :

> *The gig economy is characterized by workers contracting to complete short-term task-based work via digital platforms which facilitate labor transactions between workers and businesses. The rapid rise of the gig economy represents risks and opportunities for gig economy workers, many of whom are characterized as independent contractors rather than employees and lack workplace entitlements and protections.*
>
> *The increase in the number of gig economy workers has brought into question the appropriateness of the employee/independent contractor distinction in relation to gig economy workers and whether reforms are needed to provide better job security, income, and retirement savings for gig economy workers.*
>
> *The policy challenge for the Parliament would seem to be finding a balance that preserves much of the flexibility and advantages of digital platform-enabled gig work for both busi-*

nesses and workers in a way that also provides appropriate protections, rights, and benefits for workers participating in the gig economy.
(Murphey, n.d., p. para 1)

The main drivers for the expansion of the gig economy in Australia include:

- *digital platform-enabled advances in technology that increase the scope and frequency of transactions, reduce transaction costs, increase accessibility, and enhance trust regarding payment between workers and businesses*
- *changing economic behavior and increases in the number of workers seeking supplemental income*
- *workers seeking more flexible and autonomous work-life environments and businesses seeking more flexible workplace arrangements*
- *demand by consumers and businesses for the convenience of on-demand services, including improved job matching*
- *the absence of (adapted/targeted) regulation and lower barriers to entry that allow consumers and providers to switch roles easily and quickly. (Murphey, n.d., p. para 5)*

The concerns of the government about the gig economy and preserving the regulation of work for the benefit of workers are not unfounded. Despite the attractive advantages of gig work in terms of flexibility lean business models and entrepreneurial spirit, there are also significant risks for the exploitation of workers including poor working conditions (Pangrazio, Bishop, & Lee, 2023).

The rise of the gig economy represents a fundamental shift in the nature of work (Scully-Russ & Torraco, 2020). The gig economy sits outside of the traditional ideas of employment and outside of current government conceptualizations of work. It is quite different and therefore represents the emergence of new social structures as well as new tools that people engage with to work (in this case the new tools are the various platforms used – because of this the gig economy is sometimes referred to as the platform economy) (Pangrazio, Bishop, & Lee, 2023).

"Gig work is facilitated through platforms' digital ecosystems which are underpinned by matching technology (Howcroft and Bergvall-Ka⊠reborn,2018; Peticca-Harris et al., 2018; Stewart and Stanford, 2017), with algorithmic management often used to exercise varied levels of control over task allocation and performance (Cherry, 2016; Rosenblat, 2019)"
(Barratt, Goods, & Veen, 2020, p. 1644)

The platforms being used in the gig economy play a pivotal role in shaping new social structures and relationships by virtue of their designs and algorithms – that's far from the platforms being the neutral entities that they portray themselves to be (Barratt, Goods, & Veen, 2020).

The issue with algorithms is well summarised by (Marmo, Sinopoli, & Guo, 2022, pp. 181-182)

> *"One way in which gig companies create barriers that remove their responsibility is through the adoption of algorithms. An algorithm is any sequence of well-defined instructions for completing a task that repeats itself over time without explicit human intervention. In the gig economy, gig companies assign tasks through an 'algorithmic management' system to match customers with workers and evaluate workers' performance.*
>
> *As a society, we are only just beginning to grasp how big data is being assembled and used by companies, and most often algorithms are depicted as if they deliver neutrality. However, a growing number of scholars are becoming vocal about the way such data has been used to influence and control behavior through 'algorithm[ic] governance', arguing that algorithms are therefore neither objective nor neutral, with some claiming that big data is used within 'a political process involving questions of power, transparency and surveillance'.*

Another 'invisible' mechanism of control in the gig economy is the illusion of flexibility and autonomy (Marmo, Sinopoli, & Guo, 2022). This discourse gives the appearance that the responsibility for working conditions, fair work, etc is not that of the platform owner – after all the worker is apparently (but falsely so) autonomous and even entrepreneurial running 'their own business' (Marmo, Sinopoli, & Guo, 2022). The actual situation couldn't be further from the truth. The flexibility is forced and there is very little control on the part of the worker (Marmo, Sinopoli, & Guo, 2022). Furthermore, gig workers receive little training and often have little understanding of how the business model of the platform actually works (and most certainly have very little if no awareness of the algorithms and their designs). Rather than give autonomy and flexibility platforms may do exactly the opposite – restrict and foster powerlessness (Marmo, Sinopoli, & Guo, 2022). And because the gig economy models are so different than traditional work models, so far there is little protection offered by government and laws. This is not to say that nothing is being done, but there is much left to do as governments grapple with how to deal with the worker protection that is so important to the Australian work context. The union movement that has a long history in Australian work, despite limited powers, is also joining the cause to support and work to protect gig workers from exploitation (Marmo, Sinopoli, & Guo, 2022).

Conclusion

The evolution of work in Australia reflects the country's shifts from convict labor and pastoralism to industrialization, mass immigration, and service-based economies. Today, Australia's workforce is shaped by globalization, technological change, and emerging challenges like climate change, aging populations, and labor market flexibility. Understanding this evolution is crucial to anticipating the future of work in the country.

Australia's work landscape is shaped by its unique economic, social, and cultural context, which has been further influenced by global trends. This chapter delves into the nature of work in Australia, exploring how it has evolved, the role of key industries, the impact of technological advancements, and the challenges faced by the workforce. It also examines the social and cultural implications of work in Australia and considers the future of work in a rapidly changing environment.

Looking ahead, the future of work in Australia will be shaped by several key trends, including technological innovation, demographic changes, and the need for sustainable economic growth. The ongoing impact of climate change is also likely to influence the work landscape, particularly in sectors such as agriculture, energy, and tourism. As automation and artificial intelligence continue to evolve, there will be a growing need for workers to acquire new skills and adapt to changing job requirements. Lifelong learning and continuous professional development will be essential to ensure that the workforce remains competitive in a global economy.

In addition to technological change, Australia's aging population presents both challenges and opportunities. The demand for healthcare and aged care services is expected to grow, creating jobs in these sectors but also requiring careful planning to ensure that the workforce can meet this demand.

Sustainability will be another key consideration for the future of work in Australia. The transition to a low-carbon economy will require the development of new industries and the transformation of existing ones. This presents an opportunity to create jobs in renewable energy, green technology, and sustainable agriculture, while also addressing the environmental challenges facing the country.

Work in Australia and other countries is a dynamic and evolving aspect of the nation's identity, shaped by its economic history, technological advancements, and social values. As Australia navigates the challenges and opportunities of the 21st century, it will be essential to embrace change, foster innovation, and ensure that work continues to contribute to the well-being of all Australians. In considering the implications of the nature of work in Australia and across the globe, change, particularly rapid change is the consistent theme. Of all the capabilities necessary to survive and thrive in the future, it is perhaps agility that is needed most – the agility of governments to evolve vision and to ensure that policies and laws continue to change in ways that genuinely protect individuals and societies; the agility of education and training providers to align learning and training and to also anticipate what is needed for the future, and agility of individuals to engage meaningfully and positively with work and society in the future.

With emphasis on the need to develop new skills and technical proficiencies in the face of change in how work is done, and the kind of work is done, it is also necessary that governments and policymakers ensure explicit consideration is given to inclusion and diversity. Access to training and education as well as to technology and opportunities to engage meaningfully in new work contexts is central to preventing a future where changes and new technologies lead to a widening of inequalities and lack of opportunities.

Technology is and will likely remain central to shaping work and society. Hence one of the greatest burdens and responsibilities lies with those who design and develop the technologies that we will interact with and even collaborate with. These developers of technological work tools must consciously design and implement with the recognition that what they are creating is far from neutral. What's more, it must be borne in mind that the goal of these tools is not to replace humans but rather to free humans from the tedious, drudgery of tasks, enabling individuals to engage meaningfully in work in a way that will make positive changes to the human condition.

REFERENCES

Adel, A. (2022). Future of industry 5.0 in society: Human-centric solutions, challenges and prospective research areas. *Journal of Cloud Computing, 11*(40), 1-15.

Attard, B. (n.d.). *The Economic History of Australia from 1788: An Introduction.* https://eh.net/encyclopedia/the-economic-history-of-australia-from-1788-an-introduction/

Australia: Distribution of gross domestic product (GDP) across economic sectors from 2012 to 2022. (n.d.). Statistica: https://www.statista.com/statistics/375558/australia-gdp-distribution-across-economic-sectors/

Australian Government. (2024, August 26). *Right to disconnect.* Fair Work Ombudsman. https://www.fairwork.gov.au/about-us/workplace-laws/legislation-changes/closing-loopholes/right-to-disconnect

Barratt, T., Goods, C., & Veen, A. (2020). 'I'm my own boss. . .': Active intermediation and 'entrepreneurial' worker agency in the Australian gig-economy. *EPA: Economy and Space, 52*(8), 1643–1661.

Bessant, J., & Watts, R. (2021). COVID, capital, and the future of work in Australia. *AUSTRALIAN QUARTERLY, January-March 2021.* https://www.pressreader.com/similar/281913070736245

Cholbi, M. (2023). Philosophical Approaches to Work and Labor. *Standford Encyclopedia of Philosophy*, online - https://plato.stanford.edu/cgi-bin/encyclopedia/archinfo.cgi?entry=work-labor.

Department of Infrastructure and Regional Development, Australian Government. (2014). *Bureau of Infrastructure, Transport and Regional Economics The evolution of Australian towns Report No. 136.* Australian Government.

Hopkins, J., & Bardoel, A. (2023). The infiltration of digital technologies and the rise of digital platforms and apps has given birth to a growing gig economy in Australia and on a global scale. *Sustainability, 15*, 1-21.

Kontic, R. (2024, May 07). *Greater AI utilisation could add $200 billion a year to the Australian economy, according to a new report.* https://www.adelaide.edu.au/aiml/news/list/2024/05/07/greater-ai-utilisation-could-add-200-billion-a-year-to-the-australian-economy

Lebowitz, S., Ward, M., Canal, E., Knight, R., York, A., & Yip, J. (2024, September 19). *The list of major companies requiring employees to return to the office.* https://www.businessinsider.com/companies-requiring-return-to-office-rto-mandate

Lobo-Pulo, A. (2024, June 13). *How Australia's skills will evolve with Generative AI.* https://www.ceda.com.au/newsandresources/opinion/workforce-skills/how-australia%E2%80%99s-skills-will-evolve-with-generative-ai

Mangan, J. (2024). *Australia's AI Imperative.* Kingston AI group, University of Adelaide.

Marmo, M., Sinopoli, E., & Guo, S. (2022). Worker exploitation in the Australian gig economy: Emerging mechanisms of social control. *Griffith Law Review, 31*(2), 171-192.

Mobbs, S., Deady, M., Johnson, A., Nguyen, H., Yip, D., Cnnell, C., & Harvey, S. (2021). *What is modern work*? Black Dog Institute.

Murphey, J. (n.d.). *Regulating the 'gig' economy as a form of employment.* https://www.aph.gov.au/About_Parliament/Parliamentary_departments/Parliamentary_Library/pubs/BriefingBook47p/GigEconomy

National Archives of Australia. (n.d.). *Industrial development in Australia after World War II.* https://www.naa.gov.au/help-your-research/fact-sheets/industrial-development-australia-after-world-war-ii

National Museum of Australia. (n.d.). *Defining moments - the Great Depression.* https://www.nma.gov.au/defining-moments/resources/great-depression

Pangrazio, L., Bishop, C., & Lee, F. (2023). Old media, new gigs: The discursive construction of the gig economy in Australian news media. *Work, Employment and Society, 37*(3), 606–624.

Scully-Russ, E., & Torraco, R. (2020). The changing nature and organization of work: An integrative review of the literature. *Human Resource Development Review, 19*(1), 66-93.

Ungur, S., & Johnson, J. (2024). *Generative AI: How will it affect the future of work in Australia?* https://www.mckinsey.com/featured-insights/future-of-asia/future-of-asia-podcasts/generative-ai-how-will-it-affect-the-future-of-work-in-australia

CHAPTER 12

Ethical Work Practices

Viktor Wang, California State University, San Bernardino, USA

Abstract

This chapter emphasizes employers' pivotal role in cultivating a healthy work ethic among employees. Drawing on Pech's (2009) case study, it demonstrates how engaged workers can transition from unproductive to highly productive. Leaders must assess their practices, decisions, and inclusivity to combat disengagement and foster a positive workplace. Tailoring strategies based on the distinction between healthy and misguided work ethics—where X theory individuals may require more guidance and Y theory individuals benefit from autonomy—supports employee retention and drives innovation.

In a diverse global workforce, understanding cultural values and motivators is crucial for fostering strong work ethics (Association for Talent Development, n.d.; Rannala, Gorman, Tierney, Guðmundsson, Hickey., & Corney, 2024) through training and development. Ethical leaders who respect these differences create environments conducive to innovation and best practices. As technology advances, traditional work ethics evolve, with higher education pivotal in nurturing ethical leaders who facilitate employee learning and work ethic growth.

Prioritizing work ethic in education and training programs is essential, equipping individuals with skills like dependability, initiative, and interpersonal competence crucial for success in the 21st century. The evolving role of graduates underscores the importance of cultivating a work ethic tied to professionalism. Effective leadership in these programs fosters trust, credibility, and motivation, essential for organizational growth and innovation. Recognizing work ethic as a cornerstone, nearly nine out of ten hiring managers prioritize it in hiring decisions, underscoring its significance in preparing future professionals.

Introduction

In today's globalized and competitive world, characterized by rapid technological advancements and economic uncertainties, the significance of work ethics (Association for Talent Development, n.d.; Rannala, Gorman, Tierney, Guðmundsson, Hickey., & Corney, 2024) cannot be overstated in shaping the trajectory of organizations. The ability of organizations to swiftly respond to evolving information and global dynamics underscores the critical role of work ethics in maintaining integrity and ethical decision-making. Without a solid foundation in work ethics, organizations risk succumbing to unethical practices and compromised values.

While some may perceive work ethics as an outdated concept, its relevance remains paramount for both individuals and organizations striving for success (Yu & Agrawal, 2013). A cursory search on 'work ethic' reveals a plethora of resources offering guidance on developing and improving work ethics, highlighting its enduring importance in contemporary society.

This chapter explores the intricate facets of work ethics, influenced by diverse factors including leadership ethics, motivational theories, and global trends. It begins by examining different perspectives on work ethics, emphasizing their cultivation through academic exposure, leadership influence, and organizational modeling. Essentially, work ethics serve as a foundational pillar in the 21st-century landscape, guiding ethical decision-making and professional conduct.

Integral to the discourse on work ethics is the exploration of motivation—the driving force behind maintaining a robust work ethic and fostering productivity. Leaders' perspectives on motivation significantly shape organizational cultures and leadership styles. Ethical leadership emerges as a pivotal approach that not only motivates employees but also cultivates a strong sense of work ethics among them. The chapter delves into motivational theories such as Maslow's hierarchy of needs, Herzberg's two-factor theory, and McClelland's need for affiliation, elucidating their implications for organizational behavior and leadership practices.

Looking forward, the chapter considers the evolving landscape of work ethics in a culturally diverse and digitally driven world. It acknowledges the influence of generational differences on work ethics, emphasizing that work ethics encompass more than mere diligence. In the contemporary context, work ethics encompass values like integrity, professionalism, responsibility, accountability, quality, and teamwork, shaping organizational success and ethical standards.

Ultimately, within organizations, the embodiment of work ethics by employees and leaders alike fosters trust, ethical practices, and effective leadership. It sets the tone for organizational culture, influencing how individuals perceive their roles and responsibilities, and contributing to broader societal responsibilities.

The Nature and Evolution of Work

HISTORICAL PERSPECTIVES ON WORK

To fully comprehend work ethics, it is essential to explore how work has been perceived throughout history. This brief review of historical attitudes towards work provides valuable insights into the work ethics necessary for today's universities and organizations.

Wenrich, Wenrich, and Galloway (1988) observed that the Hebrews, as well as the Greeks and Romans, viewed work as painful drudgery. Early Christianity also followed the Jewish tradition, regarding work as a form of punishment. However, Christianity added a positive dimension to work, viewing it as necessary not only for earning a living but also for enabling the sharing of profits with the poor for those who wished to do so. The Church discouraged the pursuit of profit, fearing it was contrary to the 'quest for grace' and would cause the 'less skillful to suffer'. Instead, the Church encouraged work that benefited society and the less fortunate (Roth, 2014). This unpaid work was done not for earthly reward but for the forgiveness of sins and the acquisition of grace. Today, while not necessarily linked to religious reasons, the pursuit of work to help others persists in contemporary society. Many philanthropists in Western societies espouse this positive view of work by donating most of their wealth to charitable organizations. For example, Bill Gates, the second wealthiest individual in the United States, has given away 80% of his wealth to societies worldwide.

In the past, people worked primarily for livelihood—a means of subsistence. This was true for Europeans and Asians alike, and many people in developing countries still struggle to work for just this livelihood. Most Africans belong to this category. In contrast, people in developed countries often work beyond their daily bread, seeing work as the right and moral thing to do (Kazanas et al., 1973; Tilgher, 1930). DeGrazia (1962) noted that American Protestants and Puritans considered work as good and idleness as bad.

CONTEMPORARY VIEWS ON WORK

Scholars and practitioners today summarize seven well-accepted viewpoints toward work:

1. **Continuous Activity**: Work is ongoing and leads to additional activity.
2. **Productive Output**: Work produces goods and services.
3. **Physical and Mental Exertion**: Work requires both physical and mental effort.
4. **Socio-Psychological Aspects**: Work has social and psychological dimensions.
5. **Regularity**: Work is performed on a regular or scheduled basis.

6. **Constraint**: Work involves a degree of constraint.
7. **Personal Purpose**: Work is performed for personal purposes, either intrinsic or extrinsic (Petty & Brewer, 2005).

The German philosopher Marx argued that work is a social activity, with conditions and forms that are socially determined and change over time (Whelan, 1999). Marx defined work as a process between humans and nature, in which humans, through their own activities, initiate, regulate, and control material reactions between themselves and nature. More importantly, work produces surplus value (Wang, 2006).

Adding to our understanding of work, Roth (2014) conceptualizes work as one of four types, depending on the amount of control held by employees and the degree of opportunity available. Roth identifies these types as slave work, subsistence-level work, situation improvement work, and developmental work.

- **Slave Work**: Involves no control over tasks and no benefit beyond survival, carried out under threat.
- **Subsistence Level Work**: Offers minimal control, just enough pay for basic needs, and repetitive tasks with little opportunity for personal development.
- **Situation Improvement Work**: Allows some quality of life improvement, with limited control and some challenging tasks, though mostly repetitive.
- **Developmental Work**: Involves high autonomy, well-paid positions, continuous opportunities for self-development, and entrepreneurial endeavors. This type aligns with innovative work behaviors, fostering creativity, idea generation, and problem-solving (Yidong & Xinxin, 2013).

The Role of Higher Education in Shaping Work Ethics

Before entering the workforce, students' experiences within higher education set the foundation for their work ethic, values, and ethical behaviors. Much like the work environment, students navigate various departments and build relationships, learning the values of the organization. Reybold and Halx (2018) consider the university arena as the environment where students learn about ethics and their application to daily living and decision-making. Higher education institutions, therefore, bear a responsibility for developing students' sense of ethics and subsequent work ethic.

Understanding Work Ethic

DEFINING WORK ETHIC

To understand work ethics, we begin by examining its roots. The term "ethos" is the Greek translation, meaning customs, conduct, or character (Northouse, 2013, 2016, 2022; Bogale & Birbirsa, 2023). The concept of ethics can be traced back to Ancient Greek philosophers Plato and Aristotle, who focused on values and morals and why people behave as they do. Aristotle described an ethical human being as possessing virtues such as courage, temperance, generosity, self-control, honesty, sociability, modesty, fairness, and justice (Northouse, 2013, 2016, 2022). These virtues are ingrained in a person's character and, through practice, become habitual.

Similarly, Reybold and Halx (2018) found that most student affairs staff rely on their personal moral and religious standards, despite available codes of conduct. Academic leaders play a crucial role in translating virtues into ethical practice and modeling work ethics to students and staff. Lawton and Páez (2015) posit that these virtues are applied situationally in ethical leadership.

THE IMPORTANCE OF WORK ETHICS

Today's organizational and higher education leaders must instill desirable work ethics in their employees and students. One's work ethics drive their work performance. Poor work ethics can lead to organizational failure or even national decline, as illustrated by the fall of ancient Babylon (Wang, 2006). Hence, work ethics are a critical component of workforce education.

HEALTHY VS. UNHEALTHY WORK ETHICS

Defining healthy work ethics involves turning to management and education. Management education is increasingly responsive to the dynamics between businesses and society. Enhancing students' knowledge and practice of ethics influences future corporate decisions and work efforts. Universities now play a pivotal role in shaping attitudes toward corporate responsibility and ethical leadership (Setó-Pamies & Papaoikonomou, 2016; Sakr, 2022).

Leaders within organizations can drive positive or negative outcomes. Understanding the relationship between leadership and ethics promotes virtuous behaviors and ethical decision-making. Higher education provides a forum for students to explore their values and ethical principles, forming the foundation for their future work ethic (Reybold & Halx, 2018; Sakr, 2022).

BUILDING A SOLID WORK ETHIC

Fostering a solid work ethic begins with an ethical learning environment and continues through experiential learning in real-world situations. Keeping students aware of the implications of their decisions prepares them to be socially responsible and ethical leaders (Couch & Dodd, 2005). Ethical leaders encourage open dialogue and foster environments where employees and students feel secure enough to express differing viewpoints (Yidong & Xinxin, 2013).

Leaders set the platform and model work behaviors for followers, impacting organizational success. Understanding the factors contributing to the work ethic of leaders and followers is crucial for fostering a positive and productive work environment.

Contemporary Work Ethics in the 21st Century

X THEORY AND ITS IMPLICATIONS

Previous research indicates that Theory X individuals possess an unhealthy work ethic (McGregor, 1960, 1967; Knowles, 1975; Rogers, 1961, 1969, 1980, 2015, 2020). These scholars concluded that Theory Y individuals, conversely, possess a healthy work ethic. To understand this dichotomy, we must first explore the assumptions of Theory X regarding human nature (McGregor, 1960) and the assumptions implicit in current workforce education by Rogers (1961, 1969, 1980). According to McGregor, Theory X individuals inherently dislike work and will avoid it if possible. Based on this assumption, Rogers concluded that Theory X individuals, whether students or employees, cannot be trusted to pursue their learning or work, and thus, most must be coerced, controlled, or threatened to meet organizational objectives.

Rogers also posited that presentation equals learning and that education aims to build factual knowledge like bricks. In this mode of thinking, a knowledge presenter is more valued than a knowledge facilitator. McGregor further argues that the average human being prefers to be directed, wishes to avoid responsibility, has relatively little ambition, and desires security above all. Rogers concluded that truth is known and that creative citizens develop from passive learners. In this view, evaluation is education and education is evaluation. These Theory X assumptions about human nature (controlling) and implicit assumptions in current education (controlling) run contrary to what today's organizations need.

Although today's organizations do exert some control over employees, it is widely accepted that they need creative leaders who make positive assumptions about human nature, unlike the negative assumptions of controlling leaders (Knowles, Holton III & Swanson, 1998, 2005, 2015, 2020). Knowles (1978) observed that creative leaders in today's organizations have faith in people, offer them challenging opportunities, and delegate responsibility. An ethical leader, for example, sincerely demonstrates concern for employees, relates work to a higher cause, and empowers employees to work innovatively (Yidong & Xinxin, 2013). This freedom to evaluate the needs of the work environment and develop solutions is a behavior ethical leaders cultivate through their modeling of work ethic performance and ethical decisions. This is where Theory Y individuals come into play.

Y THEORY AND ITS IMPLICATIONS

The Y Theory assumptions about human nature contrast sharply with those of X Theory. Unlike the assumptions about work in X Theory, the expenditure of physical and mental effort is as natural as play or rest. From the perspective of Y Theory, human beings have a natural potential for learning. External control and the threat of punishment are not the only means of motivating effort toward organizational objectives. People will exercise self-direction and self-control in the service of objectives to which they are committed. Based on this assumption, significant learning takes place when the subject matter is perceived by the student or employee as relevant to their own purposes. Therefore, much significant learning is acquired through doing. Commitment to objectives is a function of the rewards associated with their achievement. Based on this assumption, learning is facilitated by the student's responsible participation in the learning process. The average human being learns, under proper conditions, not only to accept but to seek responsibility. Based on this assumption, self-initiated learning involves the whole person—feelings as well as intellect—which are the most pervasive and lasting. A high capacity for imagination, ingenuity, and creativity in solving organizational problems is widely, not narrowly, distributed in the population. Therefore, learning is best facilitated when self-criticism and self-evaluation are primary, and evaluation by others is of secondary importance.

The final assumption about Theory Y individuals is that under modern industrial conditions, the intellectual potential of the average human being is only partially utilized. Based on this assumption, the most socially useful aspect of learning in the modern world is the process of learning, a continuing openness to experience, and the incorporation of the process of change into oneself (Rogers, 1951). In higher education and the corporate world, leaders who foster an atmosphere of trust and psychological safety provide a gateway for employees to risk personal change and subsequent personal growth. When employees are supported to take risks in the process of learning and doing, innovative work behavior surfaces, contributing to the overall effectiveness of the organization (Yidong & Xinxin, 2013). Through this discussion of the dichotomy of X and Y individuals, it is clear that for today's organizations to remain competitive in a global economy, Theory Y individuals possess the healthy work ethic most organizations desire. To determine whether an organization has acquired a healthy work ethic, Wang (2006) developed a valid and reliable instrument. This tool can be used to identify where employees fall within the dichotomy of X and Y individuals, providing valuable information for leaders who need to assign staff according to tasks and projects. Tasks requiring little innovation and considerable repetitiveness may suit X individuals, while tasks requiring ongoing learning and problem-solving may better fit Y individuals.

TABLES

TABLE 1. X-Work Ethic

Statements	Likert Scale						
1. I have an inherent dislike of work and will avoid it if I can.	7	6	5	4	3	2	1
3. I must be coerced, controlled, directed, and threatened with punishment to put forth adequate effort toward the achievement of organizational objectives.	7	6	5	4	3	2	1
4. I do not learn under proper conditions to accept or seek responsibility.	7	6	5	4	3	2	1
6. Under the conditions of modern industrial life, my intellectual potentialities are widely used.	7	6	5	4	3	2	1
7. I avoid responsibility and have relatively little ambition and want security above all.	7	6	5	4	3	2	1
10. I am not capable of exercising a high degree of imagination, ingenuity and creativity in the solution of organizational	7	6	5	4	3	2	1

TABLE 2. Y-work ethic

Statements	Likert Scale						
2. To me, the expenditure of physical and mental is as natural as play or rest.	7	6	5	4	3	2	1
5. I exercise self-direction and self-control in the service of objectives to which they are committed.	7	6	5	4	3	2	1
8. To me, commitment to objectives is a function of the rewards associated with their achievement.	7	6	5	4	3	2	1
9. I learn under proper conditions not only to accept but also to seek responsibility.	7	6	5	4	3	2	1
11. I exercise a high degree of imagination, ingenuity and creativity in the solution of organizational problems.	7	6	5	4	3	2	1
12. Under the conditions of modern industrial life, my intellectual potentialities are only partially utilized.	7	6	5	4	3	2	1

Understanding Motivation Theories

THE NATURE OF MOTIVATION

Osland, Kolb, and Rubin (2001) assert that all human beings are motivated; the challenge lies in identifying what drives an employee to work and maintain a healthy work ethic. A manager might perceive an employee as lazy and possessing an unhealthy work ethic. However, under different circumstances, that same employee may work diligently on a home project they find interesting or important. Managers can create an environment that inspires employees to work or engage in activities. Employees' needs must be met for them to feel satisfied. Motivation is an internal state within the employee, and everyone has control over this state. A thorough understanding of motivational theories can help managers identify the types of environments employees need and their expectations to perform well.

MASLOW'S HIERARCHY OF NEEDS

Maslow (as cited in Dinibutun, 2012) proposed a hierarchy of human needs, ranging from physiological needs at the base to self-actualization at the peak. Once a need is satisfied, the next need becomes the motivating factor, and the previous need ceases to be a motivator.

- **Self-actualization:** Realization of one's full potential
- **Self-esteem:** Confidence, strength, independence, freedom, achievement
- **Social belonging:** Affection, sense of belonging, social activities, giving and receiving love
- **Security:** Safety and security, protection from danger
- **Physiological:** Basic needs such as hunger, thirst, sleep, and sex (Dinibutun, 2012)

This hierarchy is not universally accepted, as cultural differences can affect the order of needs. For instance, in Japan and Greece, security is prioritized over self-actualization, while in Africa, social needs are deemed more important than self-esteem and self-actualization (Osland, Kolb, & Rubin, 2001). In today's global workforce, managers must recognize how cultural factors influence employee motivation.

HERZBERG'S TWO-FACTOR THEORY

Herzberg (as cited in Osland, Kolb, & Rubin, 2001) expanded on Maslow's theory, proposing that job satisfaction and dissatisfaction arise from two different sets of factors.

- **Extrinsic factors (hygiene factors):** These include supervision, working conditions, salary, and interpersonal relations. Their absence can cause dissatisfaction, but their presence does not necessarily motivate employees.
- **Intrinsic factors (motivators):** These include work tasks, degree of challenge, responsibility, achievement growth, and recognition. These factors must be present to motivate employees.

Again, these factors are not universal. For example, in New Zealand, supervision and interpersonal relationships are significant motivators (Osland, Kolb, & Rubin, 2001). Managers must consider these differences when managing a diverse workforce.

MCCLELLAND'S THEORY OF NEEDS

McClelland (as cited in Osland, Kolb, & Rubin, 2001) aimed to scientifically measure and define human motives. He identified three categories of needs:

- **Need for affiliation:** Desire for friendly and close interpersonal relationships
- **Need for power:** Desire to influence and control others
- **Need for achievement:** Desire for personal achievement and success

These needs vary among individuals, with some having a higher need for power and a lower need for affiliation, or vice versa. McClelland believed that culture and parental upbringing significantly influence these motives.

Motivation and Age

According to Nelson and Quick (2013), age influences an individual's work ethic. Employees entering the workforce today seek a healthy work-life balance, valuing family life and personal time. In contrast, Baby Boomers (born 1946-1964) often have a live-for-work attitude, driven by the need for achievement at work (Stanley, 2006). Baby Boomers are noted for their productivity and creativity.

Generation X (born 1965-1980) and Generation Y (born 1980-1994) exhibit different values. Generation X values individualism, self-reliance, and balancing work and home life. They possess a strong work ethic and commitment to organizations that demonstrate commitment to them (Lander, 2006). Quality of life is crucial for Generation X, who often experience their parents' long work hours and downsizing (Hahn, 2010). They are motivated by challenging opportunities and prefer working alone.

Generation Y values a work-to-live attitude and a flexible working schedule. They have experienced significant global events such as the Gulf War and September 11, which have influenced their preference for teamwork and a 'can-do' attitude (Hahn, 2010). Millennials embrace modern technologies for knowledge management, ongoing learning, and social interactions, seeking open and frequent communication with superiors and striving to make a difference in organizations (Au-Yong-Oliveira et al., 2018).

Motivating a Multigenerational Workforce

To effectively motivate employees from different generations, Hahn (2009) recommends the following strategies:

1. Self-assess your managerial style and generational cohort
2. Educate yourself about the generational characteristics and core values of your staff
3. Embrace commonalities
4. Create and maintain a culture of respect
5. Bridge the generational gap (p.121)

TABLE OF GENERATIONAL CHARACTERISTICS

TABLE 3. Characteristics of Different Generations

Generation	Birth Years	Characteristics
Baby Boomers	1946-1964	Achievement-oriented, live-for-work attitude, productive, creative
Generation X	1965-1980	Individualism, self-reliance, strong work ethic, quality of life
Generation Y	1980-1994	Team-oriented, flexible schedule, tech-savvy, open communication

TABLE 4. Multigenerational cohort backgrounds

Generations	Core Values	Styles
Baby Boomers 1946-1964	Strong sense of duty Team player Personal gratification Uncomfortable with conflict Immediate gratification & reward	Involvement Personal growth Optimism Mentors
Generation X 1965-1980	Self-directed Self-reliant Work and play balance Diversity Action rather than words Individual positive feedback	Think globally Techno literacy Pragmatic Asynchronous Communication Skeptical
Generation Y Millennials 1980-1994	Optimism Diversity Ambitious Can-do attitude Flexible 24-hour workplace Attentive rewards	Multitasking Technologically Savvy Outcome driven Determined

Source: Stewart, D.W. (2006) and Zemke, R., Raines, C., & Filipczak, B. (2000)

Bridging Education and Workplace Realities

Higher education research has delved into the various attributes of generational cohorts, striving to discover the most effective methods to teach and prepare each generation to become productive employees and leaders. Technological advancements have introduced online forums for classroom learning, including social media as a teaching tool. The challenge for higher education is to integrate the technological academic environment with workplace realities, where soft social skills and relationship-building often outweigh productivity in promotion considerations (Au-Yong-Oliveira et al., 2018).

PREPARING STUDENTS FOR THE WORKPLACE

Educators must explore alternative learning strategies to instill a strong work ethic, develop leadership skills, and encourage ethical decision-making in students. Understanding how generational differences in core values influence work ethics can help academia better prepare students for their future roles. As a business entity, academia can also play a crucial role in placing students in suitable work environments (Au-Yong-Oliveira et al., 2018).

UNDERSTANDING GENERATIONAL ATTRIBUTES

Employers aiming to retain and attract talent must understand the unique characteristics of each generational group. This understanding can provide valuable insights into what motivates employees to work diligently, helping employers create environments where all employees can thrive.

THE EVOLUTION OF WORK ETHICS IN A GLOBAL CONTEXT

Petty and Brewer (2005) argue that global competition has intensified the pressure to establish and sustain a positive work ethic. Employees who align with Theory Y, which assumes that people are inherently motivated and capable of self-direction, are increasingly seen as desirable. Historically, the concept of work ethic evolved during the postindustrial revolution, transitioning from an agrarian to an industrial society (Petty & Brewer, 2005, p. 100). As Marx predicted, corporations seek profit by relocating production to regions with cheaper labor. This trend highlights Marx's view that work is a social activity that changes over time (Whelan, 1999).

A future trend will involve examining whether Theory Y assumptions about human nature can effectively release employees' energy in developing countries. Au-Yong-Oliveira et al. (2018) believe that higher education, by fostering innovation, transparency, and self-actualization, can prepare students to be future change agents. However, differing social conditions in developing countries may challenge the widely accepted Western views on work ethics.

CULTURAL INFLUENCES ON WORK ETHICS

Another emerging trend is the need to understand how work ethics align with different cultural contexts. Wang's (2006) research found that within the same Chinese culture, employees exhibited both Theory X and Theory Y work ethics, while some did not fit into either category. Yidong and Xinxin's (2013) study on ethical leadership and innovative work behaviors in China highlights the significant influence of group leadership in a collectivist culture.

Pech (2009) emphasizes the importance of employee engagement for productivity. He notes that disengaged employees, who make up over 80% of the workforce, contribute to decreased productivity. These employees fulfill minimal job requirements and then disengage, leading to negative outcomes for both the organization and the employees themselves.

ETHICAL LEADERSHIP AND MOTIVATION

Yidong and Xinxin (2013) explain that ethical leadership fosters intrinsic motivation, driving innovative solutions to corporate challenges. Ethical leadership builds trust and promotes shared decision-making and citizenship behaviors (Walumbwa, Hartnell, & Misati, 2017). Conversely, favoritism and inequitable reward systems can lead to a decline in work ethic (Chapman & Lindner, 2016).

THE IMPACT OF DIVERSITY AND GLOBALIZATION

Today's organizations consist of increasingly diverse workforces and operate across various cultural contexts. Understanding and respecting cultural differences in values, such as loyalty, is crucial (Nelson & Quick, 2013). For instance, American employees may prioritize personal and family loyalty over organizational loyalty, whereas in Japan, loyalty might involve staying late to support colleagues.

THE SHIFT FROM HARD WORK TO SMART WORK

The Society of Human Resource Management notes a shift in American work ethic from hard work to smart work (Leonard, 2000). Emerging technologies facilitate work-life balance and improve work processes. Millennials, in particular, value using technology to enhance both work and personal life (Au-Yong-Oliveira et al., 2018).

ADAPTING TO AN AGING WORKFORCE

As the workforce ages, with many Baby Boomers (born between 1946 and 1964) delaying retirement, organizations must find ways to keep these experienced workers engaged. Baby Boomers are known for their loyalty and strong work ethic, seeking self-worth and fulfillment from their jobs (Cordinez, 2002). Employers can empower these workers by leveraging their creativity and understanding their motivations.

MOTIVATING DIFFERENT GENERATIONS

Understanding the motivations of different generations—Generation X (born between 1965 and 1976) and Millennials (born between 1977 and 1997)—can help organizations create environments where employees feel valued and motivated. A study of 341 Zambian employees identified key motivating factors, such as work nature, growth opportunities, and fairness, which are essential for fostering a productive work environment.

THE DIGITAL RENAISSANCE OF WORK

Miller and Marsh (2014) describe the current era as a 'digital renaissance of work,' where digital devices and connectivity enable flexible work arrangements. This shift allows for increased autonomy and a new 'digital work ethic' based on passion and fulfillment. However, the integration of work and life necessitates a reevaluation of traditional work ethics.

THE NEED FOR A DEVELOPMENT ETHIC

Roth (2014) argues for replacing the traditional Work Ethic with a Development Ethic, which emphasizes developing and enjoying one's potential to the fullest. In a digital age where technology handles repetitive tasks, employees can focus on self-learning and creative pursuits. This Development Ethic aligns better with modern values and work environments, promoting both professional and personal growth.

Conclusion

Reflecting on the lessons from this chapter, it is evident that employers play a crucial role in fostering a healthy work ethic among employees. The case study by Pech (2009) emphasizes the transformative potential of employee engagement, demonstrating that actively involved workers can shift from unproductive to highly productive. This underscores the importance of creating opportunities for employees to be involved in decision-making, potentially reducing the alarmingly high rate of disengagement, which currently stands at 80%. Addressing this issue begins with leaders taking a reflective inventory of their practices and decisions. By evaluating the ethics of their decisions, inclusiveness of diverse perspectives, and fairness in their practices, leaders can identify whether their style contributes to declining morale and productivity. Leaders must first understand their own work ethic to foster a positive environment.

The significance of distinguishing between a healthy and a wrong work ethic is clear: once employers or instructors determine the work ethic of their employees or students, they can tailor their management or teaching strategies accordingly. For instance, employees or students with an X theory work ethic may require more control and guidance, while those with a Y theory work ethic may thrive with more autonomy and opportunities to release their energy productively. Recognizing the work ethic of individuals is essential for retaining valuable employees who contribute to innovation and competitiveness. Understanding various motivational theories and the factors that satisfy or dissatisfy employees allows managers to create conditions that foster a strong work ethic, ultimately retaining effective and dedicated workers.

In a diverse and global workforce, it is crucial for organizations to understand the cultural values and motivators of employees from different backgrounds. Recognizing these factors enables organizations to invest in training and development that aligns with what motivates employees, thereby cultivating strong work ethics. Similarly, understanding the values of different age groups, such as Generation X, Y, and Baby Boomers, helps in identifying what drives them to work hard. Ethical leaders who appreciate these differences create environments where all perspectives are respected, leading to innovative improvements and best practices that enhance organizational competitiveness.

As technology advances, the traditional work ethic is undergoing significant transformation in the 21st century. Higher education institutions are increasingly responsible for developing the next generation of ethical leaders who can create environments conducive to employee learning and work ethic development. Despite modern challenges, the fundamental belief that work is a good and moral endeavor should remain unchanged. Although societal forces may challenge one's work ethic, it is essential to view work as a positive and moral activity.

Work ethic should be considered a critical element. Work aims to prepare individuals for successful workforce participation, and in the modern context, this includes more than just technical skills. Work ethic, alongside career navigation and innovation, is a pillar of college programs. College graduates must be equipped to navigate a fluid, global, and dynamic workforce, and work ethic is integral to their success. Rojewski and Hill (2014) argue that work ethic encompasses employability skills such as dependability, initiative, and interpersonal skills, all essential for 21st-century success.

As the role of college graduates evolves, nurturing work ethic becomes increasingly important. Work ethics are closely tied to professionalism, a highly desirable attribute in today's workforce. Work must go beyond traditional skills training to remain relevant and viable, addressing the diverse challenges and opportunities in the modern work environment. Understanding work ethic in the context of contemporary digital society is crucial, as technology offers new possibilities for autonomy and self-growth.

Leadership plays a pivotal role in the viability of work in the 21st century. If work ethic and professionalism are to be nurtured in college students, they must also be exemplified by college leaders. Leadership work ethic is integral to strategic management, contributing to long-term success and competitiveness. Ethical leadership fosters trust, credibility, inspiration, motivation, and accountability, all essential for growth and innovation within an organization. Therefore, colleges (American Association of Community Colleges) must embrace work ethics as a fundamental goal, recognizing it as a critical skill for the 21st-century workforce. Nearly nine out of ten hiring managers consider work ethic the most important factor in hiring, highlighting the need for colleges (American Association of Community Colleges) to prepare students with these essential skills for future success.

REFERENCES

American Association of Community Colleges. (2022). *The economic value of America's Community Colleges.* https://www.aacc.nche.edu/wp-content/uploads/2022/11/AACC_ExecSum_1920_Formatted-Finalv2.pdf

Association for Talent Development. (n.d.). *Work ethic: The critical skills for the 21st-century workforce.* https://www.td.org/videos/work-ethic-the-critical-skills-for-the-21st-century-workforce

Au-Yong-Oliveira, M., Gonçalves, R., Martins, J., & Branco, F. (2018). The social impact of technology on millennials and consequences for higher education and leadership. *Telematics and Informatics, 35*(4), 954–963. doi:10.1016/j.tele.2017.10.007

Bogale, A.T., & Birbirsa, Z.A. (2023). HR system and work ethics: A systematic review. *Cogent Business & Management, 10*(3). https://doi.org/10.1080/23311975.2023.2278848

Chapman, D. W., & Lindner, S. (2016). Degrees of integrity: The threat of corruption in higher education. *Studies in Higher Education, 41*(2), 247–268. doi:10.1080/03075079.2014.927854

Cordinez, J. A. (2002). Recruitment, retention, and management of generation X: A focus on nursing professionals. *Journal of Healthcare Management, 47*(4), 237–249. doi:10.1097/00115514-200207000-00006 PMID:12221745

Couch, S., & Dodd, S. (2005). Doing the right thing: Ethical issues in higher education. *Journal of Family and Consumer Sciences, 97*(3), 20–26.

DeGrazia, S. (1962). *Of time, work, and leisure.* NY Twentieth Century Fund.

Dinibutun, S. R. (2012). Work motivation: Theoretical framework. *GSTF Business Review (GBR), 1*(4), 133-139. http://ezproxy.fau.edu/login?url=http://search.proquest.com/docview/1038956802?accountid=10902

Hahn, J. A. (2010). Multigenerational diversity: Working together to bridge the generational gap. *Nurses First, 2*(5), 6–8.

Kazanas, H. C., Baker, G. E., Miller, F. M., & Hannah, L. D. (1973). *The meaning and value of work* (Information Series No. 71). The Center for Vocational Education. (ED 091 504)

Knowles, M. S. (1975). *Self-directed learning: A guide for learners and teachers.* Association Press.

Knowles, M. S. (1978). *The adult learner: A neglected species* (2nd ed.). Gulf.

Knowles, M. S., Holton, E., & Swanson, A. (1998). *The adult learner* (5th ed.). Gulf Publishing Company.

Knowles, M. S., Holton, E., & Swanson, A. (2005). *The adult learner* (6th ed.). Butterworth-Heinemann. doi:10.4324/9780080481913

Knowles, M. S., Holton, E., & Swanson, A. (2015). *The adult learner* (6th ed.). Routledge.

Knowles, M. S., Holton, III, Swanson, & Robinson, P. A. (2020). *The adult learner the definitive classic in adult education and human resource development* (9th ed.). Routledge.

Lander, C. (2006). Generations X & Y. *Canadian Consulting Engineer, 47*(6), 79–80.

Lawton, A., & Páez, I. (2015). Developing a framework for ethical leadership. *Journal of Business Ethics, 130*(3), 639–649. doi:10.100710551-014-2244-2

Leonard, S. (2000). Is America's work ethic changing? *HRMagazine, 45*(4), 224.

Marx, K. (1929). *Capital: A critique of political economy: The process of capitalist production* (E. Paul & C. Paul, Trans.). International Publishers. (Original work published 1890)

McGregor, D. (1960). *The human side of enterprise.* McGraw Hill.

McGregor, D. (1967). *Leadership and motivation.* The Massachusetts Institute of Technology Press.

Miller, P., & Marsh, E. (2014). *The digital renaissance of work: delivering digital workplaces fit for the future.* Gower Publishing Limited.

Nelson, D. L., & Quick, J. C. (2013). *Organizational Behavior.* South-Western.

Northouse, P. G. (2022). *Leadership: Theory and practice* (9th ed.). Sage Publications.

Northhouse, P. G. (2016). *Leadership theory and practice* (7th ed.). Sage.

Northouse, P. G. (2013). *Leadership theory and practice* (6th ed.). SAGE Publications.

Osland, J., Kolb, D. A., & Rubin, I. M. (2001). *Organizational behavior: An experiential approach.* Prentice Hall.

Pech, R. J. (2009). Delegating and devolving power: A case study of engaged employees. *The Journal of Business Strategy, 30*(1), 27–32. doi:10.1108/02756660910926948

Petty, G. C., & Brewer, E. W. (2005). Perspectives of a healthy work ethic in a 21st-century international community. *International Journal of Vocational Education and Training, 13*(1), 93–104.

Rannala, I.E., Gorman, J., Tierney, H., Guðmundsson, A., Hickey, J., & Corney, T. (2024). Ethical practice in professional youth work: Perspectives from four countries. *Ethics and Social Welfare, 18*(2), 195-210. https://www.tandfonline.com/doi/full/10.1080/17496535.2024.2312274

Resources for Employers. (n.d.). What is work ethic and why is it important for success?: https://resources.workable.com/hr-terms/what-is-work-ethic

Rojewski, J., & Hill, R. (2014). Positioning research and practice in career and technical education: A framework for college and career preparation in the 21st century. *Career and Technical Education Research, 39*(2), 137-150.

Reybold, L. E., & Halx, M. D. (2018). Staging professional ethics in higher education: A dramaturgical analysis of "Doing the Right Thing" in student affairs. *Innovative Higher Education, 43*(4), 273–287. doi:10.100710755-018-9427-1

Rogers, C. R. (1951). *Client-centered therapy.* Houghton-Mifflin.

Rogers, C. R. (1961). *On become a person.* Houghton-Mifflin.

Rogers, C. R. (1969). *Freedom to learn.* Merrill.

Rogers, C. R. (1980). *A way of being.* Houghton Mifflin.

Roth, W. F. (2014). Has the work ethic run out of steam? *World Future Review, 6*(2), 172–177. doi:10.1177/1946756714536875

Sakr, F. H. (2022). Work ethics and ethical attitudes among healthcare professionals: The role of leadership skills in determining ethics construct and professional behaviors. *Healthcare, 10*(8), 1-13.

Stanley, T. L. (2006). Baby Boomers: Why these employees matter. *Super Vision, 67*(10), 3–5. http://ezproxy.fau.edu/login?url=http://search.proquest.com/docview/195599866?accountid=10902

Stewart, D. W. (2006). Generational mentoring. *Journal of Continuing Education in Nursing, 37*(3), 113–121. doi:10.3928/00220124-20060301-06 PMID:18814392

Tilgher, A. (1930). *Homo faber: Work through the ages* (D. C. Fisher, Trans.). Harcourt Brace.

Walumbwa, F. O., Hartnell, C. A., & Misati, E. (2017). Does ethical leadership enhance group learning behavior? Examining the mediating influence of group ethical conduct, justice climate, and peer justice. *Journal of Business Research, 72*, 14–23. doi:10.1016/j.jbusres.2016.11.013

Wang, V. (2006). A Chinese work ethic in a global community. *International Journal of Vocational Education and Training, 14*(2), 39–52.

Wenrich, R. C., Wenrich, J. W., & Galloway, J. D. (1988). *Administration of vocational education*. American Technical Publishers, INC.

Whelan, F. (1999). Karl Marx (biography of Marx). Fourth Estate.

Yidong, T., & Xinxin, L. (2013). How ethical leadership influence employees' innovative work behavior: A perspective of intrinsic motivation. *Journal of Business Ethics, 116*(2), 441–455. doi:10.100710551-012-1455-7

Yu, D., Harter, J., & Agrawal, S. (2013). US managers boast best work engagement: Managers also show greatest improvement in engagement. http:www.gallup.com/poll/162062/ managers-boast-best-work-engagement.aspx

Zemke, R., Raines, C., & Filipczak, B. (2000). *Generations at work: Managing the clash of veterans, boomers, Xers, and nexters*. American Management Association.

www.ingramcontent.com/pod-product-compliance
Lightning Source LLC
La Vergne TN
LVHW080028210926
848481LV00011B/3132